A GUIDEBOOK TO THE COMPARATIVE STUDY OF ECONOMIC SYSTEMS

FREDERIC L. PRYOR

Swarthmore College

PRENTICE-HALL, INC., Englewood Cliffs, New Jersey 07632

Library of Congress Cataloging in Publication Data

Pryor, Frederic L.
A guidebook to the comparative study of economic systems.

Bibliography: p.
Includes index.
1. Comparative economics. I. Title.
HB90.P79 1985 330 84-13026
ISBN 0-13-368853-4

To Dan

Editorial/production supervision and interior design: Barbara Grasso
Cover design: Ben Santora
Manufacturing buyer: Ed O'Dougherty

Printed in the United States of America

10 9 8 7 6 5 4 3 2 1

ISBN 0-13-368853-4 01

Prentice-Hall International, Inc., *London*
Prentice-Hall of Australia Pty. Limited, *Sydney*
Editora Prentice-Hall do Brasil, Ltda., *Rio de Janeiro*
Prentice-Hall Canada Inc., *Toronto*
Prentice-Hall of India Private Limited, *New Delhi*
Prentice-Hall of Japan, Inc., *Tokyo*
Prentice-Hall of Southeast Asia Pte. Ltd., *Singapore*
Whitehall Books Limited, *Wellington, New Zealand*

CONTENTS

PREFACE

As this book represents the first genus of a new species—the economic guidebook—a certain explanation is necessary.

If you are a tourist in Paris and have a guidebook in hand, you can easily learn the city by yourself. If you pay the equivalent of a penny to buy a one-paragraph guide, you might read the following:

> Start at the Ile de la cité and visit the cathedral of Notre Dame, which is the most famous cathedral of Paris. Construction started in 1163. Note particularly the rose windows. Then cross the Seine to the right bank, walk south one-half mile along the river to the Louvre. Former home of the kings of France, it now houses the best art collection in France. The renaissance collection is particularly impressive. Take Bus 72 going south and get off at the Eiffel tower. Built in 1887 it provides a magnificent view of the city. Watch out for pickpockets.

A popular guidebook such as the *Michelin* provides more description of many of the fascinating details and rates the various touristic attractions according to their relative importance. With the help of such a guidebook, you can gain a perspective on the city's spatial and historical relationships. Although it won't tell you everything there is to know about any particular site, a good guidebook supplies enough information for you to decide what to see and whether to make the visit or not. Special books or pamphlets can be obtained for more information about any particular attraction.

The economic guidebook should serve the same function so as to permit you, the reader, to learn a particular subject matter. Such a guidebook is something less than a treatise, because the subjects covered are not treated at great length; rather, the guidebook outlines the major aspects of various important problems and issues, sketches the key relationships between them, and then refers you to more detailed or specialized books and articles about them. Such a guidebook is also something more than an annotated bibliography since great emphasis is placed on explaining the relationships between various special problems and ideas (although, it should be added, annotated bibliographies follow almost every chapter). In sum, an economic guidebook is not a textbook to be studied under the direction of a teacher and to be later forgotten; but is rather a means to encourage you to discover a particular subject for yourself, to focus on those aspects of the subject that especially interest you, and to view other aspects of the subject in a manner such that contours of individual problems can be placed in perspective.

Since guidebooks should be short, the particular attractions that are chosen depend very much on the tastes and interests (more vulgarly, the prejudices) of the author. It is not by accident that almost all interesting guidebooks, beginning with Pausanias' guide to Greece written almost two millenia ago, are idiosyncratic. To give some warning about what you are—and are not—going to read, I would like to explain briefly what I am trying to do.

I believe that comparative economic systems is the most interesting field in economics because it deals with some of the largest and most important issues. The study of this subject can provide you with a useful framework of analysis for reading critically more specialized studies of particular capitalist or socialist economies or studies of economically less developed nations, both now and in the past. Unfortunately, almost all comparative economic systems textbooks on the market are extremely dull because, as you might find, they are usually arranged in one of three different ways: Books of the first type consist primarily of potted descriptions of a number of economies—little stories of Soviet, Chinese, Indian, French, and Swedish economies—so that you are unable to connect one economy with another. Books of the second type spend inordinate amounts of time on problems of methodology or typologies or untested theoretical models, so that you are unable to determine how actual economic systems really function. Those of the third type provide comparisions between theoretical models of one type of economic system and the actual performance of other economic systems so that you cannot separate the ideological shaff from the empirical wheat. In short, very few of these textbooks are truly comparative in an empirical sense.

Since I leave the detailed descriptions of various economies to others, you will not find in this guidebook a fully shaped description of any single economy. However, I do give references to such studies, particularly with regard to Eastern Europe and China. For those of you particularly interested in the Soviet Union, I also provide references in each chapter to the relevent chapters in Alec Nove's book *The Soviet Economic System;* there are, however, other fine books on the Soviet economy that you can use instead.

I also leave a great deal of theorizing and endless discussion of methodology to others. Let me add, however, that I believe strongly in the role of theory in understanding different economic systems and I have written this book assuming that you have mastered the materials of an introductory microeconomics course at the university level. Further, I do not hestitate to introduce certain theoretical concepts and models into this discussion, both from the Marxist and non-Marxist literature. Those of you having difficulties in understanding the type of statistical analysis that is carried out might find it useful to read Appendix A, which explains these methods in a simple manner. Particular concepts and terms, with which you may not be familiar, are defined in a glossary in Appendix B.

Finally, I spend little time on ideological or normative questions. I certainly do not attempt to tell you which economic system is "best." This is a question of vital importance that only you can decide for yourself. However, I try to provide relevant data to help you in making up your mind on this problem.

In short, I focus primarily on the making of actual empirical comparisons by setting out a series of testable propositions and then summarizing or presenting the results of actual empirical comparisons for nations with different economic systems. Sometimes empirical materials to make such tests are not available, but this is noted as well. This means, of course, that the generalizations that are actually obtained are based on an analysis of the best available data, rather than on strictly ideological or theoretial considerations. Of course, this also means that I will offend readers along all points of the political spectrum, for I try to test empirically many of the common assumptions about economic systems that pass as common coin in political discourse.

Thus I have tried to combine theoretical and empirical knowledge in a manner such that you can test your judgments about the way in which economies actually function, even though these economies may not conform to our theoretical ideas and models. I have also tried to indicate subject areas where our knowledge is weak and where much more research needs to be done, rather than covering up our important blind spots by the presentation of elegant theories, the explanatory powers of which have yet to be measured against the real world.

The briefness of the guidebook also forces me to select only those attractions which, given my biases, I think are of greatest importance. In this guide you will find little about fascism, or about the current developing nations, or about the transport sector, or agriculture, or banks, or any of a number of other subjects that might be included in a standard textbook. Many important interrelations between the economic and the political realms are also not discussed. On the other hand, some of you may find too much about primitive economies or about the developed European nations in both East and West from which most of the empirical comparisons are drawn.

As noted above, reading a guidebook is no substitute for visiting the places mentioned therein. Similarly, reading this guidebook is no substitute for reading more about the problems that are discussed in the sources indicated. It is my hope that you will take this book in hand and use it as a guide in exploring the comparative study of economic systems by yourself and with others. There are many fascinating relationships to discover, many important ideas to ponder, and many propositions to dispute. You are also invited to try your hands in making the comparative analyses concerning those countries, topics, and periods that you believe to be important; and Appendix C helps you to get started along this path.

Throughout history almost every preface to every guidebook ends with the same wish on the part of the author and I follow tradition to extend that wish to you: *Bon voyage!*

Acknowledgments

I am grateful to Peter Elek, Steven Golub, Zora Pryor, and John Stevens for their extremely useful comments on the manuscript of this book. I would also like to thank Frederick Kettering, who provided the fine drawings through this study. Finally, I am greatly in debt to several generations of students at Swarthmore College with whom I have discussed and debated my ideas about economic systems; their ideas are found on many pages.

1

INTRODUCTION

A. The Study of Economic Systems

Broad questions concerning the economic system arise on many occasions in the social sciences: Can capitalism survive? Are the economic systems of the United States and the Soviet Union converging? Can goods be more efficiently allocated with or without a price mechanism? In what directions are property rights changing? To what extent are fluctuations in aggregate production due to the institutional structure of the system or to changing policies of the government that act to destabilize the economy? To what degree can fluctuations arising from either cause be dampened? What are the underlying principles of production, exchange and distribution, and consumption in traditional peasant economies? Does central planning lead to faster or slower economic growth? As this list of specific questions can be extended almost without limit, it is useful to examine more carefully the basic types of questions underlying the study of economic systems and, more briefly, the purposes for undertaking such a task.

The subdiscipline of comparative economic systems differs from other branches of economics because its primary focus of analysis is on economic institutions. (The concepts of *system* and *institution* are difficult and are defined below.) It is a broader field of study than other subdisciplines of economics and touches not only upon the usual types of economic questions but also upon questions from many of the other social sciences. Such a study uses both the analytic tool of traditional (both orthodox and nonorthodox) economic theory and also tools from other disciplines. It focuses not just on our own contemporary economy but also on market and nonmarket economies throughout history and over the face of the earth, so that its scope of inquiry is very wide. Finally, the field relies greatly on the comparative method as a tool of analysis. Those wishing to pursue the comparative study of economic systems do well to heed Dante's well-known advice: "Watch how you enter and in whom you trust; do not let the wideness of the gate deceive you."

For the most part the comparative study of economic systems deals with *positive,* rather than *normative,* questions. That is, it focuses on questions about what "is," basing its answers on appeals to facts, rather than examining questions about what "ought to be" and basing its answers on appeals to values. For instance, we might ask questions about the forces underlying the volume of social insurance expenditures, rather than whether such expenditures are desirable or not; or about the effect of the level of development on the existence of specific property rights, rather than whether or not such property rights should exist in the first place. It should be clear that positive economics is useful for normative analysis. For instance, to judge the desirability of introducing national economic planning of investment, it is important to know the relative performance of nations with and without such policies. It must also be added that normative economics is important for positive analysis because it helps to define questions that are worthwhile to examine and provides the criteria of evaluation that are used in the exercises of positive analysis.

It is also useful to distinguish between the study of *ideal* and *real* economic systems, for both can be studied (although in this book, the focus is primarily upon the latter). When we analyze ideal economic systems, we are studying simplified models of the way in which these systems function. Since economic systems are so complex, this is the only way in which we can begin to try to understand their operation. An example of an ideal economic system is the general equilibrium model of the workings of the perfectly competitive market economy, which is sometimes used to explain certain facets of the U.S. economy. But the models may be oversimplified in a sufficient number of ways so that actual economies may not behave in the predicted fashion, either because they do not incorporate all the basic institutional assumptions of the model or because the models abstract from other important influences on the behavior of the economy. However, such models may be very useful in directing our gaze toward important aspects of the economy or in setting up certain measuring rods with which to examine actual institutions. When we analyze real economic systems we empirically examine actual economies and their behavior. Of course, without the aid of models, we may be unable to explain much of what we see; however, the models may also lead to predictions at considerable variance with what we observe.

It is this tension between ideal and real analyses that advances the field because it leads to new theory and improved observations of what has actually happened. However, this tension also makes the study of economic systems difficult because with the theories in which you now believe, you may be unable to explain many of the empirical results presented in this guide and this should require you to reexamine your beliefs.

Underlying the notion that the study of economic systems is a discipline distinct from other branches of economics is an important assumption about the nature of causal forces in the economy. More specifically, we assume that economic institutions and systems can*not* be adequately explained by reference to such "economic" causes as the level of economic development or to such "technical" causes as the physical or technological environment. If, for instance, the origin and development of all the most important economic institutions were primarily a function of the per capita income of the economy, then the study of economic systems could be subsumed under the field of economic development. However, the existence of apparently viable and different economic systems among nations at the same level of development in Eastern and Western Europe appears to belie any such strict economic determinism. Similarly, if economic institutions were solely the function of soil, climate, and terrain, then the study of economic systems could be subsumed under the field of economic geography. For instance, according to the Wittfogel hypothesis,[1] arid climates and the necessity of irrigating agriculture act strongly to encourage a centralized state and economy in preindustrial societies. However, the existence of precapitalist societies with large-scale irrigation systems without any such centralized economic system and also of centralized

[1]Karl A. Wittfogel, *Oriental Despotism: A Comparative Study of Total Power* (New Haven, Conn.: Yale University Press, 1957).

economies at similar levels of development without such irrigation systems appears to belie any strict geographical determinism. Of course, the separate discipline of economic systems must take into consideration that technological, developmental, and geographical factors do have an influence on the institutions and their functioning within the society, even though such influences may not be decisive.

In the study of economic systems, we explore two groups of basic questions: (1) What is the *impact* of an economic institution or system? and (2) What are the forces underlying the establishment, *development,* and decline of particular institutions. Each of these questions deserves brief attention.

An *impact* question focuses on the extent to which the performance of an economy can be attributed to particular institutions. For example, does the allocation system currently employed in the Soviet Union and some other Eastern European nations lead to more rapid growth or to a more efficient allocation of resources than a market economy? On an *abstract* level this question can be examined by constructing models of the different types of allocation systems and by comparing them according to the designated criteria. On an *empirical* level this question requires separating out the mutual influences on the actual performance of particular economies of *environmental variables* (e.g., the level of technology, the availability of skills and resources, the climate, and so forth), *policy variables* (the choice of different policies within a given institutional structure), and *institutional variables*. Since these factors are discussed in greater detail in a few pages, one example must suffice. If we are investigating the performance of the housing sector of a given nation, we must ask whether the existence of slum housing is a function of the climate or the level of development, or a function of particular policies (regarding the interest rate, incomes, and the construction of public housing) or the different economic institutions such as the market allocation of housing that influence the allocation of housing space (e.g., can one find slums in nations with similar economic institutions?)

A *developmental* question focuses on the institution *per se* and the analysis not only of such broad causal forces as the level of development or the climate (which are discussed above) but also on many more subtle causal forces as well. For instance, if we are examining the growth of social security systems, to what extent can their creation and development be attributed to the age structure of the population, the level of development, or the political mobilization of particular groups with an interest in seeing the creation of such institutions?

If impact and developmental questions are examined together for economic institutions influencing the behavior of the entire economy, we sometimes speak of *laws of motion* of the economy. In such cases the analyst focuses first on the forces leading to the creation of particular institutions, then on the impact of such institutions on the economy, and finally on the influence of such an impact upon the further development of the institution.

It should be emphasized that such institutional analyses can be carried out at different levels of abstraction. We might, for instance, focus our attention on the micro level, that is, upon the impact of a particular institution in a particular economy (such as labor unions). Or we might focus our attention upon the macro levels, that is, upon the impact of a set of institutions upon a broad economic indicator (e.g., differential growth rates of East and West Germany). Or we might focus our attention on the meta level, that is, upon a system defined in a broad manner that transcends particular national economies. For instance, the analyses of David Ricardo, Karl Marx, Joseph Schumpeter, or, more recently, Daniel Bell on the development of capitalism would be examples of this genre. In passing it is interesting to note that most such meta-level analyses have been performed on capitalist, rather then socialist, economies.

The purpose of this book is to discuss methods and to develop concepts with which economic systems can be analyzed on both abstract and empirical levels. The book is not meant to be an exhaustive monograph. Rather, by drawing examples from a number of economies, it attempts to sensitize you to a set of issues that the author deems important. At the end of each chapter is an annotated bibliography of sources for further reading that provide contrasting views or develop particular points or present important factual materials on certain economies, particularly the socialist economies of Eastern Europe.

Given the array of important issues that are covered in the study of economic systems, it should not be surprising that each reader will approach this book with different goals and motives in mind. You may wish to gain an idea about the spectrum of possibilities for carrying out economic activities and how to evaluate the major advantages and disadvantages of different solutions so as to develop your own personal political-economic philosophy. You may approach the subject to gain a deeper understanding of basic economic laws and to determine which of these transcend individual systems and which are specific to the system. You may wish to learn a particular approach toward gaining economic knowledge, that is, to learn the comparative method and both its uses and misuses. Or you may wish to use the results of the study of economic systems to organize in a coherent manner the vast factual materials that exist about the different economies of the world. All of these are quite valid purposes and, it is hoped, all will be served by this guidebook.

B. Approaching Economic Systems Comparatively

1. An Example about Garbage Collecting

Let us consider, for a moment, a small economic system consisting of the production, distribution, and consumption of one service. A good example is garbage collecting, a common service for which the relevant technological and economic issues should be relatively familiar to most of you. This example is not chosen as a lighthearted introduction to the subject, but rather as a problem that illustrates most of the difficult analytic problems of the comparative approach and, further, one that has been the subject of some careful empirical work. Three broad systems of organizing such activity are in general use: municipal socialism, free enterprise or competitive capitalism, and regulated capitalism.

a. Municipal Socialism

In municipal socialism the city owns the means of production (the garbage trucks) and a special city department hires the workers and manages the system. By means of some political process certain parameters of the type of service provided by the system are set (e.g., how many times a week the garbage is collected, whether it is collected at the curb or at the back of the dwelling, whether garbage must be separated from other refuse, whether a special type of garbage container must be used, and so forth). All homes and apartments must be serviced and the customers are billed for such services—whether they are wanted or not—either directly (usually a flat fee per home, but sometimes per garbage container) or through the tax system. Such a system does not, of course, prevent individual home dwellers from negotiating with private companies to obtain additional garbage-collecting services.

b. Free Enterprise, Competitive Capitalism

In the free enterprise system the service is provided by any entrepreneur who wishes to enter the market. The entrepreneur owns the trucks, hires the workers, and solicits customers (usually through letters to the various homes and apartments detailing the services provided and the costs). The customers can choose the type of service they wish by setting some of the parameters of the service (certain parameters may also be specified by the city and determined through the political process); they pay according to the negotiated price. In order to prevent the potential health menace that might occur if some home dwellers tried to save money by burying their garbage in their back yards, such systems are generally accompanied by laws requiring garbage disposal of some specified sort at all homes and apartments.

c. Regulated Capitalism or a Mixed System

Although regulated capitalist systems can cover a variety of arrangements, one common system is for the city to hold an auction or bidding system for private enterpreneurs every few years. The entrepreneur offering to supply the service at the lowest cost per customer obtains an exclusive franchise. As in the case of municipal socialism, the city can set certain parameters of the service. All home dwellers are required to subscribe to the service; according to the way in which the system is set up, the customers might pay the company directly or else they might pay the city which in turn transfers the funds in a block to the entrepreneur. Again, such a system does not prevent the customers from negotiating either with the winning entrepreneur or with other companies to obtain additional services.

2. Evaluation Problems

Before you and your fellow citizens can make the momentous choice of which is a better system for collecting garbage—municipal socialism, free enterprise capitalism, or regulated capitalism—it is necessary to establish some criteria for judgment. Otherwise, you may be arguing forever. Although the following list is not exhaustive, it provides a useful starting point:

    a. Monetary costs of the system
    b. Quality of the service—reliability, punctuality, cleanliness, etc.
    c. Degree to which the parameters of the service correspond to consumer desires
    d. Flexibility of the system if growth occurs (occasioned either by a rising population or by a growing amount of garbage per person)
    e. Distributional aspects, such as the inequality of the consumption of the service by home dwellers and also the degree to which unconscionable profits are being made by certain people as a result of the system
    f. Treatment of garbage workers in a humane fashion

It should be clear that all the above criteria rest on particular value judgments. Sometimes their subjective nature is quite apparent (e.g., "unconscionable profits"); sometimes they are more subtle. The difficulties arising from such a subjective basis for selecting these six criteria are particularly apparent in trying to weigh the relative importance of each. Obviously, if one of the three systems discussed above performed the best on all six criteria, no problem would occur; but such a fortunate circumstance is highly unlikely. If, for instance, free enterprise capitalism had the best rating with regard to correspondence with consumer desires, but had the lowest rating with regard to various distributional issues, then our judgment about the "best" system would depend on the degree to which these different criteria are important to us.

3. Relevant Theoretical and Empirical Evidence

Let us focus, for a moment, on just the first criterion which concerns the cost of the system. How would we determine which is the least expensive?

Having studied economic theory, some people might be inclined to set up some economic models and, by studying them, determine the lowest cost. Certainly the existing models would help us in isolating the most important cost elements. For instance, it should be clear that the system of free enterprise capitalism might result in the trucks of five companies collecting garbage on the same street, while the other two systems would have only one truck on that street, thereby saving wages and gasoline expenditures. Furthermore, negotiation costs between the customers and the providers might be much higher than in the other two systems. However, the entrepreneurs might have much more incentive to hold down labor costs than in the case of municipal socialism. The regulated market capitalism and the municipal socialism solutions may also be more open to corruption than the free enterprise capitalism solution; and corruption has an impact on the costs paid by consumers.

Economic theory can help us isolate many such factors; but no theory yet proposed can tell us very much about the relative magnitudes involved. Clearly we need a more empirical approach, and two options are open to us: (1) an engineering approach and (2) a statistical approach.

An *engineering approach* would require us to sit down and, with the usage of various service norms, to try to figure out what the costs would be. For instance, given the "norm" that with a given type of truck, an average garbage-collecting team can service a house in five minutes, then total collection costs can be calculated. Unfortunately, many such norms are quite unreliable and, further, are based on conditions that may not exist in particular towns. If the population density is high, a garbage collection team may be able to service houses in less than five minutes; if houses are some distance from each other, the reverse may be true. Further, there are no norms to tell you the impact of the systemic elements outlined above.

A *statistical approach* is rather different. First we specify the major cost elements; then we obtain data from a variety of cities and calculate a cost function from these data. This involves calculating a regression equation with some dummy variables, a procedure that deserves a short explanation.

If we are calculating a cost curve in a situation where the wages in all cities in the sample are the same and the cities all have the same characterictics, then we might need only to relate one independent (or explanatory) variable—namely, total cost—to one dependent (or explained) variable—namely, quantity of service provided. We can plot the various observations of price and quantity of garbage collecting in the different cities on graph paper and then draw a line that seems to fit these points. To shortcut this tedious procedure, we can handle the observations by employing some simple formulae derived by statisticians to determine the line that "best fits" the observations. This line is called the *regression line;* the criteria for the "best fit" are rather tricky and are best left to the study of statistics. (If you are unfamiliar with this technique of statistical analysis, which is used extensively throughout this guidebook, then it is important for you to read Appendix A which explains these matters in much greater detail.) If, in this example of a cost curve, the wages in the cities are different, then this can be easily taken into account by adding an additional variable into the regression analysis so that costs of service depend on both wages of the workers and the quantity of services provided. In this case, we have a multiple regression with two independent (or explanatory) variables.

A simplified cost function for garbage collecting in our sample of cities can be a calculated as a multiple regression that looks something like this:

$$C = a + b_1W + b_2P + b_3D + b_4N + b_5T + b_6S_1 + b_7S_2,$$

where C is cost per person per year; W is average wages paid to garbage collectors; P is the population of the city (a variable to capture any economies or diseconomies of scale); D is the population density; N is the number of times the garbage is collected each week; T is a variable designating the type of collection system and is set up as a *dummy variable* which is given a value of one if the city collects the garbage in the backs of dwellings and zero if the city only has a curbside service (dummy variables are treated in the same manner as other variables); and the S's are dummy variables representing the economic system (this is explained below). The lowercase letters are coefficients that are calculated from the observations. The a is a constant and the b's are coefficients that show the impact of the accompanying variable on C with other things being equal. For instance, if b_1 is 16, this means that the cost of collecting garbage per person per year rises $16 for every $1 rise in hourly wages, other variables held constant.

This still does not answer the question of which system of garbage collecting has the lowest cost. Let us, therefore, make our base line of comparison the case of municipal socialism. In every city for which we collect data that has municipal socialism, we set both S_1 and S_2 equal to zero. If the city has free enterprise capitalism, we set S_1 equal to one and S_2 equal to zero. Therefore, the calculated b_6 signifies the difference in costs between municipal socialism and free enterprise capitalism, other things being equal. If it is positive, then the former is less expensive; if it is negative, the latter is less expensive. Similarly, if the city has regulated market capitalism, we set S_1 equal to zero and S_2 equal to one. In this case the calculated b_7 signifies the difference in costs between municipal socialism and regulated capitalism; other things being equal, if it is positive, municipal socialism is less costly; if it is negative, regulated capitalism is less costly. If we want to compare free enterprise and regulated capitalism, we need only compare the calculated values of b_6 and b_7. Other things being equal, if the former is larger, free enterprise capitalism is more expensive; if the latter is larger, regulated capitalism is more expensive.

A calculation of such a cost curve for garbage collecting that includes the systemic variables specified above has been made for a group of cities in the U.S. state of Connecticut in a very systematic manner.[2] The results are quite interesting: The lowest garbage-collecting costs occur, on the average, in systems of regulated capitalism and the highest cost occur, on the average, in systems of municipal socialism. Although such results may hold for Connecticut, many serious problems arise in trying to generalize such results to other situations; some of these are discussed below.

Turning back to the list of criteria by which systems should be evaluated, we find that collecting relevant quantitative information for making judgments is very difficult. In some cases we can make certain judgments on the basis of a theory: For instance, it seems likely that the free enterprise system would have garbage-collection systems more tailored to the individual wants than the other systems, especially if the city's population or housing are heterogeneous. On the other hand, we have very few clues from theory about the relative quality of the service between municipal socialism and regulated capitalism except for scattered anecdotal evidence and horror stories: "I lived in Chicago, which has a municipal garbage collection system, and let me tell you. . . ."

For garbage collecting it may turn out that the most important criterion is the relative costs since the systems are quite similar in other respects; if this is the case, we can sidestep most of the problems in trying to quantify particular types of information for the purpose of making comparisons according to the other criteria listed. But if this is not the case and if the most important criteria do not lend themselves

---

[2]John Quigly and Peter Kemper, *The Economics of Refuse Collection* (Cambridge, Mass.: Ballinger, 1976).

easily for the making of quantitative comparisons, then considerable difficulties arise.

In making such overall judgments, two pieces of wisdom are important to observe: First, if we cannot easily quantify variables that have relevance to the criteria we hold to be the most important, we must never allow our judgments to be based on those comparisons that *can* easily be made. Second, we should never compare *actual* performance of one system with the *theoretical* or *ideal* behavior of another.

4. The Meaning of the Results from a Comparative Analysis

Let us suppose that the cost functions obtained for cities in Connecticut are correct. To what extent can we generalize such results to other areas or to activities other than garbage collection? To what extent do the results obtained allow us to understand the major systemic questions about the service? In short, what do our results mean?

a. Generalizing from the Results

On a very abstract level, the performance of an economic system can be said to be a function of three variables: (1) the social and physical environment within which the system is located, (ii) the system itself, and (iii) the policies followed by the government and private individuals to make the system work. These three factors mutually influence each other but can usually be separated for the purpose of empirical analysis. In the comparisons made for garbage collecting in cities in Connecticut, the environment variable is roughly the same (except for those variables such as population density that are taken into account in the regression); further, governmental policies followed except with regard to garbage collecting are also roughly similar. Therefore, the empirical analysis focuses primarily upon the system.

If we broaden the basis of our comparison to include more cities in the United States or in other countries in the world, the environmental and policy variables might be quite different. For instance, in societies where native entrepreneurship is very weak and the government can provide services relatively efficiently (i.e., the social environment is quite different from that in Connecticut), municipal socialism might be the best solution. Or where the climate and road conditions (the physical environment) change drastically over the year (e.g., in very northerly climates), not only are costs of collecting garbage higher but risks in supplying garbage collecting might be sufficiently great that one or the other system might not be viable.

Similarly, the policies followed by cities utilizing the various systems may be different. Consider, for example, different variants of municipal socialism. Administrators in some cities with such a system may not be able to fire incompetent or lazy garbage collectors; in other cities they can. In some cities the garbage collectors may belong to a powerful labor union that has been able to obtain high wages for the workers; in other cities, the city might have been able to resist demand for higher wages. In some cities, the garbage-collection department may provide different services for different people (for a price, of course), so as to tailor collection more closely to the needs of the people; while in other cities the same service is provided for all. These different policies can greatly influence costs of garbage collection. Similarly, in cities with a system of regulated capitalism, policies concerning the time period between auctions, the area that is covered in each auction, the monitoring of the services of the franchise holder, the manner in which contract enforcement is carried out, and other aspects can also considerably influence costs. In the capitalist system, the policies concerning the activities of entrepreneurs (e.g., when a company can drop a customer, or the setting of minimum service requirements) similarly influence costs.

What all this means is quite simple: Because performance is a function of environment, system, and policies, the Connecticut results cannot be easily generalized, either to different areas or to different activities (in which the production and consumption environments are different). Unless the observations are drawn from a sample embracing a large area, skepticism about the relevance of the results of empirical comparisons of economic systems is in order because of difficulties in determining the influences of differences in environment and policies. It should also be added that quite often a sufficient number of difficulties in data collection and analysis arise in making even a set of small-scale comparisons that a certain skepticism should be exercised when examining the statistical results themselves.

b. Unanswered Questions

Suppose that we have been able to make valid empirical comparisons about costs and other criteria used in evaluating economic systems. We still have not answered all important questions because we have only focused on *impact* questions. A whole range of *developmental* questions has not been posed. For instance, to produce garbage-collection services why have some cities opted for municipal socialism, others for free enterprise capitalism, and still others for regulated capitalism? How often, why, where, and when do we find revolutions, that is, important and sudden changes in the system? Do the systems have their own natural life cycles? It does not appear that such questions have been addressed with regard to garbage-collection systems, but illustrative examples can be found for other services that show what kind of analyses can be made.

For solving the problem of old age pensions, we can also specify a variety of solutions that can be labeled socialism, free market capitalism, and regulated capitalism (or mixed systems). For instance, if we look at the 25 economically most developed nations in 1913, we find that roughly half of them had adopted some type of old age insurance that was run by the central government (which might be considered "socialistic"). The other half did not adopt such governmental programs until much later (e.g., the Social Security program in the United States was not set up until the mid-1930s) and had adopted solutions based either on principles of free market or regulated capitalism. What were the important causal elements underlying adoption of such governmental social insurance programs?

Again, models may give us some ideas about possible causal elements but they are no substitute for empirical investigation. The causal forces underlying the adoption of social insurance are, perhaps, most easily isolated by investigating the differences between the two groups of developed nations and, indeed, an empirical investigation of this question has been made.[3] It showed that certain "obvious" factors such as the relative level of economic development, urbanization, and the percentage of the aged in the population did not distinguish the two groups of nations (i.e., did not play a causal role) but that the results could be explained by one variable representing the political mobilization of the workers, as measured by the relative importance of membership in labor unions among members of the work force. If one reads case studies of the adoption of social insurance, one finds confirming evidence that the labor unions played an important political role in the establishment of such systems or that such social insurance systems were adopted in order to counter the growing political power of the unions, as Chancellor Bismark did in Germany in the 1880s.

Inasmuch as such a measure of political mobilization of workers is valid (i.e., if the "proxy variable" of unionization really represents political moblization), this result raises an important difficulty in the study of comparative economic systems. In many instances, we must look beyond the economy narrowly defined in order to isolate causal variables. These variables may be political or social (e.g., in primitive societies it has been shown that the presence of a system of plural wives has an important impact on the presence or absence of systems of land rental[4]). Their possible importance requires us to cast our net widely in

[3]Frederic L. Pryor, *Public Expenditures in Communist and Capitalist Nations* (London: Allen and Unwin, 1968), pp. 473–75.

[4]Frederic L. Pryor, *The Origins of the Economy* (New York: Academic Press, 1977), chap. 5.

the search for causal forces, even at the cost of losing the theoretical elegance found in the more narrowly defined economic models.

5. Some Conclusions

These examples have been presented to show in a concrete fashion most of the important methodological problems that arise in the study of comparative economic systems. Much more can be said; but it seems more interesting to discuss such problems in the context of specific problems, rather than on an abstract level with a few illustrative examples.

It should be clear that our first task is to pay close attention to the criteria of evaluation of economic systems and the relationship between policy and institutional tools on the one hand and economic goals on the other hand. Therefore, these topics serve as the focus for the next chapter. Most of the remaining chapters of this guidebook are arranged around one or more of the criteria of evaluation of economic systems. The analysis is both theoretical and empirical; its purpose is to permit you to read case study materials with greater sensitivity and discrimination.

C. Definitions and Problems
of Labeling Economic Systems

Since this guide is about economic institutions and systems, it will be useful to have some definitions of what these entities are. The definitions discussed below are highly abstract, but they may provide some aid in defining our subject matter.

1. Institutions: Definitions and Examples

An *economic institution* is a pattern of recurrent and regularized relations between two or more people who are carrying out some economic function (production, distribution or exchange, consumption). Such relations are shaped by the values of the participants (the beliefs legitimizing such interactions), norms regularizing the interaction (e.g., property laws, customs and class mores, rules, and so forth), sanctions and rewards, and the specific motives of the individuals involved.

Institutions can be *concrete* or *embodied* in the sense that they are represented by some "visible" evidence (e.g., factories, banks, collective farms, or hunting and gathering parties). They can also be *abstract* or *disembodied* and more difficult to observe directly, although they influence observable behavior (e.g., the price mechanism or a physical allocation mechanism). They can be *formal* and operate by means of published rules; or they can be informal and operate by means of shared understandings. They can be *narrow* and concern only one or a few activities (e.g., the rules and procedures for obtaining a license or permission to export); or they may be *all-embracing* and concern many activities (e.g., the set of property laws of a nation).

According to one's analytical interests, particular institutions can be designated in quite different ways. For instance, looking at distributional institutions we can classify them according to whether transactions are predominantly characterized by equivalent or nonequivalent movements of goods and services (i.e., by *exchange* or by *transfer*), or whether particular media of exchange are involved in such transactions, or whether such distribution is carried out by individuals or groups, or whether such distribution is carried out in a personal or impersonal manner, and so forth. Each designation cuts reality in a different fashion; each may or may not be useful, depending upon what behavior the analyst is trying to explain. The purpose of different delineations of institutions is not to develop typologies for their own sake but to gain insight into human behavior; if that goal is not met, the delineation is not very useful.

2. Economic System: A Definition

What is an economic system? If the problem is stated in such a general fashion, it should not be surprising that the answer is quite general as well.[5] An *economic system* consists of those parts of political, social, and economic institutions, organizations, laws, rules, and beliefs that interact in a manner directly or indirectly to affect consumption, distribution or exchange, and production (what is produced, how much is produced, and how it is produced).

Several aspects of this definition should be noted. First, the economy is not separated from the society or polity; rather it is an aspect of behavior of the participants and is imbedded in their individual behavior and social interactions. Second, it covers both formal and informal behavior as well as concrete and abstract institutions. Third, it emphasizes the interaction of individuals and different types of organizations. Finally, this definition can be applied to a variety of different circumstances: We could, for instance, consider a troop of baboons or chimpanzees as an economic system and examine their production, distribution or exchange, and consumption activities, even though they have no formal economic institutions. Or we could examine a university in the same manner. Or, as shown above, the production, distribution or exchange, and consumption of garbage-collection services can be examined as a small-scale economic system as well.

[5]This definition is a modification of that proposed by J. M. Montias, *The Structure of Economic Systems* (New Haven, Conn.: Yale University Press, 1976).

3. The Labelling of Economic Systems

Two major methods of labeling economic systems have come into common use. The first looks at the processes of economic activity and growth and distinguishes various economic systems in this context. The second defines certain crucial characteristics and defines economic systems in terms of these. Such characteristics may, in turn, be derived from some model or theory of economic activity; or the characteristics may be chosen in an ad hoc manner.

A brief examination of the development of the concept of economic system allows us to see these approaches more concretely, to understand the importance of the distinction between *ideal* and *real* economic systems (terms discussed in Section A), and to appreciate the uses and misuses that the concept of economic system currently enjoys.

a. Some Very Brief Historical Notes

The term *economic system* arose in the discussion of continental economists, especially of the German historical school, in the second half of the nineteenth century. The major focus was the development of economies from primitive to modern stages. The participants of these debates were all influenced by the "evolutionism" in the intellectual air at that time, stemming from the twin influences of Charles Darwin in the field of biology and of G. W. F. Hegel in the fields of history and philosophy. They were reacting against the use of physics as a model for economic analysis where analysts (such as David Ricardo) attempted to reduce the economy to a set of interacting but bloodless decision makers and where neither economic institutions nor economic history were ever seriously discussed. Indeed, using this physics model, analysis focused on a single abstract "economy" and all differences between economic systems disappeared.

In contrast, these continental social scientists focused on different questions and attempted to apply ideas about evolution to explain the growth and development of institutions and economic systems; in such attempts they often constructed various types of "stage theories." Some nineteenth-century stage theorists such as Friedrich List focused primarily on production and made a simple distinction between hunting and gathering, agricultural, industrial, and commercial economies. Others focused on distribution, and differentiated economic systems by the "distance" between producers and consumers; for example, Karl Buecher distinguished three major stages of development: (i) the household economy of antiquity, which produced all of its own needs; (ii) the town economy of the Middle Ages, where producers and consumers of a particular good were usually different people, but were in close contact;

and (iii) national economies of modern times, in which consumers and producers are separated by many middlemen and agencies. Such ideas were attacked by contemporaries who supplied other sets of differentiating characteristics between economic systems. For instance, Bruno Hildebrand declared that the key was the role of money and, as a result, he distinguished economies using only barter, those with simple token money, and those with credit and more complicated monetary instruments.

Unfortunately, most of these stage theories served not as theoretical constructs with which to generate hypotheses, but rather as sets of descriptive labels with which to classify the growth of "real" economies during the course of their history. They have little analytical content and the argument between such economists was, literally, a battle of labels.

Before much of this battle had taken place, Karl Marx and Friedrich Engels had proposed a different classification that was based on the major technological relations and accompanying property relations. According to the simplistic interpretation of their ideas given by Joseph Stalin, five economic systems can be distinguished: (i) primitive communism where there is no private property, class structure, division of labor, money, or trade; (ii) slave-holding economies, a class society where the most important factor of production is labor; (iii) feudalism, a class society where the major factor of production is land that is owned by a small group of aristocrats; (iv) capitalism, a class society where the major factor of production is machinery and buildings that are owned by a small group of capitalists; and (v) developed communist economies where private property is eliminated, where class domination has been eliminated, and where the division of labor has been sharply reduced. Unlike the stage theorists mentioned above, Marx and Engels attempted to derive testable propositions about at least one of these economic systems (capitalism); furthermore, they based their predictions on the basis of a theoretical model and looked for verification in actual economies. In short, they distinguished between ideal and real economic systems for the purpose of analysis and tried to use the systems concept as an economic tool. Whether their attempt was successful is, of course, open to question.[6] In the twentieth century other examples of attempts to construct a stage theory with testable hypotheses can be found, for example, in some of the writings of W. W. Rostow.

Almost all stage theorists assume a unilineal line of economic development so that economic institutions and systems are primarily a function of the level of per capita income. But once economies are found

[6]An extensive discussions of these matters is found in Frederic L. Pryor, "The Classification and Analysis of Precapitalist Economic Systems by Marx and Engles," *History and Political Economy*, 14, No. 4 (December 1982), pp. 521–42.

that seem to skip certain stages or that have certain institutions at particular level of development which are not in accordance with the stage theory, some obvious analytical difficulties arise. Empirical research reveals not only an imperfect correlation of many features of economies with the level of economic development but also long periods in which the level of economic development has fallen rather than risen so that the assumption of unilineality is also open to doubt for another reason.

To escape such difficulties, some economists broke the link between the systems labels and the development of real systems. For instance, at the end of the nineteenth century Werner Sombart proposed a more complicated classification system with three major criteria: (i) the prevailing technologies, (ii) the organization of economic activity, and (iii) the "spirit" of the individuals engaged in economic activities. By sorting actual economies into different boxes based on these criteria, he hoped to group economies whose basic economic behavior was similar in major respects. Although he never provided a coherent explanation of the ways in which those economies falling in the same classification would be similar or dissimilar, his breaking of the link between classification of economic systems and their level of economic development and his attempt to use the system labels in an analytical fashion set the stage for more modern analyses. Many decades later Alexander Gerschenkron attempted to show how the behavior of particular economic systems at a given stage of development is modified by the international environment in which they are found, a fruitful approach that has focused attention on the relationship of the development and behavior of economic institutions and forces external to the economy.

b.   Three Major Analytical Difficulties in Labeling

(i) Problem 1: The Continuum Problem.   We can define an economic system according to any criteria we want. However, the characteristics may not be manifested in a real economic system in a discrete fashion (100% or 0%) but rather over a continuum. Suppose, for instance, that we define capitalism and socialism in terms of governmental ownership of the means of production (the concept of "public ownership" is somewhat more vague than "governmental ownership" and most statistical data on the subject do not make this distinction). We can then attempt to classify the economic systems of different countries by examining some appropriate data. In Table 1–1 some such data for a number of countries in East and West are presented. Some problems of classification became immediately apparent.

It should be clear that the various real economies fall along a continuum and that in the first two columns certain "socialist" nations such as

TABLE 1-1
The Relative Importance of Government Ownership

Country	Year	Ratio of Economically Active Population in Enterprises and Facilities Owned by the Government to Total Economically Active[a]			
		Total	Total Material Production[b]	Total except Agriculture, Forestry, Fishing	Total Material Production except Agriculture, Forestry, Fishing
West Germany	1950	9%	7%	12%	10%
Japan	1960	10	5	14	9
Switzerland	1960	11	8	12	9
United States	1960	15	5	16	6
France	1954	17	10	22	15
Sweden	1960	20	6	22	7
Israel	1959	24	8	28	11
United Kingdom	1962	25	17	26	19
Yugoslavia	1953	30	18	75	80
Austria	1966	31	27	33	30
Finland	1965	34	25	36	26
Bulgaria	1956	37	27	92	88
Poland	1960	48	40	84	86
Soviet Union	1959	59	49	96	95
East Germany	1964	71	69	80	84

[a]"Economically active" refers to all men and women who participate in the labor force or who are looking for employment.
[b]"Material production" refers to total production excluding services. "Ownership" refers to the formal holding of a title pertaining to 50 percent or more of the assets of the estblishment under consideration.

Source: The sources for these data are given in Frederic L. Pryor, *Property and Industrial Organization in Communist and Capitalist Nations* (Bloomington: Indiana University Press, 1973), app. B–2.

Yugoslavia have a lower degree of governmental ownership than certain "capitalist" countries such as Austria and Finland. This result occurs because of a high percentage of the labor force in private agriculture in Yugoslavia. (In the last two columns the picture is different.)

Even the data themselves present problems because certain enterprises and facilities are only fractionally owned by the government. As a cutoff point in the calculations, a "50 percent or more" public ownership criterion was employed.

The continuum problem is another way of saying that most real economic systems are "mixed" to some degree. In classifying real economies according to a group of characteristics derived from some ideal model, it is generally useful to approach the problem in terms of such characteristics being more or less realized, rather than trying to impose some absolute standard of "all or nothing." Of course, once the problem is stated in terms of degrees, rather than extremes, the fascinating question of the optimal place to draw the boundary between two sets of economic systems arises.

(ii) Problem 2: Discrepancies of Meaning of System Labels. A major problem in the modern discussion of economic systems is the variation in meaning of the various systems labels. Two illustrations of this problem will be given.

The term *feudalism,* which has been in usage for over two centuries, has been defined in a large number of ways. If we are referring to a feudal economic system, it is useful to see what some of these differences are so that we can correctly classify particular economies. Some "materialistic" definitions of the term (i.e., definitions focusing on behavior or institutions, rather than what participants in the economy think or believe) culled from various books and articles about feudalism published since 1960 are presented in Table 1–2. It should be clear that many of the 30 or so definitions conflict and that many of the definitions cover quite different real economies. If we are trying to decide whether Japan in 1700 was feudal or not, the answer would depend very much upon the definition chosen.

When we turn to the definition of capitalism or, more fruitfully, the distinction between capitalism and socialism,[7] we run into the same problem. Some of the major distinctions that are made are the following:

• In capitalism the means of production are owned by private individuals or groups; in socialism the means of production are owned by the government or by social groups.

---

[7]According to a distinction made by Marx and others, in "socialism" each gives according to his ability and receives according to his work; while in "communism" each gives according to his ability and receives according to his need. This useful distinction is maintained throughout the book.

- In capitalism the allocation of productive resources is unplanned by the central government and is coordinated through a market mechanism; in socialism the allocation of productive resources is planned by the central government and is centrally administered.
- In capitalism most consumer goods and services are bought by the consumers and, further, governmental transfers of income are relatively small; in socialism more consumer goods and services are financed by the government through the tax system and allocated to the consumers and, further, governmental transfers of income are relatively large.
- In capitalism the major driving forces for undertaking economic activities are material incentives (e.g., additional income) and production is primarily motivated for the sake of profit; in socialism the major driving force for undertaking economic activities are moral and production is for use.
- In capitalism the major sources of income are activities initiated by the individual so that large inequalities of income are tolerated; in socialism the major sources of income are activities initiated by the state or social groups and large inequalities of income are not tolerated.
- In capitalism political life is dominated by a competition between political parties: in socialism political life is dominated by a single party.
- In capitalism/socialism (take your pick) people are free and unalienated; while in socialism/capitalism (take your pick), people are unfree and alienated.

This list can, of course, be considerably extended. The different definitions would not be disturbing if the phenomena to which they refer were correlated; but below it is shown that this is *not* the case. This lack of coherence means, in turn, that for discussions about capitalism and socialism to make any sense, the terms must first be defined; otherwise it is difficult to know what the discussion is all about.

(iii) Problem 3: The Coherence Problem. To what extent do the characteristics designated above describe the same economies? Some types of theories suggest that there is a high coherence; however, the issue cannot be solved in such a manner and we must turn to some data.

Table 1–3 refers to the first two distinctions between capitalism and socialism, namely, the ownership of the means of production and the method by which resources are allocated. Given these two sets of distinctions, four combinations of characteristics are generated and concrete examples of each are provided. These examples suggest that there is certainly no logical connection between the two sets of distinctions.

Table 1–4 refers to the first and third distinctions between capitalism and socialism, namely the ownership of the means of production and the relative importance of public consumption expenditures. To make the problem concrete, some data are supplied. Pairs of nations with roughly the same per capita income are presented on each line so that this causal factor underlying public consumption expenditures is held

TABLE 1–2

Materialistic Defining Characteristics of Feudalism

A. Society

1. Economic, political, and social institutions are not sharply differentiated.
2. Society is primarily divided into two groups of actors: those actually carrying out agricultural production (lower group) and those living upon the fruits of this labor (upper group).
   a. The upper group obtains this income through some type of property rights upon the land.
   b. Such property rights are obtained from those higher in the upper group in return for the performance of services.
   c. Such services are usually military but could include administrative or fiscal services as well.
   d. The enjoyment of income and social privileges is correlated with this ranking of lower and upper groups.
   e. Only members of the upper group are allowed to participate in warfare as leaders and to bear a certain type of arms.
3. The upper group is organized hierarchically.
   a. Personal oaths of fealty bind individuals on higher and lower levels of the upper group.
   b. Such oaths are only between individuals of adjoining levels of the upper group (in contrast to a situation where such an oath is sworn not only to an immediate superior but also to the superior's superior).
   c. Such oaths of fealty are accompanied by contractual specification of rights and duties of each partner. Although a strong element of reciprocity is defined in such an oath, there is an implied social hierarchy through which the major activities of society are structured.
4. The lower group is organized as a pool of dependent laborers and is both economically and juridically under the landlords.
   a. The laborers are tied to particular pieces of land (rather than to particular individuals) by extraeconomic means.
   b. They generally own their own tools of production
   c. They produce more than they consume, with the difference given to the upper groups:
      i. Such extractions (their form is discussed below) are based or justified primarily as payment in return for the use of land (i.e., a rent on land) rather than in terms of political allegiance (i.e., a tax arising from political subjectship) or in terms of religious duties.
      ii. Such extractions can, however, also take the form of taxes and service duties to the government (e.g., the corvée) or compulsory payment of tithes to the church imposed on the individual.

B. Polity and Law

1. Sovereignty is parcelized in a vertically articulated system.
   a. The top of the social, political, and economic hierarchy (the king) is de facto politically weak.
   b. Parcelization occurs primarily through immunities granted to landlords.
   c. Parcelization can occur horizontally as well; that is, members of the lower groups could have different seigneurs for rent payment, for the system of local justice, or for the "banalities."
   d. The governmental bureaucracy is highly underdeveloped.
   e. Laws are primarily customary and the legislative function of the top is highly limited.
2. Land tenure by members of the upper group is generally combined with legal, fiscal, and police powers.

a. Law is enforced for members of the lower group through courts that are primarily under the jurisdiction of landholding groups.

b. Fiscal exactions by the top are relatively small in comparison to other types of exactions and members of the upper group are generally immune from most of these.

3. Land is held conditionally (i.e., rights in land are shared) in comparison to the Roman concept of ownership implying absolute powers.

a. Land tenures may or may not be formally inheritable but usually they extend through many generations of the same family; further, primogeniture is the primary form of inheritance.

b. Violations of the service conditions of land tenure are defined as a breach of contract, rather than a crime.

4. A polity dominated by a landlord class is able to prevent peasants from obtaining land-ownership or control over rents, from organizing the conditions of production and the use of the means of production in the manner they see fit (e.g., controlling the size of their plots or the character of their work or cooperation with others), and from obtaining political power.

C. Economy

1. The benefits of landholding provide the major source of income for the upper groups; and direct agricultural production provides the major source of income for the lower groups. Economic activities other than agriculture are relatively unimportant.

2. Both land and labor productivity in agriculture are relatively low; agricultural techniques are generally quite primitive.

3. The major unit of production is the large estate (the manor).

a. It is relatively self-contained so that only a small percentage of total production is exchanged with people outside the manor.

b. Such exchange of produce occurs through a market.

c. The land is managed directly or indirectly by the rent receiver.

4. The members of the upper group exact a certain share of production from members of the lower group and this exaction takes the form of:

a. Labor services:

   i. In the form of agricultural work on the land (service to the demesne).

   ii. Other services (at the table, collecting firewood, or corvées, etc.)

b. Produce rents:

   i. A fixed amount of agricultural goods.

   ii. A share of agricultural production.

   iii. Other goods (e.g., craft work).

c. Money rents:

   i. A fixed amount.

   ii. A variable amount dependent on income.

d. Extractions through the exchange process (monopolies: members of the upper group force members of the lower group to use a mill or buy liquor only from certain sources).

e. Extractions through the administration of justice.

5. The feudal landlord is much more interested in the "prestige" of landholding than in "profit" or productivity.

6. The economy has only a very limited market for land or labor services.

Note: The division between social, political, and economic factors is rather arbitrary. In addition, I omit various defining characteristics based primarily upon ideological characteristics of particular sub-groups. The elements also exhibited a certain redundancy.

Source: Frederic L. Pryor, "Feudalism as an Economic System," *Journal of Comparative Economics,* 4, No. 4 (December 1980), pp. 56–77.

TABLE 1–3
Ownership and Public Planning and Administration of the Economy

Ownership	Public Planning and Administration of the Economy	Examples
Private	Low	United States in early 1980s
Private	High	Nazi Germany; many wartime economies
Public	High	Soviet Union in early 1980s
Public	Low	Yugoslavia in late 1960s (market socialism)

constant. These results suggest that for 1962 there were no significant differences in such expenditures in the two sets of nations as a whole, although, of course, there are noticeable differences within each pair. If just health, education, and welfare expenditures are isolated,[8] the same results are obtained. In 1976 the same type of calculation for health, education, and welfare expenditures reveals that the "capitalist" nations have somewhat more such governmental expenditures for these purposes than the East European "socialist" nations, a matter discussed in greater detail in chapter 7. It should be added that the single most important change occurring in the economic systems of "capitalist" nations of Western Europe in the three decades following 1950 has been the rise of government expenditures for goods, services, and transfers in the gross national product from about 28 percent of the GNP in the mid-1950s to over 41 percent of the GNP in the early 1980s.[9]

To gain additional perspective on the coherence of the first three distinctions between capitalism and socialism, a more complicated typology is constructed in Table 1-5. In this table, a sample of 12 countries in Western Europe in the mid-1960s is utilized. For the ownership and allocation criteria available data for the relevant indicator were obtained and the countries were ranked according to the results. A line was drawn between the sixth and seventh country in these rankings so that those countries ranking "relatively high" or "low" could be distinguished. A similar procedure was followed for the "degree of national economic planning" but the data were average rankings according to this scale by a group of comparative economists. (Warning: truth does not necessarily lie in the majority opinion of experts.)

The results show that there is some coherence of these indicators; that is, half the countries fall on either extreme. However, this coher-

[8]Frederic L. Pryor, "Interpretation of Public Expenditure Trends in East and West," in Gustav Ranis et al., *Comparative Development Perspectives* (Boulder, Colo.: Westview Press, 1984), pp. 362–89.

[9]OECD, *Public Expenditure Trends* (Paris: 1978).

TABLE 1–4
Public Consumption Expenditures in Western and Eastern Europe in 1962

Country	Public Consumption Expenditures as Percent of GNP	Country	Public Consumption Expenditures as Percent of GNP
West Germany	30%	East Germany	33%
Austria	28	Czechoslovakia	30
Ireland	18	Hungary	17
Italy	28	Poland	20
Greece	20	Bulgaria	22
Unweighted average	24.8%	Unweighted average	24.4%

Note: Public consumption expenditures are expenditures of all levels of government (central and local) that are financed by taxes or governmental borrowing. In this table these expenditures include the following eight functions: political administration, diplomacy and foreign aid, military, internal security, education, health, welfare, and research and development. These data exclude all private expenditures for these eight functions. Although national account data for the government sector include more expenditure functions of government, these data include not only goods and services but also transfer expenditures; thus they differ in definition from other data often presented on the subject; the calculations for both sets of nations are, however, comparable. The pairs of nations are arranged roughly in order to descending per capita gross domestic product.

Source: The data come from Frederic L. Pryor, *Public Expenditures in Communist and Capitalist Nations* (Homewood, Ill.: Richard D. Irwin, 1968), p. 61.

ence is by no means strict since the other half of the countries rank high according to some indicators of socialism and low according to others.

Table 1-6 presents some examples of different combinations of centralization of economic control and importance of material incentives. For this table examples from the experience of "socialist" nations are drawn. Again, little logical connection between the two criteria of socialism is apparent.

The political definition of socialism also has some problems. Although the countries in Eastern Europe are clearly one-party states (even though some of them have several formal political parties, none of which is independent of the Communist Party), a number of nonsocialist countries in Western Europe have also not had any effective party competition at different times in their recent history (e.g., Germany from 1933 to 1945 or Spain from the late 1930s to the early 1970s). Other problems with "political" definitions of socialism are discussed in Chapter 10 where a sample of Third World nations is briefly examined.

The distinction between capitalism and socialism that rests on the degree of alienation or freedom raises still other problems. Although ideologists of various sytems have declared the populations in the rival system as "unfree" or "alienated," it is usually unclear what type of evidence underlies such claims. Indeed, these phenomena resist empirical measurement even though they are very real and important. In this

TABLE 1–5
"Degrees of Socialism" in Western Europe in the Mid-1960s

Relative Degree of Public Ownership	Relative Degree of Public Consumption	Relative Degree of Governmental Planning and Administration of the Economy	Countries
High	High	High	France, Norway, Sweden
High	High	Low	Austria
High	Low	High	Netherlands, United Kingdom
High	Low	Low	—
Low	High	High	—
Low	High	Low	Canada, West Germany
Low	Low	High	Belgium
Low	Low	Low	Greece, Switzerland, United States

Sources: Data on the relative extent of public ownership come from Table 1–1 and other sources. The relative extent of public expenditures is determined from the ratio of current total governmental expenditures plus transfers to households to the GNP in factor prices. The data for the third column come from Myron H. Ross, "Fluctuations in Economic Activity," *American Economic Review*, 55, No. 1 (March 1965), pp. 158–61. Further details about the calculations are given in Frederic L. Pryor, *Property and Industrial Organization in Communist and Capitalist Nations* (Bloomington: Indiana University Press, 1973), p. 23.

guidebook I focus primarily on measurable phenomena so as to keep the discussion relatively concise; however, this approach may overlook some of the important differences between economic systems.

The empirical approach followed in this guidebook raises another problem that revolves around the distinction between "formal" and "nonformal" analyses. The importance of this distinction can be seen by considering, for a moment, whether labor markets are "free" in East or West. Certainly in a legal or formal sense, labor markets exist in all nations of Europe in the 1980s with the possible exception of Albania; and we find no country with industrial serfs or slaves who are legally tied to their jobs. In actuality, however, job mobility may be severely

TABLE 1–6
Incentives, Central Planning, and Administration of the Economy

Importance of Central Planning and Administration of the Economy	Importance of Material Incentives	Examples
High	High	Soviet Union in early 1980s
Low	High	Yugoslavia in late 1960s
High	Low	Cuba during mid-1960s; almost any army
Low	Low	China during Cultural Revolution in mid-1960s

limited because housing in other areas is impossible to find, or pensions or social insurance losses occur when jobs are changed, or special labor passes are required, or unemployment may be sufficiently high that other jobs are very difficult to find. It should be clear that it is necessary to look not only at the formal aspects of institutions and systems but also at their economic context if we wish to understand how such systems really function.

These exercises of examining different combinations of criteria distinguishing capitalism and socialism show quite clearly that the coherence between diffrent definitions of these two economic systems is not great, and that a country that is capitalist by one criterion may be socialist according to another. We must be careful, therefore, when using these terms for they are members of a set of fuzzy concepts (such as "centralization") that raise enormous confusion (not to mention emotions) in discussing economic systems.

It must be emphasized that there is no "correct" definition of any of these terms, and that arguing about the correct definition is futile. If, of course, one believes that capitalism or socialism is a "good" or "evil" system, then arguments about definitions are actually arguments about what is "good" or "evil."

If we define what we mean when such terms are used; and if the definitions serve some analytical purpose (i.e., if a particular proposition about the impact or development of institutions is tied to a particular characteristic of the economy by which systems can be labeled), then the systems labels can be employed in a useful fashion. If the labels are not defined or if it makes no analytical difference how the labels are defined, then such labels get in the way of serious discussion and it is not worthwhile to employ them.

D. A Final Note

The next chapter deals with various economic goals and the criteria by which economies can be judged. The succeeding six chapters then focus upon one or more "success criteria," the ways in which policy makers in different economic systems attempt to achieve these goals, and their degree of achieved success. The final two chapters take a broader view of the subject.

At no place in this guidebook is a single economy discussed as a whole. Rather, relevant parts of several economies are discussed together. Since you may have difficulty in integrating the factual materials, it is useful to study at least one actual economy at the same time as reading this guide so that a sense of the integument of a single system can be gained.

At the end of each chapter you will find an annotated bibliography. Some of these suggested readings permit you to gain more thorough knowledge of specific problems discussed in the text. Other suggested readings provide materials for the case study of one particular economy, namely, that of the Soviet Union. Whenever possible, articles with quite different ideological viewpoints are also recommended so that you can gain an appreciation of the different ways in which the subject can be approached.

SUGGESTED READINGS

A. What Is an Economic System?

1. Egon Neuberger, "Classifying Economic Systems," in Morris Bornstein, ed., *Comparative Economic Systems: Models and Cases,* 4th ed. (Homewood, Ill.: Richard D. Irwin, 1979), pp. 19–28.

2. John Michael Montias, "Types of Communist Economic Systems," in Workshop on the Comparative Study of Communism, Chalmers Johnson, ed., *Change in Communist Systems* (Stanford, Calif.: Stanford University Press, 1970), pp. 117–34. This draws upon the economic history of the Soviet Union, Eastern Europe, and China to derive to useful set of categories. In a subsequent essay, "A Classification of Communist Economic Systems," in Carmelo Mesa-Lago and Carl Beck, eds., *Comparative Socialist Systems* (Pittsburgh: University of Pittsburgh Press, 1975), pp. 39–52, Montias deals with more philosophical issues arising in such an intellectual exercise.

3. Two discussions developing some of the ideas contained in the Neuberger discussion are Paul R. Gregory and Robert C. Stuart, *Comparative Economic Systems* (New York: Houghton Mifflin, 1980), pp. 9–28; and Vaclav Holesovsky, *Economic Systems: Analysis and Comparison* (New York: McGraw-Hill, 1977), pp. 14–38.

4. Lance Davis and Douglass North, *Institutional Change and American Economic Growth* (New York: Cambridge University Press, 1971). This book, especially in the first few chapters, contains an excellent discussion of the meaning of the concept of "economic institution" and shows how the concept can be usefully employed in the analysis of important problems.

B. Approaches to the Analysis of Economic Systems

1. Morris Bornstein, "The Comparison of Economic Systems: An Integration," in Bornstein, ed., *Comparative Economic Systems,* pp. 3–18. This essay summarizes well the conventional wisdom in the West about comparing economic systems.

2. Robert A. Dahl and Charles E. Lindblom, *Politics, Economics, and Welfare* (New York: Harper & Bros., 1953), pp. 3–18. This is an extended argument against the notion that we really face "grand alternatives of the 'isms'."

3. Alexander Erlich, "Eastern Approaches to a Comparative Evaluation of Economic Systems," in Alexander Eckstein, ed., *Comparison of Economic Systems* (Berkeley: University of California Press, 1970), pp. 301–34. This selection summarizes the orthodox Marxist approach for comparing economic systems. The official Soviet view can be gained by comparing the chapters on capitalism and

socialism in O. W. Kuusinen, et al., *Fundamentals of Marxism Leninism* (Moscow: Foreign Language Publishing House, n.d.), which is a Soviet textbook. A more interesting reading is by the American Marxist Paul Sweezy, "A Crucial Difference between Capitalism and Socialism," in David Horowitz, ed., *Marx and Modern Economics* (New York: Monthly Review Press, 1968), pp. 315–26. These Marxist analyses argue in a directly opposite manner to Dahl and Lindblom.

4. John Michael Montias, "From Theory to Measurement," in his *The Structure of Economic Systems* (New Haven, Conn.: Yale University Press, 1976), pp. 53–73. This chapter discusses some problems of statistical techniques employed in modern comparative economics.

5. A number of social scientists have analyzed more general issues in using the comparative method. Of particular interest are the chapters on methodology in Neil Smelser, *Comparative Methods in Social Science* (Englewood Cliffs, N.J.: Prentice-Hall, Inc., 1976); the essay by Zelditch in Ivan Vallier, ed., *Comparative Methods in Sociology* (Berkeley: University of California Press, 1971); the first two chapters in Robert M. Marsh, *Comparative Sociology* (New York: Harcourt, Brace & World, 1967); and the introduction and first chapter in Adam Przeworski and Henry Teune, *The Logic of Comparative Social Inquiry* (New York: John Wiley, 1970).

C. Background to the Case Study Approach

In order to place the various readings in context, it is useful to understand the operations of at least one socialist economy. An interesting case study is the Soviet Union and considerable materials about the Soviet economy in English are available. For background on the political framework underlying the Soviet economy, it is useful to read Alec Nove, *The Soviet Economic System* (London: Allen and Unwin, 1978), chaps. 1–3, pp. 13–84.

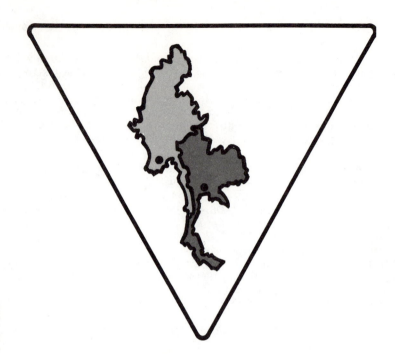

2

GOALS, PERFORMANCE CRITERIA, AND POLICY INSTRUMENTS

A. Introduction

In analyzing the impact of economic systems and institutions, we must first designate a set of criteria for making judgments about them. Such an exercise means, in essence, we are setting up a series of goals and measuring the performance of the economy against them. Studying an economic system in such a manner is, in some social sciences such as anthropology, called an *etic* analysis.

It is also important to analyze what types of performance criteria for the system are important to the participants of the economy. This requires us to examine their goals and beliefs about important performance criteria. Studying an economic system in this manner is often called an *emic* analysis.

To understand fully the impact of an economic system, it is necessary to carry out both etic and emic analyses of economic ends. In this chapter we explore some of the most important issues of both approaches. We also examine the policy instruments and the methods by which various goals can be realized in a particular economy, as well as the crucial relationship between economic ends and means available to particular economic systems or institutions. The reader is warned that the chapter requires careful study since it is one of the two in the book with difficult theoretical materials and since the concepts and the ideas generated in the pages below form the framework for analysis of the impact questions that are posed in the remainder of the study.

Although the study of developmental questions—those questions covering the origins and important causal forces in the continuation of particular institutions—does not appear to require such close attention to values, it should be noted that in choosing particular aspects of economic systems and institutions to study we require some criteria for the selection of "important" phenomena; and this, in turn, rests on value judgments. Thus our selection of developmental questions to analyze is also strongly influenced by our values and the economic ends that we believe to be important.

B. Criteria for Evaluating Economic Systems

1. A Hierarchy of Criteria

The selection of economic phenomena to investigate and the criteria used in evaluating them forces us to make value judgments; indeed, a value-free economics is impossible. But if the values underlying a comparative study of economic systems are made explicit, the analysis can be placed in perspective by others so that its limitations and merits can be more easily judged. Further, by attempting to make our values explicit, we become more self-aware of what we are really doing. For instance, although most economists in East and West implicitly seem to place a positive value on economic growth, by discussing this matter explicitly, it becomes quickly apparent that such a goal is not an unmixed blessing and that certain religious groups, who believe that exclusive focus on economic growth leads to the neglect of spiritual development, have an idea worth considering.

There is, of course, a hierarchy of ends, ranging from very general to very concrete goals. It is useful to consider briefly some aspects of this hierarchy.

a. General Political-Economic Ends

Discussions of general political-economic ends for a society are common. One analysis of economic policy in Western Europe and North America lists nine such ends: material welfare, equity, reduction in social tensions, promotion of human values, encouragement of ethics and religion, law and order, external security, political order, and international solidarity.[1] To such a list we can add a large number of other political-economic ends including freedom, democracy, security, and stability. Of course, many of these general goals may seem to overlap and others may seem to be of secondary importance.

Analyzing an economy in terms of these general political-economic ends is almost impossible because the specific content of many of these goals is not entirely clear. Furthermore, it is often difficult to link any particular economic phenomenon to such goals. For instance, the relationships between a high rate of growth and the promotion of human values, or reduction of social tensions, or security, or stability, or democracy, or encouragement of international solidarity are far from clear.

b. Specific Economic Goals

An alternative procedure for analyzing the impact of an economic system is to designate a series of specific economic goals or objectives such as full employment, price stability, expansion of production, promotion of internal competition, coordination of economic activities, an equilibrated balance of international payments, mobile capital and labor, encouragement of the international division of labor, satisfaction of collective needs, elimination of poverty, protection of certain regions or industries, a stable source of supply of necessary raw materials, reduction of working hours, or certain institutional goals (such as a low degree of private ownership of the means of production or heavy usage of the market for allocating goods and resources).[2]

Examining the relative degree to which various economies meet these goals allows us to make comparisons. Of course, it should be apparent that some of these policy goals are still stated much too broadly

---

[1]These are the most general aims listed by Etienne S. Kirschen and Lucien Morrisens, "The Objectives and Instruments of Economic Policy," in Bert G. Hickman, ed., *Quantitative Planning of Economic Policy* (Washington, D.C.: Brookings Institution, 1964), pp. 111–33; this is reprinted in Morris Bornstein, ed., *Comparative Economic Systems: Models and Cases,* 4th ed. (Homewood, Ill.: Richard D. Irwin, 1979), pp. 28–47.

[2]These particular economic goals serve as the basis of an extensive empirical analysis of Western European economies by Etienne S. Kirschen et al., *Economic Policy in Our Time* (Amsterdam: North Holland, 1964). For the Soviet Union, however, these goals are not suitable and must be modified; such an exercise is carried out in Z. Frank and J. Waelbroeck, "Soviet Economic Policy Since 1953: A Study of Its Structure and Changes," *Soviet Studies,* 17 (July 1965), pp. 1–43.

for making comparisons (e.g., protecting certain regions or industries), and that other common goals raise considerable problems of analysis (e.g., an equilibrated balance of international payments). Although it is often very important to determine the relative degrees to which certain of these institutional goals are achieved, other items in the list above seem to be of secondary importance or peripheral to more general institutional arrangements (e.g., mobile capital and labor).

In certain circumstances where one is comparing a set of quite similar economies, comparing performance according to such specific economic goals might be carried out; but for use in comparing a broader range of economies, the disadvantages of such an approach become more apparent and a somewhat different approach is required.

c. Performance Indicators

In this study a series of performance indicators (or criteria) for the economy form the framework for analysis and evaluation. These indicators have relatively well-defined meanings and can be applied to any type of economic system, independent of particular institutional arrangements. These indicators are (1) economic growth, (2) dynamic efficiency, (3) economic stability, (4) static efficiency of production, (5) consumer sovereignty (or consumer efficiency), and (6) an equitable distribution of income and wealth such that basic human needs can be met. The specific meanings of these six performance indicators are discussed in detail in Section C.

To avoid misunderstanding about what such performance criteria mean, four observations must be made.

(i) Other Performance Indicators. This list of six performance indicators is by no means complete and others can be added: a high degree of economic security (i.e., a low percentage of people below a certain minimum income); a low level of unemployment or underemployment; a lack of exploitation (defined in some way); a low incidence of bribery and economic corruption (difficult to measure!); a low degree of vulgar commercialism; few shortages of consumer goods; little necessity for consumers spending long hours in queues to obtain necessary goods and services; a high degree of participation and hard work by *all* adult members of the society in the production of goods; or a low degree of concentration of economic power and a high degree of participation by all members of society in the making of important economic decisions. The exact indicators included can be defined only on the basis of subjective value judgments and you are invited to add your own to the list. I have chosen the six criteria in my list according to some (but not all) of my values and also for convenience of exposition.

(ii) Relation to More General Goals.   Although the relation of these indicators to the specific economic goals mentioned above should be relatively clear in most cases, their relationship to the general political-economic ends is considerably more vague. None seem directly related to the promotion of human values, and none seem either directly or indirectly related to such ends as encouragement of ethics and religion, or international solidarity. The concentration in this guidebook on just the six indicators specified above means, therefore, that the discussion is not sufficiently complete to enable final judgments about the desirability of particular economic systems to be made. In short, if an economy scores high on all of these economic performance indicators but turns out rotten human beings, according to most people it is *not* a successful system.

(iii) Conflicting Goals.   Some of these performance indicators may conflict with each other. For instance, there may be tradeoffs between productive efficiency and equity, or between economic growth and stability on either a micro- or macroeconomic level. In certain cases such as the growth/macrostability tradeoff, tests are made in this guidebook to determine whether or not such a competition between goals actually exists. If there are tradeoffs, then we must have some way of weighting these six indicators if we wish to make an overall evaluation of the performance of economic systems.

(iv) Etic versus Emic Approach.   The setting up of such indicators is an etic approach since we are imposing our criteria of judgment on the economy. Some of these indicators may conflict with the values of the members of the economic system. For instance, some societies may not favor rapid economic growth, particularly if severe social strains are caused by this growth.

2.   Actual Economic Goals

It should be clear that unless we know what goals the participants of an economic system deem important, we will find it difficult to understand many of the policy measures that are taken in that economy. But how do we discover the actual goals of an economy?

a.   Study of Official Pronouncements and Documents

One obvious method is to study the relevant official pronouncements of the top political officials to determine the nation's desired economic goals. Unfortunately, these are often self-serving statements designed for political purposes, rather than to specify the actual goals of the person making the pronouncement. Further, such statements are quite often specifications of what the economic goals should be, rather than what such goals actually are.[3] Rather than look at pronouncements, we might study instead the goals specified in important official governmental documents (e.g., the preambles of the yearly economic budget or plan); unfortunately, these are also quite often of a propagandistic nature, designed to hide, rather than to illuminate, the goals being followed. Although study of official pronouncements and documents cannot be neglected in trying to determine national economic goals, supplementary approaches are also necessary.

b. Use of Sample Survey Data

Another method of determining national economic goals is to examine the results of public opinion polling of the country in which a representative sample of members of the economy is questioned to determine how they view the economic goals of their nation. Of course, if positive goals are stated in a general fashion, most will subscribe to them. (Do you believe we should have more, the same, or less unemployment, inflation, economic security, etc.?) To avoid this problem, some questions must be stated in a more open-ended fashion so that the hierarchy of goals or values can be established, and other questions must be posed in a manner to reveal tradeoffs between goals.

A good deal of public opinion information is available for such purposes. For instance, in early 1975 a business group conducted a study of 1990 Americans about their "understanding and attitudes" toward their nation's economic system.[4] When asked what is particularly good about the U.S. economic system, 54 percent emphasized personal mobility, freedom, and opportunities; 12 percent mentioned the high standard of living; 9 percent specified the free enterprise, capitalistic economy (and 5 percent also mentioned that the government doesn't dictate purchases and/or permits private property). When asked what is not particularly good about their economic system, 27 percent specified inflation, 18 percent mentioned dubious business practices, 8 percent mentioned unemployment and business cycles, 7 percent said that the wealthy have unfair advantages, 5 percent mentioned the uneven distribution of wealth, and so forth. With regard to more specific issues such as governmental regulation, 43 percent said there is not enough, 22

---

[3]A great many studies of economic goals abound for every nation and most are terribly dull to read. For instance, for the United States, such an exercise is found in Edgar O. Edwards, ed., *The Nation's Economic Objectives* (Chicago: University of Chicago Press, 1964). Often when U.S. presidents find themselves under attack for being shortsighted, they form grandiose commissions to study U.S. national goals; the reports of these commissions are seldom read by any but their authors.

[4]Compton Advertising, Inc., *National Survey on the American Economic System* (New York: The Advertising Council, Inc., 1975).

percent said there is too much, 19 percent said there is the right amount, 13 percent gave nuanced answers (e.g., not enough in some areas, too much in other areas), and 3 percent had no opinion. A series of specific questions in this survey probed attitudes toward regulation in particular areas. Such survey exercises have also been carried out by public opinion polling companies in many other nations. Indeed, certain international polling enterprises have posed similar questions to respondents in several countries so that some internationally comparable data are available.

Certainly, these sample survey results provide some interesting and useful information. However, it should be emphasized that employing this approach to determine the actual economic goals of a nation has many problems; and these deserve brief mention.

First, such public opinion polls have not been designed for our purposes; in most cases the questions are not framed in a manner such that values that interest us can be easily extracted. Indeed, to frame the questions to elicit answers that would reveal national economic values is extremely difficult.

Second, because questions must be posed in a relatively simple manner, many contradictions arise. For instance, in asking questions about attitudes toward fiscal policy, pollsters have found that a majority of U.S. citizens favor lower taxes, more public expenditures, and a balanced governmental budget.[5]

Third, many of the individuals in the society may have put little thought on the questions of economic goals for the society as a whole since they are so far removed from the decision-making process. To elicit a consistent set of their ideas on the topic would take a long interview which might be prohibitively expensive.

c. Focusing on the Values of Elites

In several countries social scientists have conducted interviews with a sample of the elites who play major roles in the making of economic policy. Some of these researchers have made considerable efforts in structuring the questions to reveal value tradeoffs. For instance, decision makers have been asked questions such as, If there is a marginal tradeoff such that the inflation rate rises 2 percent for every 1 percent decrease in unemployment, what combination of unemployment and inflation would you prefer to see in your country? If, instead, the

---

[5]Eva Mueller, "Public Attitudes toward Fiscal Programs," *Quarterly Journal of Economics,* 77, No. 2 (May 1963), pp. 210–35. In the 1980 U.S. presidential campaign, Ronald Reagan appeared to hold the same incompatible goals for the short run; given the large deficit in the governmental budget in that year, one of his opponents at that time, George Bush, labeled this notion "voodoo economics."

tradeoff is really 1 percent increase in inflation for 1 percent decrease in unemployment, how would your answer differ?

Unfortunately, the number of respondents in such studies is generally quite small, not only because of the costs involved but also because many decision makers do not wish to be pinned down in such a manner. Further, the results are seldom comparable internationally.

Another technique is to study the values expressed in publications circulating among various elites. For instance, for the United States and the Soviet Union, a team of sociologists counted the number of times that certain ideas relating to values appeared in leading newspapers (e.g., in the Soviet Union, *Pravda;* in the United States, *The New York Times*) and journals during the 1950s and early 1960s. Several examples of the results of such research are presented in Table 2–1. They suggest, for instance, that in comparison with U.S. elites, the Soviet elites seem to favor more not only the socialization of the means of production (which is not a surprise) but also the introduction of more nonequalitarian wages.

Such a method of assessing the values of the political and economic elites suffers from several difficulties. First, the newspapers and journals may be controlled by the government in a manner such that only articles favorable to certain values will be published; thus the results correspond only to the values of a particular segment of the elite. Second, considerable differences between expressed and actual values may occur. For instance, it is true that the degree of governmental ownership of the means of production is higher in the Soviet Union than in the United States. However, later in this book data are presented showing that, contrary to expressed values, money wage inequalities are greater in the United States than in the Soviet Union. Such a discrepancy between values and reality may be attributable to a different reference point with regard to "some degree of inequality" and "rewarded much more" so that the results are really not comparable. It might be also added that, although Soviet elites appeared to favor less egalitarian wages, wage spreads narrowed in the Soviet Union during this period.

d.   A Revealed Preference Approach

The body politic is not a unitary entity that can be easily psychoanalyzed to reveal its underlying hopes, fears, values, and neuroses. Rather, various groups are contending in a struggle for power and such groups have quite different values and goals. It is practically impossible to investigate the values of each contending group and then to aggregate them in some manner to determine national values. However, we could try a different approach and actually look at the results of the political process. More specifically, just as we can analyze the preference

TABLE 2–1

Examples of Values of Elites in U.S. and Soviet Publications

	Prevalence of Position[a]	
Value Position	United States	Soviet Union
Value: Ownership of the Means of Production		
a. Socialization of the means of production should be the norm; exceptions should be very few.	0%	100%
b. Our society has been too dogmatic in its property principles. We should accept some modifications that will bring us nearer a mixed system of private and public ownership.	25	0
c. Private ownership of the means of production should be the norm with only rare exceptions, e.g., the postal service.	75	0
Value: Distribution of Labor Income		
a. Everyone contributes what he can to the working of the economic system; therefore, all positions should be rewarded substantially equally.	0%	2%
b. Some degree of inequality of reward to various occupations or to various degrees of productivity is necessary for the satisfactory working of the economic system, but this inequality should be kept to a minimum.	73	16
c. High productivity is so important to the economic system that persons of the highest productivity should be rewarded much more than those of low productivity.	8	81
d. The different occupations are of very unequal importance to the economy and should, therefore, be rewarded very unequally.	8	1

Note: The data refer to the period 1957–60.

[a]The columns may not add to 100 percent because of rounding.

Source: Data are from Robert C. Angell, "Social Values of Soviet and American Elites: Content of Elite Media," *The Journal of Conflict Resolution,* 8 (December 1964), pp. 330–86.

structure of consumers by examining their behavior, we can apply the same techniques to governmental bodies. Indeed, such a method has been tried, not only for small agencies but for nations as well.[6]

The results of such studies permit us to carry out the very valuable task of separating what governmental decision makers do from what they say. However, such an approach also has some problems: First, such types of statistical analyses are very difficult to carry out; empiri-

[6]Such an exercise is carried out for Israel by Howard Pack, *Structural Change and Economic Policy in Israel* (New Haven, Conn.: Yale University Press, 1971).

cal and theoretical problems abound. Second, the results do not lend themselves easily to comparative analysis because the environments in which the various national decision makers are operating are very different. One government (e.g., the Swiss) may do very little to lower unemployment, not because the policy makers like unemployment but rather because unemployment in the country is so low (for reasons unrelated to governmental policy) that it is not considered to be a major problem. Another government may appear to do a great deal because the problem is quite acute, even though in the final anlysis they may place a lesser value on a low unemployment rate than other countries.

e. Analysis of Ideologies

A traditional type of approach toward the determination of national values is the analysis of the value content of the dominant ideologies, as reflected in the writings of the most widely published ideologues. Unfortunately, many of the values in which we have interest may not be mentioned at all in such ideological discussions; indeed, the agenda for ideological discussion in many societies is relatively short and may be shaped more by current political problems than by the desire for philosophic coherence. Thus, for example, we may never learn what the ideologues believe to be the optimum balance between hard work and sloth. Further, in many cases such ideological discussions are not focused in a manner to permit us to resolve certain questions. For instance, an important component of all ideologies is the clarity of their image of a significant and exciting future, as well as the measures necessary to achieve such a state of affairs.[7] If, however, the ideologues of a particular group or party differ in their understanding of the mechanisms of the economy that would achieve such ends, their discussion may focus so much on the appropriate means that the ends are totally obscured.

f. Some Conclusions

Although we have discussed the major methods of approaching the study of actual national goals our list is not complete. Moreover, it should be clear from this brief discussion that no single method to determine actual economic goals of a society is sufficient and that all contribute to our understanding since each provides a quite different jigsaw piece to this difficult puzzle. What is most surprising is that research in this fascinating area is still quite underdeveloped, few empirical studies are available, and so much remains to be done.

[7]The importance of this element of ideology is emphasized and analyzed in Fred Polak, *The Image of the Future* (New York: Oceana Press, 1960); and Kenneth E. Boulding, *The Meaning of the 20th Century* (New York: Harper & Row, 1964), chap. 8.

3. The Importance of Subjectivity

If you study the economic performance of an economy according to the values that are shared by the population or by the key policy makers, you have some useful information for understanding the mechanisms of change in that system. But such study may not reflect in any way those aspects of the economy that you believe to be important.

It is, of course, an act of supreme egotism to judge an economic system according to one's own subjective criteria, rather than the more "objective" criteria of the society itself or, for that matter, the criteria of the author of this guidebook. But if you want to make comparisons between economic systems that are truly of interest to you, you must take this step. You are encouraged to consider values that are not included in the discussion of this book, to derive performance indicators of such values, and to make your own empirical comparisons. This guidebook can be of help to you in showing how such comparisons can be made, even if you choose different criteria and indicators.

C. Performance Indicators in Detail

Applying the six performance indicators mentioned above to different institutions and systems serves as the focus of analysis in the next six chapters. Before starting such an exercise, it is useful to explore not only what the indicators mean but also some of their major interrelations and implications.[8]

1. Economic Growth

Since the early 1950s, policy makers in almost every nation of the world have proclaimed economic growth to be an important economic goal. Two difficult questions arise in using economic growth as a performance indicator: What should be measured? And how should the individual items be valued? Each deserves brief examination; more concrete problems of comparing the economic growth in different economic systems are discussed in Chapter 3.

In the West a commonly used indicator of economic growth is the gross domestic product (GDP), which is the total production of goods and

---

[8]Many of the ideas in this section are argued in greater depth by Kenneth Boulding, "Welfare Economics," in Bernard F. Haley, ed., *A Survey of Contemporary Economics,* Vol. 2 (Homewood, Ill.: Richard D. Irwin, 1952); and Bela A. Balassa, *The Hungarian Experience in Economic Planning* (New Haven, Conn.: Yale University Press, 1959), pp. 5–24.

services, or the GDP per capita.[9] Among the centrally planned economies of Eastern Europe and Asia, the most commonly used indicator is
net material production (NMP), which is, roughly speaking, the total
production only of goods. But do either of these aggregates measure
what you want to measure? If you're really interested in welfare, then it
might be better to focus on total consumption plus some omitted "goods"
such as leisure or particular home-produced services such as house-
cleaning (which are omitted from both the GDP and the NMP) minus
certain "bads" such as pollution. Depending on your value judgments,
you might further define consumption to omit expenditures on ciga-
rettes, liquor, arcade games such as Pacman, periodicals such as comic
books or *The New York Times,* all records of punk rock groups or of
Gustav Mahler, and sales of all paraphernalia concerned with Dungeons
and Dragons. Of course, the more your definition of *consumption* devi-
ates from the official definitions (which, of course, embody other value
judgments), the more difficult it is to make empirical comparisons between nations.

The question of valuation of the goods included in the volume
index whose growth is to be measured raises a second set of difficulties
that concern the *index number problem.* This type of problem arises
whenever we wish to compare two groups of dissimilar items, such as
two baskets that have different mixes of apples and oranges. The problem of calculating volume indices focuses on the set of prices to be used
as weights for the various quantities of goods and services so that they
can be placed on a comparable basis, for example, in terms of dollar
value. Usually prices at the beginning or the end of the period are used.
The nature of the problem is illustrated in Table 2–2, where the upper
half of the table shows an economy producing two goods at two points in
time. If the prices in the base year are used as weights for the physical
amounts, the calculated volume index shows a growth of 175 percent; if
prices in the end year are used, the volume index shows a growth of only
66 percent. This simple numerical exercise is not merely a hypothetical
example to confuse students. If the growth rate of the Soviet Union
between 1928 and 1937 is calculated using 1928 prices the GNP growth
is 175 percent, while 1937 price weights yield a growth of GNP of 66
percent.[10] It is important to realize that both of these conflicting growth

[9]Often the gross national product (GNP) is used instead of the GDP. The former is a
consumption concept; the latter is a production concept. They differ only in the handling of
income flows to and from foreign countries. Since this item is very small in most countries,
especially the socialist, centrally administered economies, the results of empirical analyses using either concept are very similar.

[10] These data come from Abram Bergson, *The Real National Income of Soviet Russia
since 1928* (Cambridge, Mass.: Harvard University Press, 1961).

TABLE 2–2
Illustrations of Index Number Problems

	A. Comparisons between Two Points in Time				
	1. Production and Price Data				
	1928		*1937*		
	Production	*Price*	*Production*	*Price*	
Good A	10	10	40	2	
Good B	10	10	15	30	

	2. Quantity Indices		
	1928	*1937*	*Ratio: 1937/1928*
Price Weights			
1928 prices	200	550	2.75
1937 prices	320	530	1.66

	B. Comparisons between Two Countries				
	1. Production and Price Data				
	United States		*Soviet Union*		
	Production	*Prices*	*Production*	*Prices*	
Good A	10	10	8	1	
Good B	10	10	2	11	

	2. Quantity Indices		
	United States	*Soviet Union*	*Ratio: Soviet/U.S.*
Price Weights			
U.S. prices	200	100	.50
Soviet prices	130	30	.25

rates are correct; there is no unambiguous answer to the question of what was the Soviet growth between those two years.

Three comments must be appended to this discussion of index number problems. *First,* such problems are greatest when there are major structural transformations of the economy such that the price and production structure change greatly. For the Soviet Union, for instance, such index number problems are not severe in the years following this period; and for the United States, such index number problems are severe only when measuring economic growth in the nineteenth century. *Second,* for a period of rapid growth, use of base-weighted volume indices generally gives a higher growth rate than current weighted indices, a fact well known to those wishing to use statistics for propagandistic purposes. *Third,* such index problems are exactly the same when one compares total production to two nations and must choose the prices of one nation or another to make the comparison. A numerical example is given in the bottom half of Table 2–2 and the numbers are chosen to reflect roughly the results obtained in comparing Soviet and American GDPs. It must be added that the relative production of a given nation almost always appears greater if the prices of the other nation in the comparison are used.

The meaning of a high rate of growth in GDP per capita requires attention to three major factors underlying such performance.

a. *Increase in Productive Inputs.*

The first factor, increase in productive inputs, includes not only an increase of the capital stock through investment but also an increase in the labor force participating in production (i.e., through an increase in the *participation ratio* of various sex-age groups), an increase in the use of land (which includes both renewable and nonrenewable resources), and an increase in the quality of the inputs (resulting, for instance, from more training of workers). Per capita growth may be achieved not only in benign ways but also by the impressment of children, nursing mothers, and old people into the work force, by extension of the hours of the working day, or by using up all one's supply of certain key minerals.

b. Increase in the Use of New Technologies

Increase in the use of new technologies refers not only to obtaining new technologies (either through original research and development or else from purchase from other countries) but also increasing the speed at which they are adopted. The optimal institutional arrangements to achieve such ends are far from clear.

c. Increase in Efficiency

Economic growth can come by moving closer to the production possibility curve, (i.e., achieving greater *static efficiency* of production) or by using the new inputs in a better way (i.e., achieving greater *dynamic efficiency*). Both of these concepts of efficiency are discussed in detail below.

It must be emphasized that economic growth is not an unmixed blessing if there are tradeoffs with other performance indicators. Rapid growth, for instance, might be incompatible with economic stability, a proposition argued by Joseph Schumpeter[11] and tested in Chapter 3.

---

[11]Joseph A. Schumpeter, *The Theory of Economic Development* (Cambridge, Mass.: Harvard University Press, 1949).

Such growth might also be incompatible with an equitable distribution of income or consumer sovereignty if it is achieved through a liberal use of economic incentives or forced savings. Some have also argued that economic growth is incompatible with the static efficiency of production since achieving such efficiency requires resources that could also be used in investment;[12] with our current data we cannot empirically test this iconoclastic proposition. Economic growth might also involve important human costs as well, and disillusionment with growth on these grounds has served as the starting point for several interesting studies.[13]

2. Dynamic Efficiency

Dynamic efficiency is a concept that has given rise to considerable confusion since it is defined in somewhat different ways by various economists. On the most abstract level most economists generally consider that dynamic efficiency is reflected by a growth path such that consumption per capita in any given future period cannot be increased without decreasing consumption per capita at another period. Figure 2-1 shows the growth of consumption per capita in economies that are initially identical in all respects. According to this definition, economy A is dynamically more efficient than economies B and C, and economy B is dynamically more efficient than economy C.

This kind of rigorous definition is, unfortunately, very difficult to use in empirical analysis. It seems obvious that greater dynamic efficiency occurs when investment is placed in the "proper" industries or in more "rational" locations, or when the labor force learns new skills faster or works harder or when new technologies spread more rapidly. If efficiency in a static sense can be achieved without using resources, it also seems clear that dynamic efficiency is greater where static efficiency is higher. But it is very difficult for an economist looking at the situation from the outside to know what industries are "proper," or what locations are "rational," or how much the labor force works, or how fast new technologies are spreading, or how many resources are required to increase static efficiency.

To circumvent these problems, dynamic efficiency is often analyzed in terms of the growth of output per unit of input. Quite simply, an

[12]Peter Wiles, "Growth versus Choice," *Economic Journal,* 66 (June 1956), pp. 244–55.

[13]These issues are discussed in an interesting fashion in Klaus Knorr and William J. Baumol, eds. *What Price Economic Growth* (Englewood Cliffs, N.J.: Prentice-Hall, Inc., 1961); and Edward Mishan, *The Costs of Economic Growth* (London: Staples Press, 1967). In recent years the popular press has featured a number of articles arguing that the very rapid growth of Iran in the 1960s and early 1970s led to such social strains and unhappiness that a fundamentalist Islamic ideology gained many new adherents and eventual political power.

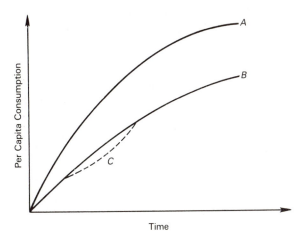

FIGURE 2–1
Paths of Per Capita Consumption in Three Economies

       At the initial point, all three economies appear identical in all respects. Economy *A* manifests the highest dynamic efficiency; and economy *C*, the lowest, all other circumstances being equal.

output index such as the GDP is divided by an input index (combining such productive inputs as labor, capital, and land). It must be emphasized that a definition based on this total factor productivity approach is rather different from the more abstract definition given above and it is not clear that rankings of economies would always be the same if calculations could be made using both. In most cases, however, it seems likely that the two definitions would give roughly similar rankings of different countries if the proper data could be obtained. Unfortunately, even the output input approach raises many serious problems because often we do not have very good data on productive inputs (either the flow of capital services or, for that matter, the number of hours worked by the labor force). In such cases we must try to make judgments about dynamic efficiency by using even more imperfect indicators.

3. Economic Stability

Economic stability refers to certain properties of the time path of prices and production and also to absolute levels of unemployment and of imbalances in the international accounts of the nation.

a. Stability of Prices

    On a macroeconomic level, stability of prices means zero inflation. That is, aggregative indicators of the price level (such as the consumer price index) mantain the same level over time. Among the major problems arising with this performance indicator, two deserve brief mention.

(i) Price Stability Tradeoffs. Although most people might agree that a zero rate of inflation is "good," certain economists have argued that economic growth is encouraged by inflation. If this is correct, then policy makers face a tradeoff between price stability and economic growth. Whether or not such a tradeoff occurs is examined empirically in Chapter 4. A similar policy dilemma might occur if it turns out that most debtors in the economy are numbered among the poor and most creditors among the wealthy; in this case a mild inflation might act to redistribute income in a progressive fashion so that there is a tradeoff between price stability and a more equal distribution of income.

(ii) Noncomparable Data. Although data to make such calculations are readily available for most nations, caution must be exercised in using these data since there are great differences in the manner in which such series are calculated. An example of different calculation methods is presented in Table 2–3, which gives Soviet data for two different types of price indices for the same commodity groups and which yield quite different results.

TABLE 2–3
Two Different Calculations of 1980 Price Indices in the Soviet Union (1970 = 100)

Product	Official Price Indices[a]	Price Indices Derived from Official Series on Sales Values and Volumes[b]
Bread and products	100	109.3
Sugar	100	99.8
Meat and products	102	113.3
Confectionery	104	110.1
Butter	100	100.5
Fabrics	100	131.8
Leather footware	100	133.6
Television sets	66	113.9
Watches and clocks	105	176.6
Cameras	100	201.2
Sewing machines	100	180.6

[a]Prices are for specific qualities of the particular goods.

[b]Prices are average values and can reflect either higher prices or a voluntary move by consumers to higher-quality goods (in which case the higher unit values do not reflect prices) or a response by producers to shortages by deliberately shifting away from cheaper toward more expensive qualities of the good, regardless of consumer demand.

Source: The data are taken from Alec Nove, "When Is a Price Increase Not a Price Increase," *Soviet Studies*, 34, No. 3 (July 1982), pp. 440–43, who cited statistics found in Soviet periodicals and government documents.

b.   Stability of Production

Stability of production generally refers to fluctuations around a trend of a volume index of production. As we shall discover in Chapter 4, theoretical knowledge of the causal mechanisms underlying such fluctuations in nations with different economic systems is quite incomplete; nevertheless, empirical analyses of the extent of such fluctuations can be easily made. A close analysis of such results requires us to separate instabilities arising from endogenous causes (i.e., causal factors arising from within the economy) from those that can be traced to factors outside the economy such as foreign trade or, for that matter, the weather.

c.   Changes in the Rates of Unemployment
    or Underemployment of Labor

It is unfortunate that almost all of the socialist, centrally administered economies do not publish data on labor force unemployment or underemployment, so that this potentially useful indicator cannot be employed in comparisons between different economic systems.

d.   Imbalances in the Accounts
    of International Payments

Since the statistics on international transactions are presented in a manner as to be always in balance, only certain parts of these statistics can be used to measure imbalances, for example, the payments on current account. Two problems discourage the discussion of such problems in this guidebook: First, since most socialist, centrally adminstered economies do not publish complete balance of payments information, empirical comparisons are impossible to make. Second, distinguishing those imbalances in the balance of payments that adversely influence the functioning of the economy is an extremely difficult analytical task that is best left for specialized monographs. The same may be said for considerations of fluctuations of exchange rates between currencies.

4.   The Static Efficiency of Production

According to the common definition, production is efficient in a static sense if it is impossible to rearrange the factors of production (land, labor, capital) so as to produce any more of one good or service without reducing the production of another.[14] In terms of the familiar production

---

[14]Several assumptions underlying this analysis must be emphasized. It is assumed that production functions are "smooth" and twice differentiable; and that all producers use all factors of production. Further, there are no indivisibilities or corner solutions and all factors can be transferred costlessly. Although these are very restrictive assumptions, they can be relaxed without essentially changing the conclusions.

possibility (or production transformation) curve, this means simply that the economy is producing on the curve and not in the area between the curve and the origin. In terms of an Edgeworth box diagram of production, with which some of you may be familiar, it means that production occurs on the contract curve.

Since we generally do not have the requisite information to determine whether the production possibilities curve has been reached, other tests must be devised to enable judgments about whether efficiency has been achieved. A variety of indicators and tests has been used, ranging from quite simple (and misleading) to quite complex.

A rather simple test revolves around the existence of unemployment or underemployment of labor. However, this indicator raises certain problems. *On the one hand,* a small degree of unemployment or underemployment can be favorable to the economy by permitting changes in the pattern of production to occur more easily. Further, frictional unemployment reflecting the unemployment of workers in transition from one job to another is a sign of a matching process between workers and jobs that has many positive aspects for the functioning of the economy and, indeed, can be a result of rapid economic growth and change. *On the other hand,* unemployment or certain types of underemployment can result from a lower aggregate demand for goods and services than the productive potential of the economy, and other types of underemployment can result from a higher aggregate demand than the productive potential. In the latter case factory managers are induced to hoard labor so that workers are available when needed, even if such resources could be more effectively used by others. Added to these conceptual problems are measurement problems: Although the governments of most market economies publish an imperfect measure of the involuntarily unemployed, very few comparable data are available on underemployment which, in terms of the static efficiency of production, may be a more serious problem.

If quantitative tests of static efficiency are difficult to make, certain qualitative tests are available. One such method is to determine whether certain marginal conditions have been met. Although these conditions are stated in a highly abstract fashion, they can be applied to many concrete situations. In the discussion below six important tests of this nature are described; in order to make the discussion more concrete, a series of examples are presented of cases in which such tests are *not* met.

a.   Equality of the Marginal Physical Productivity
     of a Single Production Factor for All Producers
     of a Given Good or Service

The *marginal physical productivity* is the additional production occurring when one unit of a factor of production (such as labor) is added to the production process. If the marginal physical productivity of any factor of production is not the same for any two producers using this factor to produce a given good or service, then production can be increased by moving the factor to the producer where the marginal productivity is higher. This condition can be understood more clearly in the following simple numerical example (where the formula $1L = 1Q$ means that one additional unit of factor L leads to an increase in production of one unit of Q):

	Marginal Productivity of Factor L to Produce Q	Initial Situation		Type of Change	Final Situation	
		Factors	Production		Factors	Production
Producer M	$1 L = 1 Q$	50 L	110 Q	Transfer of factor from	49 L	109 Q
Producer N	$1 L = 2 Q$	50 L	110 Q	one producer to another	51 L	112 Q
Total		100 L	220 Q		100 L	221 Q

By transferring one unit of factor L (e.g., labor) from producer M to producer N, a net production gain of one unit of Q is obtained. Further production gains will continue to be made by such a transfer until the marginal productivity of the factor is the same for both producers.

One obvious situation where the condition is violated occurs where labor is involuntarily unemployed in one place (so that its marginal productivity is, in essence, zero) but where there is full employment in another place (i.e., where the marginal productivity of labor is some positive amount); such unemployment could be the result of lack of capital in the former area, or lack of sufficent regional aggregate demand, or laws in one region forbidding certain segments of the labor force from accepting particular types of work (e.g., laws to "protect" minors and women). Other cases violating the condition occur in economies with profit-maximizing enterprises where similar factors of production receive different factor payments. For labor resources, this might arise where certain factories are unionized and pay higher wages while others do not, or where certain segments of the labor force are discriminated against and receive lower wages for the same work, or where the economy is characterized by dualism (i.e., where city wages are much higher than wages in the country for the same type of work), or where the wages of certain groups of workers are subsidized. For capital resources, this could occur where particular types of enterprises (e.g., large enterprises) could borrow at lower interest rates, or where capital is rationed to certain areas (e.g., the case of "redlining" in the housing industry). The marginal condition is also not met if the factors are allocated centrally and if they are arbitrarily distributed to various producers of a given good or service. Another case where the marginal condition is violated occurs where the users of the factors are not profit maximizing and where there are no strong forces pushing factor users to employ land, labor, and capital in the most productive manner (e.g., an incentive system basing managerial bonuses on gross output measured in physical terms, which encourages enterprises to "hoard" factors of production and continue to employ them, even if the costs of production are very high and the enterprise is not making any monetary profits). Laws or customs making factor mobility more costly (e.g., laws to prevent labor migration or language barriers between regions) would similarly lead to an inequality of marginal productivities.

b. Equality of the Marginal Rate of Substitution
    of Any Two Factors for All Producers

The *marginal rate of substitution* of two factors reflects the least number of units of one factor of production that can replace one unit of another factor such that production remains constant. This marginal condition refers to all producers, not to just the producers of a particular good or service. If this condition is not met, then production can be increased by reallocating factors between producers. This proposition can be more easily understood in a simple numerical example of substitution between labor, L, and capital, C. It is assumed in this example that the marginal physical productivity of one unit of L is one unit of Q_1 or one unit of Q_2. Further, the formula $1L = 1C$ means that one unit of L can be replaced by one unit of C in such a manner that production remains the same.

	Marginal Rate of Substitution between L and C	Initial Situation		Type of Change	Final Situation	
		Inputs	Outputs		Inputs	Outputs
Producer *M*	$1L = 1C$	10 *L* 6 *C*	10 Q_1	Rearrangement of productive	8 *L* 9 *C*	11 Q_1
Producer *N*	$1L = 3C$	4 *L* 6 *C*	10 Q_2	factors among producers	6 *L* 3 *C*	11 Q_2
Total		14 *L* 12 *C*			14 *L* 12 *C*	

Producer M gives up two units of L and gains three units of C; his overall production increases because two units of C "replaces" two units of L and the additional unit of C leads to an increase of production of one unit of Q_1 (since $1C = 1L = 1Q_1$). Producer N gives up three units of C and gains two units of L. Her production also increases because, for her, one L "replaces" three units of C and the additional unit of L leads to an increase of production of one unit of Q_2.

This marginal condition is violated so that efficiency is not achieved in almost all of the situations specified above which also lead to a violation of the first marginal condition. However, this marginal condition is often violated in cases of "economic dualism" in developing nations where highly capital-intensive methods of production are adopted in industry (so that the marginal productivity of labor is very high) and highly labor-intensive methods are used in agriculture (where the marginal productivity of labor is sometimes very low). This marginal condition is violated in nonmarket economies where resources are allocated between industries on the basis of priority ratings (e.g., favored sectors such as energy production obtain capital more easily than light industry). The condition is also not met when there is some type of discrimination between industries (and not within industries, which is the case for the first marginal condition). For instance, such discrimination sometimes occurs when there is general unemployment and where the marginal substitution of capital for labor differs from industry to industry, depending on the relative fall of demand for the products of that industry.

c. Equality of the Marginal Rate
   of Transformation between Any Two Products
   for Any Two Producers

The *marginal rate of transformation* represents the least production of one good that must be given up in order to produce one unit of another good. This marginal condition refers to the production of two different products by sets of producers and, strictly speaking, it refers only to those producers who are capable of producing two different products at reasonable costs. If the condition is violated, production of both products can be increased for the economy as a whole by changing the product mix of both producers. This proposition can also be understood in a simple numerical example with goods Q_1 and Q_2, where the formula $1Q_1 = 1Q_2$ means that one unit of either product must be given up to produce an additional unit of the other.

	Marginal Rate of Transformation of the Two Products	Initial Situation: Output per Period	Type of Change	Final Situation: Output per Period
Producer M	$1 Q_1 = 1 Q_2$	$10 Q_1$ $6 Q_2$	Reallocation of production between products in enterprises	$12 Q_1$ $4 Q_2$
Producer N	$1 Q_1 = 3 Q_2$	$4 Q_1$ $8 Q_2$		$3 Q_1$ $11 Q_2$
Total		$14 Q_1$ $14 Q_2$		$15 Q_1$ $15 Q_2$

Producer M, by producing two units less of Q_2, can produce two units more of Q_1. Producer N, by producing one unit less of Q_1, can produce three units more of Q_2. By carrying out this change in the product mix of both producers, more of each good is produced.

The meaning of this marginal condition can also be concretely seen by examining a series of situations where it is violated. For instance, this condition is not met in cases where a producer who can make a particular good or service is prevented by nonmarket forces from producing as much of it as wished, a situation arising because of the presence of guild regulations, or of governmental monopolies (e.g., where only a single enterprise is given a franchise to produce and sell electricity in an area), or of differential quantitative restrictions placed on different producers (by a cartel, or by a government planning agency, or by governmental regulations preventing certain types of producers, such as those without unions, from competing on certain types of construction projects). Other cases violating this marginal condition arise where sales taxes (or import duties) are placed on the products of some producers but not others, or where different producers must pay quite different prices for raw materials.

d. Some Major Empirical Problems in Analyzing Static Efficiency

From standard welfare economics it can be demonstrated that these three marginal conditions are necessary and sufficient conditions for achieving static efficiency of production.[15] Although static efficiency has received great attention in the comparative study of economic systems, especially by those of a non-Marxist persuasion, it must be recognized that this criterion raises a good number of difficulties, of which several deserve brief discussion.

One major problem is that it is very difficult to measure the *relative degree* of inefficiency. The marginal conditions do not offer much help here. If we know where the production possibilities frontier lies and how much of each good is produced, then we can measure its relative distance to this frontier on a ray that goes through the point designating the set of produced goods and the point where nothing is produced. In the left-hand side of Figure 2–2, it should be clear that the economy at point A is more efficient than the one at point B according to this measurement.

Unfortunately, we generally do not know where the production possibility frontier lies, which makes comparisons of economies with different product mixes more difficult. If we are comparing economies with the same amount of factors of production and the same production possibilities frontier, we can try to measure relative efficiency by deter-

---

[15]See Kenneth Boulding, "Welfare Economics," in Bernard Haley, ed., *A Survey of Contemporary Economics*, Vol. 2 (Homewood Ill.: Irwin, 1952), chap. 1.

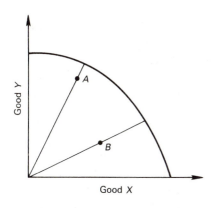

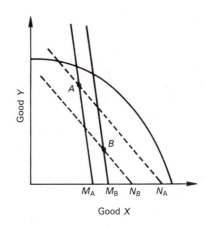

FIGURE 2–2
Problems in the Measurement of Inefficiency

The curves in the two diagrams indicate the production possibility frontier. One country produces at A, another at B. According to the left-hand diagram, A is relatively closer to the production possibility frontier than B.

In the right-hand diagram lines representing two sets of relative prices are drawn through A and B. The total production of the two goods in terms of good X is indicated by the intersection of the price lines with the good X axis. Whether or not A represents more or less production depends, according to this method, on which set of relative prices is considered "best." These index number problems are shown in a different context in numerical examples in Table 2–2.

mining the relative levels of production; this requires us to weigh somehow the production of each good by some price in order to calculate an output index so as to compare levels of production. The problem becomes more difficult if the economies have the same technological knowledge but have different amounts of the factors of production. In this case we can try to measure relative efficiencies by calculating the relative productivities; this requires us to combine the factors of production in some manner so as to calculate an input index, which is divided into the output index to determine relative productivities. If we are comparing economies that do not have the same technological knowledge, then the problem of determining relative efficiencies is almost insurmountable unless we have highly detailed data about production in that economy.

At this point you might begin to suspect that the calculation of output and input indices to measure such static inefficiency raises an *index number problem* that is similar to that discussed with regard to the measurement of economic growth and dynamic efficency. If so, you are perfectly correct; this problem can be shown geometrically in the right-hand side of Figure 2–2. Suppose we must compare two economies, A and B, that produce the same two products, X and Y, that have the same inputs and production possibility frontier. We calculate an output index by weighting the products according to a set of relative prices indicated by the unbroken lines. Geometrically this involves drawing lines with slopes indicated by the ratio of the price of one good to the price of the other good through the points indicating the product mix of a countries A and B. The total amount of production of A and B in terms of good X are indicated by the intersection of these lines at points M_A and M_B; and it is clear that such production is higher at B. If, however, the price ratios are indicated by the dashed lines so that total production of the two products are indicated at points N_A and N_B, it is clear that production is higher at point A. Since we do not know which prices are more valid for the comparison (each price line may correspond to the domestic prices of the given economy) and since we do not know where the production possibilities frontier lies, we cannot unambiguously determine the relative efficiencies of the two economies in such a manner.

We might try to sidestep such index number problems and measure inefficiencies by determining the degree to which the marginal conditions are not met. However, according to the theory of "second best," if one marginal condition is not met in the economy, then the economy might produce more if several other marginal conditions are not met as well. For instance, take a situation where a tax is placed on labor inputs in one part of the country but not another (i.e., one district imposes a special payroll tax). This would lead to a violation of the first two marginal conditions. Under certain circumstances, the country might move closer to the production possibilities curve if additional distorting taxes were imposed as well. Unfortunately, a number of theoretical problems concerning the theory of "second best" have not yet been resolved, so a more precise discussion of this problem is not possible.[16]

Another major problem is of quite a different order. The static efficiency of production may be achieved at the cost of some other success criteria. Many have argued that there is an important tradeoff between equity and efficiency—that static efficiency can only be achieved by creating unacceptable inequalities. Still others have argued that institutions leading to a high degree of static efficiency (e.g., a laissez faire market economy) may also lead to greater instabilities on an aggregative level; however, the theoretical foundations of this argument are far from being rigorously specified. As noted above, some others have maintained that devoting resources to obtaining the infor-

---

[16]The theory of second best was originally proposed by Richard G. Lipsey and Kelvin Lancaster, "The General Theory of Second Best," *Review of Economic Studies,* 24, No. 1 (1956–57), pp. 11–32. Certain aspects came under attack, e.g., Otto A. Davis and Andrew B. Whinston, "Welfare Economics and the Theory of Second Best," *Review of Economic Studies,* 32, No. 1 (January 1965), pp. 1–14 (an article that contains an outdated but nevertheless useful bibliography on the topic); or G. Santoni and A. Church, "A Comment on the General Theorem of the Second Best," *Review of Economic Studies,* 39 (October 1972), pp. 527–30.

mation necessary to achieve static efficiency may lower investment and the overall growth rate of the economy.[17]

5.   Consumer Sovereignty (Consumption Efficiency)

I shall define *consumer sovereignty* as occurring when the consumption pattern of goods and services among the consumers cannot be changed, nor can the production pattern be changed, without decreasing the level of utility of at least one person. This definition, which some have also labeled *consumption efficiency,* differs somewhat from the way the term is occasionally used by others. With my approach it is analogous to static efficiency on the production side except, of course, it refers to a different group of participants in the economy. Two necessary and sufficient marginal conditions must be met for consumer sovereignty to occur; these are discussed in turn.

a.   Equality of the Marginal Rate of Substitution in Consumption of Any Two Goods for Any Two Consumers

The *marginal rate of substitution in consumption* represents the least additional amount of one good that must be consumed if one unit of the other good is removed and if the consumer's utility of consumption remains the same. This condition means that for any two individuals the amount of one product that a person is willing to exchange for one unit of another product must be the same. Otherwise, the welfare of both individuals can be increased by exchanging goods and, therefore, the overall consumption pattern is changed. This proposition can be easily understood by means of a simple numerical example, where the formula $1Q_1 = 1Q_2$ means that one unit of Q_1 can be substituted for one unit of Q_2 and utility remains the same.

	Marginal Rate of Substitution	Initial Situation: Stock of Goods	Type of Change	Final Situation: Stock of Goods	Utility
Consumer M	$1 Q_1 = 1 Q_2$	$10 Q_1$ $6 Q_2$	Exchange of goods between con-	$9 Q_1$ $8 Q_2$	+
Consumer N	$1 O_1 = 3 Q_2$	$4 Q_1$ $8 Q_2$	sumers at rate of $1 Q_1 = 2 Q_2$	$5 Q_1$ $6 Q_2$	+
Total		$14 Q_1$ $14 Q_2$		$14 Q_1$ $14 Q_2$	

Since the marginal utility of Q_1 and Q_2 are the same for the consumer *M,* with a price ratio of $1Q_1$ for $2Q_2$, he increases his utility by

[17]Another difficulty not mentioned in this discussion is the problem of "X-inefficiency," for which several suggested readings are given in the list of suggested readings.

exchanging $1Q_1$ for $2Q_2$. Since the marginal utility of one-third unit of Q_1 is the same as one unit of Q_2 (or two-thirds of Q_1 for two units of Q_2) for consumer N, she increases her utility by exchanging $2Q_2$ for $1Q_1$. This marginal condition is, of course, quite analogous to the second marginal condition for static efficiency of production.

It must be noted that if one of the two "goods" involved is leisure, this marginal condition means that consumer sovereignity occurs when the marginal wage rate for any two individuals is the same (i.e., the marginal substitution of goods for leisure is the same for all individuals). One of the two "goods" might also be a future good; in this case the condition of consumer efficiency means that all individuals have the same marginal tradeoff between present and future goods.

Certainly this condition is *not* met when any type of nonprice consumer rationing system occurs where people are forbidden to consume more than a particular amount of a given good or service. Such a rationing system can either be quite formal or else introduced in some legal guise so that it is not labeled as a rationing system at all. Examples of the latter are numerous: laws forbidding consumption of certain goods such as drugs, or sumptuary laws limiting consumption to certain groups of the population (e.g., in medieval times in certain places, only the nobility could carry long swords), or goods where users may consume only a certain amount (e.g., a system of monogamous marriage where a person can have only one legal spouse; or medicines, which require a physician's prescription); similarly, industrial systems where a worker can only work a certain number of hours a day (with no chance to work more or fewer hours) violates this condition. Different kinds of violations of this marginal condition occur in the market economies where price or wage discrimination between different groups occur or where informal rationing devices (gasoline purchases only on even days; or distribution of scarce goods by queuing methods) are found. The marginal condition is also violated wherever differential sales taxes by regions occur, or where full information about prices is not available. It is quite likely that wherever a well-functioning market for a particular good or service does not exist the condition is violated, since exchange between consumers to achieve equality of the marginal rates of substitution is hindered. A special case occurs for *public goods,* which are goods or services that an additional person can consume without diminishing the quantity consumed by others and which others cannot be prevented from consuming (e.g., the military security provided by an intercontinental missile force, or the services of a lighthouse). Such services are often provided by a government and financed by taxes; this means that for any given individual the amount produced may be too little or too much. However, it is impossible for a person wishing the government to produce more to make a payment to other people so that they will support a production (and tax) increase since everyone wishing to avoid higher taxes would claim that they would not support such an increase without payment (this difficulty is called the "free rider problem").

b. Equality of the Marginal Rates of Transformation with the Marginal Rates of Substitution in Consumption

Both the *marginal rate of transformation* and the *marginal rate of substitution in consumption* are defined above. This marginal condition requires that the subjective marginal exchange rates of consumers between any two goods must be the same as the marginal rates of transformation of producers between the same goods. If this condition is not met, then welfare can be increased by changing the pattern of production and consumption. This proposition can be seen more clearly in the following simple numerical example.

	Marginal Rate:	*Initial Situation:*	*Type of Change*	*Final Situation:*	*Util-ity*
	Of Substitution	*Consumption*		*Consumption*	
Consumer M	$1\ Q_1 = 1\ Q_2$	$10\ Q_1\ 6\ Q_2$	Change pattern of production and consumption	$9\ Q_1\ 8\ Q_2$	$+$
	Of Transformation	*Production*		*Production*	
Producer N	$1\ Q_1 = 2\ Q_2$	$10\ Q_1\ 6\ Q_2$		$9\ Q_1\ 8\ Q_2$	

Since the last unit of Q_1 and Q_2 have the same utility, the consumer gains utility by exchanging one unit of Q_1 for two units of Q_2. Since with the same inputs producers can increase the production of Q_2 by two units without decreasing production of Q_1 more than one unit, then this restructuring of the product mix results in higher utility with no greater use of productive resources.

This marginal condition can be extended by considering one of the "goods" to be leisure. In this case the proposition tells us that the marginal rate of substitution of work (nonleisure) for income must be the same as the marginal productivity of this work. Simlarly, one of the "goods" can be considered as a good in the future, in which case the proposition tells us that the tradeoff between present and future goods (i.e., the time rate of preference of an individual) must be equal to the tradeoff between present and future production (i.e., the marginal productivity of capital).

Most of the cases violating the marginal condition concerning the equality of marginal rates of substitution would also violate this condition. In addition, however, other circumstances would also lead to a violation of this condition. Any type of monopolistic pricing in a market economy or administered pricing in a centrally administered economy usually leads to a situation where this marginal condition is not met. A blockage of the flow of information between consumers and producers so that the latter do not know what the former want and cannot respond to these wishes may cause inequalities in this marginal condition. Further, a sales tax or subsidy that is placed at a different rates on each good would lead to a violation of this condition. If the two "goods" are income and leisure, an income tax (in contrast to a head tax) has the same distorting effect. Or if the two "goods" are present and future goods, the equivalent distorting tax would be a special tax on interest income (i.e., on future consumption). In the goods market, various types of nonprice rationing systems would usually violate this marginal condition. Similarly, in the labor market various sytems of involuntary labor (e.g., serfdom, slavery, army conscription) or, for that matter, involuntary unemployment would lead to an inequality of the marginal rates of transformation and substitution in consumption.

c. Some Problems in Empirically Analyzing Consumer Sovereignty

Like static efficiency of production, consumer sovereignty is difficult to measure quantitatively with the economic data that are usually available. Although it is relatively easy to determine whether the marginal conditions are met or not, the exact loss in utility cannot be easily measured.

Some conceptual problems arise because, in certain cases, consumer sovereignty may not be desirable. For instance, households or individuals may demand certain products that are "bad" for them (e.g., narcotics) or consumers might not have sufficient knowledge about certain goods and services (e.g., medicines or medical services) to make rational decisions so that the government feels it necessary to set minimum standards. Certain economists such as A. C. Pigou have also argued that individual consumers are unable to place a "correct" value on the future; that is, their "telescopic faculty" leads to an undervaluing of the economic well-being of future generations. (Whether or not governments are any better in this respect is unclear.) Other economists have argued that consumers are not as autonomous as this type of approach implies and that they are being manipulated by producers or governments through advertising and propaganda. In this case, the marginal rates of substitution are not "real." This is, of course, a controversial argument and is discussed in Chapter 7.

It must also be emphasized that tradeoffs exist between consumer sovereignty and other performance criteria. If the population strongly prefers present to future consumption, economic growth may be low. Similarly, consumer sovereignty may be achieved through institutions that also bring about a highly unequal distribution of income; or a high degree of consumer sovereignty may conflict with certain goals of economic stability if consumers' tastes often change.

6. Optimal Distribution of Income and Wealth

Many criteria for judging the optimality of the income distribution can be found in the economic literature; three deserve special mention.

a. Equality

The data on values of elites presented in Table 2–1 show very clearly that there are considerable disagreements both within and between systems as to what is the optimal degree of equality in the distribution of income. The same might be true concerning wealth. A very minimal criterion of equality is that labor income should be roughly equal for those who perform the same job at the same level of intensity and that those who work less intensely deserve less labor income. The optimal degree of income inequality between different jobs is much more difficult to determine.

b. Adequacy

Adequacy of income is usually defined as some fraction of income above the minimum subsistence level. According to this criterion an income distribution can be quite adequate if everyone in the economy has an income above a certain level, even though the distribution of income may be highly unequal. Such an state of affairs is, of course, easier to achieve for a country that has a high average per capita income than for another with a low average per capita income. To apply the criterion of adequacy, however, one needs some designation of a minimum adequate income and data on individual incomes. Such conceptual simplicity raises some empirical problems, especially because in most modern welfare states considerable income is "invisible" and comes in the form of entitlements to free services (e.g., medical services) if need for such services arises. Once, however, we begin to consider need, then it should be clear that a meaningful application of the adequacy criterion would focus primarily on need and not on a blanket level of minimum income applicable to all: A person who is ill has need of much more income than a person who is well. If the economies under consideration have perfect mechanisms to provide special income (either in terms of cash or of services) to those in need, then this need factor is not a problem in our empirical analysis; if such mechanisms are not perfect, then some obvious difficulties arise.

c. Correspondence of Total Income to Labor

In most economically developed Western nations, rents, interest, and profits constitute roughly one-fifth to one-fourth of pretax personal income. In most Eastern European economies, in-kind income in the form of privileges and perquisites (e.g., special medical care, better apartments, ability to obtain certain scarce foodstuffs at low prices) are associated with particular job positions.[18] If it is an important performance criterion that total income should correspond to the real labor performed by the recipient, then judging an economic system according to its income distribution requires taking the existence of such nonlabor income into account. Some obvious problems of measuring nonlabor income in the form of privileges and perquisites arise, not only in determining the monetary importance of such in-kind income but also in deciding whether some parts of such income are independent of or dependent on job performance.

7. A Final Comment

This survey could be considerably extended to cover many other performance indicators. Many important problems in using such indicators should now, however, be quite apparent. Although the long list of difficulties may be depressing, it should be a warning against the facile comparisons that one often finds and an encouragement to read further in this guidebook to see how such problems can be overcome or sidestepped.

D. Policy Goals and Policy Instruments

An economic system or institution can function without any explicit central economic policy-making body, for example, a perfectly competitive market economy. In all countries, however, the system is sufficiently centralized that economic policy makers can be distinguished.

If the policy makers of a system or institution actually have sufficient power to influence the course of events, then analysis of the performance of the economic system requires us to separate the impact of particular policies on the system from the autonomous behavior of the system (i.e., how the system would behave without such policies). This

---

[18]Michael Voslensky, *La nomenklatura: Les privilégiés en U.R.S.S* (Paris: Belfond, 1980).

task, in turn, requires a consideration of the goals of the policy makers and the means with which they have to achieve such goals. If the policy makers do not have sufficient power to influence the course of events, then it may not appear necessary to know anything about their goals. However, to determine whether they have any power, it is still necessary to examine their goals and the policy tools available to them.

Determination of whether or not the policy tools available can be used to influence the course of events requires some type of theory about the way in which the economy functions. For instance, according to Keynesian theory, a government can combat unemployment in an advanced market economy by increasing expenditures (current expenditures, subsidies, transfers, or investments), or decreasing taxes (either indirect or direct), or lowering the interest rate, or loaning more to the private sector (to encourage investment and consumption), or devaluing currency (to encourage exports).

To determine the relationship between policy ends and policy means, the *first* step is to determine in a qualitative fashion the major policy goals of the key decision makers and the policy tools that are open to them.[19] The *second* step is to determine—if possible in a quantitative fashion—the key functional relationships linking the variables and the policy tools. The *third* step is to examine the impact of each tool on each end in order to see whether the policy tools are sufficient for the required tasks. It is shown below that the number of policy tools must generally be equal to or larger than the number of goals if all of the goals are to be achieved. The *final* step is to investigate the actual policy decisions taken. To make this approach more concrete, let us consider a simple model of an economically developed market economy.[20]

Consumption, C, is a function of disposable income (total income, Y, minus taxes, T) and a constant term, A_1, which is influenced in some manner by governmental monetary policy:

(2–1) $$C = A_1 + 0.7 (Y - T).$$

Taxes, T, are a linear function of total income, Y, and a constant term, A_2. The relationship is determined by the tax law of the nation:

(2–2) $$T = A_2 + 0.2Y.$$

[19]Kirschen et al., *Economic Policy*, analyze 12 policy goals and 61 policy instruments for nine Western European and North American nations. This study shows the potentialities of such an approach.

[20]This discussion draws heavily on a simple model discussed by Daniel B. Suits, "Forecasting and Analysis with an Econometric Model," *American Economic Review*, 52, No. 1 (March 1962), pp. 104–32. Suits also presents an analysis of the U.S economy using a 32-equation model.

There are only two uses of total income: private consumption, C, and government expenditures, A_3 (for simplicity, investment and the foreign trade sector are omitted):

$$(2\text{–}3) \qquad\qquad Y = C + A_3.$$

Assuming that we know A_1, A_2, and A_3, we can solve for the three unknowns C, T, and Y by employing simple techniques for solving simultaneous equations.[21] The following results are obtained:

$$(2\text{–}1a) \qquad\qquad C = 2.273A_1 - 1.591\,A_2 + 1.273\,A_3$$

$$(2\text{–}2a) \qquad\qquad T = 0.451\,A_1 + 0.682\,A_2 + 0.454\,A_3$$

$$(2\text{–}3a) \qquad\qquad Y = 2.273\,A_1 - 1.591\,A_2 + 2.273\,A_3$$

By substituting the known A's into the equations, we can easily determine C, T, and Y. Since the A's either represent policy tools (coefficients in the tax function or government expenditures) or constants influenced by policy, we can now procede to try to determine the impact of the three policy measures.

Suppose, for instance, that the policy makers wish to change personal consumption so that it is one unit higher than the current amount. They can achieve this end by raising government expenditures, A_3, by 0.786 (i.e., 1/1.273), or by lowering the constant term in the tax schedule, A_2, by 0.628 (i.e., 1/1.591), or by carrying out monetary policy which will raise A_1 by 0.440 (i.e., 1/2.273). In short, to increase consumption, it appears that the government can use one or more policy tools. Of course, if certain constraints are placed on such tools (e.g., taxes can not be lowered by more than 0.20) then tax policy alone will not achieve the desired goal and at least two policy tools must be employed.

---

[21]Simple substitution methods can be employed. To derive equation 2–1a, start with equation 2–1 in the text:

$$C = A_1 + .7\,(Y - T) = A_1 + .7Y - .7T$$

Now substitute equations 2–2 and 2–3 for Y and T at every occasion:

$$C = A_1 + .7\,(C + A_3) - .7\,(A_2 + .2Y)$$
$$= A_1 + .7\,(C + A_3) - .7\,[A_2 + .2\,(C + A_3)]$$

Expand and collect terms:

$$C = A_1 - .7A_2 + .56A_3 + .56C$$
$$.44C = A_1 - .7A_2 + .56A_3$$
$$C = 2.273A_1 - 1.591A_2 + 1.273A_3$$

The others equations can be solved in like manner.

If they wish to raise consumption by a certain amount and the total GNP by another amount, then only in rare circumstances will the policy makers be able to achieve such goals using one policy tool. The combination of policy tools necessary to achieve two goals can be determined by solving equations 2–1 and 2–3 for two of the three unknowns, leaving the third unknown at its original level. Similarly, three goals (i.e., specified levels of C, T, and Y) can generally be achieved only with the use of three policy tools (A_1, A_2, and A_3).

From considerations such as these Jan Tinbergen formulated the simple rule that at least N policy tools are generally needed to achieve N policy goals.[22] Thus we must compare the number of policy goals to the available policy instruments to determine whether such goals are feasible. Problems arise when constraints are placed on the use of the policy tools, in which case even more tools than goals may be needed. Similarly, if limits are placed on the amount by which any of the variables (C, T, and Y) can rise, this may require more policy tools than goals.

This analysis assumes policy makers have a certain set of fixed goals. However, they may be willing to trade off achieving one goal at the expense of another. In such a case it is often useful to try to formulate a preference function of the policy maker, that is, the decline in utility if the performance of the economy is at various distances from the goals. The model is then used to determine what set of means will maximize the policy maker's utility function, given a certain cost for using each policy tool. If, for instance, it is extremely costly to utilize any policy tool, and if three performance goals are set, the policy maker's utility may increase if only one tool is used that places the economy near the three goals, rather than if three policy tools place the economy exactly at these goals.[23] As mentioned before, certain economists have tried to determine such preference functions for different political groups by means of interviewing decision makers in these groups to determine their tradeoffs of goals; from such information it is possible to formulate different policy bundles that would maximize the utility of each of the major groups.

The analysis of policy problems is further complicated when different government agencies control different policy tools. In many cases, the order in which these measurements are employed strongly influences the results. In other cases, the relationship of the goal upon which the agency focuses and the particular policy instrument that it controls

---

[22]This rule was originally formulated by Jan Tinbergen and is well illustrated with examples from the Dutch economy in his *On the Theory of Economic Policy* (Amsterdam: North Holland, 1955); and his *Economic Policy: Principles and Design* (Amsterdam: North Holland, 1956).

[23]Such an approach is illustrated in considerable detail by Hans Theil, "Linear Decision Rules for Macrodynamic Policy," in Hickman, ed., *Quantitative Planning.*

can influence the result. For instance, the central bank (in the U.S., the Federal Reserve) may control the interest rate and focus on using this to achieve a balance of payments with no gold outflow or inflow, while the ministry of finance (in the U.S., the Department of the Treasury) may control the level of taxes and focus upon using this to achieve full employment. Given certain parameters of the economy, this may result in the economy moving further from full employment and external equilibrium than before; and it might be better for the central bank to use the interest rate to achieve full employment and the ministry of finance to use tax policy to achieve external balance.

If uncertainty is introduced into the analysis, other interesting complications arise.[24] Suppose, for instance, that we have the following relationship between a particular policy at a given time, P_t, and a desired policy goal which we will designate as Y:

$$Y_t = (X_t + e'_t) + a P_t,$$

where $(X_t + e'_t)$ is the Y that would have occurred if no policy measure had been taken; e'_t is a random variable reflecting outside forces that cannot be predicted; and a shows the relationship between the policy measure P and the change in Y.

Suppose we wish to use P to achieve a given level of Y and also to offset fluctuations in Y arising from e'. If no policy measures are taken ($P_t = 0$), the economy will fluctuate according to e', and Y will be some distance from its desired level. Use of P_t (which involves a certain cost) will change Y_t and, if used judiciously, can also be used to offset fluctuations in e'_t. If we have these two goals of influencing the level and fluctuations of Y, it can be easily shown mathematically that the best policy does not aim toward achieving the desired Y_t, but rather some lower amount.

Another type of uncertainty is introduced when policy makers are not certain of the impact of their policy measure on the goal, that is, when there is a fluctuation in a so that they must consider $(a + e'')$, where e'' is a random variable. Although this makes the analysis more complex, essentially the same results as before are obtained. In cases where e'_t and e''_t are correlated, it can be shown that a higher level of utility is often obtained when policy measures in the ostensibly "wrong" direction are taken. From such an approach it can also be argued it is better to employ a number of policy tools in a small way than several policy tools in a big way; that is, the policy makers should diversify their use of policy tools.

[24]Various articles on the subject are cited in the list of selected readings.

The number and type of policy tools are an integral part of any institution or economic system. A centrally planned and administered economy offers a great many more possibilities to public policy makers to try to affect economic performance than a market economy, where the policy instruments are fewer. Whether or not the availability of more policy instruments leads to better performance is, of course, a different matter that is not easy to answer. A central bank that cannot carry out open market operations (either because of the lack of a capital market in the nation or because of a lack of legal authorization) is in a much different position for dealing with problems of inflation or unemployment.

It should be clear that the equations demonstrating the linkage between the policy instruments and the performance of the economy rest on the institutional framework of the economy. If the economic system or any part of it is changed, the equations most likely must be changed as well if the model is to retain its predictive powers. For instance, the form of the capital market in a nation—particularly the role and importance of banks, insurance companies, mutual funds, as well as the tax and other laws influencing the possibilities of internal financing by corporations—is extremely important in determining the impact of a change in the money supply on the level and fluctuations of interest rates and other variables.

The performance of the economic system also determines the need for certain policy tools. For instance, every economic system offers to its members the possibilities for economic misfortunes such as unemployment, industrial accidents, or sickness. To counteract the ill effects of such occurrences, many nations have created extensive social insurance systems so that such members can receive public support. However, if the institutions of an economy were so arranged that unemployment and accidents were minimized, medical care was free, and wages continued even though workers could not work, then formal social insurance institutions would be much less necessary.

If it is possible that some policy instruments can be used by political and economic policy makers to achieve an adequate economic performance and if these instruments are not available, then clearly the system must be faulted for the performance of the economy. If the policy instruments to achieve an adequate economic performance are available and are either not used or incorrectly used, then clearly the economic policies must be faulted for any poor performance of the economy. If things were this simple, the comparative study of economic systems would be easy. However, it is often difficult to determine whether such instruments would be effective. It is also difficult to determine the quantitative impact of the use of such tools.

E. Summary and Conclusions

The evaluation of economic systems can be carried out using many types of criteria. Although broad or general political-economic goals may be interesting to discuss, it is difficult to give such goals a sufficiently precise meaning to facilitate economic comparisons of different economic systems. Even specific economic goals may still be too broad for analysis and we must, instead, focus upon particular performance criteria if we wish to have something to say of scientific value.

We can, of course, impose our own performance criteria and measure an economic system against it. We can also try to determine the performance criteria, values, or goals of the participants of the economic system, a task that raises many problems.

Six performance criteria are defined and discussed in this chapter: economic growth, dynamic efficiency, economic stability, static efficiency of production, consumer sovereignty, and an optimal distribution of income. Except for the last, these indicators have relatively specific meanings and yet are broad enough to be of interest in evaluating economies. They certainly do not include all the types of economic performance that are important to the investigator; rather, they represent a subjective judgment about what the author regards as useful and manageable indicators. In many cases these performance indicators conflict with each other; that is, one can be achieved only at the expense of others. Further, there are many conceptual and quantitative difficulties in trying to apply them, so that considerable caution on the part of the investigator is important.

The performance of any economic system is not only a result of its structural elements and environment, but also of the measures taken by certain important policy makers in the system. There is a relationship between particular policy goals and the instruments available to achieve them. Determining these ends and means and how they interact is a crucial aspect in trying to separate the influence of the system *per se* and the choices facing the participants within the economy.

SUGGESTED READINGS

A. Goals and Assessment of Economic Performance: Theoretical Viewpoints

1. Bela Balassa, *The Hungarian Experience in Economic Planning* (New Haven, Conn.: Yale University Press, 1959), pp. 3–24. Balassa sets out a number of success criteria and discusses how they may be applied. For a more technical discussion, see John Michael Montias, *The Structure of Economic Systems* (New Haven, Conn.: Yale University Press, 1976), chap. 4, pp. 39–70.

2. Kenneth E. Boulding, "Welfare Economics," in American Economic Association, Bernard Haley, ed., *A Survey of Contemporary Economics,* Vol. 2 (Homewood, Ill.: Richard D. Irwin, 1952), chap. 1. Boulding's essay analyzes in much greater detail the marginal conditions of static efficiency that are discussed in this chapter. It is a difficult but important piece.

3. Peter Wiles, "Growth versus Choice," chap. 11 in his book, *The Political Economy of Communism* (Cambridge, Mass.: Harvard University Press, 1962), pp. 206–22. This selection provides an approach almost totally in conflict with that the Boulding article cited above.

4. Harvey Leibenstein, "Allocative Efficiency versus 'X Efficiency' ", *American Economic Review,* 56 (June 1966), pp. 392–415. Leibenstein argues that the traditional approach to efficiency is much too narrow and that a broader range of phenomena must be included; he includes a number of interesting empirical cases to argue his point.

5. E. F. Schumacher, "Buddhist Economics," chap. 4 in his *Small Is Beautiful* (New York: Harper & Row, 1973), pp. 53–63. Schumacher presents a set of values for evaluating economic systems that are totally different from those traditional bourgeois or Marxist economists. A more developed, but different, system based on many of the same values is proposed by Amritananda Das, *Foundations of Gandhian Economics* (New York: St. Martin's Press, 1979). Some theoretical problems of such systems are discussed by David Collard, *Altruism and Economy: A Study in Non-Selfish Economics* (New York: Oxford University Press, 1978).

6. Finding a good Marxist discussion of economic goals in English is extremely difficult. Sources such as *Fundamentals of Marxism Leninism* (a Soviet textbook) are very diffuse. Although some Marxist speak about goals in terms of obeying certain developmental laws (these are summarized by Morris Bornstein, "Ideology and the Soviet Economy," *Soviet Studies,* 18 [July 1966], pp. 74–81) or achieving communism in the most expedient manner, these analyses are not completely relevant to our topic. Yugoslav economist Branco Horvat, *Toward a Theory of Planned Economy* (Belgrade: Yugoslav Institute of Economic Research, 1964), pp. 17–33, has some interesting remarks about goals. A Maoist view is presented by John Gurley, "Maoist Economic Development: The New Man in New China," *The Center Magazine,* 3 (March 1970), pp. 25–33.

B. Goals and the Assessment of Economic Performance in Practice

1. Peter H. Sturm, "The Systems Component in Differences in Per Capita Output between East and West Germany," *Journal of Comparative Economics,* 1 (March 1977), pp. 5–25. Some of the difficulties in comparing quite similar economies should be manifest from this discussion.

2. Richard Easterlin, "Does Economic Growth Improve the Human Lot?" in Paul David and Melvin W. Reder, eds., *Nations and Households in Economic Growth* (New York: Academic Press, 1974), pp. 89–120. This essay uses survey data to compare empirically the degree of (subjective) happiness in various nations.

3. Abram Bergson, "Comparing Productivity and Efficiency in the U.S.A. and the U.S.S.R.," in Alexander Eckstein, ed., *Comparison of Economic Systems* (Berkeley: University of California Press, 1971), pp. 161–219. This is a superb but difficult study of the difficulties in making aggregate comparisons of efficiency. A technical criticism of Bergson's methods is made by Domar in the same volume, pp. 219–33, which is also important to read. A shorter version of this essay, as well as other essays on the same theme, is contained in Abram Bergson, *Productivity and the Social System: The USSR and the West* (Cambridge, Mass.: Harvard University Press, 1978).

4. Alan Abouchar, *Economic Evaluation of Soviet Socialism* (New York: Praeger, 1979). A more extended development of his analysis of spacial efficiency, using linear programming techniques, is found in his book *Soviet Planning and Spatial Efficiency* (Bloomington: Indiana University Press, 1971). Gregory Grossman, "Notes on the Illegal Private Economy and Corruption," in U.S. Congress, Joint Economic Committee, *Soviet Economy in a Time of Change,* Vol. 1 (Washington, D.C.: GPO, 1979), pp. 834–55, examines some negative values that are actualized in the Soviet economy. An attempt to evaluate economic and political values together is Wlodzimierz Brus, "Political System and Economic Efficiency: The East European Context," *Journal of Comparative Economics,* 4, No. 1 (March 1980), pp. 40–56.

5. E. S. Kirschen et al. *Economic Policies Compared: West and East* (New York: American Elsevier, 1974). In Chapter 1 an interesting attempt is made to determine national preferences for particular economic policies in different economic systems. Two other quite different studies for determining "national values" are Compton Advertising, Inc., *National Survey on the American Economic System* (New York: American Advertising Council 1975). This book contains the result of an extensive public opinion study of American views toward their own economy. Such information can be used to develop goals of the system as viewed by the participants. A much different approach using content analysis of mass media to derive economic values is Robert C. Angell, "Social Values of Soviet and American Elites," *The Journal of Conflict Resolution,* 8 (December 1964), pp. 330–86.

C. Implementation of Goals

1. Etienne S. Kirschen and Lucien Morissens, "The Objectives and Instruments of Economic Policy," in Morris Bornstein, ed., *Comparative Economic Systems: Models and Cases,* 4th ed. (Homewood, Ill.: Richard D. Irwin, 1979), pp. 28–49.

2. There are a number of analyses of the relation of economic goals and policy tools. Many of these are quite technical, especially when considerations of uncertainty are introduced. Some of the simpler discussions are Jan Tinbergen, *Economic Policy: Principles and Design* (Amsterdam: North Holland, 1956); and Henri Theil, "Linear Decision Rules for Macrodynamic Policy," in Bert G. Hickman, ed. *Quantitative Planning of Economic Policy* (Washington, D.C.: Brookings Institution, 1965), pp. 18–42. The introduction of uncertainty is handled in an elegant way by William C. Brainard, "Uncertainty and the Effectiveness of Policy," *American Economic Review,* 57, No. 2 (May 1967), pp. 411–25. A description of how the tradeoff between macro goals can be determined is contained in Pan A. Yotopoulos and Jeffrey B. Nugent, *Economics of Development: Empirical Investigations* (New York: Harper & Row, 1976), pp. 424–27.

3

ECONOMIC GROWTH AND DYNAMIC EFFICIENCY

A. An Overview of the Problem

In modern history, economic growth has been proclaimed an important national goal by a number of individual politicians and statesmen such as Colbert in seventeenth-century France and Peter the Great in eighteenth-century Russia. Indeed, both of these men are well known for the institutional changes and new policies they introduced to achieve growth. However, the period following World War II is unique in the almost universal interest of *all* political leaders in achieving this economic goal.

Although the institutional arrangements for encouraging economic growth are quite different in nations with different economic systems, I show below that the institutions themselves appear to make little difference in the final growth rates achieved. Such a surprising result occurs because many of the difficulties in achieving growth are the same in all nations and many of the effective policies that lead to growth can be carried out in very different institutional settings.

Because governments play a central role in promoting growth in many modern economies, it seems useful to approach the topic of growth by examining the interactions between government and the productivity sectors of the economy. (If the empirical emphasis were on societies and nations with much lower levels of economic development, a different approach might be more useful.) This analysis begins, therefore, with a brief look at the most important economic institutions which influence growth, the various types of governmental planning for growth, and the mechanisms through which governmental policies affect growth. To place these institutional details in perspective, this discussion is followed by a brief survey of the economic growth experience of a number of nations. The more lengthy following sections deal with the elements of particular strategies for attaining more rapid economic growth, as well as the institutional prerequisites to facilitate such policies.

B. Institutions, Planning, and Growth Rates

1. Some Important Institutional Considerations

One highly centralized method for achieving economic growth is for the central government of a nation to mobilize and to direct the resources of the country toward growth. The necessary resources for investment would be obtained by taxing individuals and production units and would be allocated according to some national economic plan to particular regions and economic purposes; the labor force would also be assigned to the appropriate work places; and the necessary land would be requisitioned from its current users. The plan itself would be based on calculations of the most effective uses of the factors of production for achieving growth, constrained by certain political necessities such as maintaining a given standard of living.

A highly decentralized method for achieving economic growth is for the government to do little except to facilitate individual saving and the mobility of land, labor, and capital to their most productive uses. No national plans would be promulgated, and investment would be entirely individually financed and directed toward those uses that offer the highest chance of gain for the investors.

All economically developed or semideveloped nations fall between these two extremes. As I point out in greater detail in Chapter 8, labor is allocated through some type of market mechanism in all nations of

Europe and North America (with the possible exception of Albania). Further, in all countries capital is allocated partly by the central government and partly by lower-level institutions such as enterprises and banks. In nations with national economic plans, not all investment is covered in these plans; in nations without a formal economic plan, certain investment carried out by various levels of governments are administered through their budgets, which serve the same function as a plan.

In general, most of the central governments of the socialist, centrally administered nations of Eastern Europe obtain about 75 to 90 percent of total resources for investment from taxation and organize most of the spending of these funds through their national economic plan. In the capitalist, market economies of Western Europe and North America, it seems likely that this percentage of governmental mobilization of investment funds is between 30 and 70 percent. Some idea of the difficulties in making such estimates can be gained by looking briefly at the United States.[1] In 1975, for example, direct investments by local, state, and federal governments amounted to roughly 24 percent of total gross investment in this nation. However, governmental agencies on the federal level also lent out funds amounting to about 26 percent of total gross investment and, further, guaranteed a group of loans that amounted to an additional 13 percent of total gross investments. Since the degree to which these loans and loan guarantees were used for investment purposes is quite unclear, all we can say is that U.S. governmental involvement in capital formation was somewhere between 24 and 63 percent of total gross investment; and inclusion of loans and guarantees by state and local governments would raise the upper limit a little higher. The only "central" planning of this governmental participation occurred for the direct capital investment of the federal government that was specified in the federal budget.

Since the institutional details of the investment process differ considerably from nation to nation, these are best learned by reading case studies. It seems more useful to turn to some general problems of planning designed to achieve rapid economic growth in all nations.

2. Planning for Economic Growth

Planning is a magic word that is used in various incantations about economic growth. Usually it is defined as an attempt to achieve rational political and economic actions by designating and by using the most suitable means to achieve desired goals.

---

[1]The data come from U.S. Bureau of the Census, *Statistical Abstract, 1978* (Washington, D.C.: GPO, 1978); and Murray L. Weidenbaum, "An Economic Analysis of the Federal Government's Credit Program," Working Paper 18 (St. Louis: Center for the Study of American Business, January 1977).

Economic growth is an important national goal and, in the last three decades, almost every developed nation in the world has established special organs devoted to planning the national economy. Even in some of the nations without such official planning organizations, national development plans have also been produced by one or another governmental agency.

Among the nations in Europe and North America, the planning processes vary considerably.[2] The planning organs differ in their place in the governmental structure: In some cases, the planning agency is a separate organ reporting to the head of the government; in other cases it is attached to a ministry; while in still other cases it is "semi-independent" and serves in an advisory capacity. The various "development plans" differ in their time horizons (5 years, 10 years, 15 years), their comprehensiveness, and their orientation (production goals, regional development goals, trade goals, social consumption goals). The conception of planning also differs, for in some cases planning is conceived in *genetic* terms (i.e., as an attempt to guide growth along some preconceived equilibrium path, which involves some concept of balanced growth), while in other cases planning is conceived in *teleological* terms (i.e., as an attempt to break away from current economic relations, which involves some concept of unbalanced growth).[3] And of course, the planners differ in their power to enforce the plan, so that plans range from those based totally on voluntary compliance to those having the power of law.

In Eastern Europe the situation is more uniform. All nations have a central planning agency empowered to draw up plans for different time intervals. In most countries the plan has the power of law and usually the central government tries to enforce it.

Are these planning organs in different nations doing anything serious and useful? Or is the exercise of planning nothing more than an exercise in political propaganda with no important impact on either the rate of direction of economic growth (a type of exercise that throughout this discussion I call *epiphenomenal planning*)? Although it is often difficult for an outsider to determine whether the governmental planning effort in a particular country is serious or epiphenomenal, the

---

[2]Two interesting but somewhat outdated sources that summarize the relevant institutional information about Western European planning agencies are Jan Tinbergen, *Central Planning* (New Haven, Conn.: Yale University Press, 1964); and Albert Waterston, *Development Planning: Lessons of Experience* (Baltimore: Johns Hopkins University Press, 1965).

[3]The terms *geneticist* and *teleologist* were coined to describe two sides of a planning debate in the Soviet Union in the 1920s as described by Alexander Erlich, *The Soviet Industrialization Debate, 1924–28* (Cambridge, Mass.: Harvard University Press, 1960). Such issues of planning strategies that were raised in this early debate have not yet been completely resolved; these labels are used to emphasize the continuing history of the arguments.

answers to certain questions will aid us in reaching a judgment.[4] To make the discussion more concrete, selected examples are given from the experience of Western Europe and Japan.

a. Incorporation of Planning in Government Decisions

It is quite likely that the planning exercise is epiphenomenal if the planning process is outside of normal intragovernmental decision making (e.g., it is done by a group of outsiders or by a single ministry that cannot enforce its will on the other ministries); if the plan forecasts governmental decisions rather than embodies decisions already made; if the plan consists of a summary of projects of individual departments before they are given priorities by the top-level governmental authorities; if planners have been given few guidelines by the highest political authorities on which to build the plan (the case with certain national plans in Japan); if the planning for a given ministry is made without direct participation by most ministries (as in Sweden); or if the development plan is formulated after the most important economic policy decisions (such as the budget) have been made (as in the Netherlands).

b. Provisions for Implementation of Plan

Certainly the planning exercise is epiphenomenal if it is not implemented; however, the degree of implementation depends on the sanctions available and the desire to use such sanctions to carry out the plan by the highest political authorities. In Japan the planning agency has no powers of enforcement and must rely on the outcome of political infighting with other ministries to determine if the plan is enforced. In Sweden the enforcement of the plan is weakened by several agencies (such as the Labor Market Board) that appear independent of the plan.

c. Specification of Targets and Instruments

The feasibility of the plan can be analyzed by determining the consistency between targets and instruments. A number of the plans promulgated in the West such as the French Fourth Plan have contained little analysis of the policy instruments to achieve the goals. An American economist once posed to a group of Latin American planners the question of how their plans would vary if the published growth rate targets were 2 percentage points lower or higher; in most cases it

[4]This discussion, as well as the examples from Western Europe, draws heavily on Peter Murrell, "Planning and Coordination of Economic Policy in Market Economies," *Journal of Comparative Economics,* 3, No. 2 (June 1979), pp. 145–67.

appeared that the plans would have been essentially the same.[5] Obviously such plans are epiphenomenal. In certain cases, of course, the goals and instruments can be specified but the plan may be impossible to achieve since the premises underlying the plan are incorrect. With limited information, however, it is often difficult for an outsider to make such judgments.

d. Exploration of Alternative
   Goals and Instruments

In the plans of a number of Western nations (e.g., in the past, France, Japan, and the Netherlands), the growth rate and other targets of the plans are chosen before the planning work is begun. In dealing with only one major variant, planners forego the opportunity to make an informed choice between alternatives.

e. Response to Changing Circumstances

This flexibility of the planning process in meeting uncertainty is important in determining the degree to which the plan is an operational document. In many cases, development plans are maintained long after the economic premises of the plan have been superseded; as a result, yearly plans differ considerably from the long-term plan. Most Western countries (or, for that matter, countries in Eastern Europe) have not developed effective mechanisms for generating rolling long-term plans so that the development plans would always rest on realistic premises related to the current economic situation.

3. The Results of Planning: Comparisons of Growth Rates

It is unfortunate that official statistics in most nations in Eastern Europe embody rather different concepts from those in nations in the West and, further, that the various aggregates are calculated in somewhat different ways. In all the growth rate statistics presented below, the aggregates refer either to the gross domestic product (GDP) or gross national product (GNP), even though this required a very wearisome recalculation of all statistics from Eastern Europe in order to base them on the same concepts and methods used in the West.[6]

---

[5]Communication from Carlos Diaz-Alejandro.

[6]The national accounts data from Eastern Europe are not comparable with those from the West for three major reasons. First, most of their aggregate series for the volume of production omit services and focus exclusively upon "material production." Second, the components of these volume series are weighted by market prices that are distorted in a fashion often to reduce the importance of some of the most slowly growing sectors and industrial branches. Third, in some countries for certain periods, gross production for each branch was aggregated without any attempt to eliminate intermediate products. Since all

In the last century the rate of aggregate economic growth has varied considerably.[7] In Western Europe and North America, for instance, the unweighted average annual growth of the GNP per capita was about 1.6 percent in the period from 1870 to 1913, and about 1.1 percent from 1913 to 1950. Certain areas of Eastern Europe seemed to have shared in the growth surge during the latter part of the nineteenth century. For instance, the per capita GNP of European Russia grew at an average annual rate of 1.4 percent from the early 1860s to the eve of World War I and total industrial production during this time increased at a 5 percent annual average. Czechoslovakia and East Germany also appeared to follow the Western European pattern at this time. During the interwar period, most of the Eastern European nations appeared to experience a growth equal to, or more than, the Western European average.

By 1950 the reconstruction work from the damage of World War II was almost completed in all European nations. Their growth rates since that time have been very much higher than in the past and are summarized in Table 3–1.

Although the unweighted averages appear roughly the same for the countries in East and West, such a comparison is not valid. It is well known that after a certain level of economic development, the aggregate growth rates appear inversely related to the levels of economic development. This is because countries with lower per capita GNPs have a greater potential for moving labor force from low productivity agriculture to high productivity industry; because they can borrow or buy technology rather than having to spend the resources to develop new technology; and because they often have a smaller service sector which, due to the way in which output is measured, appears to have a lower productivity growth rate than agriculture or industry. Further, when starting from a relatively small base, any given increment of production yields a higher growth rate. In order to compare the experience of East and West, it is therefore necessary to hold constant the level of per capita GDP. Although we might try to hold constant a number of other variables as well, experiments along these lines have shown that such vari-

---

factors lend an upward bias to production series, it is necessary to use the data on physical quantities of production in these countries and recalculate the volume indices using "adjusted factor prices." For the Soviet Union, the Greenslade indices are used; for the other centrally administered economies, the recalculations of Thad Alton and his colleagues at the Research Project on National Income in East Central Europe are used. Most of the sources of these recalculations are listed in Appendix D.

[7]The generalizations in this paragraph are based on material from Angus Maddison, *Economic Growth in the West* (New York: Twentieth Century Fund, 1964), p. 30; Raymond Goldsmith, "The Economic Growth of Tsarist Russia, 1860–1913," *Economic Development and Cultural Change*, 9, No. 2 (April 1961), pp. 441–75; and B. R. Mitchell, *European Historical Statistics, 1750–1970* (New York: Columbia University Press, 1976).

TABLE 3–1
Average Annual Growth Rates in East and West, 1950 through 1979

Country	Relative per Capita GDP 1970	Average Annual Growth Rates[a]					
		GDP	GDP per Person	GDP per Economically Active	Industrial Production	Agricultural Production	Gross Fixed Capital Investment
Socialist, centrally administered economies							
Bulgaria	37.3	5.43%	4.69%	4.91%	9.48%	2.51%	10.89%
Czechoslovakia	62.0	3.67	3.02	2.80	4.38	0.62	6.11
East Germany	63.9	3.77	4.04	3.71	4.68	1.54	8.52
Hungary	42.7	3.64	3.22	2.96	4.81	1.20	8.85
Poland	35.4	4.12	2.98	2.61	6.78	1.56	9.70
Romania	31.2	5.81	4.78	4.71	9.45	2.39	11.33
Soviet Union	46.9	4.95	3.64	3.62	6.99	3.04	8.02
Unweighted average		4.49%	3.77%	3.62%	6.65%	1.84%	9.06%
Yugoslavia	25.8	5.87%	4.84%	4.91%	8.93%	2.66%	7.48%
Capitalist, market economies							
Australia	69.6	4.54%	2.56%	2.15%	—	—	4.43%
Austria	63.1	4.74	4.38	4.76	5.35%	1.82%	5.95
Belgium	72.0	4.00	3.51	3.53	5.11	0.61	4.36
Canada	81.9	4.57	2.69	1.88	5.46	1.49	4.36
Denmark	83.3	3.81	3.15	2.97	4.79	0.87	5.42
Finland	63.1	4.48	3.92	3.95	5.82	1.06	4.54
France	73.2	4.86	3.93	4.24	5.84	1.79	6.41
West Germany	78.2	4.85	3.87	4.31	5.55	1.93	5.69
Greece	38.7	6.20	5.51	6.40	8.74	2.92	7.16
Ireland	40.5	3.45	3.06	3.75	—	—	5.66
Italy	49.2	4.92	4.22	4.62	6.71	1.91	4.79
Japan	59.2	8.35	7.23	7.06	—	—	11.43
Netherlands	68.7	4.58	3.39	3.59	5.92	3.18	5.10
New Zealand	64.6	3.46	1.78	1.38	—	—	—
Norway	68.4	4.15	3.37	3.53	4.88	−0.16	4.93
Portugal	27.1	5.43	5.07	4.72	7.63	0.86	6.49
Spain	48.9	5.53	4.52	4.86	7.81	2.49	7.43
Sweden	86.6	3.69	3.08	2.88	4.60	0.22	4.18
Switzerland	72.4	3.72	2.52	2.33	—	—	4.63
United Kingdom	63.5	2.72	2.29	2.39	2.67	2.17	4.29
United States	100.0	3.39	2.05	1.67	3.46	1.18	3.09
Unweighted average		4.54%	3.62%	3.66%	5.65%	1.52%	5.52%

[a]The data for the socialist, centrally administered economies are drawn from Western recalculations for their national accounts, except for the series on gross fixed capital investment which are official data.

Sources are specified in Appendix D.

ables do not appear to have much explanatory value.[8] The results of regression experiments to determine the explanatory role of the economic system and the level of economic development are presented in Table 3–2. If you have questions about the meaning of the various terms or how to interpret the results, an explanation of the statistical method is given in Appendix A.

From these regression experiments, several important conclusions can be drawn: *First,* for all series except for gross fixed capital investment (this result is discussed in a later section), there are no significant differences between the growth rates in the socialist, centrally administered and those in the capitalist market economies. This can be seen by examining the calculated regression coefficient for the systems variable that shows the impact of economic system when the level of per capita income is held constant. Although it is negative in the first five cases (i.e., the socialist, centrally administered nations have a lower growth rate), this result is not statistically significant and could have occurred by chance.[9] If official Eastern European data are used for industrial and agricultural production, rather than series recalculated in the West, the results are not greatly different:[10] Agricultural production is still lower in the East than in the West, industrial production appears higher, but in neither case is the systems coefficient statistically significant. In short, there do not appear to be important differences between the growth rates of the socialist nations and those of the capitalist nations.

Second, as predicted, the growth rates are significantly and inversely related to the per capita GDP. This can be seen by examining the calculated regression coefficient, which reflects the influence of per capita income when the systems variable is held constant. According to the calculated coefficient, if the measure of GDP per capita is higher by 10 units (for instance, if Bulgaria has a per capita GDP that is 43.7

[8]Some of these experiments are reported by Frederic L. Pryor, "A Quasi-Test of Mancur Olson's Hypothesis," in Dennis Mueller, ed., *The Political Economy of Growth* (New Haven, Conn.: Yale University Press, 1983), pp. 90–109. The regression results presented in Table 3–2 differ slightly from those in this source because a somewhat different time period is covered, and the estimates for the level of GDP per capita was calculated for a different year and in a different manner.

[9]An interesting problem of interpretation arises in this regard. Since the regressions include all of the OECD and Eastern European nations, the sample represents practically the entire universe of economically developed and semideveloped nations in the world. Therefore, it might be argued, significance levels are not important. If, on the other hand, one considers the nations in the sample as *representative* of *possible* developed and semideveloped nations that could have arisen in world history, then significance levels are important. This latter interpretation is, in essence, followed throughout this guidebook.

[10]Such experiments are reported in Frederic L. Pryor, "Growth and Fluctuations of Production in O.E.C.D. and Eastern European Nations," *World Politics*, 37, No. 3 (January 1985). In the same article it is shown that there is no difference in the retardation of growth among the OECD and Eastern European nations except for agriculture, where retardation was greater in the East. The regressions on growth retardation serve as the basis for the analysis of fluctuations of aggregate production that is presented in Chapter 4.

TABLE 3–2
Results of Regression Experiments with Average Annual Growth Rates

Dependent Variable (average annual growth rates)	Constant	Relative Level of per Capita GNP	Systems Variable	R^2	n
GDP	+6.549* (0.846)	−0.0307* (0.0125)	−0.666 (0.517)	.1954	28
GDP per person	+6.016* (0.837)	−0.0366* (0.0123)	−0.579 (0.511)	.2627	28
GDP per economically active	+6.744* (0.936)	−0.0471* (0.0138)	−0.977 (0.572)	.3182	28
Industrial production	+10.558* (1.087)	−0.0737* (0.0156)	−0.541 (0.648)	.5601	23
Agricultural production	+2.780* (0.766)	−0.0189 (0.0110)	−0.079 (0.457)	.1519	23
Gross fixed capital investment	+9.237* (1.240)	−0.0569* (0.0182)	+2.419* (0.760)	.6116	27

Note: For the capitalist, market economies, the systems variable is zero; for the socialist, centrally administered nations, one; Yugoslavia is omitted from the regressions. R^2 is the coefficient of determination; *n* is the number of nations in the sample. The standard errors are placed in parentheses below the calculated coefficients and an asterisk designates statistical significance at the .05 level.
Source: The data come from Table 3–1.

percent of that of the United States, rather than 33.7 percent) the aggregate growth rate of production decreases roughly 0.3 to 0.5 percent, depending on whether we are talking about growth on an absolute basis or on the basis of per member of the population of the labor force.

Third, the degree to which growth rates can be explained by the two variables increases as we move from GDP to GDP per capita to GDP per economically active. This is shown by examining the coefficient of determination, which reflects the degree to which the dependent variable is explained by the two variables. Since a change in the labor supply is an important input to a change in the level of production, this result is quite understandable.

Although it would be interesting to attempt to link the "seriousness" of development planning to the growth rates presented in Table 3–1, developing a ranking of the relative seriousness that is more detailed than the systems variable included in the calculations would be very difficult. Further, it is likely that such a variable would have little relation to the actual growth rates.

Certainly a government can carry out a series of policies that effectively act to increase the average annual growth rate without generating such policies in a formal planning exercise. Indeed, higher growth may be the byproduct of a policy based on a quite different aim in mind. These policies, however, may create institutions favorable to growth; or they may provide incentives for the private sector to take steps to increase economic growth; or they may remove bottlenecks to more rapid growth. Therefore, in the remainder of this chapter it seems useful to focus our attention on the policy variables and other factors that appear to influence the growth rates of the individual countries, rather than the planning system per se.

C. Economic Growth by Increasing the Factors of Production

Regardless of the economic system, one method of raising the level of GDP is to increase the quantity and quality of the factors of production. After examining each of the production factors in turn, important similarities and differences between economic systems can be clearly identified.

1. Labor

Increasing the utilized labor supply can be accomplished in a variety of ways including increasing the population, encouraging immigration (or discouraging emigration), decreasing unemployment or underemployment, and increasing the participation of the population in the labor force (i.e., raising the *participation ratio*). Each is discussed in turn.

a. Increasing Population

In the long run, increasing the population by encouraging births may increase the total GDP; however, it does not seem likely to change greatly the per capita GDP. In the short run, moreover, encouragement of births might reduce the number of women in the labor force (i.e., the mothers of small children) so that the per capita GDP is reduced. Aside, perhaps, from Nazi Germany, no modern country has tried to increase the population by direct means; nevertheless, a number of countries have offered pronatalist incentives including children's allowances (a feature of the social insurance systems in almost every one of the nations of Europe); special privileges for mothers of small children (e.g., maternity pay plus the possibility of returning to the same job within so many months after the birth of the child); and restrictions against abortions and the sale of contraceptives.

Certain countries in both systems have followed pronatalist policies, for example, France (albeit for reasons other than increasing the labor force) and Czechoslovakia (in recent years). In the case of Czechoslovakia, one of the specific reasons offered to justify the policy was to increase the labor force in the long run. On the other hand, other countries in both systems have adopted antinatalist policies, for example, Japan and the People's Republic of China.

It is quite possible to increase the population by decreasing the death rate. Almost all countries in both East and West have taken special measures to prevent deaths among infants, children, and those in the working ages, not only to increase the labor force but for humanitarian reasons as well. For reasons which are not completely clear, the Soviet Union appears an exception to this generalization. During the late 1960s and the decade of the 1970s, infant mortality rates rose dramatically so that they are considerably higher than many capitalist nations with very much lower levels of economic development. Further, in most Eastern European nations the mortality rates for working age men (but not women) rose in the 1970s, but the causes remain obscure.

b. Immigration and Emigration Policies

The use of immigration as a means of increasing the labor force appears much more prevalent in the capitalist, market economies than in the socialist, centrally administered economies. In Western Europe *guest workers* have been a prominent feature of the labor market for several decades; and in the United States, it has been estimated that there are roughly 10 million foreign workers, a considerable proportion of whom entered the country illegally. Immigration between the socialist nations of Eastern Europe has been much less extensive and limited to brief episodes—for example, the planned exportation of workers from Bulgaria to the Soviet Union, from Poland to Czechoslovakia and East Germany, or from Vietnam to the Soviet Union, and the flight of Vietnamese of Chinese origin to China in the mid and late 1970s. (It should also be noted that considerable emigration has taken place from socialist countries such as Afganistan, Cuba, East Germany, Kampuchea (Cambodia), and Vietnam to the West, and that such flight has often been carried out at risk of life). Political considerations appear to play the major role in the differences between Eastern and Western Europe with regard to labor flows between countries with the same economic system and this does not seem to have anything to do with the economic system *per se*. Within individual socialist nations, there have been important regional shifts of the population and labor force, of which only part has been "planned" or anticipated by the planners.

c. Reducing Unemployment

Increasing the utilized labor force by decreasing unemployment or underemployment can be carried out in a variety of ways. However, the incidence of these types of underutilization of the labor force have been quite different.

(i) Unemployment due to a Lack of Aggregate Demand. Keynesian-type unemployment has never been important in the centrally planned, socialist economies of Eastern Europe. Moreover, until the late 1970s, such unemployment was not extensive in most capitalist, market economies either and thus did not seem a characteristic of either economic system. Indeed, among the capitalist nations under consideration, only the United States and Canada seemed to suffer such unemployment difficulties; therefore the causes seemed to lie in the particular economic circumstances, institutions, and policies of these two countries. The worldwide economic decline in the early 1980s which has led to unemployment rates of more than 8 or 9 percent in most developed, capitalist, market economies requires rethinking of this problem. For the 1980s, reduction of this type of unemployment appears to provide an important source of economic growth; unfortunately, the means by which this can be accomplished are difficult to specify.

(ii) Frictional Unemployment. Frictional unemployment and structural unemployment are difficult to discuss due to a lack of appropriate and comparable statistics. It appears, however, that these types of unemployment have been low in almost all nations in Eastern and Western Europe except in the early 1980s and, therefore, reduction of these types of unemployment has not been provided an important potential for growth in the 1950–80 period except for a few countries.

(iii) Underemployment. Underemployment, where the employed labor force is not used to full capacity, appears to be more important in the East than in the West. Such underemployment can be the result of a situation where the demand for labor is greater than supply at the market wage. In this case underemployment occurs because many workers do not work very hard and, as a result, have very low productivity. Such behavior is premised on the assumption that alternative work is easy to find, a situation that does not apply in all areas within the socialist nations. (This kind of underemployment has occurred in the Soviet Union and has led certain Soviet industrial managers to request the right to fire some workers and to create a certain "artificial unemployment" that would permit them to increase labor discipline). Underemployment of

labor can also arise due to lack of capital equipment and other necessary inputs, a situation that occurs not only in many developing nations but one that seems to have occurred in Bulgaria and Poland in the 1960s and other times.[11] Certainly reduction of underemployment could be an important source of economic growth in the socialist, centrally administered economies; and the first secretary of the Soviet Communist Party, Yuri Andropov, pursued just such a goal in his first few months after succeeding Leonid Brezhnev to power. However, the means to reduce such underemployment without employing some very unpleasant compulsory means are difficult to specify and the success of his program to reduce underemployment appeared debatable at the time of his death somewhat more than a year later.

d. Increasing Participation

Increasing the labor force by raising the participation ratio is a method of achieving growth that permits some interesting comparisons; and some relevant data are presented in Table 3–3. The 1970 unweighted average participation ratios are dramatically higher among the socialist, centrally administered economies than among the capitalist, market economies. The table reveals that the cause of such differences is the greater participation of women in the labor forces of the former set of nations. Compared to Western nations, the centrally administered nations appear to have given much greater direct encouragement to women to work outside the home, focusing considerable efforts on providing public nurseries and child day-care centers so that mothers can work without sacrificing too much of their salaries for such services. (Such a result should not, however, by interpreted to mean that women have higher economic positions in the East compared with the West or that average women's wages *vis-à-vis* those of men are any higher, a mattered discussed in Chapter 8).

In Table 3–4 the results of some regression experiments are presented so that more features of the data in Table 3–3 can be highlighted. The first regression shows that average participation ratios are higher in the East than the West. Per capita income does not appear to be an important causal factor (either in the equation presented in the table or when the equation is recalculated with the addition of a squared income term). The second regression equation shows that the rate of change of the participation ratio is higher in the socialist, centrally administered nations than in the capitalist, market economies and that this difference is statistically significant, even though it is

---

[11]Considerable information exists on the Polish underemployment problems in the 1960s which is analyzed by Michael Garmarnikov, "Poland's Unemployment Problem," *East Europe,* 13 (June 1964), pp. 30–33.

TABLE 3–3
Level and Changes of Labor Force and Participation Ratios

	Relative per Capita GDP 1970	Average Annual Growth Rates 1950 through 1980			Participation Ratios 1970		
		Total Participation Ratio	Working Age Population	Economically Active	Total	Men	Women
Socialist, centrally administered economies							
Bulgaria	37.3	−0.317%	+0.648%	+0.329%	.790	.906	.673
Czechoslovakia	62.0	+0.469	+0.524	+0.995	.747	.840	.657
East Germany	63.9	+0.627	−0.438	+0.186	.819	.961	.698
Hungary	42.7	+0.242	+0.325	+0.568	.719	.855	.591
Poland	35.4	+0.140	+1.209	+1.351	.796	.885	.712
Romania	31.2	+0.257	+0.860	+1.119	.855	.967	.748
USSR	46.9	+0.197	+1.398	+1.597	.762	.825	.710
Unweighted average		+0.230%	+0.647%	+0.878%	.784	.891	.684
Yugoslavia	25.8	−0.451%	+1.198%	+0.741%	.694	.901	.497
Capitalist, market economies							
Australia	69.6	+0.243%	+1.925%	+2.172%	.707	.939	.465
Austria	63.1	−0.074	+0.122	+0.047	.661	.853	.489
Belgium	72.0	+0.208	+0.320	+0.528	.630	.860	.402
Canada	81.9	+0.561	+2.128	+2.701	.645	.857	.432
Denmark	83.3	+0.268	+0.612	+0.882	.750	.918	.580
Finland	63.1	−0.247	+0.809	+0.560	.720	.831	.614
France	73.2	−0.166	+0.725	+0.558	.677	.874	.506
West Germany	78.2	+0.005	+0.648	+0.653	.695	.925	.481
Greece	38.7	−0.539	+0.773	+0.230	.578	.869	.302
Ireland	40.5	−0.464	+0.341	−0.124	.657	.965	.343
Italy	49.2	−0.259	+0.592	+0.331	.595	.868	.335
Japan	59.2	−0.052	+1.534	+1.481	.720	.894	.554
Netherlands	68.7	−0.453	+1.293	+0.835	.583	.862	.301
New Zealand	64.6	+0.253	+1.731	+1.989	.649	.919	.374
Norway	68.4	+0.353	+0.599	+0.955	.641	.890	.388
Portugal	27.1	+0.191	+0.532	+0.724	.647	1.034	.308
Spain	48.9	−0.240	+0.816	+0.574	.621	.964	.292
Sweden	86.6	+0.346	+0.454	+0.802	.743	.888	.594
Switzerland	72.4	+0.144	+0.982	+1.127	.764	1.005	.521
United Kingdom	63.5	+0.189	+0.189	+0.379	.724	.943	.508
United States	100.0	+0.372	+1.422	+1.800	.677	.871	.489
Unweighted average		+0.030%	+0.883%	+0.914%	.671	.906	.442

Note: The participation ratio is the ratio of economically active (those in the labor force or looking for work) to the population from 15 to 65 (the working age population). The growth rates of the participation ratios are calculated from the growth rates of the economically active and the working age population. The participation ratio can be over unity if many under 15 or over 64 are in the labor force.

Source: The sources of data are described in Appendix D.

TABLE 3–4
Results of Regression Experiments with Labor Force Data

Dependent Variable	Constant	Relative Level of Per Capita GNP	Systems Variable	Average Annual Growth of Working Age Population	R^2	n
Total participation ratio, 1970	0.600* (0.041)	.00108 (.00060)	0.135* (0.025)	—	.5445	28
Average annual growth of total participation ratio, 1950–80	−0.726* (0.214)	.0113* (.0031)	0.428* (0.127)	0.0196 (0.0865)	.4182	28
Average annual growth of economically active, 1950–80	−0.101 (0.530)	.0155* (.0078)	0.270 (0.324)	—	.1370	28

Note: For the capitalist economies the systems variable is zero; for the socialist economies, one; Yugoslavia is omitted from the calculations. R^2 is the coefficient of determination; n is the number of nations in the sample. The standard errors are placed in parentheses below the calculated coefficients and an asterisk designates statistical significance at the .05 level.

Source: The data come from Tables 3–1 and 3–3.

small. The growth of the participation ratio is also a function of the level of per capita GDP. The third equation shows little relationship between the growth of the labor force and either the level of per capita income or the economic system. This means that the Eastern European nations have had to increase their participation ratio so as to keep their labor force growing at roughly the same rate as in the West. This, in turn, implies that the age structure of their population for increasing the labor force has been more unfavorable than in the West.

In examining the experience of different nations in Table 3–3, we can see enormous differences between nations with the same economic system. Since both groups of nations have relatively free labor markets where indirect, rather than direct incentives for labor force participation must be employed, such differences must be due to a variety of policies and institutions that cannot be easily disentangled without a much more detailed analysis.

It should be added that overall participation rates can be raised not only by increasing the participation of people in particular age and sex cohorts, but also by encouraging greater participation of those outside the working ages (specified as 15 to 65 in the table). Because of the need to provide education to young people, such a policy is hardly feasible with regard to those below 15, except for unskilled work in agriculture during school vacations. In most countries there are also irrational prejudices against child labor. For those over 65, however, such a policy is quite feasible as life expectancies increase and the health of this segment of the population improves with changes in medical technology. Although most countries in Eastern Europe have relatively low formal retirement ages (60 for men and between 55 and 60 for women), older workers are encouraged to continue to work. In the West, policies are more mixed. On the one hand, in the United States, during the late 1970s, the formal retirement age was raised to 70 in many fields (although no corresponding changes in the social security system were made); on the other hand, in France, during the early 1980s, systems of early retirement were introduced into the social insurance system to encourage workers to leave the labor force before 65 (in order to solve, unsuccessfully as it turned out, a short-run unemployment problem).

A measure producing the same effect as a rise in the participation ratio is increasing the number of hours that each person in the labor force works each year. But the effect of such a measure is difficult to assess since there is considerable empirical evidence that a loss in hourly productivity accompanies each increase in the workweek. Since the workweek has declined in all economically developed nations, this policy alternative for increasing the growth rate of the GDP has not been utilized in the past few decades. It should be added that the number of days in the workyear varies considerably among nations, but this matter seems more related to the level of economic development, religious traditions, and governmental regulations than to differences in the economic system *per se.*

Since it is often difficult for goverments to increase the size of their national labor forces, qualitative improvements of the labor force to raise the level of GDP may be more effective policies. As discussed in Chapter 7, government expenditures on education (measured as a percentage of GDP) appear roughly the same in both socialist and capitalist nations (they were somewhat higher in the socialist countries in 1956 and somewhat lower in 1976). Private expenditures for education appear higher in the West. There are also no significant differences between the two groups of nations, either with regard to enrollment rates in primary and secondary schools or to student teacher ratios in these schools.[12] For institutions of higher learning, it appears that enrollment rates are slightly greater in the East than the West, but the data are not sufficiently comparable for such a conclusion to be drawn with much certainty.

2. Land

In most discussions of economic growth, *land* means not only land used for agriculture but also raw materials and land used for mineral exploitation. This is a difficult aspect of growth to discuss in a quantitative

[12]Frederic L. Pryor, *Public Expenditures in Communist and Capitalist Nations* (Homewood, Ill.: Richard D. Irwin, 1973), chap. 5.

fashion because of the lack of comparable statistics for anything but agricultural land; and even comparisons of agricultural land must be taken with caution because of comparability problems (e.g., the definition of *arable* as opposed to *waste* land is often difficult to apply). Certain relevant data are presented in Table 3–5.

Although growth achieved by increasing agricultural land is cer-

TABLE 3–5
Average Annual Changes in Arable Land in East and West

	Relative 1970 GDP per Capita	Average Annual Change in Arable and Permanent Cropland, Late 1940s to 1979	Arable and Permanent Cropland (hectares) per Capita, 1979
Socialist, centrally administered economies			
Bulgaria	37.3	−0.020%	.533
Czechoslovakia	62.0	−0.179	.372
East Germany	63.9	−0.012	.282
Hungary	42.7	−0.237	.541
Poland	35.4	−0.237	.472
Romania	31.2	+0.374	.519
Soviet Union	46.9	+0.094	.959
Unweighted average		−0.031%	.525
Yugoslavia	25.8	−0.004%	.403
Capitalist, market economies			
Austria	63.1	−0.414%	.226
Belgium	72.0	−0.552	.092
Canada	81.9	+0.385	2.028
Denmark	83.3	−0.040	.543
Finland	63.1	−0.056	.591
France	73.2	−0.362	.377
West Germany	78.2	−0.498	.133
Greece	38.7	+0.564	.445
Ireland	40.5	−1.432	.388
Italy	49.2	−0.711	.279
Netherlands	68.7	−0.782	.067
Norway	68.4	+0.081	.210
Spain	48.9	+0.213	.863
Sweden	86.6	−0.747	.380
Switzerland	72.4	−0.701	.061
United Kingdom	63.5	−0.244	.130
United States	100.0	+0.075	.937
Unweighted average		−0.307%	.456

Note: Arable and permanent cropland includes fallow land and orchards but excludes permanent meadows and pastures, forest and woodlands, and unused but potentially productive land. For most countries the series run from 1948 or 1949 to 1979 (for Canada, 1956 to 1976); although the data for the beginning and end years come from the same source, their comparability is unknown.

Sources: The GDP per capita in a common currency come from Table 3–1; the cropland data come from Food and Agricultural Organization, *Production Yearbook* (Rome: various years).

tainly a possibility, in both East and West such policies were utilized by only a few nations. Indeed, as shown by Table 3–5, the amount of arable land has decreased in most countries, a feature that is probably due to two factors: a growing urbanization or conversion of lands to recreational usages, and the increasing conversion of croplands to meadows in order to meet the growing demands for meat and dairy products occurring with rising incomes. We might also suspect that the possibilities of increasing arable land would also be influenced by the present degree of utilization of such land, as measured crudely by the arable land per capita. To investigate such matters, the following regression can be calculated from the data:

$$AR\% = \underset{(0.380)}{-0.515} + \underset{(0.217)}{0.223\,S} + \underset{(0.201)}{0.555\,{}^*AR/P} - \underset{(.00580)}{.00067\,YCAP} \quad \underset{.3367}{R^2} \quad \underset{24}{n}$$

where:

$AR\%$ = percentage change in arable and permanent croplands, late 1940s to 1979

S = economic system: 0 = capitalist, market economy; 1 = socialist, centrally administered economy

AR/P = arable and permanent croplands per capita, 1979

$YCAP$ = per capita GDP in 1970 in a common currency

R^2 = coefficient of determination

n = size of sample

( ) = standard error

* = statistical significance at the .05 level

This regression calculation shows that the percentage increase of arable land appears significantly related only to the amount of such land per capita; that is, the higher the population density per arable acre, the lower the increase in such land. The increase in arable land in the Soviet Union can be attributed to the New Lands program instituted by N. S. Khrushchev in the mid-1950s; the increase in arable land in the United States and Canada is atrributable to its relative availability and to the increase in irrigation. The dramatic increase of arable land in Greece seems surprising and may be, in part, the result of a change in the definition by which such land is estimated. It should be noted that any increase in arable land via reclamation of irrigation is often accompanied by vast capital expenditures.

The extent of the discovery and utilization of new mineral deposits lends itself less to quantitative measurement. In a careful study of this factor in the growth of eight Western European nations and the United States, Edward Denison suggests that such increased mineral exploitation was not an important growth factor in some major Western European nations, even though geological exploration in some of these countries was quite extensive.[13] There are some important exceptions to this generalization, especially for those countries with oil such as Norway (or, in other parts of the world, Nigeria, Indonesia, and the OPEC nations). Because of lack of hard information, it is difficult to discuss differences between nations with different economic systems.

3. Capital

If growth of per capita GDP cannot be traced to important increases in the per capita land utilization, which seems to be the case in most economically developed nations, then the crucial factor is the growth of the capital stock, that is, of buildings, tools, equipment, and inventories. A certain historical perspective on the topic is useful.

Over the twentieth century the relative importance of investment as a share in the gross national product has risen dramatically over time. Between 1914 and 1949 the average ratio of gross investment to the GNP in Western Europe was about 14 percent; between 1950 and 1960 this ratio was about 21 percent and it has risen even higher since then. Unfortunately, these data are in current prices and do not indicate the real extent of the rise, especially since the prices of many capital goods (residential housing appears as an exception) have risen less than prices in other sectors (or, conversely, the productivity in the capital goods sector has increased relatively more). An interesting illustration of this problem can be seen in the case of the Soviet Union, where the share of gross investment in the GNP remained about the same in current prices between 1928 and 1937, but increased from 25 percent to 44 percent in constant 1928 prices (and from 12.5 percent to 26 percent in constant 1937 prices).[14] This kind of price effect also makes international comparisons of such investment GNP ratios very suspect so that we cannot compare East and West in this fashion.

What are the differences in the growth of the capital stock between the two economic systems?[15] Although the official data in Table 3–1 suggest that gross fixed investment has grown faster in the East, the data for the Eastern European nations appear to have a considerable upward bias and, therefore, such results must be adjusted. Without entering into the wearisome debate on this topic, it appears most likely

[13]Edward F. Denison and Jean-Pierre Poullier, *Why Growth Rates Differ: Postwar Experience in Nine Western Countries* (Washington, D.C.: Brookings Institution, 1967), chap. 14.

[14]Abram Bergson, *The Real National Income of Soviet Russia since 1928* (Cambridge, Mass.: Harvard University Press, 1961), p. 237.

[15]A more extensive discussion of these issues, along with supporting data, can be found in Frederic L. Pryor, "Growth and Fluctuations of Production in O.E.C.D. and Eastern European Nations," *World Politics*, 37, No. 3 (January 1985).

that the growth of the net fixed capital stock has been roughly the same in the two sets of nations, although it is possible that the capital stock has grown slightly faster in the socialist, centrally planned economies. This conclusion has some important implications for the discussion below on dynamic efficiency.

D. Economic Growth by Increasing Factor Productivity

1. Empirical Evidence about Dynamic Efficiency

As noted in Chapter 2, it is difficult to measure dynamic efficiency directly. One alternative measure is the growth of total factor productivity, that is, the increase in an output index per unit of an input index.

We have already observed that the two economic systems appear to have roughly the same increases in the labor supply, the amount of arable land, and the net fixed capital stock. Such data, however, represent *stocks,* while to measure total factor productivity we need information on flows, that is, on the amount of labor, capital, and land per unit of time. It seems reasonable to assume that the stocks of land and capital are proportional to their flow of services. Since the workweek has been decreasing in all economically developed nations, the flow of labor services (i.e., labor hours) has been decreasing in relation to the stock of labor (i.e., the labor supply at any one point in time). Unfortunately, we have no comparable data on the change in work hours for nations in East and West. However, it also seems reasonable to assume that the process of reduction of the workweek has proceeded at roughly the same pace in both the socialist, centrally administered economies and the capitalist, market economies. Given these facts and assumptions, we can conclude that the flow of factor inputs has been roughly the same in both sets of nations.

As shown in the first equation in Table 3–2, the growth in the gross domestic product appears to be roughly the same in the two economic systems. Therefore, we must conclude that the growth in total factor productivity appears roughly the same as well. It must be stressed that this conclusion about the similarity of dynamic efficiency in the two sets of nations flies against not only the conventional wisdom on the topic but also a considerable number of industry and sectoral case studies. Therefore, certain interpretative comments appear in order.

This unorthodox conclusion about similar dynamic efficiency may be simply an artifact of our data. If, for instance, the capital stock in the socialist, centrally administered nations has actually grown more quickly than in the West, or if their working week has declined less rapidly than in the West, then their total factor productivity has grown less rapidly than in the West and the paradox is resolved.

A more likely interpretation of this unlikely conclusion about the similarity of dynamic efficiency rests on an interesting *composition effect.* If the socialist, centrally planned nations have placed a higher percentage of their factors of production in sectors where the growth of recorded total factor productivity has been more rapid (e.g., industry in contrast to services), then it is possible for their aggregate factor productivity to be the same as in the West, even though the factor productivity *in each individual sector* is lower than in the West. I present evidence below that this, indeed, appears to have been the case.

2. Policies to Increase Productivity

Since dynamic efficiency appears to vary considerably among nations with the same economic system, it is worthwhile to consider briefly the types of policies that are used to increase total factor productivity in nations with either economic system.

a. The Use of More Advanced Technologies

Use of more advanced technology can be manifested either in the use of new capital embodying such technology or in the use of old capital in a new manner. Such an advance in technology can occur either from an increase in general knowledge throughout the world (e.g., a new scientific or engineering discovery) or by the use of already existing technologies more extensively.

Other things being equal, governmental research and development expenditures appear greater among the socialist, centrally administered economies than among the market economies.[16] Of course, nongovernmental expenditures on R & D are much higher in the latter nations and, unfortunately, comparable data on total R & D expenditures do not seem to be available for a sufficient number of nations in the two systems to allow us to make any generalizations about total expenditures. Although the number of published scientific papers in chemistry and physics per capita appears to be higher in Eastern Europe than in the West, there is no indication that there are more scientific discoveries in these nations or that new technologies are employed more rapidly. For instance, the oxygen converter for producing steel was discovered in Austria in the late 1940s. By 1976 more than half the steel in Austria, West Germany, Japan, and the United States was produced with this new process; in Czechoslovakia, Poland, and the Soviet Union, such a process was used in less than one-fourth of the total production of

---

[16]Data are presented and analyzed in Pryor, *Public Expenditures,* chap. 6.

steel.[17] Other examples can be cited. Unfortunately, we are limited by anecdotes and no overall picture can be drawn from such an approach. However, case studies of certain centrally administered economies reveal some powerful disincentives for adopting new technologies by industrial managers,[18] and this type of evidence appears to contradict the conclusion drawn above about the similarities in dynamic efficiency.

b. Improving the Static Efficiency
of the Allocation of Resources

As I argue in Chapter 5, it appears (but we cannot be completely certain) that the socialist, centrally administered economies have a lower static efficiency than the capitalist, market economies. Although the former group of nations have instituted a series of institutional and policy changes, there is no convincing evidence that the "efficiency gap" (if it exists) has been significantly closed except, perhaps, in the area of foreign trade (which is discussed in Chapter 6). Increasing the static efficiency of production provides, however, only a one-shot increase in dynamic efficiency.

c. Economies of Scale

Economies of scale can play an important role in generating economic growth. For seven Western European nations we are fortunate to have a comparative study of growth that attempts to attribute in absolute terms (e.g., factor X accounted for a growth of Y percent of the GDP) the impact of various factors underlying growth including such scale effects.[19] From 1950 to 1962, national income grew at an annual rate of 4.78 percent. According to these rough estimates, increases in labor, land, and capital accounted for 1.69 percentage points of growth; economies of scale, 0.93 percentage points of growth; technological change, 0.76 percentage points of growth; improved allocation of resources (moving labor from less to more productive sectors, reduction of international trade barriers, etc.), 0.68 percentage points of growth; economies of scale and all other, 0.72 percentage points of growth. Given the importance of economies of scale in this sample of Western European nations, we can hardly doubt that they have played an important

[17]Jiří Sláma, "Technologische Luecke und Technologietransfer zwischen Ost und West," in Deutsche Gesellschaft fuer Freidens- und Konfliktforschung, *DGFK-Jahrbuch 1979/80: Zur Entspannungspolitik in Europa* (Baden-Baden: Nomos Verlagsgesellschaft, n.d.), p. 624. See also Ronald Amann et al., *The Technological Level of Soviet Industry* (New Haven, Conn.: Yale University Press, 1977), chap. 2–3.

[18]These are explored in a number of essays in Stanislaw Wasowski, ed., *East-West Trade and the Technology Gap* (New York: Praeger, 1970); and also in Joseph S. Berliner, *The Innovation Decision in Soviet Industry* (Cambridge, Mass.: MIT Press, 1976).

[19]Denison and Poullier, *Why Growth Rates Differ,* p. 300.

role in the economic growth of Eastern Europe as well, even though we do not know the relative importance of this factor in most nations.

d. Placement of Investment in the Most Productive Sectors

It should be clear that faster growth and greater dynamic efficiency can be obtained by placing investment in those sectors requiring the least amount of additional capital to achieve one additional unit of output.

E. Special Aspects of National Growth Strategies

1. The Allocation of Investment Funds

Nations differ considerably in their use of gross fixed investment. Indeed, in the current economic literature the direction of investment is considered to be a crucial aspect of growth and there is a great deal of discussion about this question. For the most part, however, the technical discussion focuses on the normative side of the problem, especially the methods by which optimal decisions about the particular directions of investments can be made, rather than the sectors and industries in which investment has actually been placed.

Before considering the institutions and policies that might influence the allocation of investment funds, it is useful to glance briefly at some relevant data which are presented in Table 3–6. Although these data are not completely comparable, several differences and similarities appear quite evidence for the three decades covered by the table.

First, the socialist, centrally planned nations have invested proportionately more in both manufacturing, mining and utilities and also agriculture, forestry, and fishing than the capitalist, market economies. Further, the ratio of investment in agriculture to manufacturing appears considerably higher in the former than in the latter group of nations.

Second, the two groups of nations appear to have invested roughly the same proportion in transportation and communication facilities.

Third, the capitalist, market economies have invested proportionately more than the socialist, centrally administered nations in "other" sectors, which include housing, construction, trade, finance and real estate, and public and private services. In these "other" sectors, residential housing accounts for the greatest amount of investment. Such investment data also correspond to labor force studies that show a greater proportion of workers in agriculture and industry in the former group of

TABLE 3-6
Distribution of Gross Fixed Investment in East and West, 1950-79

Country	Number of Years	Agriculture, Forestry, and Fishing	Manufacturing, Mining, and Utilities	Transportation and Communications	Other[a]
Eastern European nations					
Bulgaria	30	16%	38%	16%	30%
Czechoslovakia	30	11	41	14	34
East Germany	30	12	50	11	27
Hungary	30	13	38	12	37
Poland	30	13	41	11	35
Romania	30	15	51	10	24
Soviet Union	30	17	37	9	37
Unweighted average		14%	42%	12%	32%
Yugoslavia	28	10%	35%	12%	43%
OECD nations					
Australia	20	10%	29%	19%	42%
Austria	19	6	29	16	49
Belgium	27	3	30	11	56
Canada	30	7	29	17	47
Denmark	26	9	18	18	55
Finland	30	11	25	19	45
France	24	6	26	10	58
West Germany	29	5	30	15	50
Greece	30	11	22	23	44
Ireland	30	13	28	15	44
Italy	30	8	30	10	52
Japan	27	5	26	11	58
Netherlands	30	5	28	13	54
New Zealand	—	—	—	—	—
Norway	30	8	26	23	43
Portugal	25	9	38	17	36
Spain	—	—	—	—	—
Sweden	30	5	30	18	47
Switzerland	—	—	—	—	—
United Kingdom	30	4	35	12	49
United States	30	4	19	13	64
Unweighted average		7%	28%	15%	50%

Note: These data were calculated from official statistics for each country by determining the percentage distribution of gross fixed investment in current prices for each year and then averaging. They are comparable only in the roughest sense for several reasons. First, the definitions of the various sectors differ somewhat, not only between East and West but also at different times for individual nations. Whenever possible, rough adjustments were made to achieve intertemporal comparability by trying to follow the definitions used in the late 1960s for each nation. Second, among the OECD nations, data on governmental investment by sector are incomplete for many nations, especially in the 1970s, and therefore had to be estimated. For the United States, such estimates had to be made for the 1950s and early 1960s and are particularly crude. Third, for various countries other estimates had to be made, especially where national statistics did not separate investments by the sectors designated in the table above.

[a]"Other" sectors include housing, construction, trade, finance, and public and private services.

Source: The major sources of data are presented in Appendix D.

nations and a correspondingly lower proportion of workers in services and trade.[20]

It is important to note that the "other" sector generally requires a much higher amount of capital per unit of output than manufacturing and agriculture. Further, since output of much of the "other" sector is measured in terms of inputs, growth of measured total factor productivity is much lower than in other sectors. Thus, as I noted above, a much higher share of factors in the West are placed in the sector that shows the lowest growth of total factor productivity and, because of the *composition effect*, it is possible for aggregate dynamic efficiency to be the same in both systems, even though the dynamic efficiency of all individual sectors is greater in the West.

It should also be noted that placing a greater share of investment in those sectors yielding more output per unit of input might lead to higher economic growth, but it might also be undesirable from a social point of view. For instance, a relatively small amount of investment in the trade sector might increase difficulties in shopping and cause considerable wasted time, a phenomenon investigated in Chapter 8. Further, relatively low investments in the "other" sector might lead to an ill-housed population. In 1970 in the Soviet Union there were 1.23 households per housing unit (i.e., apartment or house) and in 1977 there were 8.2 square meters of living space per capita (a space about 3.1 by 3.1 yards for sleeping, eating, and entertaining). At roughly the same time in capitalist nations with similar levels of development there was roughly one household per housing unit and the amount of space per capita was very much higher.[21]

It is certainly not outside the realm of possibility for governments in capitalist, market economies to direct the flow of investment to certain crucial sectors as they have in the centrally administered economies. Indeed, this idea underlies the various schemes for "industrial policies" that have been discussed and, to a certain extent, implemented in the West for the last several decades.[22] Such a redirection of investment funds can be carried out directly by governmental investment in crucial sectors or indirectly by setting up targeted governmental loan guarantees or by the establishment of special investment banks with directives for channeling funds in particular directions. Additional tools

[20]This has been specially studied by Paul Gregory, *Socialist and Nonsocialist Industrialization Patterns: A Comparative Appraisal* (New York: Praeger, 1970).

[21]The data in this paragraph come from Henry W. Morton, "The Soviet Quest for Better Housing—An Impossible Dream," in Joint Economic Committee, U.S. Congress, *Soviet Economy in a Time of Change,* Vol. 1 (Washington, D.C.: GPO, 1979), pp. 759–90; and United Nations, Economic Commission for Europe, *The ECE Region in Figures* (New York: 1972), pp. 75.

[22]Raymond Vernon, ed., *Big Business and the State* (Cambridge, Mass.: Harvard University Press, 1974).

include the use of tax incentives, interest rate subsidies, and other devices to encourage investments being placed in priority areas.

Another aspect of the direction of investment funds is the spatial dimension. Although direct indicators of investment funds going into particular areas within countries are seldom available, we do have information about the spatial dimensions of production and labor force. Comparisons carried out on these data show that, other things being held equal, there are few differences between the centrally administered, socialist economies of Eastern Europe and the capitalist, market economies of Western Europe with regard to the preferential channelling of industrial investment into the poorest areas.[23]

2. The Financing of Investment[24]

a. Some Institutional Considerations

As noted above in a brief discussion of the United States, determining the degree of governmental participation in the financing of investment in capitalist nations is rather difficult. In many Western European nations, the governmental role in investment is strong and there are a number of governmental entities focusing on the financing of investment in particular sectors. For instance, in most of these capitalist nations, roughly half or more of housing investments are in some manner governmentally financed. Further, in some of these countries, such as France, the banking sector is mostly nationalized and these governmentally owned banks play a major role in the financing of investments in other sectors as well. Moreover, the role of governmental loan guarantees, interest rate subsidies, and special tax incentives to encourage borrowing and lending for investment purposes is also strong. As noted above, in the mid-1960s in most of the economically developed capitalist nations, about 30 to 70 percent of total fixed capital investment appears to have been directly or indirectly financed, subsidized, or guaranteed by the government. Further, between 1950 and 1980 this role of government in investment appears to have risen—a very important change in the economic system.

Among the socialist, centrally administered economies of Eastern Europe, the share of investment financed by the central government was well over 75 percent in most nations in the mid-1960s; further, most of the remaining investment was financed from funds of public enterprises. However, to increase dynamic efficiency, some of these countries

[23]See particularly Frederic L. Pryor, *Property and Industrial Organization in Communist and Capitalist Nations* (Bloomington: Indiana University Press, 1973), pp. 290–97.

[24]These generalizations are derived from scattered data from national sources, as well as from Economic Commission for Europe, *Economic Survey of Europe in 1959* (Geneva: 1960), chap. 5.

have begun to finance a smaller share of investment by the central government and a larger share by the enterprises. Nevertheless, marked differences of the role of government in East and West still persist, many of which are traceable to the higher degree of public ownership and the more activist policies adopted by the centrally administered economies in directing economic growth.

Whether or not the increasing governmental role in the West in the financing of investment has actually raised the volume of investment depends upon the degree to which privately financed investment is cut back as publicly financed investment increases. Some "supply side" economists argue that the governmental participation has led to little rise in total investment, for if governmental funds are raised on capital markets, the interest rate rises and this leads to a cutting back of private investment. They further argue that if governmental investment funds are raised through the tax system, privately financed investment might also fall as savings decline because disposable income and enterprise cash flow fall. The empirical evidence underlying these arguments is mixed and controversial. If the government establishes banks or raises taxes to obtain investment funds in areas where little private savings and investment have occurred, then total investable funds definitely rise through such governmental activity. However, this argument assumes imperfections in the capital market that, in most developed capitalist nations, are difficult to demonstrate.

b. The Role of Foreign Funds

The role of international financing of investment in particular nations has received a great deal of quantitative attention. Such foreign investment played an extremely important role in the nineteenth century when, for example, about half of U.K. savings were invested abroad and when developing countries such as Australia, Argentina, Canada, and the United States benefited enormously. In 1900, for instance, about 10 percent of total reproducible tangible assets in the United States were directly owned by foreigners and, further, foreign loans had financed a very much larger share of the remainder.[25] In the first two post–World War II decades, U.S. grants, loans, and direct investments played an important role in the investment picture in Western Europe. However, in Japan such international capital flows appeared as a much less important source of economic growth. In the centrally administered nations in Eastern Europe, international flows of capital were generally small (excepting reparation payments) during the post–World War II

---

[25]Considerable data on these matters can be found in U.S. Bureau of the Census, *Historical Statistics of the United States* (Washington, D.C.: GPO, 1975).

era and, with the exception of Albania, did not appear to play an important role in the growth of the capital stocks in the individual nations.[26] However, among the socialist nations elsewhere, international grants and loans have played important roles at various times in investment in China, Cuba, North Korea, Vietnam, and Yugoslavia (the last nation has received investment aid from both the East and the West). Whether or not investment is financed through international lending or grants appears to be a matter of policy that is not tied directly to systemic aspects of the economy.

c. The Costs of Investment

If more investment takes place, on whom do the costs of lower consumption fall? In the case of financing the investment from funds abroad or from voluntary savings, there is no problem in answering this question. However, there is a crucial ambiguity arising in cases where saving is not voluntary and investment is financed through taxation or other forced means. The problem is especially acute when we try to determine which sector of the economy "really paid" for this investment. A great deal of attention has been focused on the degree to which industrial investment has, in essence, been "financed" by other sectors such as agriculture.

If we say that "the agricultural sector financed industry," we can mean either (1) net flows of agricultural products to the other sectors of the economy increased; or (2) a fall in net income from the farmers and peasants provided the funds for investment in other sectors. These are not the same thing and, for the Soviet Union, this ambiguity has given rise to many pages of unnecessary scholarly controversy. As shown in Table 3–7, net flows of agricultural production to the rest of the economy between 1928 and 1937 (the time of the all-out drive for industrialization in the USSR) decreased and, in this sense, agriculture did not finance industry. This decline occurred partly because of the need to replace the livestock killed during collectivization with tractors. On the other hand, if peasant incomes fell by as much as 40 percent during these years and production decreased less, then in this sense the agricultural sector did contribute to the financing of investment in the economy. It should also be noted, however, that industrial wages fell in the Soviet Union in this period and did not reach the level of the late 1920s until the early 1950s, which means that industrial workers also, in this sense, financed part of the massive investment program of that nation.

Although the terms of trade between agriculture and industry can

---

[26]Some data on these matters are found in Marshall I. Goldman, *Soviet Foreign Aid* (New York: Praeger, 1967); and Pryor, *Public Expenditures,* chap. 6.

TABLE 3–7
Contributions of Agriculture to Soviet Growth in the 1930s

A. Estimate of Contribution of Agriculture to Other Sectors (million 1926/7 rubles)

Year	Gross Agricultural Production	Estimated Current Inputs from All Sectors	Estimated Investment in Equipment and Construction	Net Agricultural Production[a]
1928	13,607	2,824	812	9,971
1932	11,117	2,307	1,635	7,175
1933	11,525	2,392	2,509	6,624
1937	15,349	3,186	5,014	7,149

B. Estimate of Rural Sector's Contribution to Other Sectors[b]

Year	Net Agricultural Production[a]	Assumed Income Levels in Rural Sectors		Net Goods Flowing out of Rural Sector	
		Assumption X	Assumption Y	Assumption X	Assumption Y
1928	9,971	9,971	9,971	0	0
1932	7,175	7,999	5,983	−824	1,192
1933	6,624	7,999	5,983	−1,355	639
1937	7,149	7,999	5,983	−828	1,161

[a]Net contribution of agriculture is gross production minus current input and investment.

[b]It is assumed that in 1928 there was no flow of goods out of the rural sector. Assumption X assumes a 20 percent fall in farm income after 1928; assumption Y assumes a 40 percent fall. If the fall was only 20 percent, the rural sector (peasants) was a net receiver of goods; if the fall was 40 percent, there was a net outflow of goods out of the rural sector. The 40 percent decline appears much more realistic.

Sources: The index of gross agricultural production comes from D. Gale Johnson and Arcadius Kahan, "Soviet Agriculture: Structure and Growth," in U.S. Congress, Joint Economic Committee, *Comparisons of the United States and Soviet Union,* Part I (Washington, D.C.: GPO, 1959), pp. 237–57.

For 1928, estimated current inputs for all sectors come from input-output calculations presented by Holland Hunter, "The Overambitious First Soviet Five-Year Plan," *Slavic Review,* 23, No. 2 (June 1973), pp. 201–79. The proportions of inputs to gross production in 1928 were assumed to hold for all other years.

Investment in equipment and construction come from Richard Moorsteen and Raymond Powell, *The Soviet Capital Stock 1928–1962* (Homewood, Ill.: Richard D. Irwin, 1966). Although they are in 1928 prices, these are assumed to be sufficiently similar to 1926/7 prices to use in this calculation. They also provide estimates of livestock investment (in the four years, respectively −100, −700, 0, and +400).

be manipulated by means of collectivization of agriculture and the enforcement of agricultural delivery targets at specified prices (a process occurring in the long run in all of the centrally administered economies except Poland), many other measures can also be devised to achieve the same ends in either centrally administered or market economies which, while less dramatic, might be more suitable for accomplishing the same ends. For instance, the rural sector can be assessed special taxes, either on the goods they buy or on the products they sell, to generate investable funds. Fixed prices at which agricultural products are bought by government agencies can also be set to serve the same purpose; indeed, in recent years a number of articles in the field of economic development have analyzed the beneficial and adverse effects of development strategies in capitalist, market nations with an "antirural bias." Again, the degree to which investment is financed by one sector or another appears more a policy matter than a feature of the economic system.

3. The Choice of Technology

In the capitalist, market nations the choice of technology is usually left up to the individual investors who, allegedly, are guided by profit considerations. For certain types of investments, however, constraints on these decisions are imposed by the establishment of certain environmental and other standards. In certain capitalist nations attempts have been made to influence the capital/labor ratio of private investments by influencing the relative prices of the different factors of production.

In the centrally administered, socialist economies of Eastern Europe, governmental tastes in technology have played a more important role than in the West. This has meant, for instance, that factories and enterprises are usually larger in size.[27] In general, special industrial priorities have been established so that certain industries are able to obtain investable funds more easily. Since the ranking of industries by capital/labor ratios is roughly the same in East and West, the influence of such policy measures is open to doubt.

Although it might be felt that standardization of products and processes should be much greater in the centrally administered economies than in the West, given their greater degree of governmental direction of investment funds, variations can be found among countries in both systems. For instance, in China it appears that the specification of product characteristics of many industrial goods is much more tied to local demand than in the Soviet Union.[28]

4. Other Aspects of Growth Strategies

Brief mention has been made of the fact that, in early years, foreign trade played a much less important role in the centrally administered socialist economies than in the capitalist, market economies (see also Chapter 7 for a more extended discussion). However, among the capitalist nations considerable differences occur in the degree to which economic growth is influenced by foreign trade considerations. An extensive debate has arisen over the relative success of growth strategies

[27]Comparative data on these matters can be found in Pryor, *Public Expenditures*, chaps. 5–6, and p. 441.

[28]This is discussed in American Rural Small Scale Industry Delegation, *Rural Small Scale Industry in the People's Republic of China* (Berkeley: University of California, 1977).

based on import substitution (i.e., the substitution of domestically produced goods for imports) in contrast to growth strategies based on the encouragement of export production.

Another aspect of the growth strategy concerns the building of social overhead capital (such as roads, railroad lines, harbors, schools, sewage lines, and so forth) ahead of, concurrently with, or behind demand or need for them. Such timing of social overhead capital was varied considerably among nations, even within the same economic system. For instance, it has been argued that in nineteenth-century America, the canal building of the various state governments in the early part of the century and, in the latter part of the century, the huge land grants to railroads in exchange for constructions of such lines (not to mention the land grants by the federal government for the establishment of various universities) seem to have occurred ahead of, or concurrent with, demand and thus provided a very important impetus for investment and economic growth. Some of the railroad building in Russia in the latter part of the nineteenth century might be considered in the same light. In the twentieth century, however, some nations of both systems have preferred to build such social overhead capital behind demand so that precious investment funds could be placed were they were allegedly most needed (BAM, the new trans-Siberian railroad line in the Soviet Union, appears to have been built behind demand).

Other elements of growth strategy and the ways in which governments have tried to influence, channel, and coordinate economic growth could be discussed and illustrated by appropriate empirical comparisons. Some of these relate to the development of human capital (health and education) and are discussed in Chapter 7 in other contexts. Still other ways are analyzed in the suggested readings listed at the end of this chapter.

F. Final Remarks

A growth strategy does not need to be a matter of conscious design on the part of the government or any other decision makers in the economy. The growth of the U.S. economy during the nineteenth century was channeled by a series of institutions in both the private and the public sectors, many of which were not designed with economic growth in mind. A further important role was played by private and governmental policies, most of which were quite uncoordinated with each other and/or focused on goals other than economic growth.

Formal developmental planning efforts, while perhaps indicative of some commitment to the goal of economic growth, may be epiphenomenal rather than serious. Further, in many cases the actual strategies differs from the stated strategy. This means we must not only look at the policies that were promulgated and the institutions established, but must also investigate what actually happened to see if the measures taken were more effective than other policies that could have been followed.

The comparisons of output growth reveal few important differences between the socialist, centrally administered economies and the capitalist, market economies. The comparisons of input growth also reveal few important differences, although the data underlying this conclusion are much less reliable. Given the similar growths in inputs and outputs, dynamic efficiency in the two systems appears similar. However, because the proportion of investment placed in sectors such as housing (where the relation of output to capital is low) is greater in the West than in the East, this suggests that dynamic efficiency within the manufacturing and agricultural sectors is higher in the former than in the latter group of nations.

The important differences in growth rates appear not between the systems but rather among the nations with the same economic system. This suggests that particular economic policies might have a considerable influence on the growth rate and, for this reason, a series of measures to increase factor inputs and to raise the output per unit of input for nations with different economic systems are investigated. To gain a more rounded picture, attention is also given to other factors of a growth strategy—the allocation of investment funds, the financing of investment, the costs of investment on particular segments of the population, and the timing of investment.

Economic growth appears in many instances to be a useful means by which to alleviate the grinding poverty that characterizes so many countries, both now and in the past. We have much to learn about how this growth can be carried out most effectively and with the lowest social costs.

SUGGESTED READINGS

A. Centrally Administered Growth Strategies

    1. Nicholas Spulber, *Soviet Strategy for Economic Growth* (Bloomington: Indiana University Press, 1964), pp. 53–118. This is a useful survey of the economic arguments leading up to the first Soviet five-year plan. A more detailed study of these issues is Alexander Erlich, *The Soviet Industrialization Debate 1924–28* (Cambridge, Mass.: Harvard University Press, 1960).

    2. Some loose ends on the Soviet strategy are picked up by Alec Nove, "Was Stalin Really Necessary?" in his *Economic Rationality and Soviet Politics* (New York: Praeger, 1964); and Holland Hunter, "Optimal Tautness in Developmental Planning," *Economic Development and Cultural Change,* 9 (July 1961,

Part 1), pp. 561–72. For a Marxist perspective on these matters see Maurice Dobb, *Soviet Economic Development since 1917* (London: Routledge and Kegan Paul, 1960), chap. 8, pp. 177–208; or Charles K. Wilber, *The Soviet Model and Underdeveloped Countries* (Chapel Hill: University of North Carolina Press, 1969), chaps. 5–6, pp. 76–137.

3. K. C. Yeh, "Soviet and Communist Chinese Industrialization Strategies," in Donald Treadgold, ed., *Soviet and Chinese Communism: Similarities and Differences* (Seattle: University of Washington Press, 1967), pp. 327–63. This is a superb comparison of the contrasting approaches of the two nations. Another selection that focuses more on China is Benjamin Ward, "The Chinese Approach to Economic Development," in Robert F. Dernberger, ed., *China's Development in Comparative Perspective* (Cambridge: Harvard University Press, 1980), pp. 91–120.

4. The growth strategies adopted by other planned economies differ considerably from the Soviet and Chinese patterns in many respects. For Eastern Europe, see Gur Ofer, "Industrial Structure, Urbanization and Growth Strategy of Socialist Countries," *Quarterly Journal of Economics*, 90, No. 2 (1976), pp. 219–44; George W. Hoffmann, *Regional Development Strategy in Southeast Europe* (New York: Praeger, 1972); and John Michael Montias, *Central Planning in Poland* (New Haven, Conn.: Yale University Press, 1962). For Cuba an informative discussion can be found in Carmelo Mesa-Lago, *The Economy of Socialist Cuba* (Albuquerque: University of New Mexico Press, 1981).

5. Growth strategies imply certain political and administrative conditions. Many of these are analyzed by Warren Ilchman and R. Bhargave, "Balanced Thought and Economic Growth," *Economic Development and Cultural Change*, 14 (July 1966), pp. 385–399.

B. Empirical Analyses of Selected Growth Experiences

1. Abram Bergson, "Development under Two Systems: Comparative Productivity since 1950," *World Politics*, 23 (July 1971), pp. 579–617. This is a classic comparative analysis. An article along the same lines but with more recent data is Frederic L. Pryor, "Growth and Fluctuations of Production in O.E.C.D. and Eastern European Nations," *World Politics*, 37, No. 3 (January 1985).

2. Stanley H. Cohn, "Analysis of the Soviet Growth Model," in Morris Bornstein and David Fusfeld, eds., *The Soviet Economy*, 4th ed. (Homewood, Ill.: Richard D. Irwin, 1974), pp. 246–69. A more technical analysis is Abram Bergson, "Notes on the Production Function in Soviet Postwar Industrial Growth," *Journal of Comparative Economies*, 3, no. 2 (June 1979), pp. 116–27.

3. Paul Gregory, *Socialist and Non-Socialist Industrialization Patterns* (New York: Praeger, 1971). A more recent study of Western nations along these lines is Hollis Chenery and Moises Syrguin, *Patterns of Development, 1950–70* (London: Oxford University Press, 1975).

C. Selected Aspects of Growth Strategies

1. The issues of import substitution versus export led growth are discussed in a wide literature, of which the following provide a good sampling: Albert O. Hirschman, "The Political Economy of Import Substituting Industrialization," *Quarterly Journal of Economics*, 82, No. 1 (February 1968), pp. 1–33; Henry J. Bruton, "The Import Substitution Strategy of Economic Development," *Pakistan Development Review*, 10, No. 2 (1970); Gustav Ranis, "Industrial Sector

Labour Absorption," *Economic Development and Cultural Change,* 21, No. 3 (April 1973), pp. 387–408; and Michael Roemer, "Resource-Based Industrialization in the Developing Countries: A Survey," *Journal of Development Economics,* 6, No. 2 (June 1979), pp. 163–203. Empirical studies of these issues are provided by Irving B. Kravis, "Trade as a Handmaiden of Growth: Similarities between the Nineteenth and Twentieth Centuries," *Economic Journal,* 80, No. 320 (December 1970), pp. 850–73; William G. Tyler, "Growth and Export Expansion in Developing Countries," *Journal of Development Economics,* 9, No. 1 (August 1981), pp. 121–30; and Jagdish N. Bhagwati and T. N. Srinivasan, "Trade Policy and Development," in Rudiger Dornbusch and Jacob A. Frenkel, eds., *International Economic Policy* (Baltimore: Johns Hopkins University Press, 1979), pp. 1–30.

2. Problems associated with the choice of technology in a development strategy are surveyed by Lawrence J. White, "The Evidence on Appropriate Factor Proportions for Manufacturing in Less Developed Countries," *Economic Development and Cultural Change,* 27, No. 1 (October 1978), pp. 27–59. For the centrally planned, socialist nations there is a considerable literature on the choice of technology. Many issues are surveyed by Alec Nove, *The Soviet Economic System* (London: Allen and Unwin, 1977), chap. 6, pp. 149–72. Some specialized studies include Robert Campbell, "Problems of Technical Progress in the USSR," and Richard Judy, "The Case of Computer Technology," both in Bornstein and Fusfeld, *Soviet Economy,* pp. 348–87; Joseph S. Berliner, "Prospects for Technological Progress," Stanley Cohn, "Deficiencies in Soviet Investment Policies and the Technological Imperative," and Robert Campbell, "Issues in Soviet R & D: The Energy Case," all in U.S. Congress, Joint Economic Committee, *Soviet Economy in New Perspective.* See also John A. Martins and John P. Young, "Soviet Implementation of Domestic Invention," in U.S. Congress, Joint Economic Committee, *Soviet Economy in a Time of Change* (Washington, D.C.: GPO, 1979), pp. 472–510; and Leslie Dienes, "Soviet Energy Policy," in the same volume, pp. 196–230. Three longer studies are J. Wilczynski, *Technology in Comecon* (New York: Praeger, 1974); Joseph Berliner, *The Innovation Decision in Soviet Industry* (Cambridge, Mass.: MIT Press, 1976); and Raymond Hutchings, *Soviet Science, Technology, Design* (New York: Oxford University Press, 1976).

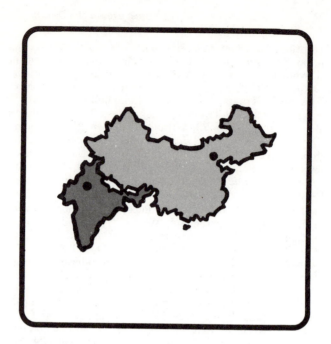

4

ECONOMIC STABILITY

A. Introduction

On both theoretical and empirical levels we have much to learn about economic stability in various economic systems.

The inadequacies of our theoretical knowledge with regard to such stability in capitalist, market economies are perhaps most glaringly manifested by our inability to understand fully and, therefore, to counter successfully the various mechanisms underlying inflation and macroeconomic fluctuations of production in the capitalist, market economies. Our theoretical knowledge about inflation and macroeconomic fluctuations for socialist, centrally adminstered economies is even less developed; and the construction of theoretical models that would aid us in understanding these phenomena is only in the beginning stages.

On the empirical side, our knowledge about economic stability is much more extensive, at least for the capitalist, market economies. However, empirical studies of fluctuations or inflation for the socialist, centrally administered economies are very few, not the least because some of the most basic statistics (e.g., adequate price indices) are not readily available.

Most of the analysis in this chapter focuses on two aspects of economic stability: the fluctuation of aggregate production and inflation. Both theoretical and empirical materials are introduced. Several other types of economic instabilities are discussed much more briefly.

B. Fluctuations of Aggregate Production

Empirical comparisons of production fluctuations for a number of nations in East and West are presented below. Fluctuations of aggregate production are analyzed with annual data and measured in terms of deviations from a trend. Such deviations can last one or more years above or below the trend values and do not necessarily follow a regular sine wave pattern around the trend. Before turning to these data, it is useful first to consider some of the underlying causes of such fluctuations.

1. Causes of Production Fluctuations from a Theoretical Standpoint

Although analyses of the causes of fluctuations of aggregate production can be quite complex, on a general level it is possible to isolate four different but complementary sources of fluctuations for both centrally planned and market economies, each of which is briefly discussed below on both micro- and macroeconomic levels.

a. External Causes

External causes of productions fluctuations lie outside the economic system under analysis. They cause fluctuations not only directly but also indirectly by setting up adjustment reactions that take some time to settle down to equilibrium again. A physical analogy is the well-known example of disturbing a pendulum from its stationary position; if undisturbed thereafter, it will continue to oscillate for some time until friction brings it to rest again.

On a microeconomic level, a very common external cause underlying production fluctuations—especially in agriculture—is the weather. Any deviation of the weather from the long-term average usually results in a deviation of production from the long-term average. An economy faces three basic ways of modifying the actions of such an external cause: (1) diversifying its production so that a variety of goods and crops are produced that are differentially affected by the particular underlying cause; (2) making particular types of investments to minimize such effects, for example, to minimize adverse effects of climate, making investments for irrigation canals, development of drought-resistant crops, smudge pots to minimize frost damage, and so forth; (3) holding inventories so as to bridge over production losses or to absorb oversupply in good years.

Another type of external cause of microeconomic fluctuations occurs in the case of echo cycles. An example can be found in the United States after World War II when there was a tremendous pent-up demand for new automobiles and sales were brisk for several years. Seven or eight years later, as these early postwar automobiles wore out, there were another few years of brisk sales, and another seven or eight years later the same phenomenon was repeated. Each time, of course, the relative changes in sales were less; in the same manner each echo is progressively weaker. These cycles are much more difficult to offset than the weather cycles discussed above.

On a macroeconomic level, a cumulation of external shocks can generate cycles. This is demonstrated in an interesting fashion in an article where the authors take one of the well-known multiequation econometeric models of the U.S. economy, subject it to a series of *random* shocks every year in various sectors (consumption, foreign trade, external capital flows, investment), and generate macroeconomic fluctuations remarkably resembling actual business cycles.[1] A more dramatic example of an external shock causing macrofluctuations is a war, which not only changes the pattern of demand but often leads to destruction of human and physical capital which, in turn, further affects production. Still another type of external influence is the bunching of invention and innovations; this can lead not only to increases in aggregate investment but also, at the same time, to the destruction (through obsolescence) of other capital. Such a Schumpeterian approach toward business cycles in capitalist, market economies[2] yields the prediction that growth and fluctuations of production may be positively related to each other, an empirical proposition that is tested below and shown to have some merit.

It is important to recognize that the ill effects of external causes are often easier to offset on the microeconomic than the macroeconomic level. Further, it should be recognized that such external causes can

[1]This exercise is carred out by Irma Adelman and Frank L. Adelman, "The Dynamic Properties of the Klein-Goldberger Model," *Econometrica,* 27 (October 1959), pp. 596–625.

[2]Joseph A. Schumpeter, *Capitalism, Socialism, and Democracy,* 3rd ed. (New York: Harper, 1950).

influence production on a macroeconomic level in *both* capitalist, market and socialist, centrally administered economies.

b. "Semiexternal" Causes

By "semiexternal" causes I refer to causal forces influencing production fluctuations that are external to production per se but arise from some interaction between the producers and other sectors of the society.

On both micro- and macroeconomic levels, changes in economic expectations that are induced by political events can strongly influence production of particular products or overall investment, which in turn can influence not only aggregate production but also political events.

The government can also cause fluctuations, particularly on a macroeconomic level, in several different ways. In order to increase its popularity before an important electoral campaign, the government may increase its expenditures or carry out an expansionary monetary policy, actions that might have considerable influence on aggregate production in future years. In socialist, centrally administered economies where elections are not important, a counterpart to such a "political business cycle" is the bunching of investment in the first few years of a five-year plan, a phenomenon of considerable importance in the Soviet Union.[3]

Even with the good motive of trying to dampen the business cycle, the government can act in a manner to increase the severity of macroeconomic fluctuations. For example, suppose that the GDP fluctuations occur naturally in the form of a sine wave. Suppose also that there are lags by the government in *recognizing* such changes in production, lags in *responding* by setting up programs to combat such changes, and finally lags in *implementing* these programs. With such lags the government might increase its expenditures at a time in which production is already on the rise; and decrease its expenditures at a time in which production has already begun to fall. In these cases, production fluctuations are made more severe by "remedial" government action, not better. This is not merely a theoretical possibility; governments in a number of Western European nations appear to have acted in such a procyclical manner.[4]

c. Disproportionalities

If we examine a tribal or peasant economy where a kin group essentially produces almost of the goods that it consumes, problems of disproportionalities do not often arise. If the kin group functions intelli-

---

[3]See Donald N. Green and Christopher I. Higgins, *Sovmod I: A Macroeconometric Model of the Soviet Union* (New York: Academic Press, 1977), chap. 5.

[4]Bent Hansen, *Fiscal Policy in Seven Countries, 1955–1965* (Paris: OECD, 1969).

gently, the inputs that are needed for producing a particular good are usually made before production of the product is attempted. Total production is equal to total consumption; total investment is equal to total savings; and there is little discrepancy between planned and actual production or investment.

As a society becomes economically more developed, greater possibilities for macroeconomic disproportionalities arise because different people make decisions about production and consumption or investment and savings. On a microeconomic level a division of labor in the production of different goods could lead to situations where the necessary inputs for making a particular good are not at hand. On a macroeconomic level in market economies, Keynes pointed out that the separation of investment and savings decisions can result in planned savings being quite different from planned investment, and that this imbalance gives rise to macroeconomic fluctuations. Marx pointed to a different type of macroeconomic disproportionality, namely, that in capitalist, market economies, changes in the distribution of income over time might result in differences in aggregate demand and aggregate supply, and that such possibilities become more serious at higher levels of economic development.

The proposition that higher levels of economic development are accompanied in capitalist, market economies by greater macroeconomic instability appears at first glance to be convincing. When it is tested empirically, however, as in the exercise carried out below, we find the empirical support for this proposition is not very impressive. If we examine the economic experience of individual nations, the proposition does not appear to receive much empirical support either.[5]

Problems due to disproportionalities are not, of course, limited to capitalist market economies, but can occur in socialist, centrally adminstered economies as well. Consider, for instance, this remarkably prescient statement of Joseph Stalin in the mid-1920s:

> There, in the capitalist countries . . . the errors of single capitalists, trusts, syndicates, or this or that capitalist group are corrected through the elementary forces of the market. . . . No really important error, no considerable overproduction, no appreciable discrepancy between production and . . . demand can occur in the capitalist countries without the mistakes, errors, and discrepancies being corrected by this or that [microeconomic] crisis. . . . With us it is quite different. Every important disturbance in trade or in production or each error of calculation in our economy does not end with just a partial crisis, but effects the whole economy.[6]

[5]For the United States, comparisons over time are made by Martin Neil Baily, "Stabilization Policy and Private Economic Behavior," *Brookings Papers on Economic Activity,* No. 1, 1978, pp. 11–61.

[6]Cited in an East German article "Soll oder Muss," *Der Aussenhandel,* 3, No. 22 (1953), pp. 507–8.

The mechanism by which such microeconomic disproportionalities ripple through the economy and cause macroeconomic waves can be seen by an example that assumes a very high degree of centralization. Suppose that all inputs of an enterprise and the technology by which these inputs are combined are designated by some central agency. If, for some reason, a sufficient amount of a designated input is not available, then the firm must receive permission from the central agency to make some substitution. Further communication between the enterprise and the central agency is required to search out and buy the substitute input because purchasing and sales functions are centralized. If such substitutes are not immediately available, a new plan for all enterprises must be made for the particular disporportionality to be closed; otherwise, for lack of the input, production of those goods requiring this input and of the products requiring such goods for their production must be cut back as well. It should be added that such extreme centralization impedes the substitution of inputs because of information costs. Or, to put the matter in a different way, slowness in bureaucratic decision making can make the final impact of any isolated shortfall extremely disruptive to the economy as a whole.

d. Problems Arising from Negative Feedbacks

Negative feedback can serve not only as an independent source of fluctuations, but also as a mechanism to exacerbate fluctuations arising from external causes or from disproportionalities. It is a phenomenon that occurs in many self-correcting mechanisms and its nature can be most easily seen in a parable of the thermostat.

An ordinary wall thermostat is set at a particular temperature; if the room temperature falls below this limit, the furnace is turned on; if the room temperature rises above this limit, the furnace is turned off. If one plots on graph paper the temperature of the room, it will reveal a cyclical pattern around the on-off limit: When the temperature is falling and the furnace is turned on, the room temperature continues to plunge until the furnance has had time to warm up and begin to heat properly, until the pipes conducting the heat are also warmed, and until the entire system starts to function at capacity. When the temperature is rising and the furnace is turned off, the room temperature continues to rise until the furnace and the pipes have had a chance to cool down.

Can the temperature cycle be modified? Suppose that the level at which the furnace is turned on is set below the level at which the furnace is turned off. This would lead to greater temperature cycles in the room than before, which does not seem desirable. If, instead, the two on-off levels are reversed so that the level at which the furnace is turned on is higher than the level at which it is turned off, the system might

the sense that if the temperature in the room rises *above*
it might further rise until the limits of the systems are
e temperature falls *below* the *off*-level, it may cool until the
)erature is reached. This does not seem like a good idea
either. ᴜᴜ. ᴜnly choice is to make changes to the sytem so that it heats
up and cools down more rapidly, which may be very costly. In short, we
have a tradeoff between costs and cyclical variation.

The thermostat is an example of a "centrally adminstered economy" based on the principle of negative feedback; that is, if certain
variables fall below or above prespecified limits, corrective actions are
taken. The cycles arise because there are lags in the system; that is,
certain actions require time to take effect. Such a system can be described mathematically by a two period difference equation of the form:

(4–1) $$X_t = a - b \, X_{t-1},$$

where X is the variable moving through time, t is the time period, and
the lowercase letters (in all equations) represent constants. The "negative" feedback describes the sign of the X_{t-1} coefficient.

Such a simple system can generate three different types of cycles
and numerical examples of each are provided in Table 4–1. These cycles
are respectively damped, regular, and exploding. If we modify equation
4–1 by adding an external shock each time period and, further, a floor
below which X_t cannot fall and a ceiling above which X_t cannot rise,
then all three equations will, given sufficient random shocks, generate
fluctuations between the two limits. Such an experiment reveals the
complementarity of fluctuations generated by negative feedback and by
external shocks. To show concretely the application of this idea to economic systems, two examples are presented, both of which refer to market economies.

The "cobweb" model of the hog cycle is a well-studied microeconomic phenomenon in the agriculture literature.[7] Let us suppose that
the quantity of a good (e.g., pork) demanded in time period t (Q_t^d) is a
linear function of price (P_t). The demand function is

(4–2) $$Q_t^d = a - b \, P_t.$$

Suppose also that it takes one time period to produce or grow a good or
product (e.g., hogs) so that the amount coming onto the market today
(Q_t^s) is the result of a decision taken in the previous time period on the

---

[7]It is called the "cobweb" model because tracing the various combinations of price
and quantity over time on a supply and demand diagram yields (if done well) a drawing
that resembles a cobweb.

TABLE 4–1
Arithmetic Examples of a Simple Negative Feedback Model

Period	Damped Cycles $X_t = 180 - 0.8\,X_{t-1}$	Regular Cycles $X_t = 200 - 1.0\,X_{t-1}$	Explosive Cycles $X_t = 220 - 1.2\,X_{t-1}$
1	80.0	80.0	80.0
2	116.0	120.0	124.0
3	87.2	80.0	71.2
4	110.2	120.0	134.6
5	91.8	80.0	58.5
6	106.6	120.0	149.8
7	94.8	80.0	40.3
8	104.2	120.0	171.7
9	96.6	80.0	14.0
10	102.7	120.0	203.2

General formula: $X_t = a - b\,X_{t-1}$, where a and b are constants, X is a variable changing through time, and t refers to the time period.
Coefficients: Set so that equilibrium of system (where $X_t = X_{t-1}$) = 100
Starting value: $X_1 = 80$

basis of an expected price (P_t^e) which the good is expected to obtain. Thus the supply function is

(4–3) $$Q_t^s = c + d\,P_t^e.$$

Further, suppose that the producer bases his price expectation on the price that is prevailing in the market at the time the production decision is made:

(4–4) $$P_t^e = P_{t-1}.$$

Finally, assume that the market clears, that is, that the price adjusts so that the quantity demanded in this period is equal to the quantity supplied.

(4–5) $$Q_t^d = Q_t^s.$$

Equations 4–2 through 4–5 can be combined and simpled to yield

(4–6a) $$P_7 = x' - y'\,P_{t-1},$$

where $x' = (a - c)/b$ and $y' = (d/b)$, and

(4–6b) $$Q_t = x'' - y''\,Q_{t-1},$$

where $x'' = (cb + da)/b$ and $y'' = (d/b)$. Both of these have, of course, the same form as equation 4–1 and yield the same type of cycles.

A macroeconomic case of negative feedback can be seen in the well-known accelerator-multiplier model. Consider an economy where the GNP (Y_t) consists only of consumption (C_t) and investment (I_t):

(4–7)
$$Y_t = C_t + I_t.$$

Assume that consumption in period t is a function of income in period t in a linear fashion, so that the consumption function is

(4–8)
$$C_t = a + b\,Y_t.$$

Finally, assume that investment is a function of the change in income. This can arise when the ratio of desired capital to production is a constant (c) and, if production changes because of changes in consumer demand, the producer tries to invest (or disinvest) an amount which is equal to the change in production times the desired capital-production ratio so that his overall capital-output ratio is at the desired level. This is the *accelerator* theory of investment and leads to the following investment function:

(4–9)
$$I_t = c\,(Y_t - Y_{t-1}).$$

Taking equations 4–7 through 4–9 and solving, we obtain

(4–10)
$$Y_t = x' - y'\,Y_{t-1},$$

where $x' = a/(1 - b - c)$ and $y = c/(1 - b - c)$. This, of course, has the same form as equation 4–1.

To what extent do such models apply to socialist, centrally planned economies? Since producer prices of most goods (such as hogs) do not greatly vary from year to year, it does not seem as though such a model would be very applicable. If, however, production is based on quantity plans and if quantity plans are based on previous production, then a model with negative feedback that generates cycles could be constructed. With regard to the accelerator-multiplier model it may seem strange that the central planners would follow an investment policy that is implied by equation 4–9. However, if planners based their investment for this year on a target in the five-year plan plus or minus a further amount based on the degree to which aggregate production last year exceeded or fell short of the target in the five-year plan, we can derive an investment function that not only has some similar features to equation 4–9 but also generates similar cycles; moreover, such an equation appears to fit in a rough way the experience of Czechoslovakia.[8] Although doubt can be cast on the degree to which these highly simplied cobweb or accelerator-multiplier models accurately describe either economic system, they nevertheless provide a useful starting place for analysis.

2. Some Empirical Comparisons

In neither the Eastern nor Western economic literatures on production fluctuations do we find any serious theories telling us whether micro- or macroeconomic fluctuations are greater in one economic system or another. In some of the Eastern European press we do sometimes find claims that "socialism is characterized, above all, by the absence of cyclical disturbances in production,"[9] but these assertions are not supported by believable empirical or theoretical evidence. It seems worthwhile, therefore, to look at some empirical evidence on the subject.

a. Microeconomic Evidence

The study of microeconomic fluctuations of production appears almost totally neglected. The only recent comparative study apparently available concerns the behavior of hog production in various nations in Eastern and Western Europe over a quarter-century period.[10]

The time paths of the number of hogs and also the production of pork appears quite jagged but cycles can be statistically discerned in the data of various countries with different economic systems. Rather intricate statistical methods must be used to determine the properties of these cycles but the general conclusions can be easily summarized: There are no significant differences in hog cycles (either in length or the amplitude of the cycle) between Eastern and Western Europe. Given the cobweb model presented above and the fact that hog prices fluctuate more in market economies than in centrally administered economies, how can this be?

One possible explanation is that the cobweb cycle is at work in the

[8]Oldrich Kyn, Wolfram Schrettl, and Jiří Sláma, "Growth Cycles in Centrally Planned Economies: An Empirical Test," in O. Kyn and W. Schrettl, eds., *On the Stability of Contemporary Economic Systems: Proceedings of the 3d Reisenburg Symposium* (Goettingen: 1979).

[9]G. I. Libman, cited by George Staller, "Fluctuations in Economic Activity: Planned and Free-Market Economies, 1950–60," *American Economic Review*, 54, No. 3 (June 1964), pp. 385–95. A brief review of Marxist doctrine on these matters is presented by Alexander Bajt, "Investment Cycles in European Socialist Economies: A Review Article," *Journal of Economic Literature*, 9, No. 1 (March 1971), pp. 53–63.

[10]Frederic L. Pryor and Fred Solomon, "Commodity Cycles as a Random Process," *European Journal of Agricultural Economics*, 9, No. 3 (1982), pp. 327–47.

capitalist, market economies, but other types of negative feedback mechanisms generating cycles are at work in the socialist, centrally administered nations. Unfortunately, we do not know exactly what these are.

Another explanation casts doubt on the cobweb theory and looks for other sources of fluctuations. The cobweb model discussed above is based on an assumption about the formation of price expectations on the part of producers that implies very unintelligent behavior: In every period the price expectation and the actual price appear on the opposite sides of the price trend. However, if individual hog growers simply assume that the actual price will be equal to the long-run average of price in the past (i.e., the trend value), they have a much better guide to action than the price expectations formula presented in equation 4–4. Given this new price expectations formula, the fluctuations of production induced by fluctuating prices would be very much dampened.

Production cycles can still occur in both sets of nations as a result of the impact of chance factors such as the weather. It seems likely that the direct impact of the weather on the production of hogs is not very strong; however, the impact of weather variations on the supply of foods eaten by hogs may be sufficiently strong that total hog production could fluctuate considerably from year to year. Further, since a low production of hogs in this year lowers the stock of breeding sows in future years, multiyear cyclical behavior can be generated.

Currently there is not sufficient empirical information to decide which explanation is correct. Nor is there sufficient evidence on the production of other goods and services to know whether or not production fluctuations are greater in East or West. However, one conclusion is clear: "Obvious" expectations that microeconomic production fluctuations are greater in the capitalist, market economies than in the socialist, centrally administered economies may be quite incorrect.

b. Macroeconomic Evidence

The comparisons below are based on the same data used in Chapter 3 to compare rates of economic growth. The data cover a 30-year period and, for the socialist, centrally administered economies, most series have been recalculated from official data so that they are comparable with the data from the West. For each series, a curve was fitted that contains a factor reflecting compound economic gowth and another factor to take into account a gradual retardation of this growth. More specifically, the following regression was calculated:

(4–11) $$\log Y_t = a + bt + ct^2,$$

where log Y_t represents the logarithm of the series under investigation (GDP, industrial or agricultural production, or gross fixed capital investment), t represents time, and a, b, and c are calculated coefficients.[11] Attention should be focused on the degree to which the pattern of production over time is *not* explained by this formula.

The statistic to measure unexplained production fluctuations is the standard error of estimate (SEE), which defines the confidence limits within which one can predict $ln\ Y_t$ in formula 4–11. The larger the SEE, the greater the unexplained production fluctuations.[12] The relevant data are presented in Table 4–2.

The data reveal that, in general, the GDP shows the lowest fluctuations, followed by industrial production, then gross fixed capital investment, and finally agricultural production. The SEE statistic is relatively low (.0300 corresponds to average deviations from the trend of about 3 percent; .0500, about 5.1 percent; .0700, about 7.2 percent; and .0900, about 9.4 percent). Further, the unweighted averages of the two economic systems do not appear very different. Finally, when similar regression experiments are performed on official, rather than recalculated, data from Eastern Europe for GNP, industrial production, and agricultural production (the gross fixed capital investment series is taken from official data), very similar numerical results are obtained.

To analyze these data in a more systematic fashion, it is necessary to hold the most important causal variables constant. Unfortunately, there is no general agreement among economists as to what these causal variables might be and, therefore, a number of possible candidates were explored: (1) You might expect that the economic system plays a role and, therefore, this variable is entered into the regression; such a conjecture receives little support. (2) From Schumpeterian considerations discussed above, you might expect that the fluctuations would be positively related to the growth rate; this conjecture receives partial support. (3) From the notion that the rising level of economic development and growing complexity of the economic structure introduces greater possibility of disproportionalities, a growth variable is entered; this conjecture receives so little support that the results are not presented except in one case.

For particular series, other possible causal variables were ex-

[11]The features of this formula can be seen by differentiating both sides with respect to t, obtaining an expression equating the percentage rate of growth of Y to $[b + (2c)\,t]$, where b represents the compound growth factor and $(2c)$ represents a growth retardation factor.

[12]Another measure of fluctuations can be derived from the coefficient of determination. However, this measure is related to the variance of the dependent variable which, in turn, is a function of the growth rate; since the growth rate was one of the explanatory variables, it seemed more appropriate to use the SEE in these experiments.

TABLE 4–2

Fluctuations in Production in East and West, 1950–1979

Country	GDP	Standard Errors of Estimate (SEE) Industrial Production	Agricultural Production	Gross Fixed Capital Investment
Socialist, centrally administered nations				
Bulgaria	.0442	.0641	.0776	.1955
Czechoslovakia	.0283	.0524	.0638	.0999
East Germany	.0311	.0401	.0669	.0706
Hungary	.0235	.0451	.0680	.1639
Poland	.0364	.0204	.0543	.1044
Romania	.0364	.0456	.0897	.1017
Soviet Union	.0192	.0170	.0694	.0458
Unweighted average	.0313	.0407	.0700	.1117
Yugoslavia	.0521	.0592	.0908	.0903
Capitalist, market economies				
Australia	.0352	—	—	.0724
Austria	.0268	.0432	.0563	.0716
Belgium	.0332	.0575	.0631	.0682
Canada	.0317	.0502	.0688	.0720
Denmark	.0378	.0480	.0529	.0993
Finland	.0376	.0716	.0526	.0756
France	.0275	.0428	.0463	.0776
West Germany	.0245	.0365	.0393	.0636
Greece	.0382	.0608	.0631	.1268
Ireland	.0291	—	—	.1277
Italy	.0262	.0446	.0367	.0608
Japan	.0637	—	—	.1370
Netherlands	.0325	.0587	.0461	.0839
New Zealand	.0375	—	—	—
Norway	.0187	.0272	.0497	.0754
Portugal	.0428	.0583	.0412	.0780
Spain	.0575	.0783	.0493	.1110
Sweden	.0319	.0693	.0554	.0488
Switzerland	.0449	—	—	.0864
United Kingdom	.0176	.0310	.0405	.0824
United States	.0309	.0549	.0258	.0812
Unweighted average	.0346	.0520	.0492	.0850

Sources: These statistics are taken from the time-series regressions described in equation 4–11 in the text. The data used for the GDP, industrial production, and agricultural production for the socialist, centrally administered nations are Western recalculations; the gross fixed capital investment data come from official sources. More details on sources are found in Appendix D.

plored: (1) For fluctuations of the GDP it can be hypothesized that the openness of the economy, as reflected by the ratio of exports or imports to the GDP, would be positively related to fluctuations since greater possibilities of introducing economic shocks from the outside world are available. Such an hypothesis receives no validation. (2) For agricultural production you might expect that the weather has an important influence. More specifically, the lower the average temperature or the shorter the growing season, the greater the agricultural fluctuations. This hypothesis also receives no support. (3) For agriculture you might also expect that the greater the land area devoted to agriculture, the less influence local weather calamities would have on overall agricultural production, a conjecture receiving weak empirical support.

Some of the most important results of these statistical experiments are presented in Table 4–3. The most important conclusion is that, other things being equal, there are *no* statistically significant differences in fluctuations of GDP, industrial production, or gross fixed capital investment in the capitalist, market economies and the socialist, centrally planned economies. Fluctuations of agricultural production are *greater* in the socialist than in the capitalist nations.

Although these results for aggregate production or for individual sectors roughly parallel the findings of others, the conclusion about similarities of fluctuations of gross fixed capital investment is quite novel and, moreover, quite unexpected. Since many Keynesians (following the logic of the accelerator-multiplier model presented above) believe that fluctuations in investment are the single most important cause of business cycles in market economies, these results suggest either (i) fluctuations in investment are independent of the economic system and they cause aggregate fluctuations not only in capitalist, market economies but in centrally administered economies as well; or (ii) modern fiscal and monetary policies used in the West have succeeded in dampening the business cycle and fluctuations in investment so that they are roughly the same as in the centrally planned economies of Eastern Europe.

With regard to the other hypothesized relationships, no statistically significant results are found. However, the signs of the per capita income variable and also the land area variable are in the predicted direction and, at least for the land area, begin to approach respectable limits of confidence.

c.   Some Interpretations

The similarities in fluctuations of gross fixed investment in nations with different economic systems appear to stem from quite different causes. In the centrally adminstered economies, such fluctuations

TABLE 4–3

Results of Regression Experiments with Fluctuations Data

Dependent Variable	Constant	Average Annual Growth of Dependent Variable	Systems Variable	Other Independent Variables	R^2	n
GDP	+.00847 (.00690)	+.00574* (.00146)	−.00291 (.00371)		.3927	28
Industrial production	+.00855 (.03083)	+.00474 (.00265)	−.0109 (.0078)	+.000251 YP (.000270)	.2524	23
Agricultural production	+.0691* (.0147)	+.00236 (.00277)	+.0220* (.0051)	−.00274 log L (.00177)	.5127	23
Gross fixed capital investment	+.0293 (.0185)	+.01008* (.00316)	−.0090 (.0166)		.3836	27

Note: YP = level of per capita GDP; log L = logarithm of arable land. For the capitalist, market economies, the systems variable is zero; for the socialist, centrally administered economies, one. Yugoslavia is omitted from the sample. R^2 is the coefficient of determination; n is the number of nations in the sample. The standard errors are placed in parentheses below the calculated coefficients and an asterisk designates statistical significance at the .05 level.

Source: The data for the dependent variable come from Table 4–2.

appear to be the result of policy decisions by the government. In some countries over the course of the five-year plan, there is a rapid increase of investment in the first few years, accompanied by a slow growth in wages. However, it is often difficult to absorb a great deal of investment quickly because bottlenecks develop and, as a result, considerable wastage of investment funds occurs. After a point, investment is cut back so that the attention can be focused primarily on widening the bottlenecks; at the same time, real wages are allowed to rise rapidly to provide greater encouragement for people to work hard and remain in the labor force.[13] In other centrally administered economies, as noted above, cycles appear to be introduced by planners basing a certain amount of investment on differences between expected and actual aggregate production in the previous period. A further cause of the fluctuations of gross fixed investment can lie in the foreign trade sector and the relationship between imports of investment goods from the West and Western business cycles which

---

[13]Ideas similar to these are argued in much greater detail by Bajt, "Investment Cycles," and Peter Wiles, "Are There Any Communist Economic Cycles?" *The ACES Bulletin,* 24, No. 2 (Summer 1982), pp. 1–21.

influence the volume of exports used to finance many such machine good imports.[14]

In the capitalist, market economies the fluctuations in gross fixed investment arise, in part, for reasons associated with the accelerator-multiplier model. However, such investment is also influenced by a number of other factors including the interest rate, the state of foreign trade, governmental fiscal and monetary policies, and economic expectations. These are discussed in detail in most macroeconomic texts.

Further regression experiments with the data in Table 4–3 reveal, as one might expect, that the fluctuations of gross fixed investment and of GDP are signficantly related. However, since both types of fluctuations seem to play a causal role in the fluctuations of the other, an investment variable cannot be included in the regression to explain GDP fluctuations.

The greater fluctuations in agriculture in the socialist, centrally adminstered economies are difficult to explain. One might suspect, however, that the central planning of agriculture has led to a greater specialization of crops and animals than might be desired, leading to greater sensitivity to weather conditions. Also, rigidities of the supply system in providing necessary inputs, spare parts, pesticides, and so forth might also play a role. These are, however, conjectures that have not yet received convincing support.

Although the fluctuations in both systems appear quite similar in most respects, one major difference must be pointed out: Declines in production in capitalist, market economies are often accompanied by unemployment of workers, while apparently in socialist, centrally administered economies they are most often accompanied by variations in the degree of underutilization of labor. Since most of the Eastern European nations do not publish unemployment statistics or, for that matter, data with which underemployment can be calculated by industry, we cannot be completely sure about this conclusion. Nevertheless, if this generalization is true, then the welfare impacts of production fluctuations are somewhat different unless the unemployed in the West receive their former wage as unemployment compensation. To view the matter from a somewhat different perspective, in the West declines in production are often accompanied by higher state welfare expenditures to the unemployed; in the East such declines are accompanied by greater underemployment within the productive units and, in essence, part of the wage represents a welfare expenditure.

[14]A model of this interaction is presented by John Michael Montias, "Socialist Industrialization and Trade in Machinery Products: An Analysis Based on the Experience of Bulgaria, Poland and Romania," in Alan A. Brown and Egon Neuberger, eds., *International Trade and Central Planning* (Berkeley: University of California ᴾress, 1968), pp. 130–59.

C. Price Inflation

Economists have advanced a considerable number of hypotheses to explain the rising level of prices in capitalist, market economies. The various discussions are, however, confusing to read because they deal with so many levels of causation. Some point to very immediate causes of inflation such as a rise in wages in particular industries; others point to less proximate causes such as an increase in the money supply by the central bank; while still others point to causes of a more fundamental structural nature.

1. Structural Causes of Inflation

International comparisons of price inflations are particularly useful for isolating the structural causes and it is worthwhile to consider briefly some of the factors which have been advanced.

a. The Role of Foreign Trade

It is often argued that more open market economies are less prone to inflation because any actions taken by the government or various groups in the private sector resulting in a rise in prices are immediately reflected in balance of payments difficulties (if the nation has a fixed exchange rate) or a change in the exchange rate (if the nation has a floating exchange rate). Therefore, domestic groups are more hesitant about taking such actions. In a less open economy, impacts of such single actions on the balance of payments or the exchange rate are relatively smaller and, therefore, provide a less important deterent to any single group when considering actions that might raise prices. Other things being equal, we would expect an inverse relationship between the relative importance of trade in the GNP and price increases. Although this hypothesis is based on a number of assumptions which can be challenged, it does receive empirical confirmation below.

b. The Role of Economic Development

It is sometimes argued that the relative degree of economic development in a market economy influences the inflation rate. Two different mechanisms are offered to support this argument. *First,* the higher the level of development, the more developed is the financial system and the more able it is to absorb governmental monetary actions (particularly with regard to changes in the money supply) without translating them into price changes. *Second,* policy makers in more developed economies presumably have better statistics and policy tools in dealing with inflation. From these rather loose arguments one would expect an inverse relationship between the relative level of GDP per capita and the inflation rate, an hypothesis that also receives confirmation below.

c. The Role of Economic Growth

It is also sometimes argued there is an inverse relationship in market economies between economic growth and inflation. The direction of causation, however, can be both ways. It is possible that inflation discourages growth; it is also possible that high growth absorbs purchasing power that would otherwise lead to price increases. This latter argument seems considerably more plausible. Therefore, a growth variable is included among the explanatory variables and, as shown below, the hypothesized inverse relationship receives confirmation.

d. The Role of Government

It is often claimed, both in East and West, that inflation problems in centrally administered nations are less serious. Governmental authorities in these nations are supposed to have more and better policy tools to combat inflation. Equally important, they also appear to have a greater political will to dampen aggregate price increases and to prevent wage-price spirals, even if their policies bring about short-run shortages of specific goods and services. Differences in inflation rates in the capitalist, market economies and the socialist, centrally administered economies are certainly worth investigating. However, therein lies a very difficult empirical problem.

2. Testing the Hypotheses

The study of price changes in Eastern Europe is hindered by the very uncertain nature of the official price statistics, particularly the cost of living indices. As shown for the Soviet Union in Table 2–3, the unit value data (i.e., the price derived by dividing the *value* of sales by the *volume* of sales) reveals much greater price increases than cost of living data. This discrepancy can be attributed to three factors: (1) Although prices remain the same, the consumers are buying higher-quality (and higher-priced) goods either voluntarily or involuntarily (because the lower-priced goods are not available) and this change in quality is not taken into account by the volume index. (2) Most prices are actually changing but the prices of the small number of specific goods contained in the index are not. (3) The cost of living index is being manipulated by the government to show lower price increases than are actually occurring (a practice also sometimes occurring in the West). It is unfortunate, but at the present time we do not have sufficient information to solve the mysteries underlying the official cost of living index in most of the Eastern European nations.

Rather than dealing with cost of living indices, a slightly different path is useful to follow. Most of these nations publish indices for total *value* of private consumption in current prices. For the period 1960 through 1980, *volume* indices for total private consumption have also been calculated in the West for all Eastern European nations except Romania. By dividing the former by the latter, we can derive a price index for consumption.[15] For the Western nations, we can also calculate price indices for total private consumption by dividing indices of the *value* of consumption by the *volume* of consumption. The result of these calculations are presented in Table 4–4.

The data show that, on the average, price increases have been almost 4 percentage points higher in the capitalist, market economies than in the socialist, centrally adminstered economies. However, the highest price increase occurred in Yugoslavia, a socialist economy with strong market elements. To investigate these matters more deeply, it is necessary to examine the effect of some of the structural elements on inflation discussed above. The first three structural elements focus on capitalist, market economies and, therefore, the regression exercises are carried out with this set of nations. The relevent results are presented in the first equation in Table 4–5.

As predicted, price increases are inversely related to the relative openness of the economy, the average growth rate, and the level of economic development; further, the last two relationships are statistically significant at the .95 level of confidence and the first relationship is statistically significant at the .90 level of confidence. Of particular importance is the negative relation between inflation and economic growth. This means that there is no tradeoff between these two important macroeconomic goals and, indeed, they complement each other.

Although there are no particularly strong reasons for believing that these structural elements influence relative inflation rates in socialist, centrally adminstered economies, we can calculate a similar regression for the six socialist nations to see what happens. When we do this, the results are quite surprising. It appears that price increases are inversely related to both the openness of the economy and the level of economic development and, further, that the calculated regression coefficients are roughly similar to those in the West (the coefficient for the level of economic development is even statistically significant). For the per capita income variable, the calculated coefficient is slightly positive

---

[15]These Eastern European nations also publish their own estimates of the volume of consumption, so price indices were calculated with these data as well. Although they result in inflation rates about 1.5 percentage points lower than those presented in Table 4–4, the results of the regression analyses reported below are quite similar.

TABLE 4-4

Average Annual Change in Prices of Aggregate Consumption in East and West, 1960–80

Country	Average Annual Change		Ratio of Exports and Imports to GDP in 1970	Per Capita GDP Index 1970
	Consumption Prices	GDP Growth		
Socialist, centrally adminstered economies				
Bulgaria	4.05%	5.43%	12.6%	37.3
Czechoslovakia	2.79	3.67	8.8	62.0
East Germany	1.21	3.77	9.0	63.9
Hungary	3.70	3.64	11.4	42.7
Poland	4.97	4.12	6.5	35.4
Romania	—	—	—	—
Soviet Union	2.30	4.95	4.1	46.9
Unweighted average	3.17%	4.26%	8.7%	
Yugoslavia	14.97%	5.87%	5.0%	25.8
Capitalist, market economies				
Australia	6.73%	4.54%	10.8%	69.6
Austria	4.70	4.74	14.2	63.1
Belgium	5.05	4.00	33.4	72.0
Canada	5.05	4.57	17.6	81.9
Denmark	7.32	3.81	19.1	83.3
Finland	8.06	4.48	17.8	63.1
France	6.75	4.86	10.4	73.2
West Germany	3.95	4.85	14.1	78.2
Greece	7.82	6.20	8.0	38.7
Ireland	9.24	3.45	22.8	40.5
Italy	9.08	4.92	11.2	49.2
Japan	7.03	8.35	6.5	59.2
Netherlands	5.91	4.58	29.4	68.7
New Zealand	8.25	3.46	14.2	64.6
Norway	6.26	4.15	24.2	68.4
Portugal	9.34	5.43	11.3	27.1
Spain	10.05	5.53	4.5	48.9
Sweden	6.53	3.69	20.7	86.6
Switzerland	4.52	3.72	26.8	72.4
United Kingdom	8.51	2.72	12.2	63.5
United States	4.71	3.39	4.2	100.0
Unweighted average	6.90%	4.54%	15.9%	

Sources: The sources for the data on the price increases of aggregate consumption are discussed in Appendix D. The data on GDP growth and GDP per capita come from Table 3–1. The trade-GDP ratio represents the arithmetic average of the dollar values of exports plus imports, divided by the dollar value of the GDP (calculated in a common set of prices).

TABLE 4–5
Results of Regression Experiments with Consumption Price Increases

Dependent Variable	Constant	Systems Variable	Trade Variable	Average Annual GDP Growth	Per Capita GDP	R^2	n
Capitalist, market economies only							
Average annual consumption price change	15.818* (2.109)		−0.511 (0.261)	−0.0761* (0.0360)	−0.0824* (0.0167)	.6376	21
All nations in sample							
Average annual consumption price change	15.887* (1.880)	−5.853 (0.637)	−0.500* (0.230)	−0.0694* (0.0325)	−0.0859* (0.0147)	.8084	27

Note: For the capitalist, market economies, the systems variable is zero; for the socialist, centrally administered economies, one; Yugoslavia is omitted from these experiments. R^2 is the coefficient of determination; *n* is the number of nations in the sample. The standard errors are placed in parentheses below the calculated coefficients and an asterisk designates statistical significance at the .05 level.

Source: The data come from Table 4–4.

but has a very high standard error so that no inferences can be made. The reasons underlying this unexpected similarity with the West remain unclear; however, such results suggest a fertile territory for further exploration. (Textbook writers have to pretend to know everything; guidebook writers can be honest and can tell you about interesting areas to investigate by yourself because there are not yet any guides.)

Given this remarkable similarity between the two systems, the two samples of nations can be combined and the regression recalculated, an exercise reported in the second equation in the table.[16] The most important result is that the rate of inflation is, other things being equal, about 5.9 percentage points higher in the West than in the East. With regard to this success criterion, the socialist, centrally planned economies perform remarkably better than the capitalist, market economies.

However, is this conclusion the end of the story? It has been argued by many economists that, although inflation is not "open" in the Eastern European nations, it occurs in a "suppressed" form. Manifestations of such a phenomenon are the scarcities of goods and the corresponding long waiting lines, and the great differences in food prices in state stores and on the *kolkhoz* (farmer) markets. However, the longer shopping

---

[16]In combining samples it is important to determine whether or not the slope variables have the same values in the two sets of nations. Such tests can be carried out in several different ways and are described in most standard econometrics textbooks. None of these tests revealed any statistically significant differences in the different slope variables of the two economic systems.

times can have a quite different and more benign explanation; and the variations in food prices in different markets might reflect disequilibria for specific goods or sets of goods, rather than a general suppressed inflation. All such matters about the availability of consumer goods receive much greater attention in Chapter 7.

The only way to determine the degree of suppressed inflation is to carry out statistical investigations to investigate some of the predicted symptoms of such a phenomenon, for example, declines in the labor force, the occurrence of forced savings, and a higher stock of money per unit of production than we would ordinarily expect. Given the high labor force participation ratios in Eastern Europe that are discussed in Chapter 3, the probability of finding the first symptom does not seem promising. The second and third symptoms are difficult to investigate statistically because suppressed inflation represents, in essence, a disequilibrium situation. That is, the quantity of goods and services supplied and demanded are not equated by price. Therefore, normal regression models of supply and demand cannot be used and rather advanced statistical techniques must be applied; unfortunately, these techniques are too involved to discuss here.[17] However, the most recent studies of the matter suggest that consumption functions for Eastern Europe and also consumer demand functions for money appear to have roughly the same coefficients as in the West. Such results suggest that suppressed inflation in these centrally administered nations does not seem present for the period as a whole. Of course, this does not preclude the occurrence of suppressed inflation at particular points in time, or individual shortages of particular goods and services. It must be further noted that enormous controversy rages among economists about whether suppresed inflation does or does not occur in the socialist, centrally adminstered nations and, therefore, the conclusions set forth in this paragraph must be considered as highly tentative.

D. Other Types of Instabilities

In the field of foreign trade, several studies have been made of fluctuations of exports and imports, but most of these are now somewhat outdated.[18] The general conclusions of these studies are quite similar

---

[17]The major articles in this literature are cited in the list of selected readings.

[18]These studies include Raymond F. Mikesell and Jack N. Behrman, *Financing Free World Trade with the Sino-Soviet Bloc* (Princeton, N.J.: Princeton University Press, 1958); Egon Neuberger, "Is the U.S.S.R. Superior to the West as a Market for Primary Products?" *Review of Economics and Statistics,* 46, No. 4 (August 1964), pp. 287–93; and George J. Staller, "Patterns of Stability in Foreign Trade: OECD and Comecon, 1950–1963," *American Economic Review,* 57, No. 4 (September 1967), pp. 879–88.

and can be easily summarized: Fluctuations in total exports or imports are *greater* in the socialist, centrally administered than capitalist, market economies and, moreover, this difference is statistically significant. One particularly important part of this trade, namely the trade with the Third World, has been investigated separately; Third World trade with the economically developed socialist nations also manifests greater fluctuations than Third World trade with economically developed, capitalist economies.

The reasons behind these greater fluctuations in Eastern Europe are not completely clear. For at least some of the Eastern European nations such as Romania, import substitution policies appear to be explicitly designed so that foreign trade fluctuations are greater than fluctuations in domestic production or investment; that is, the foreign trade sector absorbs shocks arising in the domestic economy.[19]

One study has also been made of fluctuations in public consumption expenditures among various socialist and capitalist economies.[20] Although such fluctuations appear greater in the former set of nations, the differences are not statistically significant. Further, in neither set of nations does it appear that such expenditures are used countercyclically, that is, increased when production in the rest of the economy is depressed and decreased when the reverse conditions hold. Again, the reasons behind these differences and similarities are not clear and, like many topics discussed in this chapter, require much more research.

Up to now comparative studies on the income side, that is, on the income stability of individual households, have not been carried out. As pointed out above, unemployment appears greater in the capitalist, market economies than the socialist, centrally planned economies; so we might expect individual income instabilities to be greater in the former set of nations. A number of aspects of the way in which governments attempt to even out household income flows by using different types of welfare payments are discussed in Chapters 7 and 8.

E. Summary and Conclusions

As noted in the introduction to this chapter, our theoretical knowledge about comparative fluctuations and inflation in different economic systems has many gaps. However, empirical investigations are still possible and provide some tantalizing clues.

[19]This has been argued by Montias, "Socialist Industrialization"; the argument has received comment by Pryor in the same volume, (Brown and Neuberger, *International Trade*), pp. 160–66.

[20]Frederic L. Pryor, *Public Expenditures in Communist and Capitalist Nations* (London: Allen and Unwin, 1968), chap. 7.

The comparisons of various aggregates of production show that there are few major differences between the fluctuations in the capitalist, market and those in the socialist, centrally adminstered economies, except in agriculture where the fluctuations are greater in the latter set of nations. Of particular importance is the finding that fluctuations in gross fixed capital investment are roughly the same. The Schumpeterian hypothesis about growth and fluctuations being directly related receives only slight support; thus any alleged tradeoff between growth and stability appears limited. Other hypotheses linking fluctuations with the level of economic development or other variables receive even less support.

The comparisons of aggregate price behavior in various economically developed nations shows a much lower rate of increase in the socialist, centrally administered economies than in the capitalist, market economies. These comparisons also reveal that high economic growth is associated with lower rates of price increases; thus nations do not face tradeoffs in achieving both growth and price stability.

SUGGESTED READINGS

A. Cyclical Behavior in Centrally Administered Economies

1. Alexander Bajt, "Investment Cycles in European Socialist Economies: A Review Article," *Journal of Economic Literature,* 9 (March 1971), pp. 53–63. Although somewhat dated, this is an excellent survey of the literature.

2. Peter Wiles, "Are There Any Communist Economic Cycles?" *The ACES Bulletin,* 24, No. 2 (Summer 1982), pp. 1–21. This is primarily empirical, but with a number of interesting interpretative remarks. Other general essays with both empirical and interpretative remarks are somewhat less current and include Josef Goldman, "Fluctuations in the Growth Rate in a Socialist Economy and the Inventory Cycle," and the following comment by Francis Seton in Martin Bronfenbrenner, ed., *Is the Business Cycle Obsolete?* (New York: John Wiley, 1969), pp. 332–50; and N. Cobeljić and R. Stojanović, "A Contribution to the Study of Investment Cycles in the Socialist Economy," *Eastern European Economics,* 2, Nos. 1–2 (1963–64).

3. Two excellent recent studies combining both theoretical arguments and econometric evidence are Oldrich Kyn, Wolfram Schrettl, and Jiří Sláma, "Growth Cycles in Centrally Planned Economies: An Empirical Test," in O. Kyn and W. Schrettl, eds., *On the Stability of Contemporary Economic Systems: Proceedings of the 3d Reisenburg Symposium* (Goettingen: 1979); and Reinhard Uffhausen, "Simulation von Investitions– und Planungszyklen in der sowjetischen Wirtschaft," forthcoming.

4. Empirical comparative studies of fluctuations in centrally administered economies include George Staller, "Fluctuations in Economic Activity: Planned and Free-Market Economies, 1950–60," *American Economic Review,* 4, No. 3 (June 1964), pp. 385–95; Josef Goldman, "Fluctuations and Trends in the Rate of Economic Growth in Some Socialist Countries," *Economic of Planning,* 4,

No. 2 (1964), pp. 88–98; Julios H. G. Olivera, "Cyclical Economic Growth under Collectivism," *Kyklos,* 13, No. 2 (1960), pp. 229–55; J. M. Montias, "Socialist Trade and Industrialization," in Alan Brown and Egon Neuberger, eds., *Foreign Trade and Central Planning* (Berkeley: University of California Press, 1968), pp. 130–59; Alexander Eckstein, "Comment on Fluctuations," in Gregory Grossman, ed., *Value and Plan* (Berkeley: University of California Press, 1960), pp. 262–66; and Bogdan Mieczkowski, "The Unstable Soviet-Bloc Economies," *East Europe,* 16, No 10 (October 1967), pp. 2–7.

5. Interesting articles focusing on the experience of one or a few countries include Alexander Eckstein, "Economic Flutuations in Communist China's Domestic Development," in Ping-ti Ho and Tang Tsou, eds., *China's Heritage and the Communist Political System: China in Crisis* (Chicago: University of Chicago Press, 1968), pp. 691–754; Branko Horvat, *Business Cycles in Yugoslavia* (White Plains, N.Y.: IASP, 1971); Warren Nutter et al., *Growth of Industrial Production in the Soviet Union* (Princeton, N.J.: Princeton University Press, 1962); and Eugene Zaleski, *Planification de la crossance et fluctuations économiques en U.R.S.S.,* Vol. I (Paris: SEDES, 1962).

B. *Price Stability*

1. A good survey article of the major issues is Richard Portes, "The Control of Inflation: Lessons from East European Experience," *Economica,* 44, No. 174 (May 1977), pp. 109–29; a slightly shortened version is reprinted in Morris Bornstein, ed., *Comparative Economic Systems: Models and Cases,* 4th ed. (Homewood, Ill.: Richard D. Irwin, 1979), pp. 448–69.

2. The detection of hidden (or suppressed) inflation in centrally planned economies has given rise to a fascinating but very difficult literature. David Howard, "The Disequilibrium Model in a Controlled Economy: An Empirical Test of the Barro-Grossman Model," *American Economic Review,* 66, No. 5 (December 1976), pp. 871–79, reviews Soviet evidence and finds the presence of a disequilibrium in the goods and labor markets that strongly suggests the presence of suppressed inflation. However, quite opposite conclusions are arrived at through the examination of savings and demand for money behavior. These articles include Joyce Pickersgill, "Soviet Household Savings Behavior," *Review of Economics and Statistics,* 58, No. 2 (May 1976), pp. 139–47; Richard Portes and D. Winter, "The Supply of Consumption Goods in Centrally Planned Economies," *Journal of Comparative Economics,* 1, No. 4 (December 1977), pp. 351–65; Richard Portes and D. Winter, "The Demand for Money and for Consumption Goods in Centrally Planned Economies," *Review of Economics and Statistics,* 60, No. 1 (February 1978), pp. 8–18; and Richard Portes and David Winter, "Disequilibrium Estimates for Consumption Goods Markets in Centrally Planned Economies," *Review of Economic Studies,* 47 (1980), pp. 137–59. For Yugoslavia, a first-rate study is Laura D. Tyson, "The Yugoslav Inflation: Some Competing Hypotheses," *Journal of Comparative Economics,* 1, No. 2 (June 1977), pp. 113–46.

3. The problem of suppressed inflation is approached in a quite different way in two essays dealing with planning pressure: Holland Hunter, "Optimal Tautness in Development Planning," *Economic Development and Cultural Change,* 9 (1961), pp. 561–72; and Herbert Levine, "Pressure and Planning in the Soviet Economy," in H. Rosovsky, ed., *Industrialization in Two Systems* (New York: John Wiley, 1966), pp. 266–86. More theoretical treatments of the problem of tautness or disequilibrium raise some extremely difficult issues and three quite different approaches have been proposed: János Kornai, *Anti-Equi-*

librium (Amsterdam: North Holland, 1981); David H. Howard, *The Disequilibrium Model in a Controlled Economy* (Lexington, Mass.: Lexington Books, 1979); and J. Muellbauer and Richard Portes, "Macroeconomic Models with Quantity Rationing," *Economic Journal,* 88, No. 4 (December 1978), pp. 788–821.

4. The measurement of hidden inflation in Eastern Europe raises a number of difficulties and a venomous technical debate on the subject has raged. These articles started with David Howard, "A Note on Hidden Inflation," *Soviet Studies,* 28, No. 2 (April 1976), pp. 599–608; followed by a critique by Steven Rosefielde, "A Comment on David Howard's Estimate of Hidden Inflation in the Soviet Retail Sales Sector," *Soviet Studies,* 32, No. 3 (July 1980), pp. 423–28; and a subsequent reply and rejoinder in *Soviet Studies,* 32, No. 4 (October 1980), pp. 580–86; and Vol. 333, No. 4 (October 1981), pp. 610–16.

5. Several interesting articles focus on inflation in socialist countries in their early years. These include Franklyn D. Holzman, "Soviet Inflationary Pressures, 1938–57," *Quarterly Journal of Economics,* 74, No. 2 (May 1960), pp. 167–88; and Andrzej Brzeski, "Forced Draft Industrialization with Unlimited Supply of Money, Poland, 1945–64," in Gregory Grossman, ed., *Money and Plan* (Berkeley: University of California Press, 1968), pp. 38–56.

C. Banking and Finance

In inflationary processes in any type of economic system, the banking system plays an important role. The following sources provide information about banking in the East European nations.

1. A useful comparative survey of banking systems is Egon Neuberger, "The Role of Central Banking under Various Economic Systems," *Public Policy,* 8 (Cambridge, Mass.: Harvard University Graduate School of Public Administration, 1958), pp. 227–54. This is reprinted in Bornstein, ed., *Comparative Economic Systems,* 1st ed. (1965), pp. 278–310.

2. For the Soviet Union a short but excellent summary of banking and finance is found in Alec Nove, *The Soviet Economic System* (London: Allen and Unwin, 1977), chap. 9, pp. 227–51. Other useful studies are George Garvy, "Finance and Banking in the USSR," in Morris Bornstein and Daniel Fusfeld, eds., *The Soviet Economy,* 4th ed. (Homewood, Ill.: Richard D. Irwin, 1974), pp. 117–48; and Igor Birman, "The Financial Crisis in the USSR," *Soviet Studies,* 22 (January 1980), pp. 84–105 (which presents a much more pessimistic view).

3. For other Eastern European countries a number of studies are available. These include Gregory Grossman, ed., *Money and Plan* (Berkeley: University of California Press, 1968); D. Dimitrijević and G. Macesich, *Money and Finance in Contemporary Yugoslavia* (New York: Praeger, 1973); T. M. Podalski, *Socialist Banking and Monetary Control* (Cambridge: Cambridge University Press, 1973); and NATO, *Banking, Money and Credit in Eastern Europe* (Brussels: 1973).

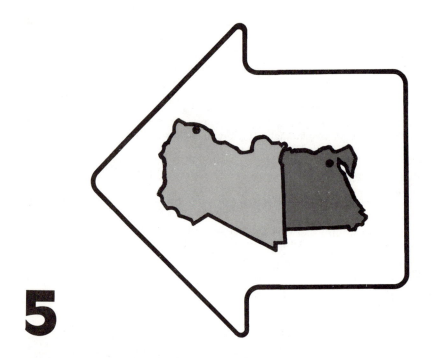

5

STATIC EFFICIENCY AND THE ALLOCATION OF PRODUCTIVE RESOURCES: NONPRICE METHODS

A. Introduction

For those brought up in a complex market economy, the allocation of resources without the use of prices and markets may seem either impossible or inefficient. However, nonprice methods of allocation have been and are still extensively employed in many economies. To evaluate their efficiency, it is first necessary to understand how they function; and this task, in turn, requires some patience and hard work.

Nonprice methods of allocation are not difficult to understand in very simple economies. Consider the allocation of resources in a tribal society at a low level of economic development. In such a society labor is relatively homogeneous and most capital equipment (spears, digging stocks, baskets) is easily produced. Most goods produced are for consumption and intermediate goods and services are new. Further, the level of technology is such that few methods for producing any particular good are known, the actual goods and services produced are few, and the division of labor occurs primarily along the lines of sex and age. In such societies most goods and services are produced by particular kin groups for their own consumption and exchange and transfers between kin groups are limited.

These societies allocate few (if any) goods and services by a price system. Indeed, a good argument can be made that a price system in such an economy is not at all necessary for achieving static efficiency (defined in Chapter 2). If, for some reason, production in this society is centrally directed by a chief or priest, such an administrator would not need to consider many production variants (either in terms of the usage of factors of production or the output mix) or to worry very much over complications arising from the interdependencies of production. Although you might consider that there is a great deal of "wastage" in the economy, especially in the form of seemingly useless ceremonial expenditures, this concerns the consumption side of the economy. From the viewpoint of production, such economies probably feature a high degree of static efficiency; that is, given their technological knowledge and their supplies of land, capital, and labor of various skills, they are producing at their production possibility curve.

However, the administrator of a centrally planned and administered industrial economy faces a much more difficult task since his economy is much more complex. In such an economy, the division of labor is more extensive, a great many goods are produced, many methods are known for producing most goods, and interdependencies of production are important (that is, capital equipment and intermediate goods play an important role of the production process). Serious problems arise in obtaining information and using such information to arrive at an efficient pattern of production for the economy as a whole.

The purpose of this chapter is to consider the methods by which such an administrator could allocate resources using nonprice methods. To illustrate how nonprice allocation can be carried out in a complex economy, the discussion starts with a theoretical model of an economy described by a simple input-output table. So that the discussion remains concrete, a series of numerical examples are presented to illustrate the key theoretical points. After showing how central planners in such an economy can allocate resources, the results are evaluated by applying the marginal conditions outlined in Chapter 2.

Then the practices of physical allocation in the socialist, centrally administered economies of Eastern Europe are examined so that you can view actual problems in using nonprice allocation methods. Particular attention is placed on the Soviet allocation system using material balances, which is a variant of the input-output model. Finally, some additional examples are briefly reviewed to show how some of the short-comings of the Soviet material balance system can be overcome or to argue how in some cases physical allocation methods give more efficient results than price allocation methods.

These various physical allocation systems are contrasted in Chapter 6 with price allocation systems. Once both nonprice and price allocation methods are described, we can turn to the empirical evidence on the relative degree of static efficiency in the two different types of allocation systems.

One warning must be given. All possible attempts have been made to cast the subject in a form so that it is understandable to those without a great deal of mathematical background. However, this short chapter contains some difficult theoretical materials and many of the ideas expressed are complex. You are asked to persevere; the path is very much less steep in the remaining chapters of the book.

B. Input-Output Methods of Physical Allocation of Resources

1. Theory

Suppose that we have an economy with four sectors that produce agricultural goods, basic industrial goods, finished goods, and services.[1] A key question for the planners can be simply stated: How much should be the total production of each good, given the fact that many of these goods are used in the production of goods from other sectors? In the examples of solutions to this problem in a four-sector economy described in the following pages, this question is restated in the following terms: What must be the total or gross production (i.e., production for both interindustry and final use) if net production (i.e., production for end use) is as follows: a = agricultural productions $=200$; b = basic industrial goods $= 200$; f = final goods $=100$; and s = services $= 25$.

We could start with a given sector, for example, basic industrial goods, and work through the interrelations. For instance, to make such goods we require a certain amount of agricultural goods, finished goods, and also basic industrial goods as inputs. To produce these, in turn, we require a certain amount of agricultural goods, finished goods, basic industrial goods, and services. Tracing through such interdependencies

---

[1]The discussion and numerical examples of this section are drawn heavily from Hollis B. Chenery and Paul G. Clark, *Interindustry Economics* (New York: John Wiley, 1959).

can be extremely tedious and time consuming unless done in systematic fashion.

The first step, therefore, is to draw up a table showing the present flow of goods between all sectors of the economy; this is called an *input-output* (I-O) table. Part of the I-O table reflects merely the flows between industrial sectors, and the data from this part of the I-O table is used in the calculation of the *technology matrix*.[2] So that the flows between industrial sectors can be related to the other facets of the economy, the factors of production used in such production and the end use (consumption, investment, export) of the various products must be included. An example of the results of such an exercise is shown in Table 5–1.

In the northwest quadrant of the table, each industry appears as a user of goods and factors of production. We can see, for instance (by moving down the first column), that to produce 250 units of agricultural goods, the agricultural sector needs 25 units of agricultural goods (e.g., seeds), 25 units of basic industrial goods (e.g., tractors), 25 units of services (e.g., repairs), 150 units of labor (defined in terms of their total wages), and 25 units of capital services (depreciation and profits). We can see also (by moving along the first row) that 25 units of agricultural output are used in agriculture itself, 120 units in finished goods (e.g., canned foods), and 105 units are used for consumption and investment (i.e., inventories). The total production of 250 is equal to total usage of 250. The sum of total final production of all sectors and also of total usage is the gross national product which is, in this table, 525. (The 1,000 represents "gross-gross production" and reflects not only production but the structure of the economy; it has little economic meaning but was once used to measure aggregate production in some Eastern European nations in the 1950s. This is why it is necessary to recalculate some of the early data from Eastern Europe.)

[2]For those unfamiliar with the concepts of *matrix* and *vector* a few words of explanation are in order. A matrix is merely a two-dimensional array of numbers. For instance, consider a set of simultaneous equations:

$$x + y = +3$$
$$x - 2y = -3$$

An example of a matrix is the array of numbers in the left hand side of these equations, namely:

$$\begin{array}{cc} 1 & 1 \\ 1 & -2 \end{array}$$

A vector is merely a one-dimensional array of numbers. For instance, in the above equations, the numbers on the right-hand side constitute a vector:

$$\begin{array}{c} +3 \\ -3 \end{array}$$

Various types of systems of linear equations can often be handled more easily by writing them in the form of vectors and matrices, rather than as equations.

TABLE 5–1
A Simple Input-Output Table

Producing Sectors	Using Sectors				Total Intermediate Use	Final Use (net output)	Total Use (intermediate and final)
	A Agriculture	B Basic Industries	F Finished Goods	S Services			
A Agriculture	25	0	120	0	(145)	105	250
B Basic industries	25	45	40	0	(110)	40	150
F Finished goods	0	0	80	0	(80)	320	400
S Services	25	15	80	20	(140)	60	200
(Total purchases)	(75)	(60)	(320)	(20)	(475)		
Labor services[a]	150	30	40	160		380	
Capital services[b]	25	60	40	20		145	
(Total primary inputs)	(175)	(90)	(80)	(180)		(525)	
Total gross output[c]	250	150	400	200			1,000

Note: The numbers in the table reflect approximately the relative sectoral relations of Italy around 1950. The numbers are expressed in value terms so that the various aggregate relations underlying the table can be more easily seen. The upper left quadrant can, however, be expressed in physical terms just as easily; but in this case global aggregates could not be calculated.

[a]Labor services include all payments to labor.

[b]Capital services include depreciation and profits from capital.

[c]The total gross output for each sector equals the total use of that product (last column).

Source: The example comes from Hollis B. Chenery and Paul G. Clark, *Interindustry Economics* (New York: John Wiley, 1959), Chaps. 1–3.

The total intermediate use and the total final purchases are included in the table only to show relative magnitudes; they are not necessary and are not included in the calculations made below.

If we are dealing with an open economy, exports are treated as a final use and imports can be treated in several ways, for example, either as a producing sector (in the northwest quadrant) or as an input like labor or capital (in the southwest quadrant). In either case, the equality of production and usage is maintained. If sales taxes or other indirect taxes or subsidies are placed on production, they can also be handled by treating such activities as a special row along with capital and labor; other methods of handling such distortions are also used.

This table, combined with some assumptions about the nature of technology, can be used to develop a powerful tool of economic analysis and planning. In specifying the five major assumptions underlying this (or any other) input-output analysis, we can also gain some idea of the limitations of this analytic tool:

a. Only one major method is used in producing the goods in a particular industrial sector and, furthermore, the composition of production within the sector does not greatly change.

b. The production function is such that all the factors of production and all inputs are used in fixed proportions; further, production is zero if the inputs are zero.

c. The production function features constant returns to scale.

d. There are no external economies or diseconomies of production.

e. The coefficients in the production function remain fixed over the time period for which the analysis is made.

The second step in tracing interdependencies between economic sectors to solve the planning problem posed above is to calculate the total amount of each good that is used to produce one unit of every other good. For instance, it takes 25 agricultural goods (e.g., seeds) to produce a gross output of 250 agricultural goods, so the calculation yields a coefficient of 0.1; similarly, it takes 120 agricultural goods to produce a gross output of 400 units of finished goods, so the coefficient is 0.3. The results of such calculations are called the *technology matrix* and are presented in the top part of Table 5–2.

The third step is rearranging the rows and columns (if you change a row, you must change the column) in order to shift as many zeros as possible into the northeast part of the matrix above the diagonal running from the northwest to southeast corner. This step, while not necessary, greatly aids the solution of the problem. This process is called *triangularization* and is shown in the middle part of Table 5–2. In the example shown in the tables, the matrix can be perfectly triangularized; this is not always possible.

The final step in solving the planning problem posed above is to attack the problem directly. In order to do this, we might employ any one of the methods discussed below.

a. Simultaneous Equation Method

One obvious approach is to employ the techniques used for solving simultaneous equations. In the example under consideration, this is very easy. We need merely solve first for finished goods (net finished goods are set at 100); and the result is the gross production of finished goods necessary to produce this, namely 125 (since 25 units of the fin-

TABLE 5–2
An Illustrative Triangularized Technology Matrix

	Original Matrix of Coefficients			
	Using Sectors			
Producing Sectors	*A*	*B*	*F*	*S*
A Agriculture	0.1	0.0	0.3	0.0
B Basic industries	0.1	0.3	0.1	0.0
F Finished goods	0.0	0.0	0.2	0.0
S Services	0.1	0.1	0.2	0.1

	Triangularized Matrix			
	Using Sectors			
Producing Sectors	*F*	*A*	*B*	*S*
F Finished goods	0.2	0.0	0.0	0.0
A Agriculture	0.3	0.1	0.0	0.0
B Basic industries	0.1	0.1	0.3	0.0
S Services	0.2	0.1	0.1	0.1

Solving by simultaneous equations:
$f = 100 = F - 0.2\,F$
$a = 200 = A - 0.3\,F - 0.1\,A$
$b = 200 = B - 0.1\,F - 0.1\,A - 0.3\,B$
$s = 25 = S - 0.2\,F - 0.1\,A - 0.1\,B - 0.1\,S$

Solutions:
$F = 125.0$
$A = 263.9$
$B = 341.3$
$S = 122.8$

Source: The technology matrix is based on the input-output table presented in Table 5–1.

ished goods are used up in producing finished goods (e.g., automobiles are a finished good but are also used in producing automobiles). Given a gross production of *F* of 125, we then proceed to determine how much gross agricultural production is necessary (since agricultural goods are used not only in producing other agricultural goods but also finished goods such as canned tomatoes). The remaining sectors are then solved in order, as shown in the bottom part of Table 5–2.

Of course, if we cannot perfectly triangularize the matrix, then solving a set of simultaneous equations using traditional methods taught in high school algebra can become extremely tedious—especially for large matrices with 400 sectors (so that the matrix is 400 × 400, not just 4 × 4, and 400 simultaneous equations must be solved).

It must be noted that if we wish to determine the gross output pattern needed to end up with a different new net output pattern, it is necessary to repeat the process and to solve the simultaneous equations over again.

b. Iteration Techniques

Another method for solving the equations involves iteration techniques, that is, a trial and error method followed in a very consistent manner as shown in Table 5–3. This numerical example is very tedious to follow; however, it illustrates an extremely important aspect of the operation of the material balance systems in Eastern Europe and, therefore, is useful to work through. Starting with the first product class in the triangularized matrix (F = finished goods), we first assume that gross output of finished goods equals the net output of finished goods (i.e., 100). Taking the technology coefficient matrix (top part of Table 5–2), we calculate that we need 20 units of F, 30 units of A, and 20 units of S to carry out such production. Then we take the next product class in the triangularized matrix (A = agriculture) and assume that to have 200 units of net production, we need 200 units of gross production of A plus the 30 units needed to produce the 100 units of F which we just calculated. Similarly, to produce a net output of 200 units of B (basic goods), we assume that we need not only 200 units gross output of B but an additional 10 units of B to produce 100 units of F and, further, 23 units of B to produce the 200 units of A. We proceed in this fashion through the entire list of products and then start again, always taking into account the amount of that product which was necessary to produce the last assumed gross production of that product, as well as the assumed gross production of the three other products as well. Given some rather unrestrictive assumptions about the nature of the technology matrix, the process will converge upon a solution—in the table, at the ninth iteration.

Such a method, while requiring a considerable amount of pencil work, is extremely easy to carry out and, moreover, can be easily programmed for a computer so that relatively large matrices can be quickly solved. In addition, the process can be speeded up by a number of tricks. For instance, instead of starting with the extremely simple-minded assumption that gross output equals net output plus the necessary inputs for the net outputs of the other goods, we could start with a more realistic set of initial conditions. Further, it is possible to extrapolate some of the series so as to skip several iterations.

However, for a given size matrix, the number of iterations necessary to solve the problem increases not only with the numerical values of the production coefficients but also with the number of interindustry relations above the diagonal (northwest to southeast corner) in the tran-

TABLE 5–3
An Iterative Solution to Balancing the Economy

Problem: Calculate gross production where net f = 100; net a = 200; net b = 200; net s = 25.

Estimated Gross Production: Net Production + Intermediate Demands of Previously Planned Production		Amounts Required for Production			
		F	A	B	S
First iteration					
F = 100.0	= 100.0	20.0	30.0	10.0	20.0
A = 200.0 + 30.0	= 230.0	0.0	23.0	23.0	23.0
B = 200.0 + 10.0 + 23.0	= 233.0	0.0	0.0	69.9	23.3
S = 25.0 + 20.0 + 23.0 + 23.3	= 91.3	0.0	0.0	0.0	9.1
Second iteration					
F = 100.0 + 20.0	= 120.0	24.0	36.0	12.0	24.0
A = 200.0 + 23.0 + 36.0	= 259.0	0.0	25.9	25.9	25.9
B = 200.0 + 69.9 + 12.0 + 25.9	= 307.8	0.0	0.0	92.3	30.8
S = 25.0 + 9.1 + 24.0 + 25.9 + 30.8	= 114.8	0.0	0.0	0.0	11.5
Third iteration					
F = 100.0 + 24.0	= 124.0	24.8	37.2	12.4	24.8
A = 200.0 + 25.9 + 37.2	= 263.1	0.0	26.3	26.3	26.3
B = 200.0 + 92.3 + 12.4 + 26.3	= 331.0	0.0	0.0	99.3	33.1
S = 25.0 + 11.5 + 24.8 + 26.3 + 33.1	= 120.7	0.0	0.0	0.0	12.1
Fourth iteration					
F = 100.0 + 24.8	= 124.8	25.0	37.4	12.5	25.0
A = 200.0 + 26.3 + 37.4	= 263.7	0.0	26.4	26.4	26.4
B = 200.0 + 99.3 + 12.4 + 26.4	= 338.2	0.0	0.0	99.3	33.1
S = 25.0 + 12.1 + 25.0 + 26.4 + 33.8	= 122.3	0.0	0.0	0.0	12.2
Fifth iteration					
F = 100.0 + 25.0	= 125.0	25.0	37.4	12.5	25.0
A = 200.0 + 26.4 + 37.5	= 263.9	0.0	26.4	26.4	26.4
B = 200.0 + 101.5 + 12.5 + 26.4	= 340.4	0.0	0.0	102.1	34.0
S = 25.0 + 12.2 + 25.0 + 26.4 + 34.0	= 122.6	0.0	0.0	0.0	12.3
Sixth iteration					
F = 100.0 + 25.0	= 125.0	25.0	37.4	12.5	25.0
A = 200.0 + 26.4 + 37.5	= 263.9	0.0	26.4	26.4	26.4
B = 200.0 + 102.1 + 12.5 + 26.4	= 341.0	0.0	0.0	102.3	34.1
S = 25.0 + 12.3 + 25.0 + 26.4 + 34.1	= 122.8	0.0	0.0	0.0	12.3
Seventh iteration					
F = 100.0 + 25.0	= 125.0	25.0	37.4	12.5	25.0
A = 200.0 + 26.4 + 37.5	= 263.9	0.0	26.4	26.4	26.4
B = 200.0 + 102.3 + 12.5 + 26.4	= 341.2	0.0	0.0	102.4	34.1
S = 25.0 + 12.3 + 25.0 + 26.4 + 34.1	= 122.8	0.0	0.0	0.0	12.3
Eighth iteration					
F = 100.0 + 25.0	= 125.0	25.0	37.4	12.5	25.0
A = 200.0 + 26.4 + 37.5	= 263.9	0.0	26.4	26.4	26.4
B = 200.0 + 102.4 + 12.5 + 26.4	= 341.3	0.0	0.0	102.4	34.1
S = 25.0 + 12.3 + 25.0 + 26.4 + 34.1	= 122.8	0.0	0.0	0.0	12.3
Ninth iteration					
F = 100.0 + 25.0	= 125.0	25.0	37.4	12.5	25.0
A = 200.0 + 26.4 + 37.5	= 263.9	0.0	26.4	26.4	26.4
B = 200.0 + 102.4 + 12.5 + 26.4	= 341.3	0.0	0.0	102.4	34.1
S = 25.0 + 12.3 + 25.0 + 26.4 + 34.1	= 122.8	0.0	0.0	0.0	12.3

Note: The production assumptions underlining these calculations are the same as in Tables 5–1 and 5–2.

TABLE 5–4
Numerical Examples of Convergence Using a Gauss-Seidel Iteration Method

Problem: Calculate gross production where net $a = 100$ and net $b = 60$.

| Producing Sectors | Using Sectors | | Number of Required Iterations |
	A	B	
Technology matrix 1			
A	0.1	0.0	
B	0.2	0.1	
			3
Technology matrix 2			
A	0.1	0.1	
B	0.2	0.1	
			5
Technology matrix 3			
A	0.2	0.2	
B	0.4	0.1	
			7

Note: Convergence is measured as occurring when the solution values of the gross output vector are within 0.1 of each other on two consecutive iterations.

gularized matrix, that is, the extent of the interdependencies.[3] This can be seen in Table 5–4, which features a series of 2×2 technology matrices and where the same iterative techniques as used in Table 5–3 are applied. In the three illustrations, the coefficients in the technology matrix are varied in order to increase interdependencies. Of course, if the matrix increases in size, more iterations are also required to achieve convergence.

It must be emphasized that if we change the set of net outputs, we must solve the problem again by starting from the beginning and iterating through to a new solution.

c. Inverse Matrix Method

A much more general solution to the problem at hand is based on the use of a special type of matrix called the *inverse matrix*. The inverse of the matrix [A] is labeled $[A]^{-1}$ and has the special property that if [A] is multiplied by $[A]^{-1}$, they yield an identity matrix, that is, a matrix composed all of zeros except for the diagonal running from northwest to

---

[3]Empirical comparisons of input-output tables of various nations are made by Hollis B. Chenery and T. Watanabe, "International Comparisons of the Structure of Production," *Econometrica,* 24 (October 1958), pp. 487–521. These show that the degree of interdependency (measured in several different ways) within the table increases up to a certain point with a rising level of per capita income; after this point, however, the degree of interdependency remains roughly constant.

southeast which is composed of ones. More specifically if [A] is a 3×3 matrix, then

$$[A] \times [A]^{-1} = \begin{matrix} 1 & 0 & 0 \\ 0 & 1 & 0 \\ 0 & 0 & 1 \end{matrix}$$

An analogy to this operation is found in simple arithmetic: A fraction multiplied by its inverse yields one.

A special inverse matrix for our purposes is shown in Table 5–5. Here we start with the technology matrix, calculate the so-called Leontief matrix by substracting the technology matrix from an identity matrix (see above) and then calculating the inverse of this Leontief matrix. The method by which this inverse is calculated is a bit tricky and is not necessary to know; however, the reader can find such an explanation in every elementary textbook on linear algebra; and computer programs to permit you to make such calculations are readily available.[4]

This inverse Leontief matrix is now used to solve the problem. We need merely multiply this inverse by the vector of final outputs in the manner that is shown in the lower part of Table 5–5, and out comes the answer. If we have another net output bundle that we wish to investigate, we carry out the same type of matrix multiplication and derive the answer. In short, once the inverse is obtained, we can use it in a very simple manner to derive the gross outputs necessary to obtain a bundle of given net outputs and we need neither to solve another set of simultaneous equations nor carry out a long iterative procedure again.

This method of using an inverse matrix illustrates an important property of the inverse. Each number in the inverse matrix gives the amount of gross output necessary to produce one unit of net output of the product specified by the column. For instance, to produce one net unit of finished goods, we need 0.417 units of gross agricultural production, 0.238 units of gross basic industrial production, 1.250 units of gross finished goods production, and 0.351 units of gross production of services. Similarly, to produce one net unit of services, we need only 1.111 units of gross production of services. Such calculations of gross units for each type of product necessary to obtain one net unit of some product include, of course, all the intermediate products necessary.

Once we have the gross outputs necessary to "support" the production of some bundle of net outputs, we can calculate the necessary labor and capital services to obtain such output. All we need to do is to calcu-

---

[4]Inverting a large matrix is not easy. One method that is suitable for use with a computer is to calculate the sum of the following power series: $([I] + [A] + [A]^2 + [A]^3 + [A]^4 \ldots)$. where $[I-A]$ is the matrix to be inverted, and $[I]$ is the identity matrix.

TABLE 5–5
Illustrative Leontief and Inverse Leontief Matrices

	Original Matrix: [A]			
	Using Sectors			
Producing Sectors	*A*	*B*	*F*	*S*
A Agriculture	0.1	0.0	0.3	0.0
B Basic industries	0.1	0.3	0.1	0.0
F Finished goods	0.0	0.0	0.2	0.0
S Services	0.1	0.1	0.2	0.1

	Leontief Matrix: [I − A]			
	Using Sectors			
Producing Sectors	*A*	*B*	*F*	*S*
A Agriculture	+0.9	0.0	−0.3	0.0
B Basic industries	−0.1	+0.7	+0.1	0.0
F Finished goods	0.0	0.0	+0.8	0.0
S Services	−0.1	−0.1	−0.2	+0.9

	Inverse Leontief Matrix: [I − A]$^{-1}$			
	Using Sectors			
Producing Sectors	*A*	*B*	*F*	*S*
A Agriculture	1.111	0.0	0.417	0.0
B Basic industries	0.159	1.429	0.238	0.0
F Finished goods	0.0	0.0	1.250	0.0
S Services	0.141	0.159	0.351	1.111

Using the inverse Leontief matrix, calculate the gross outputs of *A, B, F, and S* so that
    net agricultural production   = 200
    net basic industries production = 200
    net finished goods production   = 100
    net services   =   25

$A =$ (1.111 × 200) + (0.000 × 200) + (0.417 × 100) + (0.000 × 25) = 263.9
$B =$ (0.159 × 200) + (1.429 × 200) + (0.238 × 100) + (0.000 × 25) = 341.3
$F =$ (0.000 × 200) + (0.000 × 200) + (1.250 × 100) + (0.000 × 25) = 125.0
$S =$ (0.141 × 200) + (0.159 × 200) + (0.351 × 100) + (1.111 × 25) = 122.8

late from Table 5–1 the number of units of labor and capital needed to produce one unit of gross output, and then to multiply this by the total gross output. Such a calculation is performed in Table 5–6, part A.

It should be clear that the use of an inverse input-output matrix could be a powerful tool in the hands of planners to solve the "net-gross" problem that is discussed above. If it is not clear, it would be useful at this point to reread the last few pages, for the remainder of the discussion in the next pages builds upon such an understanding.

TABLE 5–6
Exercises Using Input-Output Techniques

A. Calculation of Required Factors of Production for Each Production Sector

Desired Net Output	Gross Output	Fixed Coefficients		Required Amount	
		Labor	Capital	Labor	Capital
a = 200	A = 263.9	0.6	0.1	158.3	26.4
b = 200	B = 341.3	0.2	0.4	68.3	136.5
f = 100	F = 125.0	0.1	0.1	12.5	12.5
s = 25	S = 122.8	0.8	0.1	98.2	12.3
Total				337.3	187.7

B. Calculation of Effects of Capacity Constraints

Desired Net Output	Required Gross Output	Capacity Constraints	Ratio of Capacity Constraints to Required Gross Output	Maximum Net Output with Same Proportions
a = 200	A = 263.9	150.0	0.568	a = 113.7
b = 200	B = 341.3	300.0	0.879	b = 113.7
f = 100	F = 125.0	115.0	0.920	f = 56.8
s = 25	S = 122.8	90.0	0.733	s = 14.4
	Labor = 337.3	380.0	1.126	
	Capital = 187.7	145.0	0.772	

C. Calculation of Prices if Service Prices Increase 50 Percent

Key assumption: All sectors pass on all service price increases.

Amount of Direct and Indirect Usage of Services to Produce $1 of Goods (from inverse matrix, Table 5–5)	Additional Costs Caused by Service Price Increase
Agricultural goods	.141	.0705
Basic industrial goods	.159	.0795
Final goods	.351	.1755

Note: This table is based on the production structure presented in Tables 5–1 and 5–2.

2. Three Examples of Input-Output Analysis

Input-output techniques can be used to solve a large variety of other planning problems. To gain a more concrete idea of such potentialities, three problems for which I-O techniques have actually been used are presented below. Many other types of problems could have been selected as examples.

a. Feasibility Problems

Although a planner can use an input-output analysis to determine a consistent plan (i.e., a consistency between net and gross output bundles), the plan may not be feasible because the economy lacks either the necessary factors of production or the necessary capacity to produce a given gross output. However, several methods are available to examine such problems in a systematic fashion.

In the third column of part B in Table 5–6, both types of capacity constraints are present. For instance, given the amount of land in the economy, a gross production of only 150 units of *A* is possible. For other reasons, only 300*B,* 115*F,* and so forth, can be produced. Moreover, the economy has only 380 units of labor and 145 units of capital. Obviously, the net output specified in the first columns is impossible to produce, not only because there is not enough productive capacity in any sector but also because there is not enough capital. The ratio of the capacity constraints to the desired gross production is presented in the fourth column.

If we wish to have a production pattern where the goods are produced in the same proportions as that shown in the first column, then it is necessary to scale back net output plans. In this case of fixed output proportions, the greatest constraint (agriculture) determines how much this scaleback must be, namely, to a level 56.6 percent of that which was originally desired. If this is carried out, there would be an unused capacity for production in all sectors except agriculture.

Two other ways to circumvent such problems must also be noted. The country could enter the world market and import some of the goods, while exporting others. Or else, the planners could choose another pattern of net output that would more closely correspond to actual production capabilities. But this would mean that they might be producing more of some goods than they actually think worthwhile, an undesirable situation unless the goods can be exported to obtain desired goods.

b. Problems Concerning the Impact of Price Changes

What are the ramifications of a price increase in some product such as oil on the prices of goods and services from other sectors? This type of planning problem requires us not only to know how much oil is used in producing goods and services in other sectors but also more indirect linkages such as how much oil is used in producing other inputs to a given sector. This problem, which came into prominence after the rapid oil price rises in the 1970s, can be easily handled with input-output techniques.

To make the discussion more concrete, let us assume that service workers have been successful in obtaining a wage increase so that the price of services rises 50 percent. Let us also assume that the entire impact of a price increase is passed forward to the consumer, that is, that the price of any product using such services as an input rises an amount equal to the additional costs of obtaining such service inputs. This assumption requires us to know how many services are incorporated directly and indirectly (i.e., embodied in other inputs, or in the inputs to the inputs, etc.) in goods of other sectors.

From Table 5–2 we know, for instance, that for every dollar of agricultural production, $0.10 of services are directly used as inputs. We also know from the inverse matrix presented in Table 5–5 that for every dollar of agricultural production, $0.141 of services are directly and indirectly embodied (the extra 0.041 reflecting the services embodied in all the other inputs).

After the service price increase, the $0.141 worth of services will cost 50 percent more, that is, an additional $0.0705. Since we have assumed that all price increases are passed on, $1 of agricultural goods will now cost $1.0705. Similar calculations of the impact of a 50 percent service price increase are carried out for the other sectors in Table 5–6, part C.

A quite similar type of problem is the determination of the impact of a tax on the products of one sector on the prices in other sectors. It can be handled in exactly the same way.

It must be emphasized that this type of solution requires us to assume that the price increase is passed forward in its entirety. If a sector "absorbs" part of the price increase of its inputs and does not pass then on, then appropriate adjustments must be made in our calculations. Further, as in all input-output calculations, we must assume that no substitution between inputs takes place, that is, that inputs are combined in fixed amounts. In the short run this may be a reasonable assumption; in the long run it is not. Further, after a series of price increases have been made, the table gets out of date since it is calculated in prices that have subsequently been changed. Therefore, input-output tables must be constantly updated and the results of such calculations cannot be assumed to cover the long run unless special adjustments have been made.

c.   Problems Arising from Considerations
     of Time and Space

Up to now we have assumed that capital magically appears in the economy so that we do not need to worry about investment problems. We can introduce more realistic assumptions into the input-output analysis by taking into account the fact that capital lasts only a few periods and by calculating an input-output system that has a temporal dimension such that goods in different time periods are considered to be different goods.

An example of how such an input-output table would be set up is shown in the top part of Table 5–7 for an economy with consumer goods (A) and capital goods (B). Capital goods produced in period 2 (B_2) are used in the production of A_2, A_3, B_2, and B_3; capital goods produced in

TABLE 5–7
Different Types of Input-Output Tables

A. The Technology Matrix of an Intertemporal Table

Products: A, B
Time periods: 1, 2, 3, 4

				Inputs				
Outputs	A_1	B_1	A_2	B_2	A_3	B_3	A_4	B_4
A_1	a_{11}	a_{12}						
B_1	a_{21}	a_{22}	a_{23}	a_{24}				
A_2			a_{33}	a_{34}				
B_2			a_{43}	a_{44}	a_{45}	a_{46}		
A_3					a_{55}	a_{56}		
B_3					a_{65}	a_{66}	a_{67}	a_{68}
A_4							a_{77}	a_{78}
B_4							a_{87}	a_{88}

B. The Technology Matrix of a Regional Input-Output Table

Products: A, B, C, D
Regions: 1, 2

				Inputs				
Outputs	A_1	A_2	B_1	B_2	C_1	C_2	D_1	D_2
A_1	a_{11}	a_{21}	a_{31}	a_{41}	a_{51}	a_{61}	a_{71}	a_{81}
A_2	a_{21}	a_{22}	a_{32}	a_{42}	a_{52}	a_{62}	a_{72}	a_{82}
B_1	a_{31}	a_{23}	a_{33}	a_{43}	a_{53}	a_{63}	a_{73}	a_{83}
B_2	a_{41}	a_{24}	a_{34}	a_{44}	a_{54}	a_{64}	a_{74}	a_{84}
C_1	a_{51}	a_{25}	a_{35}	a_{45}	a_{55}	a_{65}	a_{75}	a_{85}
C_2	a_{61}	a_{26}	a_{36}	a_{46}	a_{56}	a_{66}	a_{76}	a_{86}
D_1	a_{71}	a_{27}	a_{37}	a_{47}	a_{57}	a_{67}	a_{77}	a_{87}
D_2	a_{81}	a_{28}	a_{38}	a_{48}	a_{58}	a_{68}	a_{78}	a_{88}

period 3 (B_3) are used in the production of A_3, A_4, B_3, and B_4; and so forth. Although consumer goods are primarily end products, they may also be used in production. We can calculate a technology matrix in exactly the same manner as before.

This kind of table can be used to work out a plan where we start with a given level of output of consumption and investment goods, where we wish to end up with a higher level of output of consumption and investment goods, and where we examine various mixes of consumption and investment goods in the intermediate periods to see if they are consistent with the long-term goals. Again it must be emphasized that a number of rather rigid assumptions are required to make such an analysis.

Another way in which input-output analysis is used is in analyzing the spatial impact of particular changes in the vector of final goods. To carry out such a task, divide the country into various regions and distinguish between goods and services produced in these different regions, for example, agriculture produced in region 1 (A_1), agriculture produced in region 2 (A_2), and so forth. We must make the further assumption that the proportion of inputs for any given sector that comes from any given region does not change (i.e., that for producing A_2, X percent of input B will always come from region R, no matter what the final level of production of A_2 might be).

The technology matrix of a country with four goods and two regions (respectively 1 and 2) is shown in the lower part of Table 5–7. If we wish to know how much of each good will be produced in each region, given a final output vector of A_1, A_2, B_1, B_2 . . . , we can apply the same input-output techniques as described above. The planners can also experiment with different final output vectors to see what combinations would bring total production in the various regions up to prespecified limits.

3. An Evaluation of Input-Output Systems of Planning

Consider an economy that is centrally planned and administered by means of an input-output approach. Also assume that the information system of the economy is such that the table is always up to date. How would such an economy match up against the performance indicators discussed in Chapter 2?

For many of the indicators we do not have sufficient information to make a judgment. Unless we know the division of final output between consumption and investment, we cannot say anything about the growth rate of the economy. Unless we have a good deal more information about how policy decisions in this economy (especially in the monetary sector) are made, we cannot make any evaluation of the stability of its prices or production. Unless we have more information about the distribution of wages and also the ownership of capital, we can say nothing about the distribution of income. Unless we have some information about how the vector of final consumption goods is chosen, we cannot make any judgments about consumer sovereignty in the economy. However, we can make some important judgments about the static efficiency of this economy.

Certainly the use of an input-output approach leads to a consistent pattern of production; that is, the supply of each intermediate good or service is equal to demand. However, it is highly unlikely that the economy achieves static efficiency for none of the three marginal criteria underlying such efficiency are met except in quite unusual circumstances.

a. Equality of Marginal Productivities

We have no assurance that the marginal productivity of a given factor of production would be the same for all producers of that product or, for that matter, that any factor would be fully utilized by any producer. Use of the input-output approach does not embody any mechanism that would lead to an allocation of factors of production to meet this condition.

b. Equality of Marginal Rates of Substitution

We have no assurance that the marginal rate of substitution between any two factors would be the same for any two producers. This is because the input-output table is built on the assumption that there is only one method by which any product can be produced, while in reality the producers have a much wider range of technologies to select. For example, the I-O table may embody a very capital-intensive method of producing electricity (e.g., hydropower), but a more labor-intensive method (e.g., thermal power) might give a more appropriate marginal rate of substitution of labor for capital, given the overall factor ratios in the economy. Similarly, use of the table is based on the assumption that no substitution between material inputs (e.g., aluminum for iron, plastic for wood) can be made, which does not seem realistic.

c. Equality of Marginal Rates of Transformation

We have no assurance that the marginal rate of transformation between any two products for any two producers would be the same. Use of the input-output approach does not embody any mechanism that would lead to such a condition being met.

Suppose that the input-output table is constructed on information obtained from enterprise managers who realize that their plans will be based upon such a table. They have an incentive to provide false information so as to achieve "easier" plans; and any table built on such basic information may not even lead to consistency of the pattern of production. This is not just a theoretial possibility. For instance, the Czechoslovak price reform in the mid-1960s was based on calculations made from such an input-output table and, to achieve monetary balance, was supposed to lead to a given level of enterprise profits. The managers, however, had overstated their input needs in a manner that led to a level of overall enterprise profits several times higher than planned—and to a severe inflationary potential.

Although such a nonprice method of resource allocation appears to lead to some important static inefficiences, we need also to consider some of the inefficiencies arising from price systems before judgments about the relative degrees of efficiency can be made. This task is postponed until the next chapter.

C. Actual Physical Allocation Systems

1. The Soviet Variant

The Soviet Union does not allocate raw materials and intermediate products by means of a price mechanism but rather by physical allocation methods. Although they have used input-output techniques for certain small-scale planning and allocation projects during the 1970s and early 1980s, they do not seem to employ such an approach for the economy as a whole. Rather, they use a somewhat different method which, however, can be easily understood by reference to the I-O approach.

In the Soviet Union the highest political body issues guidelines for the production goals in physical terms for some of the key commodities. It should be emphasized that these goals are for gross, not net, production. The central planning commission then draws up an annual plan for gross production of about 1,000 of the most important groups of goods and services, using as the basis of their calculations *material balances* (explained below) of these commodity groups. The goals are then divided according to the administrative units which are responsible (e.g., ministries, republics, etc.) and these governmental bodies, in turn, subdivide the plan goals and send them to still lower administrative units until very specific production and other plan goals arrive at the enterprises, which must try to implement them. The enterprises then send up a *counterplan* containing their raw material and other resource requirements, as well as counterproposals for appropriate enterprise goals. These, in turn, are aggregated and sent to the central planning commission which makes further adjustments to bring supply and demand requirements into balance so that the overall plan is consistent. At this point, the final plan is promulgated, subdivided according to administrative units, and soon sent to the enterprises.[5]

The key planning tool in drawing up consistent supply plans are *material balances,* which are essentially pieces of paper giving the various sources and uses of each commodity. A typical material balance is presented in Table 5–8. They can be drawn up in either physical or

---

[5]A detailed source of information about these matters is Herbert S. Levine, "The Centralized Planning of Supply in the Soviet Union," in U.S. Congress, Joint Economic Committee, *Comparisons of the United States and Soviet Economies* (Washington, D.C.:GPO, 1959), Part 1, pp. 151–76. Although somewhat outdated, it provides an extremely useful and detailed view of the process. A more recent view is provided by Michael Ellman, *Soviet Planning Today* (Cambridge: Cambridge University Press, 1971), pp. 60–95.

TABLE 5–8
A Material Balance of a Product

Sources of Supply	Uses
1. Production	1. As an input into production or construction
2. Imports	2. Exports
3. Other sources (e.g., scrap for metal)	3. Other final use:
	a. Personal consumption
	b. Government
	c. Investment
4. Drawing down of inventories reserves, and stocks	4. Building up of inventories, reserves and stocks

value units and at any level of the planning hierarchy. If stated in value terms (e.g., X rubles of durable household products), they can be drawn up at any level of aggregation. At the Central Planning Commission in the Soviet Union, anywhere from 800 to 1,600 of these balances are calculated; at the ministerial level, another 5,000 or so are calculated. Such material balances are used throughout the planning process—at the beginning, to obtain consistency in the preliminary plan; and at the end, to obtain consistency of the final plan.

The difficult part of such a planning system is bringing the various material balances into a consistent whole so that demand and supply for each commodity category are balanced. A two-step process is required.

First, estimates must be made of the technological coefficients linking the final products to the intermediate products and the factors of production that are necessary to produce them; for example, a ton of steel requires X tons of coal, Y tons of iron ore, and Z labor hours. In an input-output table, of course, these coefficients are contained in the technology matrix. In the material balance system these coefficients are known and maintained by the administrators of each balance; however, such coefficients for every commodity are not formally connected in any type of table.

Second, supply and demand for each product must somehow be brought into equality. Suppose the officials in charge of the material balance for steel cannot bring sources of production (supply) and uses (demand) into equality without producing more which, in turn, requires the production of 1 million more tons of coal and 2 million tons of iron ore. They might telephone the officials in charge of coal and iron ore and ask them for these additional supplies. These officials, in turn, would determine how many additional inputs they would need and would make the required telephone calls to the appropriate suppliers.

If capacity constraints are not met, such a method of operation would work in the same manner as the iteration procedure described in

Table 5–3; after enough iterations, the system would converge into a consistent solution. In other words, the officials in such a planning hierarchy might perform the motions of a gigantic bureaucratic iteration machine without being aware of the overall mechanism in which they are engaged.[6] This is an exact parallel to the market economy in which many participants may operate in the market without ever being completely aware of the overall market mechanism by which supplies and demands are all goods are simultaneously brought into equality. The iteration mechanism described previously is the parallel to the general equilibrium mechanism for a price system that is described by economic theorists.

A second method of bringing the system into balance is sometimes called "squeezing the coefficients." It is based on the assumption that the managers are engaged in *strategic behavior* and are probably overstating their input norms in order to obtain an "easier" plan. For instance, a steel enterprise may claim that it needs C tons of coal, rather than the B tons that it actually needs, because the additional coal may serve to cushion any shortfalls in coal that might accidently occur (or so that extra coal would be at hand to trade to the supplier of another input in short supply).

Assuming such behavior, the officials in charge of the material balance can "increase" production without increasing the need for inputs simply by raising the output plan and leaving all else the same, thereby increasing the pressure on the enterprise managers to save on raw materials. Although such a method is drastic, it often acts to reduce hidden reserves. Of course, it is also a risky procedure because the revised plan might be impossible to fulfill and thus, bottlenecks would be created. However, to minimize the impact of this risk of bottlenecks, state reserves can be maintained and, furthermore, a priority system for allocating inputs can be set up if shortages occur.

This bureaucratic iteration procedure appears cumbersome and time consuming. However, several features of the Soviet system reduce such ill effects and, further, allow greater static efficiency to be achieved:

a. Use of Multiple Techniques of Production

An input-output approach assumes only one technique of production; therefore, a single capacity constraint can halt production of all other commodities requiring the particular good as an input. In the

---

[6]The author had the experience of describing the iteration method of bringing a system of material balances into equilibrium to three planners from the German Democratic Republic (East Germany). The first declared that the system in that nation worked in exactly such a manner; the second denied it categorically; and the third confessed that he didn't understand what iterations were all about. The three German economists argued so violently among themselves about the issue that no definite conclusion was reached.

material balance system, if the officials in charge of the balance are unable to obtain more of a given input, they might try to obtain a substitute, for example, plastic for wood, or iron for steel.[7] Such substitution reduces the limiting nature of capacity constraints and improves the static efficiency of the system.

b. Supplementing the I-O Approach with Other Approaches

In making decisions about the choice of technique for particular production processes, it is possible for the planners to make different types of calculations to choose least-cost combinations; these, in turn, can be inserted into the decisions at various iterations so that greater static efficiency can be achieved.

c. Starting from Gross, Rather than Net Production

For many important industrial commodities the Soviet planners start with targets for gross, rather than net, production. In the iteration process to balance the system, this type of approach simplifies the balancing process. Of course, at the same time the specification of the best pattern of production for final consumption becomes more difficult.

d. Reducing the Number of Iterations

Although the Soviet planners do not employ input-output tables in their planning, they have not been content to follow exactly the tedious iteration procedure described above, for it would take an enormous amount of time. That is, an iteration involving 1000 commodities would take considerable time and effort to complete, and many iterations to balance the system might last almost as long as planning period.[8] However, many shortcuts are available. Certainly it is not necessary to start from the beginning of every iteration, but rather from the level of production already achieved after taking into account existing shortfalls. Essentially this reduces the problem to maintaining balance at the margin of production, that is, the additions to current production. Their use of extrapolation techniques also leads to further reduction in the number of iterations to balance the system.

---

[7]These issues are discussed with a number of illustrations from the experience of Poland by John Michael Montias, "Planning with Material Balances," *American Economic Review,* 49 (December 1959), pp. 963–85; and his *Central Planning in Poland* (New Haven, Conn.: Yale University Press, 1962), chap. 1.

[8]An interesting analysis of this problem is presented by Michael Manove, "A Model of Soviet-Type Economic Planning," *American Economic Review,* 61 (June 1971), pp. 390–407.

In short, the Soviet material balance system provides greater flexibility than an I-O approach and it also permits greater static efficiency to be achieved. However, the system may still lie far from the production possibility curve.

2. Physical Allocation Systems in Capitalist Economies

In many wartime situations, administrators of capitalist economies have compiled material balances of particularly scarce commodities in order to allocate them where they are most needed. Although it is difficult to determine from existing descriptions of these procedures exactly how such systems were brought into balance, you might suspect that some variant of the iteration technique described above might have been in operation.

Input-output techniques can also be used in a variety of ways; some of the most important of these deserve brief mention.

The central government in a capitalist nation can use I-O techniques to investigate the impact of a major structural change upon various industries and regions so that appropriate measures can be taken to minimize the economic dislocations during the transition period. Such a structural change could be brought about by a mobilization for a war (one of the major early uses of the I-O approach was for this purpose) or by a disarmament and transfer of expenditures and resources to other sectors.

Another policy problem arises when the government is interested in alleviating a balance of payments problem by subsidizing certain industries to increase domestic production. Using an input-output technique, it can determine the total "import content" of particular types of production and take appropriate measures. Given the scarcity of foreign exchange in economically less developed nations, input-output techniques have provided a major foundation for their development planning.[9]

Still another use of I-O methods is to project the demand for intermediate products. It is well known that the demand for such products is a function of the demand for final products, whose production can be predicted by means of information on income elasticities of demand and some estimates of growth of income and also exports. Using such information about production of final goods and an inverse input-output matrix (these are readily available for many nations), the gross production pattern for all goods can be determined.

It should be clear that use of such I-O techniques in capitalist,

---

[9]Some such methods are discussed by Chenery and Clark, *Interindustry Economics*, chap. 11.

market economies can bring about a consistent production pattern, but they do not necessarily lead to static efficiency and, thus, must be supplemented by other planning techniques.

D. Special Topics in Nonprice Planning and Control

This section provides a brief overview of three special topics concerning nonprice planning and control. Although much of the discussion found in the economic literature about these topics is highly technical, the basic ideas are relatively simple and useful insights into the operation of different economic systems can be obtained by paying brief attention to some of the leading ideas.

1. Linear Programming

Input-output techniques are based on the assumption that there is only one method by which a good or service can be produced. However, physical allocation methods permitting the choice of different production methods and the systematic introduction of various types of constraints in production have received considerable attention in both East and West in recent years since such techniques permit greater static efficiency to be achieved.

Linear programming is one such technique and involves three steps. First, we must specify a linear *objective function* to be maximized or minimized. Such an objective function might be an index of various goods to be produced (in which case the objective function should be maximized) or an index of various costs of production (in which case the function should be minimized). The "linear" part means that the objective function cannot contain squared terms, cross-products, or logarithmic transformations but rather should be set up like a standard index number formula which sums the product of different weights (e.g., prices or costs) and different quantity of goods or factors.

Second, we must specify the productive relationships in a linear fashion, that is, different fixed combinations of inputs that permit a given amount of the good to be produced. Any production process featuring considerable substitution of capital for labor can be broken up into a bundle of different processes, each with a different fixed proportion of capital and labor.

Third, we must specify constraints on the system, for example, that only so many machines and so much skilled labor are available.

The mathematical process to solve the problem cannot be described simply. However, to provide a concrete illustration, let us consider the data in Table 5–9, which demonstrates a particular real-life application

TABLE 5–9
A Simple Linear Programming Problem

A. Map of Retail Stores (R) and Wholesale Outlets (W)

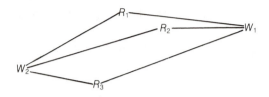

B. Unit Transportation Costs (TC)

	R_1	R_2	R_3
W_1	6	3	8
W_2	6	8	4

C. Problem (G_{ij} = goods shipped from i to j)

Minimize $TC = 6 G_{11} + 3 G_{12} + 8 G_{13} + 6 G_{21} + 8 G_{21} + 4 G_{23}$ subject to the following constraints:

	Subproblem A	*Subproblem B*
Wholesale Capacity Constraints	$\begin{cases} G_{11} + G_{12} + G_{13} \le 10 \\ G_{21} + G_{22} + G_{23} \le 50 \end{cases}$	$\begin{cases} G_{11} + G_{12} + G_{13} \le 40 \\ G_{21} + G_{22} + G_{23} \le 20 \end{cases}$
Retail Capacity Constraints	$\begin{cases} G_{11} + G_{21} \le 30 \\ G_{12} + G_{22} \le 10 \\ G_{13} + G_{23} \le 20 \end{cases}$	$\begin{cases} G_{11} + G_{21} \le 30 \\ G_{12} + G_{22} \le 10 \\ G_{13} + G_{23} \le 20 \end{cases}$

D. Solutions

$G_{11} = 0$	$G_{12} = 10$	$G_{13} = 0$	$G_{11} = 30$	$G_{12} = 10$	$G_{13} = 0$
$G_{21} = 30$	$G_{22} = 0$	$G_{23} = 20$	$G_{21} = 0$	$G_{22} = 0$	$G_{23} = 20$

E. Shadow Prices (P_{ij} = unit prices from wholesale outlet i)

$P_1 = 10$	$P_1 = 10$
$(130/18) < P_2 < 10$	$10 < P_2 < (180/14)$

Total unit costs (C_{ij} = unit costs of store i buying from wholesaler j = $P_i + G_{ij}$)

If $P_1 = 10$	If $P_2 = 8$	If $P_2 = 12$
$C_{11} = 16$	$C_{12} = 14$	$C_{22} = 18$
$C_{21} = 13$	$C_{22} = 16$	$C_{22} = 20$
$C_{31} = 18$	$C_{32} = 12$	$C_{32} = 16$

and provides some numbers. Several other illustrations in a geometrical form are presented in Appendix E.

In Table 5–9 there are two wholesale outlets (*W*) and three retail stores (*R*) and we want to minimize the total transportation costs to move the goods from the warehouses to the stores. Panel A of the table gives a map of the retail and wholesale units. Panel B presents the transportation costs (derived from distances between points and the average cost of shipment) between each store and warehouse. Each path between a warehouse and a retail store represents one technique of production and we must, therefore, select the amount of goods shipped and the particular production techniques (i.e., routes) that minimize total costs.

Panel C presents the objective function to be minimized, which is merely total transportation costs (namely the sum of the units shipped from each warehouse to each retail store multiplied by the unit transportation costs for each route). The constraints to the system are also specified in the lower part of panel C and consist of specification of the capacity at each warehouse and store. In subproblem A, warehouse 1 has a total capacity of 10 and warehouse 2 has a total capacity of 50, so that the amount of goods shipped from each can not exceed these limits. The warehouse constraints in subproblem B are different. In addition, no store can receive more than its capacity, so there are three more constraints on the solution.

The solution of these two linear programming problems are shown in panel D and are given in the form of how many goods should be shipped on which routes. It should be noted that the two solutions are different because the constraints in the two problems are different.

The central planners can, if they wish, order each warehouse to ship its goods according to the pattern derived from these solutions. However, in solving the linear programming problem, a set of prices emerge (*shadow prices*) which are presented in panel E. If prices are placed on the goods from each warehouse according to the specified inequalities and if stores are told to order from each warehouse in such a manner as to minimize their individual total costs (transportation plus goods), they will arrive at the same solution as if the planner had ordered them according to the result of the linear programming problem. For instance, if the price of goods in warehouse 1 is 10, then total unit costs (price of goods + transportation costs) = 16. Now if the price of goods from warehouse 2 is 8, then according to the data presented, stores 1 and 3 will buy from warehouse 2, and store 2 from warehouse 1, the same solution derived directly. Similarly, if the price of goods from warehouse 2 is 12, only store 3 will buy from it.

Thus if shadow prices are correctly specified, the planners do not need to send plans to each retail outlet. They merely promulgate the prices, reward the retail store for maximizing profits, and sit back. In other words, solving a physical allocation problem permits indirect, rather than direct, administrative methods to be employed. Further, in most cases this system achieves a much greater degree of static efficiency than if an input-output approach were employed.

However, the use of such a technique requires a great deal of information. In many cases such information flows can be minimized by structuring a "dialogue" between the center and the enterprises so that the solution to the linear programming problem is achieved iteratively.

We cannot easily evaluate the usage of linear programming techniques in terms of success achieved until we can place valuation on the cost of information and information processing, as well as the importance of arriving at a rapid solution. Two other factors, however, should also be added. *First,* many economic processes involve nonlinearities, so that the use of linear approximations may not allow us to obtain complete efficiency. However, although we have no assurance that the marginal conditions discussed above will be completely met (especially if the iterative process is cut off before completion), we do know that in all normal cases, the final solution will be more efficient than that achieved with input-output methods. *Second,* solving a linear programming problem becomes very difficult if many products, technologies, and factors of production are involved; therefore, the use of such techniques is confined to fairly small-scale problems. Nevertheless, linear programming techniques have been applied to solve problems of the allocation of productive resources in a variety of contexts in both East and West.

2. Price versus Quantity Signals

If a central government is attempting to direct the activities of an enterprise, it can send a quantity signal (produce Q amount of product Y) or a price signal (you must sell product Y at price P). Where there are no uncertainties and where the central government has complete information about the demand and cost curves facing the firm, it does not seem to make any difference whether a price or quantity signal is given since both can yield the same result. If, however, there are uncertainties about these curves so that the signal is given in one period and the enterprise obeys in the next period (after both the cost curve and the demand curve have shifted in ways which the government could not predict), special costs are incurred with both types of signals.

An illustration of such a situation is provided in Figure 5–1, where the firm is a monopolist, where the subscripts 1 and 2 represent respectively the time period when the signal is given and when the enterprise responds to the signal, and *MC* and *MR* represent respectively the mar-

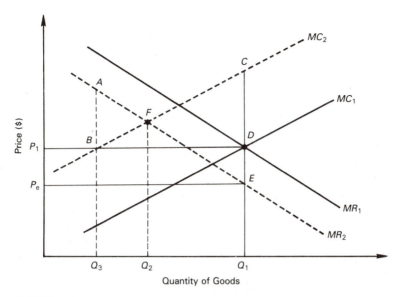

FIGURE 5–1
Costs of Price and Quantity Commands Under Conditions of Uncertainty

ginal costs of production and the marginal revenues received by the firm (which reflect the marginal benefits to the consumers of the product).[10]

If the enterprise is left to its own devices, it would choose to produce where the marginal cost and revenue curves intersect, i.e., at point D in time period 1 and point F in time period 2. In both cases the marginal benefits and costs to society are equal.

If the government imposes a quantity plan of Q_1 and if the marginal revenue curve is MR_2, Q_1 is sold at price P_e since at this point the quantity demanded equals the (planned) quantity supplied. There is a loss to society as a whole shown by triangle *FCE,* which represents the sum of the excess marginal costs over marginal benefits, given the changed cost and revenue curves.

If, instead, the government imposes price P_1, the total amount of production changes to Q_3 in time period 2 since the marginal revenue curve (represented by the fixed price line) intersects MC_2 at B. In this case, the loss to the society as a whole is shown by the triangle *FAB,* which represents the excess of marginal benefits over marginal costs which were not achieved because the enterprise set production to maximize its profits at the specified price.

[10]This illustration is drawn from Martin L. Weitzman, "Prices vs. Quantities," *Review of Economic Studies* 41, No. 1 (January 1974), pp. 50–65. See also Gary Wynn Yohe, "Comparisons of Price and Quantity Controls: A Survey," *Journal of Comparative Economics,* 1, No. 3 (September 1977), pp. 213–35.

Whether *FAB* or *FCE* is greater depends, of course, on the shape of the cost and benefit curves and their displacements. In some cases, a price signal on the part of the government would have resulted in less welfare; in other cases, a quantity signal. In the general way that the problem is set up, no decision about the superiority of one type of signal over another can be made.

In the example given, it must be pointed out that greater welfare could be achieved by no central interference at all so that production is at point *D* in time period 1 and point *F* in time period 2. However, suppose that the type of "product" that is produced is air pollution. Since the firm cannot determine the costs to society of such pollution, we do not want it to make the decision about how much pollution is produced. However, to reduce pollution should the government send the enterprise a quantity signal (e.g., you should not release more than *X* tons of sulfur dioxide into the atmosphere) or a price signal (for every ton of sulfur dioxide that you release into the air, you must pay a tax of $*Y*)? Although a majority of economists favor a price signal, most governments have opted for quantity signals. The relative costs of each, given the uncertainties about determining marginal cost and revenue curves in the future, are far from clear.

3.   Other Nonprice Controls

A very new field of research (references are given in the bibliography) is the investigation of the impact of nonprice controls in organizations. Although many enterprises operate in a market with freely fluctuating prices, they generally do not permit prices of various services and resources to fluctuate within their organization. Labor is allocated physically (worker *A* is sent to department *X* from department *Y*), rather than by a bidding system. Office space is allocated according to certain rules, rather than having executives rent them at prices so that the market is cleared. Decisions about production are made on the basis of changes in inventories of finished goods and new orders, rather than by changing some type of internal price for the product and inducing changes in this manner. Changing the example, one American graduate school of Business Administration has tried to allocate spaces in popular classes by giving each student a certain amount of scrip and having them bid on places in these classes, with the price set so that the number of students would be equal to the number of chairs in the class. However, most universities do not believe the net benefits of such an internal price system outweigh those of other allocation methods.

Although a number of theoretical properties of organizations in which physical allocation methods lead to greater efficiencies than price allocation methods have been identified, we still do not have sufficient empirical evidence to warrant further discussion of the topic. This largely unexplored territory provides a fascinating area for pioneering work, for no guidebooks are yet available.

E. Final Remarks

The allocation of factors of production and intermediate products by physical methods raises a number of problems that increase in difficulty as the economy becomes more complex and interdependent. Discussion in this chapter has focused primarily upon input-output techniques. However, other methods are also more briefly discussed such as the Soviet material balance system and linear programming.

Although input-output techniques are both simple and powerful, they are based on a number of drastic simplifying assumptions—for example, that production for a given product is carried out with only one production technique; and that for any product, all inputs enter the process in fixed proportions to each other. With the use of iterative techniques or inverse matrices, a consistent and feasible pattern of production can be determined; however, the static efficiency of the resulting solution may be quite unimpressive.

Flexibility in an input-output type of planning can be introduced in a variety of ways, of which the material balance system used in some countries of Eastern Europe illustrates one such method. The planners bring a set of supply and demand balances into a consistent pattern through a bureaucratic procedure resembling the process of solving a matrix problem through iteration. New techniques can be introduced when bottlenecks are required; further, balance is sometimes achieved by other techniques such as "squeezing the coefficients."

A more sophisticated tool of planning and coordination in physical terms is linear programming. Such a technique requires more data for solution and more computational work; therefore, such techniques cannot now be used for detailed planning on a nationwide basis. Such a technique has several advantages: First, greater static efficiency can usually be achieved than with the use of input-output techniques. Second, solution of such a problem results in a set of prices (shadow prices) which, if promulgated under certain circumstances, can lead to the physical solution provided by the linear programming problem without any orders being given.

No advanced economy relies completely on physical allocation mechanisms to obtain its pattern of production. Nevertheless, it should be clear from this chapter that extensive use of such techniques into decision making at a central level can radically change the nature of operation of the economic system. The impact on the performance of that economy is more problematic. As we saw in Chapters 3 and 4, growth and stability of production do not seem to be greatly affected; whether static efficiency is affected is explored in Chapter 6.

SUGGESTED READINGS

A. Input-Output Analysis and Some Applications

1. Hollis B. Chenery and Paul G. Clark, *Interindustry Economics* (New York: John Wiley, 1959), chaps. 1–2. This is a clear and comprehensive explanation of input-output analysis.

2. An interesting application of I-O analysis is Wassily W. Leontief and Marven Hoffenberg, "The Economic Effects of Disarmament," *Scientific American*, 104 (April 1961), pp. 47–55. Regional aspects of the same problem are investigated by Walter Isard and Eugene W. Schooler, "An Economic Analysis of Local and Regional Impacts of Reduction of Military Expenditures," *Peace Research Society Papers*, 1 (1964), pp. 15–45. International impacts of such measures are explored with such I-O techniques in Emile Benoit, ed., *Disarmament and World Economic Interdependence* (New York: Columbia University Press, 1967).

3. A quite different application of input-output analysis is James H. Noren and F. Douglas Whitehouse, "Soviet Industry in the 1971–75 Plan," in U.S. Congress, Joint Economic Committee, *Soviet Economic Prospects for the Seventies* (Washington, D.C.: GPO, 1973), pp. 206–46. This shows how I-O analysis can be used to spot possible inconsistencies in a Soviet five-year plan. Input-output analysis has been put to a variety of other uses. Several useful international surveys are International Conference on Input-Output Techniques, H. Brody and and A. Carter, eds., *Input-Output Techniques* (Amsterdam: North Holland, 1972); and International Conference on Input-Output Techniques, Karen R. Polenske and Jiří V. Školka, eds., *Advances in Input-Output Analysis* (Cambridge, Mass: Ballinger, 1976).

B. An Overall View of Physical Allocation in the Soviet Economy

1. Alec Nove, *The Soviet Economic System* (London: Allen and Unwin, 1978), chap. 4, pp. 85–118. This reviews problems of planning from the viewpoint of the firm and its administration.

2. R. W. Davies, "Economic Planning in the USSR," in Morris Bornstein, ed., *Comparative Economic Systems: Models and Cases,* 4th ed. (Homewood, Ill.: Richard D. Irwin, 1979), pp. 206–37. This article covers some of the same materials as Nove, but provides an historical perspective in order to show the rationale of some of the changes.

3. Michael Ellman, *Planning Problems in the U.S.S.R.* (Cambridge: Cambridge University Press, 1973). A somewhat difficult but informed and interesting review of the debates about mathetical planning techniques in the Soviet Union.

C. A Detailed View of Soviet Quantity Planning

1. Michael Ellman, *Soviet Planning Today* (Cambridge: Cambridge University Press, 1971), chap. 6, pp. 60–95, and app. 2, pp. 101–105. This is a highly condensed but informative discussion that cannot be read quickly.

2. Albina Tretyakova and Igor Birman, "Input-Output Analysis in the USSR," *Soviet Studies,* 28 (April 1976), pp. 157–86. The authors are emigré planners who write from an insider's viewpoint.

3. Gertrude E. Schroeder, "The 'Reform' of the Supply System in Soviet Industry," *Soviet Studies,* 24 (July 1972), pp. 97–120. This article overlaps somewhat with the Ellman essay but also contains some useful new information.

4. Herbert S. Levine, "Pressure and Planning in the Soviet Economy," in Morris Bornstein and Daniel Fusfeld, eds., *The Soviet Economy,* 4th ed. (Homewood, Ill.: Richard D. Irwin, 1970), pp. 43–61.

5. John Michael Montias, "Planning with Material Balances," *American Economic Review,* 49, No. 5 (December 1959), pp. 963–85. This article shows how flexibility can be introduced into a materials balance system.

6. Michael Manove, "A Model of Soviet-Type Economic Planning," *American Economic Review,* 61, No. 3 (June 1971), pp. 390–407. A difficult article that shows how consistency with material balance systems can be reached more quickly than previously suspected.

7. Mikhail Bor, *Aims and Methods of Soviet Planning* (New York: International Publishers, 1968). A Soviet view of planning problems.

D. Use of Linear Programming in the Planned Economies

1. Ellman, *Soviet Planning Today,* chap. 1, pp. 1–14. This is a brief overview.

2. Benjamin Ward, *The Socialist Economy* (New York: Random House, 1967), chap. 3. This chapter gives a number of geometrical illustrations of the way in which linear programming can be used in planning.

3. Chenery and Clark, *Interindustry Economics,* chap. 4.

4. János Kornai, *Mathematical Planning of Structural Decisions* (Amsterdam: North Holland, 1967). This is an extremely useful survey of the use of linear programming in Hungarian planning.

5. G. M. Heal, *The Theory of Economic Planning* (New York: American Elsevier, 1973). This is a relatively clear mathematical treatment of planning problems.

E. Other Nonprice Methods of Allocation

The discussions below contain a number of different approaches to different problems in this field.

1. Discussion about quantity versus price signals is summarized by Gary Wynn Yohe, "Comparisons of Price and Quantity Controls: A Survey," *Journal of Comparative Economics,* 1, No. 3 (September 1977), pp. 213–35. The pioneering article in this field is Martin L. Weitzman, "Prices vs. Quantities," *Review of Economic Studies,* 41, No. 4 (January 1974), pp. 50–65.

2. Other types of nonprice signaling and controls are analyzed in various essays contained in János Kornai and B. Martos, eds., *Non-Price Control* (Amsterdam: North Holland, 1981). See also János Kornai, *Economics of Shortage* (Amsterdam: North Holland, 1980).

3. Much discussion about nonprice bargaining methods of allocation is vague. Several empirical studies do, however, deal with the topic, and one informative study is by Otto Davis et al., "A Theory of the Budgetary Process," *American Political Science Review,* 60 (September 1966) pp. 529–47. This empirical study of the bureaucratic bargaining model tests a number of hypotheses on the American governmental budgetary process. This should be compared to the analysis of the Soviet planning system by Igor Birman, "From the Achieved Level," *Soviet Studies,* 30, No. 2 (April 1978), pp. 153–73.

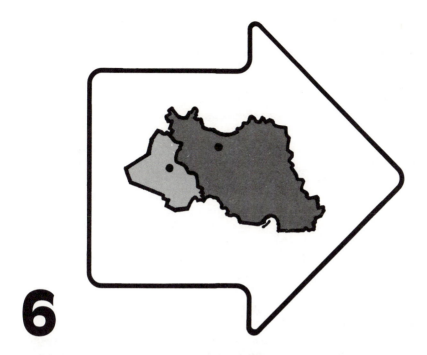

6

STATIC EFFICIENCY AND THE ALLOCATION OF PRODUCTIVE RESOURCES: PRICE SYSTEMS

A. Introduction

Although most of us have participated in market transactions for most of our lives, we should not make the mistake of believing that the price system in which we find ourselves is somehow "natural" or, for that matter, the only kind of market system that can exist. The purpose of this chapter is to provide perspective on the functioning of different kinds of markets. In this introduction a number of crucial definitions about market activity are presented. Succeeding sections discuss propositions concerning the emergence and development of markets, the variety of different types of price systems that can exist, and the types of empirical evaluations that have been made of the static efficiency of market and nonmarket allocation systems.

For any exchange of one good or service for another, we can calculate an *exchange ratio,* which is simply the ratio of the quantities of the two "things" involved. Such an exchange ratio can be implicit in the sense that it is not openly recognized as an exchange ratio. For instance, your neighbor borrows some garden tools and one of his family returns the favor by giving you a piece of recently baked cake; an exchange has taken place, but there has not been any type of formal agreement or even an explicit recognition that the exchange ratio is a loan of tools for a piece of cake. Of course, an exchange ratio can also be very explicit and, in such cases, is often called a *price.* A *price system* occurs where prices play a major role in the allocation of resources.

Four important aspects of the concept of price should be noted. *First,* prices can arise in situations where de jure ownership does not change; for instance, in large corporations certain goods are transferred between one branch and another at *transfer prices* (or *internal prices*) that may be below, or above, or at the same level as prices in the market outside the firm.[1] The problems of setting proper transfer prices are quite similar to many of the problems of setting prices between state enterprises in centrally administered economies. *Second,* the existence of prices in no way requires the existence of a price system. For instance, transfer prices can be used as an accounting device although no allocation decisions are made on their basis. In such cases, these prices are *passive,* in contrast to *active* prices, which play an important role in the decisions that underlie the allocation of resources. *Third,* prices and a price sytem can vary in extent and might include just a few goods and services. For instance, since kin groups in most tribal or peasant societies produce most of their own consumption goods and services, only a small percentage of total production is exchanged through a market. In contrast, in modern market economies, the percentage of goods and services that are exchanged through the market is very much larger. *Fourth,* a medium of exchange (money) is not necessary for prices or a price system (or a market) to exist since all transactions can be carried out by means of barter. That is, money acts as a facilitator, not as a necessary condition, of market exchange. From the four aspects it should be clear that prices need not necessarily fluctuate, that prices can occur in a variety of economic systems, and that a particular good

---

[1]A number of theoretical studies of methods by which such transfer prices should be set are presented in the suggested readings at the end of the chapter. There is also considerable anecdotal evidence about how such prices are set in reality, for example, that General Motors places transfer prices at the market level, that the DuPont Corporation used to place transfer prices below the market level, and that, in the 1960s, oil companies used to sell oil to their own dealers at a higher price than they sold this oil to independent gas stations. Unfortunately, we have few studies that survey such practices in a systematic way. One exception is David Granick, *Managerial Comparisons of Four Developed Countries* (Cambridge, Mass.: MIT Press, 1972), pp. 325–48.

can have several prices vis-à-vis other goods, depending upon which participants are involved.

A *market* is an institution that is often discussed but seldom defined. Generally it is considered to be (1) a *process* in which buyers and sellers come together to negotiate the exchange of goods and services where (2) a price exists, and where (3) the price is influenced by forces of supply and demand. A *market system* is coterminous with a *price system*. A market is *competitive* if there are many buyers and sellers, none of which has an appreciable influence on the price. Of course, neither a price system nor a market system need be competitive, although it is a well-known proposition in economic theory that degree of competition influences the static efficiency of the allocation of resources.

Although this definition is rather vague, it is important to recognize that the emphasis is on a process, rather than a concrete institution, and that markets need not necessarily occur only at formal *market places*. For instance, much buying and selling of wheat in the United States is made by telephone between dealers. Sometimes the existence of a market is difficult to determine and an interesting problem along these lines arises in analyzing marriage arrangements in certain primitive tribes where the future husband or his family must give certain gifts to the bride's family. Considerable disagreements have arisen as to whether the exchange of goods for a woman represents a transaction with primarily social and symbolic significance (and, hence, should be labeled "bridewealth") or represents a market transaction (and hence should be labeled "brideprice"). Certainly economists would not deny the important symbolic and social significance of such transactions, but such symbolic gestures occur in many important market exchanges. However, they would ask questions such as, Does the exchange ratio vary according to the relative numbr of marriageable men and women? Does the exchange ratio reflect the production which the woman provides to the man's household? Such crass questions are designed, of course, to elicit information about the possible roles of the forces of supply and demand. From an empirical examination of the answers to these types of questions,[2] it appears that such an exchange does represent a type of market transaction in a majority of these societies; however, this conclusion is very controversial.

Associated with the presence of markets are a variety of related activies such as, market research, arbitrage, mechanisms for enforcement of agreements and adjudication of disputes, and so forth. Further, a variety of markets can exist, for example, for the immediate exchange of goods and services (*spot markets*), for exchange of money for labor ser-

---

[2]One extensive cross-cultural investigation of these factors, as well as a survey of the relevant literature, is presented by Frederic L. Pryor, *The Origins of the Economy* (New York: Academic Press, 1977), pp. 347–68.

vices (*labor markets*), for exchange of goods or services in the future (*futures markets*), for lending and borrowing of money (*money markets* or *capital markets*), for renting or buying and selling of land (*land markets*), for exchange of one currency for another (*foreign exchange markets*), and so forth. Sometimes the price is called a wage or a rent or interest or an exchange rate, but these labels should not disguise the nature of the market transaction.

B. Some Propositions about the Origin and Development of Markets

Up to now in this guidebook, we have focused attention almost exclusively on *impact* propositions. However, discussion of market exchange permits us to examine some interesting *developmental* propositions as well.[3]

Most economists have considered market exchange as a universal fact of human behavior; their reasoning has often paralleled that of Adam Smith, who wrote 200 years ago:

> The division of labor . . . is not originally the effect of any human wisdom. . . . It is the necessary, though very slow and gradual, consequence of a certain propensity in human nature, which has in mind no such extensive utility: the propensity to truck, barter, and exchange one thing for another. Whether this propensity be one of those original principles in human nature . . . ; or whether, as seems more probable, it be the necessary consequence of the faculties of reason and speech, it belongs not to our present subject to enquire. It is common to all men and to be found in no other race of animals.[4]

Social scientists from other disciplines such as anthropology have seized on such careless statements and have shown without much difficulty that many societies exist with almost no market exchange and, indeed, relatively little barter or truck (peddling) as well. Such anecdotes raise a much more interesting question: What are the causal forces underlying the origins of markets? Insight into this problem can be best gained by examining some of the data on tribal and peasant societies presented in Table 6–1, one of the few existing data sets with which the origins of markets can be explored in a systematic fashion.

The table indicates that the various types of market exchange are correlated with the level of development. At very low levels of economic development, exchange takes place, but primarily in the form of recipro-

[3]This discussion draws heavily upon ibid., chap. 5

[4]Adam Smith, *An Inquiry into the Nature and Causes of the Wealth of Nations,* Book 1, chap. 3, paragraphs 1 and 2.

TABLE 6-1
The Existence of Market Exchange at Different Levels of Economic Development in Primitive and Peasant Societies

| | Number of Societies with Market | | | |
| | Groups of Societies Classified According to Relative Levels of Economic Development | | | |
Market Type	In 15 Societies at Lowest Level	In 15 Societies at 2nd Lowest Level	In 15 Societies at 2nd Highest Level	In 15 Societies at Highest Level
A. *Goods market*				
Internal market	2	3	5	13
External market	5	12	6	3.5
Total	7	12	10	14
B. *Labor market*				
Skilled labor	1	4	6	11
Unskilled labor	1	4	1	7
Total	2	7	6	13
C. *Capital and land markets*				
Occurrence of borrowing at interest	2	6.5	10	9.5
Occurrence of land sales	0	1	3	8
Occurrence of land rental	0	0	4	7

Note: A society is marked as having a goods market if 5 percent or more of produced goods are exchanged; and of having a labor market if 5 percent or more of total workers' services are purchased in market transactions. The labor market is defined only as the internal market for labor. Societies for which no judgments could be reached are coded as half a society.

Source: The data come from Frederic L. Pryor, *The Origins of the Economy* (New York: Academic Press, 1977), pp. 126–27.

167

cal exchange (in which no explicit price is present and in which the forces of supply and demand are "hidden"; cf. the example above about the loan of tools for a piece of cake). Transfers are another important mode of distribution in such societies; these are transactions in which goods are given to others without an equivalent exchange (e.g., a hunter who shares his game, a useful practice in situations where meat can not be kept very long without spoiling).

There are a number of different theories, which will not be reviewed here, that relate the development of markets to various determinants. However, to give a flavor of these arguments it is useful to focus briefly on three of them.

1. Land Market

Consider, for a moment, the problem of man possessing the rights to use more land for agriculture than he can farm himself and where he cannot easily hire outside workers. In order to increase his wealth, he has two choices: Either he can rent out the land or else he can marry several wives (if the society permits polygamy) and have them work the land for him. Such a materialistic (and crass) approach suggests that in those societies where the hiring of agricultural workers does not occur, where polygamy is customary, and where women do most of the agricultural work, we should find less land rental than in societies that have monogamy and where women do much less of the agricultural work. This type of hypothesis receives very strong statistical support, using the data base underlying Table 6–1.

2. Capital Market

For a century economists have argued that the presence of capital-intensive methods of production is an important determinant of the existence of a capital market (and of an interest rate). One might suspect, therefore, that the societies with capital-intensive methods of production (e.g., fishing from canoes instead of from shore; irrigation systems rather than rainfall agriculture; or reliance on animal husbandry rather than hunting) would be more likely to have an interest rate than those utilizing more labor-intensive production (where borrowing might be carried out without an interest being charged). This hypothesis also receives very strong empirical support.[5]

---

[5]It could be argued that the empirical relationship between an interest rate and the use of capital-intensive methods is due to a reverse causation, that is, that the occurrence of a capital market encourages the use of capital-intensive methods. Given the relative frequency of lending and borrowing in societies without an interest rate, this does not seem very likely.

3. Labor Markets for Unskilled Workers

Of all the methods by which primitive and peasant societies obtain food, herding is perhaps the most risky. In a few days an entire herd can die from disease or disappear by theft or can fall below a critical level where it can maintain itself. An opposite risk is for herd owners to have a herd that is too large to be watched by family help alone so that the herd begins to decline for neglect. A reciprocal need therefore exists between those whose flocks have fallen below the critical level necessary to maintain themselves and those whose flocks are too large. From such reasoning you might hypothesize that wherever herding is an important activity, a labor market for unskilled workers (herders) can be found. Such an hypothesis also receives statistical support.

By means of a more complicated argument, it can also be hypothesized that internal market exchange is similar to the land market and is related to the presence of polygamy and the degree to which women participate in subsistence work. These and similar hypotheses can also be demonstrated by statistical tests with the data presented above.

Determining what types of markets originated first raises some conceptual problems, because it depends on the *ceteris paribus* conditions (i.e., whether or not we hold constant the various social and economic factors acting as causal forces). Nevertheless, in a rough way it appears that goods markets emerged at the lowest levels of economic development, followed later by labor markets for unskilled labor, and lastly by land and capital markets. It is noteworthy that among the societies at the lowest level of economic development, there is little correlation between the use of money and the presence of market exchange accounting for more than 5 percent of all goods; nor is there much empirical indication that at this 5 percent level, external trade is relatively more important than internal trade. Such evidence casts in doubt the ideas of Karl Marx and others that trade originated between, rather than within, societies.

These various ideas could be probed much more deeply. However, this brief sketch should give you a feeling for some of the developmental questions that can be asked, the kind of approach that is necessary to examine these questions systematically, and the kind of data that are necessary to test them.

C. "Perfect" Price Systems and Market Failures

A "perfect" price system is one that leads to complete static efficiency (i.e., the production possibility curve is reached). Standard economic theory has demonstrated that in such a case decision makers in both production and consumption face markets where the prices of the factors of production reflect their marginal productivities and the prices of goods reflect their marginal costs.

It is useful to start the analysis of the impact of price systems by exploring where these conditions are satisfied, and what institutional implications such price systems may have.

1. A Variety of Perfect Price Systems

a. The Totally Decentralized Case

In this arrangement (often called *perfect competition*), we have a large number of buyers and sellers; individually, none have any appreciable influence on the price (i.e., there are no elements of monopoly, oligopoly, or monopolistic competititon). To achieve perfect competition, it is assumed on the institutional side that firms are profit maximizers, that individuals are utility maximizers, that the government does not interfere in the decisions of either group, and that taxes do not distort the price system (i.e., there are no sales or income taxes). It is further assumed that all factors of production are employed, that markets are complete (i.e., markets exist for all goods and services, both now and in the future), that speculation is stabilizing, that the dynamic effects of market adjustment are unimportant, and that there are no "public goods." Among the necessary technical assumptions are constant or decreasing returns to scale, diminishing returns, and no externalities or indivisibilities.

The workings of the perfectly competitive market system are the focus of most elementary economics textbooks in the West. Each enterprise faces a demand curve for its products that is completely horizontal; that is, it can sell as much as it wants at the market price without having to take into consideration the effect of its activities on other enterprises. In order to maximize its profits, the enterprise will produce amounts of each product such that the cost of producing the last unit will equal the market price. To accomplish this, the enterprises obtain a quantity of each variable factors such that the productivity of the last factor obtained is equal to its market price. Consumers with limited resources allocate their expenditures so that the utilities derived per currency unit from the last unit of each good purchased are equal. At the given price of each factor, good, and service a particular quantity is demanded and also supplied. If the quantity demanded is larger than the quantity supplied, the price rises; and in the reverse case, the price falls.

Given the various institutional and technical conditions, standard neoclassical economic theory demonstrates the proposition that complete static efficiency is achieved. Assuming the profit motive and that the working of the market in the long run will eliminate producers who do not operate at the lowest costs, there is no economic motivation for any given producer to act in a manner to violate the three marginal conditions specified in Chapter 2—that is, to employ factors in a manner such that their marginal physical productivity is lower than in other enterprises in the industry; to employ the factors in a manner such that the marginal rate of substitution is different than in the rest of the economy; or to produce different goods in a manner such that the marginal rate of transformation differs from that of the rest of the economy. Standard microeconomic textbooks present a more rigorous proof that such a perfectly competitive market achieves static efficiency.

The assumption about no externalities can be relaxed if the government is permitted to set certain sales taxes (or subsidies). Such a "price wedge" between prices paid by buyers and received by sellers permits differences in social and private costs or benefits to be taken into account.

It must be emphasized that such a model says nothing about the ownership of the means of production. Although the model is usually stated in terms of a capitalist economy, the government could own the means of production as well; indeed, Abba Lerner has spelled out in considerable detail how such an economy would work.[6] Essentially, the managers of the state-owned enterprises would maximize profits in the same manner as managers of privately owned enterprises, but would remit the profits to the government, not to the individuals.

b. A Quasi-Centralized Case

In the decentralized case discussed above, the prices are given by the market and the government is quite passive. We can, however, introduce a more active role for the government in several different ways; the model proposed by the late Polish economist Oskar Lange serves as a useful example.[7]

In the Lange model the price-setting function is taken over by a public authority. Given this change, the enterprises no longer need control only a small part of the market (as in the case above), as long as managers follow instructions to produce at the lowest costs and at a level such that the marginal cost equals the price. (As noted below, this assumption about managerial behavior is very dubious; why should they follow these instructions?) If the quantity demanded is greater than the quantity supplied so that inventories are declining, govern-

---

[6]Abba P. Lerner, *The Economics of Control* (New York: Macmillan, 1944).

[7]Oskar Lange and Fred M. Taylor, *On the Economic Theory of Socialism* (Minneapolis: University of Minnesota Press, 1938).

ment price setters raise the price; in the reverse case when inventories are rising, they lower the price. Thus the key variables entering into the decision-making process of the price setters are inventory levels of each commodity and service (in this latter case, inventories consist of unused services or queues for such services). Externalities such as pollution can also be permitted into the picture by expanding Lange's basic model. In this case, government sets one price for buyers and another for sellers so that the differences between private and social costs or benefits are taken into account. Given some additional assumptions, it can be shown that static efficiency is achieved here as well.

c. More Centralized Cases

If consumer sovereignty is not important (i.e., planners' preferences are substituted), then a variety of centralized solutions to perfect markets can be envisioned and these deserve brief mention.

Jan Drewnowski has proposed several different ways in which planners' preferences can be introduced.[8] The government can "interfere" only in the decision of consumers as to present and future consumption. If planners believe that consumers are short-sighted and consume too much so that investment is too low, they can either tax the consumers to finance additional investments, or they can offer high interest rates to induce more savings and, at the same time, lend out such investable funds at low interest rates, making up the difference by a subsidy obtained from tax funds. All other markets would function as before (either a decentralized or quasi-centralized solution). Thus the price wedge between buyers and sellers differentiates only the two sides of the capital market.

If the government has certain preferences about the structure of production, it can set different prices for the buyers and sellers of productive inputs (raw materials, machines, and so forth) so as to induce the desired pattern, letting the consumers interact with the consumer goods industry to set the final prices in this sector as before (either a decentralized or quasi-centralized solution). In this case, the price wedge between buyers and sellers differentiates the two sides of the market for producer goods.

If the government has certain preferences about the structure of consumption, it can set different prices for the buyers and sellers of consumption goods so as to induce the desired pattern. The prices of consumer goods are fixed, the consumers allocate their spendable funds among goods, and the producer is induced to produce (by proper gov-

---

[8]Citations to Drewnowski's articles and the debate around them are presented in the suggested readings.

ernmental price setting) so as to meet the consumer demand based on such prices. In this case, the price wedge between buyers and sellers differentiates the two sides of the market for consumer goods.

A different type of centralized price system possibility leading to static efficiency is mentioned briefly in Chapter 5. In this case the central planners solve a gigantic linear programming problem, derive the shadow prices, and then let enterprises maximize profits given these prices. Or else, the government and the enterprises could engage in a dialogue so that an iterative solution to the programming problem is achieved, at which time government would announce the shadow prices. In neither case are direct orders given, other than those setting up the rules by which enterprises interact with the government and then follow once the prices are announced. However, a number of conditions must be met for static efficiency under such an arrangement to be achieved, including low costs of information processing.

d. Some Institutional and Informational Implications

Certain institutional implications of the above models of perfect price systems should be quite apparent. For instance, such models are based on an assumption that factors of production, particularly labor, are mobile and move to where they obtain the highest return. Thus the various historical forms of slavery or serfdom are incompatible with the assumptions. Further, this discussion assumes perfectly competitive behavior. Clearly monopolies or labor unions (which influence the market setting of prices) or economic agents engaging in different types of strategic behavior (e.g., misleading the price-setting authorities) are also incompatible with the assumptions. Various forms of "bureaucratic behavior" (such as submaximizing, i.e., pursuing personal goals at the expense of the enterprise) would also violate the assumptions underlying these models.

Other institutional implications are more complicated to analyze, particularly those dealing with incentives. In the classical type of market economy, producers must act in a certain way or else they will be forced out of business. Where perfect competition does not obtain, managers may maximize other goals at the expense of the owners so that profit maximization does not occur.[9]

A parallel to this problem occurs in most of the quasi-centralized or centralized models where enterprise managers are told to follow certain rules. Unless incentives are carefully structured, they may not actually

---

[9]These issues are discussed in a number of recent studies in industrial organization. An interesting approach to the problem is Robin Marris, *The Economic Theory of 'Managerial Capitalism'* (New York: Basic Books, 1968).

follow these rules, preferring to maximize some of their own goals (e.g., the "easy life" or a high individual bonus) so that enterprise profit maximization does not occur. Many have also argued that where managers do not share the risks associated in any new investment, they may allocate investable funds to highly risky projects and that such behavior, in aggregate, does not necessarily benefit the economy as a whole. However, this argument is not only applicable to enterprise managers in socialist economies but also in a modified form to hired managers of large industrial firms in the West who do not own a large share of the stock.

Associated with incentive problems are problems arising from the cost of information. It has often been demonstrated that the price system serves as a mechanism for the transmission of knowledge. In a decentralized market system an enormous number of factors impinge on the demand and the supply of a particular good or service, and the resultant of all these forces is reflected in a single number: the price. A particular individual does not need to know what changes in the demand or supply forces are occurring or, in a relatively static world, why these changes are occurring. Just by knowing the price the enterprise director is given a message that induces decisions for changes in production in a particular direction; and these changes, carried out by all firms, result in the system being brought back to the production possibilities curve. For instance, in the case of a sudden scarcity of a raw material and the resulting rise in price, "without an order being issued, without more than perhaps a handful of people knowing the cause, tens of thousands of people whose identity could not be ascertained by months of investigation, are made to use the material . . . more sparingly."[10]

Although the price system acts to transmit knowledge, even in ideal systems such transmission is not costless. It takes resources to learn about the current price and the possibilities of purchasing factors of production, raw materials, and intermediate products that are necessary for an enterprise to continue production. Further, on the selling side, it takes resources to market products and to adjust the prices when demand is changing.

Of course, if the economy does not have a price system, it would also require resources to balance supply and demand by physical methods and to allocate supplies so that a consistent pattern of production would be achieved. With a price system we must have more market personnel; with a nonprice system side we must have more bureaucratic personnel.

It is an empirical, not a theoretical, question, as to whether the

[10]Friedrich A. Hayek, "The Uses of Knowledge in Society," *American Economic Review*, 34, No. 3 (September 1945), pp. 519–30.

labor resources necessary to make a market work are more or less than the labor resources necessary to make a nonmarket system function. Sufficient data are available to make some crude tests on this matter. Matching a group of Eastern and Western European nations against each other and holding per capita income constant, it does not appear that relative labor requirements for administrative personnel are much different in the two systems.[11] To put the matter differently, the personnel requirements for operating in a market economy are roughly similar to those for operating in a centrally administered economy. It must be added that such comparisons can only be made on a highly aggregative basis and that more detailed classifications of the data might reveal differences that are hidden in the comparisons on which these reported results are based.

Once we move from decentralized to quasi-centralized systems, additional costs of information occur. In the Lange model inventory information from each enterprise and warehouse would have to be relayed to the price setters, who would aggregate them and, at some time, would announce a new price. The more often that inventory information is collected and price decisions are taken by the center, the higher the information costs would be. Information costs would also be much higher for the pricing of services than for goods, because indicators for scarcity or surplus are less readily available. Additional costs of a different sort would also be involved in determining whether in response to the market signals issued by the central price-setting organization, enterprises are not engaged in strategic behavior to influence price setting.

If prices are changed only at long intervals, the planners face the risk that large surpluses or deficits would arise over time; and, further, that price changes to take care of these might induce larger errors in the opposite direction (a type of "cobweb" situation discussed in Chapter 4). For a central agency to engage in continuous changes in the price would be prohibitively expensive. Given this situation, the planners face the problem of trading off information costs and the costs induced by microecomic surpluses, deficits, and instabilities.[12]

The Lange model also seems to assume that negotiation costs between the enterprise and the price-setting agency are low. Although the process of public utility rate setting in the United States is not an exact

---

[11]These results come from Frederic L. Pryor, "Some Costs and Benefits of Markets: An Empirical Study," *Quarterly Journal of Economics,* 91, No. 1 (February 1977), pp. 81–102.

[12]The issue of how frequently and in what manner the prices would be changed by the planners was first raised by Friedrich A. Hayek, "Socialist Calculation: The Competitive 'Solution,'" *Economica,* N.S. 7 (May 1940), pp. 125–49. His approach was somewhat different from the exposition above.

parallel, it illustrates some of the time-consuming problems that might arise in negotiations to set prices that take place between the government and enterprises. Perhaps a better example might be found in the wage-price freeze in the United States that occurred in 1971–72. In this case government price setters were forced to set price ceilings for goods where scarcities were occuring and yet arrange the price structure so that overall prices did not rise.[13] The negotiation and information problems involved were formidable; and the performance of the system had many critics.

It should be clear that still more centralized price systems have increasingly greater information costs. Once the planners must know something about technologies of individual production processes or constraints about particular resources and once they must begin to solve programming problems, such costs of information rise dramatically and problems arising from lags in informational flows (which may cause difficult problems of adjustment) become more serious.

Still another important part of the problem deserves brief consideration. Once planners begin to impose their preferences onto the system, another type of informational problem arises in the translation of such preferences into prices. More specifically, a planning agency is not a unitary entity where all members have the same mind; therefore, the determination of "planners' preferences" underlying prices might involve considerable costs of negotiation.

You might, of course, ask why planners' preferences are different from consumers' preferences. Is it really of importance to planners whether straight-backed or curved-back chairs are produced? Other than to offset the effects of externalities, why should planners want to set prices different from those obtaining in a decentralized market? A number of differences can be specified: The government may believe that the savings rate is too low, or that certain industries should be fostered for national defense purposes, or that for political reasons production in a particular area should be encouraged, or that for social reasons a particular group of people should be supported, or that for environmental reasons certain technologies should be discouraged (e.g., production of electricity by utilization of atomic fission), or that to reduce information costs certain products require price standardization, and so forth.

It is unclear, however, whether such specialized purposes require some type of general price or quantity controls, rather than straight subsidies. Further, it is quite unclear whether the price and quantity

---

[13]Two studies of this experience are Arnold R. Weber, *In Pursuit of Price Stability: The Wage-Price Freeze of 1971* (Washington, D.C.: Brookings Institution, 1973); and Robert F. Lanzillotti, Mary T. Hamilton, and R. Blaine Roberts, *Phase II in Review: The Price Commission Experience* (Washington, D.C.: Brookings Insitution, 1975).

targets set forth in the plans of centrally administered economies actually reflect these preferences; the plan goals may be the result of a bureaucratic bargaining process in which other goals (e.g., the fighting for bureaucratic turf) obscure the setting of economic goals. Indeed, the final plan can be such that the quantity goals are quite incompatible with the prices that are established. In short, it is an open question whether the planned prices or quantities in the plans promulgated in Eastern Europe accurately reflect any unified set of preferences. Drewnowski's discussion, contrary to his stated intention, may be an analysis of some interesting theoretical possibilities, rather than a description of reality as it currently exists in Eastern Europe.

2. Some Market Failures

Market failures occur when a market mechanism does not allocate productive resources so that static efficiency is achieved.[14] The causes for market failures can be roughly divided into two groups, depending on the relative importance of a time element.

a. Factors Independent of Considerations of Time

(i) Externalities. An externality on the production side occurs when the physical act of production in one enterprise affects either the physical amount of production or the costs of production of another enterprise.[15] If two coal mines are next to each other, the water pumped out of one mine in the course of production lowers the costs of mining in the other mine since the latter has less mine water to contend with; if two oil drillers are both pumping oil from the same pool, the production of one driller lowers the gas pressure and hence raises the costs of the other driller. Similarly, acid wastes that one plant dumps into a river may reduce the catch of commercial fishers downstream.

In all of these cases there is a divergence between social and private costs and benefits. Given the particular type of externality, it is possible that marginal productivities of a given factor are different from producer to producer, that marginal rates of substitution between different factors vary, and that marginal rates of transformation differ between producers. Many externalities lead to divergencies between mar-

---

[14]The term *market failure* appears to have been coined by Francis M. Bator, "An Anatomy of Market Failures," *Quarterly Journal of Economics,* 52, No. 3 (August 1958), pp. 351–79. Only the major reasons for market failures are given. For more detailed discussion, see Bator or Jan de V. Graaff, *Theoretical Welfare Economics* (Cambridge: Cambridge University Press, 1957).

[15]Excluded from consideration are so-called pecuniary externalities, that is, where activities of one enterprise affect costs of other enterprises, but *only* through changes in relative prices.

ginal rates of transformation of producers and marginal rates of substitution of consumers. In short, in a decentralized market system, static efficiency may not be achieved on either the production or the consumption side (i.e., consumer sovereignty).

Since the early 1900s various economists have proposed different systems so that production decision makers would be forced to take such externalities into account (i.e., "internalizing the externality"). Some of the schemes take the form of special taxes or subsidies, for example, a pollution tax (if such a negative externality is involved) or a subsidy system (if a positive externality is considered). Other schemes rely on rearrangements of property rights, for example, auctions for pollution rights or compensation rights if externalities cause damage.

Such proposals are not without their critics and, aside from the political and administrative difficulties in instituting such systems, certain types of objections have been raised. First, if entry into a market is free or when reciprocal externalities are involved, it can be shown that even the most perfect tax-subsidy system would not lead a decentralized system to perfect efficiency in certain cases.[16]

Second, for certain kinds of production externalities it is quite advantageous for the parties involved to understate benefits (or to overstate costs) so that central administration of such systems is difficult.

Third, a number of economists such as R. H. Coase[17] have argued that such schemes are not necessary if those creating and those benefiting by (or hurting from) the externality can be brought together so that payments can be made from one group to another in a manner to prevent or compensate any harm or benefits. If either of these groups is large, however, negotiation costs are expensive; further, if payments are to be made to the polluter to stop his practices, some of those who are harmed by pollution might be tempted not to participate and to "freeload" from the payments of others. Critics of this approach have argued that the distributional impacts of such a scheme are unacceptable;[18] they argue, in effect, that it is outrageous that I must bribe my neighbors to abstain from wild parties so that I can get some sleep since they shouldn't be having such parties in the first place (and they didn't invite me either).

---

[16]Some of the major issues of these problems are discussed in Stanislaw Wellisz, "On External Diseconomies and the Government Assisted Invisible Hand," *Economica,* 31 (November 1964), pp. 345–63; Murray C. Kemp, "The Efficiency of Competition as an Allocator of Resources: 1. External Economies of Production," *Canadian Journal of Economics and Political Science,* 21, No. 1 (1955), pp. 30–42; Otto A. Davis and Andrew Whinston, "Externalities, Welfare, and the Theory of Games," *Journal of Political Economy,* 74, No. 3 (June 1962), pp. 241–63.

[17]R. H. Coase, "The Problem of Social Costs," *Journal of Law and Economics,* 3 (October 1960), pp. 1–44.

[18]For example, Wellisz, "On External Diseconomies."

Although Lange, Lerner, and Drewnowski recognize problems that externalities might bring to their models of more centralized price systems, none explain in detail how such problems can be overcome.

(ii) Public Goods. A special type of externality occurs in the case of public goods, where it is difficult to prevent anyone from consuming the product and where such extra consumption can occur almost costlessly. Examples include the services of a lighthouse or a missile force defending an area. These are discussed in much greater detail in Chapter 7.

(iii) Monopoly Elements. Monopoly elements can occur in a decentralized market system on the production side for a number of reasons, of which increasing economies of scale is particularly important. That is, if such economies of scale exist within an industry, the largest producer has the lowest costs and the highest profit rate and is thus in a position to drive all competitors out of business. Other barriers to entry may exist, either from "natural" causes (e.g., a great deal of technical know-how is required) or "artificial" causes (e.g., state franchises, patents, and so forth). Monopoly elements can also occur in the labor market through certain types of unionization practices.

If producer monopolies exist, it is only by chance that static efficiency is achieved. In maximizing profits the monopolist equates his marginal costs with the marginal revenue of the product (which is not equal to the price). Marginal rates of substitution between capital and labor are not equated for all producers, nor are marginal rates of transformation of producers equal to marginal rates of substitution of consumers.

In the socialist models of both Lange and Drewnowski, the producers are instructed to equate marginal costs with the price. But, as noted above, the setting of this price is difficult, especially if the producer restricts his output and misrepresents his marginal costs so that the central price setters raise the price. In short, monopoly distortions can exist in their systems as well.

(iv) Lack of Full Employment. Lack of full employment is a special type of market breakdown arising from various causes that have received considerable attention among macroeconomists (e.g., planned savings more than planned investment; rigidities in money wages or other crucial prices, slowness of adjustment). Whatever the source, such unemployment means that the economy is operating far from the production possibility curve, that is, inefficiently.

b. Factors Related to Time Considerations

(i) Cobwebs and Other Convergence Difficulties. If supply decisions must be made on the basis of prices of a period different from that when the good is sold (i.e., if there is a considerable lag between produc-

tion and buying decisions), then certain difficulties might occur in reaching an equilibrium price and, indeed, cycles of price and quantity supplied might be observed; these are described in greater detail in Chapter 4. Examples of cobwebs can be found in mining, in the market for certain professionals such as teachers, and in agriculture. Although the nature of the cycle depends crucially on the expectations of the producers as to future prices, the inability to predict exactly may lead to misleading price signals for future production.

A more general difficulty arises in the adjustment process when supply and demand factors have changed for a broad group of commodities. To what extent do prices and quanties throughout the system change so that equilibrium is again obtained? Theoretical studies during the last decade on the properties required for convergence are somewhat pessimistic. That is, only in particular cases does the perfect competitive model converge; in other cases, the stability of this model is open to question.[19]

(ii) Problems Related to Uncertainty. A number of decisions must be made on the basis of a considerable lack of knowledge, especially those involving future actions such as the selling of insurance. If the buying of insurance affects the future actions of the buyers so that they are less careful (the problem of *moral hazard*) or if the seller of insurance must use crude screening devices to rate risks of various groups (to avoid the problem of *adverse selection*), then serious problems of achieving static efficiency arise. Such problems would also occur in all of the more centralized price system models discussed in the previous pages.

c. What Conclusions Cannot Be Drawn?

A number of other sources of market failure can be discussed that provide further evidence that market systems do not achieve static efficiency. However, this does not mean that other allocation systems are better. Indeed, in recent years a literature has arisen that specifies and analyzes sources of failure in administered systems; and some interesting parallels can be drawn between nonmarket and market failures.[20] As of yet, we have no general theory of resource allocation failures, of which market and nonmarket failures would provide special cases.

In any case the problem of whether market or physical allocation systems result in greater inefficiency is ultimately an empirical question. In Section E of this chapter, results of several different types of

[19]For a somewhat outdated but extremely useful survey of this very complicated literature, see Tekashi Negishi, "The Stability of a Competitive Economy: A Survey Article," *Econometrica*, 30 (October 1962), pp. 635–69.

[20]Charles Wolf, "The Theory of Non-Market Failure: A Framework for Implementational Analysis," *Journal of Law and Economics*, 22, No. 1 (1979), pp. 107–39.

empirical comparisons of static efficiency in East and West are briefly reviewed.

D. Selected Allocation Problems in an Economy with Imperfect Prices

Let us assume, for the moment, that the prices of all goods, services, and factors of production are aribitrarily set by some improbable mechanism such as drawing numbers out of a hat. What would happen? In trying to answer this question by focusing on selected allocation problems, we not only gain insight into the operations of a price sytem but also see in a rather unique fashion some of the important influences of institutional constraints in the system.

1. The Choice of Outputs

Although prices are arbitrary, we still have demand and supply curves for goods. For simplicity, let us assume that firms are told to maximize profits. Although the arbitary price is not the equilibrium price, we can use the traditional analytical apparatus to see what would happen initially.

Obviously, if the arbitrary price is set below the equilibrium price, the quantity supplied is less than the quantity demanded and the market initially experiences a scarcity. If the economy has no mechanism to induce an increase in the price, such a scarcity can continue indefinitely as long as the supply curve remains fixed. Of course, the central government can try to force the firms to produce more, or it can try to induce more production by giving bonuses based on gross production, not profits. But if the firm would lose money by producing more goods at such a low price, then some institutional mechanism must be introduced which would either (a) pay the deficit that the firm would run so that the firm would be able to pay its bills, or (b) lower the costs of inputs to the firm so that, with its limited receipts, it would be able to cover its expenses. If such steps are not taken, then the quantity supplied would be determined by the producers and the economy would rest on that point where the price line intersects with the supply curve, provided that the price is at or above the level that would induce the firms to produce anything at all.

Now suppose, however, that the arbitrary price is set above the equilirium price so that the quantity supplied would be greater than the quantity demanded. The initial result, or course, is that inventories would pile up. This cannot last forever, however, unless (a) revenues are available to finance such inventories (i.e., to pay the manufacturing firm to continue such production), or (b) consumers are subsidized to buy the products. If such measures are not taken, then at some point the producing firm would have to reduce production so that only the amount that could be sold (i.e., the quantity demanded) would be produced; that is, the quantity supplied would correspond to that point where the price line intersects with the demand curve.

From this brief discussion it should be clear that the financing mechanism and the forces and incentives that can be applied to the producers are key institutional elements of the operation of such a price system. Another aspect should also be noted: Both situations open the way to special sorts of corruption that do not occur in functioning market economies.

In the case where the arbitrary price is too low, considerable efforts on the part of disappointed buyers might be invested to unearth sources of supply. Armies of purchasing agencies would scour the countryside looking for suppliers. An interesting system of black markets, bribery, or reciprocal favors (you sell me your good, which is scarce, and I'll sell you mine, which also is scarce) might arise, depending on the vigilance of the police authorities. If the government wanted to prevent such corruption without totally draconian measures, it would have to institute alternative rationing devices such as priority systems (e.g., enterprises in designated industries would receive first choice of scarce intermediate goods) or systems of waiting lists. Some of the ill effects of such low arbitrary prices might be modified if individuals and producers wanting that product could produce for themselves; in this case, a system of industrial autarky might arise.

In the case where the arbitrary price is too high, black markets might arise, operated by firms wishing to sell the product at prices lower than the official price. Armies of selling agents would scour the countryside looking for buyers. Advertising would flourish. Certain types of bribes to the consumer (i.e., rebates) would arise; a system of reciprocal favors between sellers might also occur. Again, self-production might occur for those individuals or companies that are unwilling to pay such a high price.

In short, arbitrary prices lead to arbitrary rationing and allocation devices. You should be able to determine why one or more of the three marginal conditions set forth in Chapter 2 would not be met in these various situations.

2. The Choice of Inputs

To simplify this problem, let us consider a two-good world (steel and toys), where the only inputs are labor and capital and where each good can be produced only with two technologies. Let us assume temporarily that capital has no price, so that the only costs of production is labor.

Finally, let us also assume that the economy features constant returns to scale.

The two ways of producing each of the two goods are presented in panel A of Table 6–2; for simplicity, they are labeled as the capital- and labor-intensive technologies. Panel B of the same table shows the factor constraints; that is, that only 2,000 units of capital and 900 units of labor are available for use in the entire economy.

If the steel industry is ordered to produce 200 tons of steel and the toy industry is told to produce as much as it wants, and if both industries are also told to minimize unit costs, then both industries would select the capital-intensive method of production. In the steel industry unit costs would be 0.50 (in contrast to 2.00 for the labor-intensive method) while in the toy industry the unit costs would be 5.00 (in contrast to 10.00 for the labor-intensive method). As a result, 200 units of steel and 33.3 units of toys are produced. All capital is utilized but only 266.7 units of labor are used (and 633.3 units are unemployed).

If the government designates the steel industry as a priority industry and orders the toy industry to produce the most toys that it can (or if the government gives the toy industry a gross output bonus and finances any deficits), the toy industry now selects the labor-intensive method of production. As a result, all factors of production are employed, the requisite steel is produced, and 80 toys are made as well. In short, total production is much higher although static efficiency leaves something to be desired.

If, on the other hand, a 50 percent interest rate is placed on capital and both industries are told to minimize per unit costs, the steel industry now selects a labor-intensive method (for its unit costs are 3.25, in contrast to 4.25 for the capital-intensive method) while the toy industry continues to select a capital-intensive method (for its unit costs are 12.50, in contrast to 13.12 for the labor-intensive method). In this case, all factors of production are employed, the same amount of steel is produced, but 100 toys are produced as well. Static efficiency has been achieved at last since no other combination of factors will result in more production of one good without less production of the other good.

It should be clear that arbitrary input pricing and individual decision making on the part of the firms does not lead to static efficiency. A rather arbitrary priority system combined with an arbitrary gross output bonus system considerably improves the situation. (This should warn us that certain seemingly arbitrary allocation devices in Eastern Europe may greatly improve the functioning of the system). Only if the planners physically allocate resources as a result of a linear programming calculation, or if they place a relative price on capital that reflects its scarcity value, is static efficiency achieved.

TABLE 6–2
An Example of Factor Choice with Passive Prices

A. Factor Requirements with Different Technologies

| | Amount of Production | | | |
| | 100 Units of Steel | | 100 Units of Toys | |
Production Factors	Captial Intensive Technology	Labor Intensive Technology	Capital Intensive Technology	Labor Intensive Technology
Capital	750	250	1500	625
Labor	50	200	500	1000
Unit costs with no capital charges (only labor costs)	0.50	2.00	5.00	10.00
Unit costs with a 50% interest charge on capital	4.25	3.25	12.50	13.12

B. Factor Constraints for Entire Economy

Capital = 2,000; labor = 900

C. Production and Factor Requirements When 200 Units of Steel Must Be Produced

1. Both industries minimize labor costs per unit.

| | Steel | Toys | Total Factor Use |
	Capital Intensive Technology	Capital Intensive Technology	
Amount of production	200	33.3	
Production Factors			
Capital	1,500	500	2,000.0
Labor	100	166.7	266.7

2. Steel industry gets choice of technique, full factor employment target.

	Capital Intensive Technology	Labor Intensive Technology	
Amount of production	200	80	
Production Factors			
Capital	1,500	500	2,000.0
Labor	100	800	900.0

3. Active Prices and 50% Interest Rate.

	Labor Intensive Technology	Capital Intensive Technology	
Amount of production	200	100	
Production Factors			
Capital	500	1,500	2,000.0
Labor	500	500	900.0

Note: This example is based on the assumption of totally mobile factors and constant returns to scale.

3. Special Planning Problems

If the prices of intermediate and final goods are arbitrarily set, how does one choose the technology to produce particular goods, for example, to use coal or oil as a fuel, or to use iron or aluminum as the major material? We might be tempted to make our planning calculations on the basis of calculations that purge the prices of their arbitrary elements so as to arrive at some type of average cost estimate. Not only is this procedure difficult to carry out, it is also rather one-sided because such average cost prices tell us nothing about demand. That is, such prices can tell us to use aluminum instead of iron, but if this commodity is not available, and if we are unable to be assigned a priority rating to obtain it, then we are forced to continue to use iron.

Planners in Eastern Europe do make calculations to purge the existing prices of arbitrary elements. However, in some nations such calculations have to be supplemented by information from the material balance system that tells whether the desired products are in short supply.

Similar problems arise in the field of foreign trade in the selection of exports and imports. Again, prices purged of various elements can be calculated, but demand elements are totally omitted. As a result, the material balance system or some other "outside" tool must be employed to see where the gaps in domestic production occur and what goods are in surplus that can be exported.

Investment planning only complicates matters, for unless the relative scarcity values of goods and factors of production are known, planners have considerable difficulties in deciding how much should invested in what industries. Even if we know what we wish to produce, we have to know the proper technology to choose. For example, should we select a "capital-intensive" process that has a capital cost of 20 and an ostensible profit of 5 (i.e., revenues minus labor and other costs) for the next five years, or an alternative "labor-intensive" investment that results in the same production and has a capital cost of 15 and an ostensible profit of 4 for the next five years? By investing 5 more in the capital-intensive option, we obtain an increase in profits of 1. Now if the market interest rate of 10 percent, then we might be tempted to select this more capital-intensive investment since it yields more than we could earn by lending the money at market rates. However, if the market interest rate is 25 percent, we might select the labor-intensive investment and then earn more by lending out the 5 capital units saved at the market rates (earning 1.25).

If, for ideological reasons, it is forbidden to use the concept of interest rate to make investment decisions like this, we might circumvent such restrictions by introducing pseudointerest rates such as a capital recovery coefficient (which shows how many years it would take the additional capital investment to pay for itself; in the case of the above example, 5), or "coefficients of effectiveness," which are the inverse of capital recovery rates (and look a bit more like interest rates). This is exactly what happened in the Soviet Union during most of the period when Stalin held power.

4. Several Implications for Centrally Administered Economies

Over the past two decades a number of countries in Eastern Europe have attempted to rationalize their price structures for producer goods. In many cases this has involved repricing all goods and services in the economy so as to eliminate subsidies and taxes which distort prices (at least among producer goods). After determining direct costs of production (labor, depreciation, and raw material costs), one theoretical problem in this exercise has involved deciding whether a certain "profit" should be included in each price and, if so, how this profit is determined. Proposals have varied considerably and can be classified into two groups: (1) "Single-channel" price proposals are those featuring some type of markup calculated in one of several possible ways, for example, by multiplying an interest rate times the capital involved in production (structures, machines, and inventories); or by multiplying the wage bill times some coefficient; or by multiplying the costs of production by an appropriate coefficient. (2) "Multichannel" price proposals are those featuring a markup calculated by multiplying both the capital stock by an interest rate and the wage bill by a different coefficient.

It should be clear that any of these schemes to achieve "consistent prices" (many of which have involved interesting exercises in input-output analysis) totally omit demand elements and, therefore, lead to many of the problems discussed in the previous discussion on arbitrary fixed prices.

A number of countries in Eastern Europe have also attempted to "reform" their economies by cutting back on the usage of seemingly arbitrary allocation devices so that enterprise managers have more power of decision making (e.g., by moving from gross output bonus systems to bonuses based on enterprise profits). In some cases these measures have been carried out without an accompanying price reform. From the above discussion it should also be clear that such "reforms" might, indeed, make the situation worse than before. In short, a price system responding to the forces of supply and demand appears to be a necessary condition for decentralization in any economically developed economy.

Finally, it should be clear that planning exercises involving calcu-

lations to achieve greater static efficiency are considerably more difficult to make if prices do not reflect marginal opportunity costs. If prices
do not fluctuate according to supply and demand, then various types of
substitute scarcity prices must be devised and, further, recourse to other
types of measurements must be employed as well.

E. Empirical Evaluation of Static Efficiency

The purpose of this section is to review briefly the major approaches for
comparing the static efficiency of different economies with price or nonprice allocation systems.

1. Empirical Comparisons of Producer Prices

It is sometimes asserted that distorted producer prices in Eastern Europe reflect a low degree of static efficiency of these economies. Several
aspects of this argument are worth examining.

In general, prices in the producer goods sector in most of the centrally administered economies of Eastern Europe are *passive* (since nonprice methods constitute the main allocating devices) and are based on
some variant of the average production cost; in these nations marginal
price-setting rules are not usually followed. Unfortunately, the exact
price-setting rules vary considerably from country to country and are
better left for discussion in more specialized studies of the individual
countries. It should be added that in many of these nations, the relationship between the price-setting rules and the actual prices appears
rather loose.

One way of analyzing actual prices to gain insight into static efficiency is to examine the various taxes and subsidies that affect producers and that act to distort the structure of producer price.[21] Unfortunately, on the tax side it is very difficult to distinguish between taxes on
producers and consumers and I am unaware of any comparative empirical analyses that have been made on the topic. On the subsidy side, a
different kind of problem arises.

In Hungary, an Eastern European nation trying to introduce market elements into its economy, subsidies amounted to about 21 percent

---

[21]Since we are focusing attention solely on static efficiency of production, prices in
the consumer goods sector do not concern us. In using the data on taxes and subsidies, it is
necessary to distinguish the degree to which they fall on producers and consumers. On the
tax side it appears that most are directly placed on consumers (i.e., direct taxes on incomes
or indirect taxes such as sale or excise taxes) in most nations in East and West and
probably do not greatly influence producer prices. Subsidies in many countries are given
primarily to producers (subsidies to consumers in the form of additions to income are
discussed in Chapter 8) and, therefore, receive discussion.

of total GDP in the late 1970s.[22] Although some of these subsidies were strictly on consumer goods, it appears that the producer price structure was extremely distorted. In other Eastern European nations the relative importance of subsidies appears lower. However, in most cases the available statistics for these nations are imperfect in that certain cross-subsidies appear to netted out (i.e., if a given ministry gives subsidies to one company and receives profits from another, only the net subsidies are reported).

In the late 1970s among the capitalist, market economies, governmental subsidies ranged from about 0.5 percent of the GDP in the United States to about 8 percent in Ireland. Although, private cross-subsidies are not included in this calculation, they are believed to be quite low. It seems probable that producer price subsidies are relatively less important in the West than in the East and, therefore, that average costs deviate less from average prices in the West. Thus on both marginal and average cost criteria, prices in Eastern Europe appear to deviate further from costs than in the West. This difference, in turn, increases the difficulties for planners in the centrally administered nations in comparing costs of various goods and services in order to make production decisions to achieve static efficiency.

Although this brief discussion provides a useful perspective on Eastern European producer prices, we can*not* immediately conclude that static efficiency is lower in Eastern Europe. Such an inference would be based on the assumption that resources are allocated in these nations with a (distorted) price system, but they are not. Since the socialist, centrally administered economies rely primarily on nonprice methods to allocate goods and services in the producer good sector, we must make direct comparisons in order to draw conclusions about the relative degrees of static efficiency in East and West.

2.   Direct Calculations of Static Efficiency

For capitalist, market economies a number of attempts have been made to calculate directly various types of static efficiencies.

The easiest type of efficiency calculation focuses on the production that is lost because of the single most visible source of inefficiency, namely, involuntary unemployment of labor. In the 1950s and 1960s, various economists estimated the "full employment gap" in the United States; for most years in these two decades this gap was supposed to be

---

[22]For a detailed discussion of the Hungarian price system, see Armin Bohnet, ed., *Preise in Sozialismus am Beispiel Ungarns* (forthcoming). Hungarian price subsidies receive particular attention in that volume in the essay by Pryor. The data on subsidies in capitalist, market nations presented below come from OECD, *National Accounts, 1951–80* (Paris: 1982).

between 0 and 8 percent of the GDP.[23] On the other hand, most of the capitalist, market economies of Western Europe experienced full employment during this period.

Microeconomic examinations of various sources of static inefficiency in the United States are also available. Some of these focus upon one particular aspect, for example, the costs of monopoly. Others, such as the calculation of Edward Denison that is reported in Table 6–3, try to look at all the various microeconomic inefficiencies. The methodology involved in such calculations is a combination of standard welfare economics (e.g., measurements of changes in "welfare triangles" in supply and demand diagrams), and some careful statistical work combined with some very rough and ready estimation techniques for factors for which adequate information is quite scanty.

Such calculations can be faulted not only because of the roughness of some of the estimates but also because certain crucial costs have been omitted. An influential group of economists of a neoclassical bent have argued persuasively that the methods adopted by Denison understate the inefficiencies caused by monopoly or government regulations because of failure to take into account the wastage of resources in "rent-seeking" activities (a matter discussed in greater detail in chapter 9). That is, obtaining such monopolies, or various types of governmental licenses, quotas, permits, franchises, assignments, or other permission creates scarcities by political means and high profits can be gained thereby.[24] Other economists have pointed out inefficiencies arising from failure to handle externalities correctly (e.g., pollution) or to include items such as industrial accident. Problems of estimation arise in these cases as well. Further, Marxist critics such as Paul Baran and Paul Sweezy have argued that such calculations do not take into consideration the wastes of the capitalist system as a whole. They include under this rubric wastes in distribution (e.g., too many small stores), advertis-

[23]Such calculations appear in the Council of Economic Advisors, *Economic Report of the President* (Washington, D.C.: GPO, annual). To make these estimates, some economists used such rough rules of thumb as "Okun's law," which stated that for every percentage point of unemployment over 4 percent, aggregate production fell about 3 percent (this was because existing labor was used less productively and, further, many people withdrew completely from the labor force because they were discouraged in their job search). During the 1970s, however, it became apparent that each percentage point of unemployment was associated with a smaller loss of production.

[24]Major studies along these lines have been collected in James M. Buchanan, Robert D. Tollison, and Gordon Tullock, *Toward a Theory of the Rent-Seeking Society* (College Station: Texas A&M University Press, 1980). A somewhat different approach to the same topic is presented by Mancur Olson, *The Rise and Decline of Nations: Economic Growth, Stagflation, and Social Rigidities* (New Haven, Conn.: Yale University Press, 1982). Further sources referred to later in this paragraph are K. William Kapp, *The Social Costs of Private Enterprise* (Cambridge, Mass.: Harvard University Press, 1950); and Paul A. Baran and Paul M. Sweezy, *Monopoly Capital* (New York: Monthly Review Press, 1966).

TABLE 6–3
Sources of Static Inefficiencies in the U.S. Economy About 1960

Sector	Misallocation Costs as Percent of GNP
Government Sector	
Distortions caused by taxes	0.4%
Restrictions on international trade	1.5
Retail price maintenance laws	1.0
Government subsidies of farm products	0.5
Private Sector	
Monopoly in product market	0.5
Restriction on markets for production factors	0.5
Prevention of cost effective production practices	0.5
Racial prejudice in hiring	0.8
Broader aspects of racial prejudice	4.0
Total	10.2%

Source: These data are drawn from the calculations of Edward F. Denison, *The Sources of Economic Growth in the United States and the Alternatives before Us,* Suplementary Paper No. 13, Committee for Economic Development (Washington, D.C.: 1962), p. 199.

ing, frivolous product differentiation, as well as unnecessary costs arising in the areas of finance, insurance, real estate, and the sale of legal services. In the early 1960s these authors estimated that such wastes amounted to about 10 percent of the measured GNP. It should be added that such estimates are, in turn, open to even more criticism than Denison's because of the rather casual assumptions that were made to define "necessary" and "unnecessary" costs.

Measuring static efficiency in any of the centrally planned and administered economies raises new and greater difficulties. Most economists from East and West (with the major exception of hardline Stalinists) admit that static efficiency in most of the nations in Eastern Europe is much below that of the West. This belief seems to stem not only from theoretical evidence (such as the type of analysis carried out in the previous chapter on the efficiency of various types of idealized physical allocation schemes) but also from consideration of thousands of anecdotes of economic wastage in these planned economies that are reported daily in their newspapers and popular magazines: the incredible amount of uncompleted construction, the superabundance of inventories of unwanted products, the investment in steel works on the basis of imported iron ore and coal where imported steel is less expensive (in foreign currency), the wastage of transportation by shipping uncut logs, the use of heavy tractors in situations where light tractors are clearly superior, the illogic of the spatial planning of industry, and so forth and so on.

Since anecdotes of wastage can be found for industry in the West (although in less accessible publications), it is difficult to know how to strike a relative balance. In some cases we can make systematic calculations, for example, for inventories or for efficiencies of spatial location.[25] In other cases, we have no solid bases for microeconomic comparisons at all.

Another approach to the evaluation of static efficiency for particular centrally administered economies can be made with econometric analysis. An extremely interesting study has been made by Padma Desai and Ricardo Martin, who have calculated production functions of various sectors and branches of the Soviet economy. They have asked how much more production (assuming the same output mix) could have been obtained if capital and labor resources were moved around so as to achieve equality in the marginal rate of substitution between labor and capital in each sector or branch.[26] They conclude that in the early 1970s, achieving such marginal equality could have resulted in roughly 10 percent more production. Until such an exercise is applied to some market economies, we cannot make comparative judgments following this approach.

Although direct comparisons are difficult to make, several have been attempted and two of the most interesting deserve brief attention. In the mid-1960s West Germany had a per capita output that was 19 percent higher than that of East Germany; Peter H. Sturm has attempted to isolate the most important causal forces explaining the

[25]For inventories in centrally planned economies data are available in several sources, including Robert W. Campbell, "A Comparison of Soviet and American Inventory-Output Ratios," *American Economic Review*, 48, No. 3 (September 1958), pp. 549–55; and Boris P. Pesek, "Soviet and American Inventory-Output Ratios Once Again," *American Economic Review*, 49, No. 4 (December 1959), pp. 1030–33. The debate between these authors reveals some of the pitfalls in making comparisons between systems where prices are crucial. Several examples of calculations of spatial efficiency are cited in Alan Abouchar, *Economic Evaluation of Soviet Socialism* (New York: Pergamon Press, 1979), which also summarizes other empirical studies of static efficiency in particular sectors in the Soviet Union. An interesting attempt to evaluate the efficiency of the Soviet foreign trade pattern is Steven Rosefielde, *Soviet International Trade In Heckscher-Ohlin Perspective: An Input-Output Study* (Lexington, Mass.: Lexington Books, 1973).

[26]Padma Desai and Ricardo Martin, "Efficiency Loss from Resource Misallocation in Soviet Industry," *Quarterly Journal of Economics*, (Aug. 1983), pp. 441–57. As noted, similar studies have not yet been made for other countries. However, in an unpublished Ph.D. dissertation Peter Miović has calculated and also collected other data on the marginal productivity of capital in various branches of the Yugoslav economy. These data are conveniently presented by Saul Estrin and William Bartlett, "The Effects of Enterprise Self-Management in Yugoslavia: An Empirical Study," in Derek C. Jones and Jan Svejnar, eds., *Participatory and Self-Managed Firms* (Lexington, Mass.: Lexington Books, 1982), p. 93. In this so-called socialist, market economy there is an enormous variation of such marginal productivities by sector. This suggests that considerable static inefficiencies occur which might be as great if not greater than those shown by Desai and Martin for the Soviet Union. Comparative work on this subject using the methods pioneered by Desai and Martin would undoubtedly produce some very useful results.

difference.[27] This means separating the influences of economic factors (e.g., a lower capital-output ratio, less fertile agricultural land, different composition of the labor force) from the influence of systemic factors (e.g., less efficiency in planned economies). Assuming constant returns to scale (the scale parameter = 1.000), he concludes (taking his "intermediate estimate") that nearly the entire 19 percent difference can be attributed to systemic differences (i.e., lower static efficiency in East Germany). However, if the scale parameter is 1.175 instead of 1.000, then according to his "intermediate estimate" the two systems have roughly the same efficiency and the differences in productivity result from the fact that West Germany is able to take greater advantages of economies of scale because of the larger size of its internal market.

Two aspects of these results are raise serious problems. *First,* Sturm uses only West German prices in his calculations, assuming that these reflect factor costs in both economies. Of course, because of the index number problems (discussed in Chapter 2), it is most probable that the difference in productivity would have appeared greater if East German prices had been used and, therefore, that the systemic differences would have been greater. *Second,* there is no need for a nation to experience disadvantages by a small domestic market; it can achieve economies of scale by specializing its production and exporting and, in turn, obtaining other goods through imports. The fact that East Germany has a lower volume of foreign trade than a capitalist nation of similar size and level of development is interpreted by Sturm to be a policy measure taken by the East Germans, rather than a feature of the economic system per se. This particular interpretation is open to dispute.[28]

Abram Bergson has made an interesting comparison of the relative efficiency of the Soviet Union and the United States in 1960.[29] He takes into account a variety of economic factors influencing differences in per capita output and, in addition, every conceivable type of index number problem. He examines production per unit of factor input and concludes that in the Soviet Union, this statistic is somewhere between 39 and 54 percent of its value in the United States. From this he concludes that the Soviet Union has a much lower static efficiency than the United

[27] Peter H. Sturm, "The System Component in Differences in Per Capita Output between East and West Germany," *Journal of Comparative Economics*, 1, No. 1 (March 1977), pp. 5–25.

[28] It can be argued that the very nature of central planning requires a relatively autarkical economy in order to minimize disturbances arising from the outside world. Certain data on the openness of these economies are discussed in Chapter 7.

[29] Abram Bergson, "Comparative Productivity and Efficiency in the USA and the USSR," in Alexander Eckstein, ed., *Comparison of Economic Systems* (Berkeley: University of California Press, 1971), pp. 161–219.

States. However, in a comment on these results, Evsey Domar[30] points out that similar calculations comparing Italy (which has roughly the same GDP per capita as the USSR) and the United States yield roughly the same results, so that this indicator does not reflect static efficiency.

The debate between Bergson, Sturm, and their critics focuses on a number of highly technical matters that would take us far from the theme of this chapter. One conclusion should, however, be clear: Computations of relative efficiency of different nations are very difficult and we have no unambiguous empirical evidence that price allocation systems are any more efficient than physical allocation systems. On grounds of theoretical evidence, it seems highly likely that the economies in Eastern Europe relying primarily on physical allocation methods have less static efficiency than economies relying primarily on price allocation systems. But conclusive empirical arguments to this debate have yet to be made.

F. Summary and Conclusions

Although market exchange occurs in tribal and peasant societies, such a manner of distributing goods and services is less important than in modern economic systems. Further, particular types of markets (for instance, markets for land, unskilled labor, or capital) occur in only some of these economically less developed societies.

In modern capitalist economies the movement of prices serves as the main allocating mechanism. However, the discussion of the properties of a "perfect" price system that lead to complete static efficiency should make it clear that this performance criterion is never achieved, whether in a perfectly decentralized or in various types of more centralized allocation systems. In particular, a number of market failures can arise from such factors as externalities, presence of public goods, monopoly elements, market convergence difficulties (for instance, cobwebs) and problems related to uncertainty.

To show the merits of a reasonably well-functioning price system, we briefly consider the functioning of a system in which prices are totally random. In this case consumers not only have difficulties in obtaining the goods which they want, but many inefficiencies arise on the production side as well. Such a theoretical exercise gives insight into the planning difficulties arising in the centrally planned economies of Eastern Europe, which have quite imperfect price systems.

Empirically measuring the degree to which the price systems in

[30]Evsey Domar, "On the Measurement of Comparative Efficiency," in Eckstein, *Comparison of Economic Systems,* pp. 219–33.

Eastern Europe differ from those in the West gives rise to a number of difficulties. However, we do know that rates of subsidization are much higher in Eastern Europe than in the West. Further, sales taxes in the former group of nations are also different for different categories of goods, a tax system which makes static efficiency much more difficult to achieve.

Thus, the theoretical evidence suggests strongly that static efficiency is lower in Eastern Europe than in the West. This view is also supported by thousands of anecdotes. However, the empirical calculations carried out to demonstrate this proposition yield results too ambiguous for firm conclusions to be drawn; therefore, the theoretical proposition has not yet been validated.

SUGGESTED READINGS

A. The Price System and Economic Calculation

If a socialist country does not employ physical allocation methods, is it possible for it to employ a price system to achieve static efficiency? A furious debate on the subject has raged, which has raised a number of important issues about price systems in general.

1. Two classical books on the theory of market socialism are Oskar Lange and Fred. M. Taylor, *On the Economic Theory of Socialism* (Minneapolis: University of Minnesota Press, 1938); and Abba Lerner, *The Economics of Control* (New York; Macmillan, 1944). Key parts of Lange's essay and an earlier article by Ludwig von Mises, against which Lange was arguing, are reprinted in Morris Bornstein, *Comparative Economic Systems: Models and Cases,* 4th ed. (Homewood, Ill.: Richard D. Irwin, 1979), pp. 109–26.

2. A severe critic of Lange is Friedrich Hayek. His major objections are contained in two articles: "Socialist Calculation: The Competitive 'Solution,'" *Economica,* N.S. 7, No. 26 (May 1940), pp. 125–49; and "The Use of Knowledge in Society," *American Economic Review,* 35, No. 4 (September 1945), pp. 519–30. These articles are reprinted respectivey in Bornstein, *Comparative Economic Systems,* 3d ed. (1974), pp. 140–59; and 4th ed., pp. 49–61.

3. The debate about Lange's model has been continued by Paul Craig Roberts, "Oskar Lange's Theory of Socialist Planning," *Journal of Political Economy,* 79 (May 1971), pp. 562–77; and the various criticisms and retorts in the same journal, Vol. 81, Part 1, pp. 450–70.

4. A more centralized version of the Lange model is Jan Drewnowski, "The Economic Theory of Socialism: A Suggestion for Reconsideration," *Journal of Political Economy,* 69, No. 4 (August 1961), pp. 341–54. Parts of this are reprinted in Bornstein, *Comparative Economic Systems,* 4th ed., pp. 196–206. These ideas have also generated an interesting debate in the *Journal of Political Economy;* see, for example, Paul Craig Roberts, Vol. 76 (July 1968), Part I, pp. 645–50; J. H. Petersen, Vol. 78 (March 1970), pp. 395–403; Drewnowski's reply, Vol. 79 (January 1971), pp. 196–99 and Roberts's rebuttal, Vol. 80 (May 1973), Part 1, pp. 465 ff.

6. Francis M. Bator, "The Anatomy of Market Failure," *Quarterly Journal of Economics,* 72 (August 1958), pp. 351–79, is a classical summary of the reasons why an unregulated market might not yield an optimal allocation of resources. A complementary article is Charles Wolf, Jr., "A Theory of Nonmarket Failure: Framework for Implementation Analysis," *The Journal of Law and Economics,* 22 (April 1979), pp. 107–41, which analyzes the failure of administrative allocative methods to achieve their desired goals.

B. Some Special Problems

In the text, two special problems receive brief attention: the pricing dilemmas of multidivisional firms (where one division sells products to another), and the problems of externalities such as pollution in price and nonprice systems. The materials cited below include a variety of viewpoints on these two issues.

1. Some of the actual methods used in setting internal transfer prices are discussed in David Granick, "National Differences in the Use of Internal Transfer Prices," *California Management Review,* 17, No. 4 (Summer 1975), pp. 28–40; and his essay "Internal Transfer Prices" in his book *Managerial Comparisons of Four Developed Countries* (Cambridge, Mass.: MIT Press, 1972), pp. 325–48. The business literature on such transfer prices raises some very useful theoretical issues; see especially Paul W. Cook, Jr., *Journal of Business,* 28 (April 1955) pp. 87–94; Joel Dean, *Harvard Business Review* (July 1955), pp. 65–74; Jack Hirshleifer, *Journal of Business,* 30 (April 1957), pp. 96–108; Jack Hirshleifer, *Journal of Business,* 29 (July 1956), pp. 172–84; J. Dearden, *Harvard Business Review,* 38 (January 1960), pp. 117–26; R. B. Heflebower, *Journal of Industrial Economics* (November 1960), pp. 700–23; John Menge, *Journal of Industrial Economics,* 9 (July 1961), pp. 215—33; and various articles in Charles P. Bonini et al., eds., *Management Controls: New Directions in Basic Research* (New York: McGraw-Hill, 1964), chap. 2.

2. The literature on pollution in market economies is enormous; on the other hand, the analyses of pollution in nonmarket systems is much smaller and raises some fascinating systemic problems. Useful articles on the problem include Eric Dahman, "Environmental Control and Economic System," and Marshall I. Goldman, "The Convergence of Environmental Disruption," both in Bornstein, *Comparative Economic Systems,* 3rd ed., pp. 457–80. An interesting debate on the certain critical aspects is carried on by Robert McIntire and James R. Thornton, "On the Environmental Efficiency of Economic Systems," *Soviet Studies,* 30 (April 1978), pp. 173–93; and Charles E. Ziegler, "Soviet Environmental Policy and Soviet Central Planning: A Reply to McIntire and Thornton," *Soviet Studies,* 33 (January 1980), pp. 124–34.

3. Monographs on pollution problems in planned economies include Boris Komarov, *The Destruction of Nature in the Soviet Union* (White Plains, N.Y.: M. E. Sharpe, 1980); W. A. Douglas Jackson, ed., *Soviet Resource Management and the Environment* (Columbus, Ohio: AAASS, 1978); Fred Singleton, ed., *Environmental Misuse in the Soviet Union* (New York: Praeger, 1976); Ivan Volgyes, *Environmental Deterioration in the Soviet Union and Eastern Europe* (New York: Praeger, 1974); Philip R. Pryde, *Conservation in the Soviet Union* (Cambridge, Mass.: Harvard University Press, 1972); and Marshall Goldman, *The Spoils of Progress* (Cambridge, Mass.: MIT Press, 1972).

C. Prices in the Soviet Union

Problems arising in the setting of prices in economies without market systems demonstrate in a quite unique manner many of the special properties of prices in market economies.

   1.   Alec Nove, *The Soviet Economic System* (London: Allen and Unwin, 1977), chap. 7, pp. 172–99. A more complete description of the price system is Morris Bornstein, "Soviet Price Theory and Policy," in Morris Bornstein and Daniel R. Fusfeld, eds., *The Soviet Economy,* 3d ed. (Homewood, Ill: Richard D. Irwin, 1970), pp. 85–117; and two of his subsequent essays that update this information: "Soviet Price Policy in the 1970s," in U.S. Congress, Joint Economic Committee, *Soviet Economy in a New Perspective* (Washington, D.C.: GPO, 1976), pp. 17–67; and "The Administration of the Soviet Price System," *Soviet Studies,* 30 (October 1978), pp. 466–91. An interesting collection of articles on specialized aspects of the price system is Alan Abouchar, ed., *The Socialist Price Mechanism* (Durham, N.C.: Duke University Press, 1977).

   2.   Robert W. Campbell, "Soviet Accounting and Economic Decisions," plus comments by Herbert Levine in Gregory Grossman, ed., *Value and Plan* (Berkeley: University of California Press, 1960), pp. 76–94. Although the information is somewhat outdated, these discussions raise some critical issues.

   3.   Aron Katsenellinboigen, "Colored Markets in the Soviet Union," *Soviet Studies,* 29 (January 1977), pp. 62–86. The complexities introduced by different and isolated markets, all with quite different types of prices, are explored in this amusing and highly insightful analysis.

   4.   John M. Kramer, "Prices and the Conservation of Natural Resources in the Soviet Union," *Soviet Studies,* 24 (January 1973), pp. 364–73. This is a study of what happens in situations where rents on natural resources are not calculated.

D. The Use of Prices in Planning of Nonmarket Systems

If prices do not reflect opportunity costs, how is it possible to plan in a rational manner? The articles below explore some of these issues.

   1.   Robert Campbell, "Standard Methodology for Determining the Economic Effectiveness of Capital Investment," in Bornstein and Fusfeld, eds., *Soviet Economy,* 4th ed. (1974), pp. 328–38. This is a translation of instructions to all Soviet firms. A commentary by Alan Abouchar can be found in Bornstein and Fusfeld, *Soviet Economy,* 4th ed., pp. 339–47. A fascinating account of the previous methods used in investment planning during Stalin's time is Gregory Grossman, "Scarce Capital and Soviet Doctrine," *Quarterly Journal of Economics,* 67 (August 1953), pp. 311–43.

   2.   Marvin Jackson, "Information and Incentives in Planning Soviet Investment Projects," *Soviet Studies,* 23 (July 1971), pp. 3–25. The author focuses on the investment planning agencies and their activities.

   3.   Frederic L. Pryor, "Foreign Trade Theory in the Communist Bloc," *Soviet Studies,* 14 (July 1962), pp. 41–61. This somewhat outdated study covers the use of pseudoprices in foreign trade.

E. Market Socialism

There is a large theoretical and empirical literature on market socialism, and a bibliography of useful readings is provided in Chapter 9. It should be noted, however, that most of these articles concern a type of market in which firms are not maximizing total profits, but rather profits per worker; the use of such an objective function for the firm changes in important ways the nature of the operation of the market.

F. Static Efficiency in East and West

The materials cited in footnotes 23 through 30 cover the most useful sources.

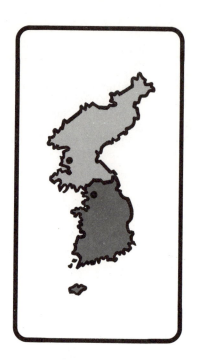

7

CONSUMPTION
AND TRADE

A. Introduction

Accompanying economic development is an increasing division of labor such that decisions concerning production and consumption become progressively more separated in time and space and, moreover, more likely to be made by different people. Mediating between the two spheres is some process by which income derived from production is transformed into consumption goods and services; in all economically developed economies—capitalist or socialist—a large portion of this mediation is accomplished through trade.

Most economic analyses of consumption focus either on models of utility-maximizing consumer behavior or on empirical studies of the pattern of consumption among various groups. In many cases these utility-maximizing models start with the notion of consumer efficiency (consumer sovereignty), the technical conditions of which are described in Chapter 2. Most of the empirical studies attempt to unearth the determinants of personal consumption for particular goods and services, to derive price and income elasticities, and so on. The focus in this chapter is, however, on some much different matters.

After a brief glance at some of the theoretical foundations of consumer sovereignty, the analysis turns to various types of institutions by which trade and consumption can be channeled. This is followed by an empirical examination of a series of selected developmental and impact propositions about trade and consumption in order to highlight important similarities and differences among economic systems. Many of the results discussed in this chapter underlie the political debate in capitalist nations about the *welfare state* and, in socialist nations, the discussion concerning the characteristics and consequences of *pure communism*.

B. Some Theoretical Considerations

1. Consumer Efficiency (Consumer Sovereignty) and its Enemies

In Chapter 2 consumer sovereignty is proposed as a performance criterion against which to measure actual economies. The two marginal conditions underlying consumer sovereignty imply that goods cannot be redistributed among consumers and the mix of products available for consumption cannot be changed to make any consumer better off without making another worse off. More simply this means that, given the distribution of income (a subject discussed in Chapter 8), the consumers are given what they want and the consumption pattern cannot be changed so that all consumers have the same or higher utility. Such a theoretical definition of consumer sovereignty is certainly compatible with different forms of ownership and, moreover, with allocating the means of production either by a market or by administrative methods.

What kinds of objections can be raised against consumer sovereignty as a goal? The issues are not as clear as they might seem and, without passing judgment on their validity, it is useful to consider some of the major arguments against such an goal, as well as certain counterarguments.

a. Consumers Show "Bad" Judgment

Consumers might want to buy goods and services that are allegedly "bad" for them, such as narcotics, prostitutes, liquor, contraceptives, abortions, useless gadgets, or games; and they might *not* buy certain goods and services that are "good" for them, such as crash helmets for motorcycle riding, seat belts for automobiles, or vaccinations. Such an argument has justified laws prohibiting the buying and selling of particular goods and services; or measures to ensure that particular goods and services are not sold in excess (e.g., removal of liquor licenses of bars if customers become rowdy); or measures encouraging the buying and selling of goods (by subsidizing them). In a redistribution of income through the tax system, this notion also underlies giving poor people income in kind (e.g., food baskets, low-rental housing, medicine) rather than in money so that they will not be tempted to waste public funds for less "worthy" purposes.

If the decision concerning such prohibitions or promotions of sales cannot not be made in some gigantic meeting by all who are affected by these measures, then the decision must be delegated. It is quite possible that the delegated subgroup making these decisions does not reflect the will of the people in any real sense: By imposing their (elitist) values on others, they inflict costs on society. Further, the costs of enforcing such regulations may be high; indeed, the inequities and costs arising from the enforcement of the prohibition of liquor sales in the United States in the 1920s numbered among the most important reasons for the repeal of this law. Finally, the lawmakers may misjudge the good and the bad qualities of the goods or services or the impact of forced usage of such items, as in the case of automobile seat belts.[1]

b.   Consumers Lack Proper Information

Consumer often lack the ability or the proper information to make an informed choice about the quality of a good or service. For this reason laws regulating the purity of foods and drugs, the labeling of furs, or the qualifications of physicians are passed. Such laws may, however, also have adverse effects. For instance, the setting of regulations for the licensing of physicians has led not only to some monopoly activity on the part of groups of physicians to restrict entry but also to the disappearance of particular types of paramedical services that can be delivered safely at a much lower cost (e.g., special paramedics to give inoculations or deliver babies).

---

[1]From data showing that drivers using seat belts experience fewer deaths in automobile accidents than drivers not using such belts, U.S. legislators concluded that compulsory sales of seat belts would lower the death rate. However, econometric evidence is supplied by Sam Peltzman, *Regulation of Automobile Safety,* American Enterprise Institute for Public Policy Research, Study 26 (Washington, D.C.: 1975) that death rates from auto accidents did not fall after the law was passed. He interprets these results as due to two factors: (1) Many people don't wear these belts, even if they have them; and (2) some people take more risks in driving when they wear such belts. These findings and interpretations are highly controversial and are used here primarily for illustrative purposes.

c. Social Needs Go Unmet

Consumer preferences do not often correspond to urgent social needs. In tense political situations such as the outbreak of war, it is often felt that restrictions on the volume and composition of consumption permits important resources to be devoted to necessary defense or war production. This argument appears in other forms as well. For instance, consumers are said to have a short time horizon and not to take sufficiently into account the needs of future generations. Such a justification is often used to help implement government taxation to finance investment (i.e., *forced savings*). However, the argument that a government, particularly one that is periodically reelected, has a longer time perspective than the individuals composing the society can be challeneged on two grounds: (i) The taxes to finance such investment distort incentives to invest for the rest of the economy, and (ii) the politicans passing the required legislation and the bureaucrats administering these laws often act to further their own ends and not those of the population as a whole. Certainly the documentation of *political business cycles* (where governmental expenditures increase shortly before elections) provides some interesting evidence on this matter.[2] Another variant of this argument about consumer preferences is that if consumers are free to select goods and services according to their income constraints, the overall pattern of production will be determined by the wealthy consumers who have more "dollar votes." If this is of concern, the situation can be rectified by redistributing income, rather than consumption.

d. Social Costs Are Incurred

Free choice of goods and services by consumers often entails high social costs. These include not only the costs of advertising for manipulating consumer tastes, but also the costs of meeting the resulting rapidly changing demand (e.g., the costs involved in annual automobile model changes[3]) or in quickly reallocating resources from one type of production to another. Again, slowness in adjusting to changes in technology or consumer tastes can also have some costs in foregone con-

---

[2]See, for instance, Bruno S. Frey and Friedrich Schneider, "An Empirical Study of Politico-Economic Interaction in the United States," *Review of Economics and Statistics,* 60, No. 2 (May 1978), pp. 174–83.

[3]The costs of model changes in the automobile industry in the United States have been calculated by Franklyn Fischer, Zvi Griliches, and Carl Kaysen, "The Costs of Automobile Model Changes since 1949," *Journal of Political Economy,* 70, No. 5 (October 1962), pp. 332–46.

The costs of not changing models is shown dramatically in the falling share of sales of domestically produced automobiles in the same nation after the 1973 oil price increases. One might also ask how much welfare was gained in the Soviet Union by producing an essentially unchanged Volga automobile between 1945 and 1957, rather than making annual changes to this car to remain abreast of changing technology and tastes.

sumer utility. In any case, the degree to which consumer tastes are amenable to significant manipulation is open to question.[4]

e. Social Class Divisions Are Obscured

Free consumer choice confounds the division of social classes or strata. As primitive societies reach a certain stage of economic development, upper classes begin to feel a desire to maintain social class distinctions by means of sumptuary laws that deny consumption of particular goods and services to lower classes or groups of people.[5] In some African societies, only those of a certain social rank (conferred by the king) can wear cloth of a certain design. Similarly, in Western Europe in past centuries the "wearing of the purple" or the trappings of the nobility were forbidden to the lower classes; indeed, one of the slogans of the French revolution was the cry to permit all to wear what they pleased. The same sumptuary idea has been used to deny education to certain groups.[6] Some modern legislation which "protects" consumers by making the mass production of particular consumer goods very difficult (but which the rich can afford to have custom made) or which prevents certain services from being sold which the wealthy can obtain by traveling to another country (e.g., safe abortions) acts in the same manner as a sumptuary law.

---

[4]Some of this literature is cited in the suggested readings at the end of the chapter concerning the controversy surrounding the theses about consumer behavior of John Kenneth Galbraith.

[5]Contrary to the assertions of many who have discussed the topic, sumptuary laws are not innate to all primitive economies. According to the empirical research of Robert L. Carneiro, "Scale Analysis, Evolutionary Sequences, and the Rating of Cultures," in Raoul Naroll and Ronald Cohen, eds., *A Handbook of Method in Cultural Anthropology* (New York: Columbia University Press, 1973), p. 834–72, sumptuary laws are a characteristic of only a few relatively developed precapitalist societies. These do include, however, a number of societies in Western Europe where some amusing remnants of these laws remain. For instance, the children's story of "Puss-in-Boots" is actually a medieval revolutionary tract in which a cat, by donning the clothes of a warrior, becomes his equal, defeats him in battle, expropriates the expropriator, and lives happily ever after. The expression "clothes make the man" comes from a German proverb that points out again the role of sumptuary laws in the class structure.

[6]In Russia in 1887 an argument for a particular sumptuary decree reflected this viewpoint quite well: "Gymnasiums and pro-gymnasiums should prevent the entrance of children of coachmen, manservants, cooks, laundrywomen, small shopkeepers, and the like; the children of whom, with the exception perhaps of unusually gifted ones, ought not to be allowed to escape from the environment to which they belong; because the experience of many years have proven that it leads them to scorn their parents and to be dissatisfied with their way of life, and that it instills hatred against the existing inequality of property status, which is inescapable by the nature of things . . ." (adapted from a citation by Arcadius Kahan, "The Development of Education and the Economy in Czarist Russia," in C. Arnold Anderson and Mary Jean Bowman, eds., *Education and Economic Development* [Chicago: Aldine, 1965], p. 370).

2. Difficulties in Achieving Consumer Sovereignty

Consider for a moment a situation where all goods and services are completely allocated to individuals by a central administration according to their determination of individual consumer desires. The administrators might attempt to achieve consumer sovereignty, but such an attempt would require an enormously complex set of communications between each consumer and the center. The costs of collecting the necessary information would be staggering; and the costs of processing such information to aid the administrators in their decisions on both the consumption or the production side would also be enormous.

On the opposite side of the institutional spectrum, we could rely on a market mechanism to structure both production and consumption decisions. However, consumer sovereignty might not be achieved in this case either. The reasons, however, are quite different and are worthwhile to consider briefly.

In its most schematic form a consumer's utility function can be specified in the following way: $u_A = f(c_A, c_{AB}, c_B)$, where u_A designates the utility of the individual A, c_A designates the set of goods and services that the individual consumes, c_{AB} is the set of goods and services that the individual *jointly consumes* with other individuals; and c_B is the set of goods and services that another individual B consumes. The first item in this utility function—what the individual consumes alone—provides few analytical difficulties; the other two arguments in the utility function require some explication.

Some types of goods and services are jointly consumed because the costs of consumption per additional person are insignificant. One subset of such goods consists of things such as movies or television programs where additional consumption is almost costless but where additional consumers can be prevented from enjoying these benefits (e.g., walls around a movie theater; a TV signal scrambler or pay cable TV); another subset consists of jointly consumed goods where others cannot be prevented from enjoying such benefits (e.g., the health benefits from eradication of malaria by draining a swamp, the security provided by an ICBM missile force, the safety for boats provided by a lighthouse). Goods and services in this second subset are often called *public goods.*

The final subset consists of goods and services where positive or negative *externalities* arise, that is, where person A's utility changes by reason of person B's consumption, even though person A does not directly consume the good. Positive externalities can arise in cases such as education or inoculation, where person A benefits from the additional knowledge in society or from the fact that there are fewer potential spreaders of a disease. Negative externalities can arise in cases such as

TABLE 7–1
An Illustration of Joint Consumption and the Exclusion Principle

	Exclusion of Benefits Possible	*Exclusion of Benefits Impossible or Difficult*
Nonjoint consumption	Roast beef, knife, suit	Education, inoculation
Joint consumption	TV or radio shows	Mosquito elimination, lighthouse

smoking in an elevator, where *A* loses utility from *B*'s consumption of the good. Positive or negative externalities can also arise from personal reasons, namely that person *A* loves (or hates) person *B* to the extent that any benefit to *B* makes *A* happy (or unhappy).[7] The various considerations discussed in the last two paragraphs can be combined in a typology that is shown in Table 7–1.

It should be clear that for those goods and services where exclusion from benefits is difficult or impossible, market allocation presents some serious problems. Some people wishing to receive the benefits from the draining of a swamp may refuse to join in a public subscription to achieve this purpose, preferring to "freeload" from the philanthropy of others. Similarly, these freeloaders may not pay for an inoculation themselves, but rather will wait for all others to be inoculated so that they do not need to make such an expenditure.

More technically, it can be easily shown that in a decentralized market system, the presence of public goods or for goods with externalities can lead to a situation where the marginal conditions for consumer sovereignty (specified in Chapter 3) are *not* met. If person *A* benefits from *B*'s consumption, *B* may reach a situation where the ratio of his marginal utilities for this good and for another are the same as the price ratios; but in achieving this optimization of his utility, *A*'s ratio of marginal utilities would be affected. That is, *B* drains a swamp or gets an inoculation and *A*'s utilities change, even though *A* has done (or paid) nothing. Only in rare cases would the proper volume of such goods or services be produced. In other words, there is a market failure. Financing the production of public goods or subsidizing the production of goods with positive externalities (and taxing those with negative externalities) is one means of escaping this problem; however, as in any case of delegated decision making, we have no assurance that this mechanism will lead to the conditions of consumer sovereignty either.

Market breakdowns also occur for a number of other reasons,

---

[7]These personal externalities have received considerable attention in the analysis of envy or altruism. An interesting analysis of the optimal functioning of an economic system with such externalities is Amartya K. Sen, "Labour Allocation in a Cooperative Enterprise," *Review of Economic Studies,* 33, No. 4 (October 1966), pp. 361–71.

among which are those associated with situations where risk and insurance are involved. In certain cases, where it is desirable to spread the costs of malign acts of fate (e.g., illness) over as wide a group as possible, insurance enterprises attempt to increase their profits by lowering prices slightly and restricting their sales to low-risk individuals. The end result is that risks are not spread evenly over the population, and certain high-risk individuals (e.g., elderly people) find it prohibitively expensive to buy such insurance (e.g., for health care). Such *risk skimming* cannot easily be regulated in a market economy. It is also possible that the purchase of insurance influences the person to behave in a manner to raise the probability of an accident. In can be demonstrated that in situations where such *moral hazard* is high, legal limitations on the amounts of insurance purchased can lead to greater social utility. Still another difficulty arises from *adverse selection,* a situation where only high-risk individuals buy the insurance, which raises the price (since the payout to this group is much greater), which leads in turn to the purchase of insurance by fewer individuals who, on the average, represent a still higher risk class.

From this discussion it should be apparent that even if consumer sovereignty is accepted as a goal, certain intrinsic properties of particular goods and services—independent of the economic system—make it difficult (if not impossible) completely to achieve it. By focusing attention on the manner in which consumption decisions are made and the institutions through which trade is carried out, we can gain considerable knowledge about the degree to which consumer sovereignty is achieved. It is these institutional matters on which attention must now be focused.

3.   Trade Institutions

As discussed in Chapter 4, the development of markets is associated not only with a rising level of economic development but also with a number of other social institutions and procedures. These include specialized judges for settling disputes, specification of regular trading days, exchange methods, standarization of products, procedures for the exchange of information, and so forth.[8] Keep in mind, however, that the buying and selling of goods and services can be accomplished not only through the kind of competitive market portrayed in textbooks (where demand and supply forces interact in a manner to influence the price and, hence,

---

[8]It is peculiar that economists have generally not paid much attention to such matters and have left such problems to sociologists and social anthropologists. For a brillant analysis, see Clifford Geertz, "Suq: The Bazaar Economy," in Geertz et al., *Meaning and Order in Moroccan Society* (Cambridge: Cambridge University Press, 1979), pp. 123–314.

the quantities demanded and supplied), but also through a variety of institutional forms that are regulated by different types of authorities in a multitude of ways (i.e., through various types of price, quality, and quantity controls).

Since trade mediates between producers and consumers, it may appear an important function of trade institutions to provide information to producers about consumer desires. However, by considering briefly the ways in which trade can be structured so that the link between producers and consumers is effectively broken, we can gain perspective on the different types of consumer good markets that exist.

a. Consumer Choice

The traders can be assigned (e.g., by the political authorities in a centrally administered economy) to sell a specified consignment of goods at any price that will clear the market and to buy a specified consignment of goods at a particular price. Such a mandate is usually accompanied by some arrangment by which the traders are subsidized (or taxed) if the goods and services sell at a price lower (or much higher) than that at which they are bought. If the traders play no role in the specification of either goods to be bought or sold, if they do not search for the lowest price at which to buy but rather play their assigned (passive) role, such an arrangement can lead to a complete separation between the original producers and consumers so that demand forces have little influence on what is produced; and costs of production have little influence on what is sold.

The situation described above is often designated as *consumer choice*. It differs from *consumer sovereignty* in that consumers can choose among available alternatives and can influence the retail price, but they have no influence on the pattern of production. It is a situation where, technically, the ratios of marginal rates of substitution between goods may be equal for different consumers but the ratios of marginal rates of substitution are not necessarily equal to the ratios of marginal rates of transformation of the producers. Where consumer *choice* but not *sovereignty* occurs, detailed data on the relative levels of the rates of profits or losses on particular goods and services, combined with information about price elasticities of demand can be used to calculate in a rough fashion the deviations both in the current pattern of production and the pattern that would be achieved under consumer sovereignty.

b. Differential Sales Taxes and Subsidies

The link between producers and consumers can also be broken in a competitive market situation if differential sales taxes and subsidies are placed on various goods. In this case, the marginal rates of subsitution between goods by consumers can remain unequal to the marginal rates of substitution by producers. "Normal" market institutions are preserved but the market forces are regulated by the fiscal authorities. In such situations, detailed information about the taxes and subsidies, combined with price elasticity data, can also permit us to calculate in a rough fashion the difference between the current pattern of production and that with consumer sovereignty.

c. Nonprice Rationing Devices

The link between supply and demand forces can also be broken if nonprice rationing devices are utilized. Such devices can be quite *informal* and are often associated with situations where prices are fixed. For instance, when shortages develop at fixed prices, the scarce goods and services can be allocated by first-come, first-served methods, which result in queueing behavior and the use of waiting time as a rationing device. Or the scarce goods can be allocated by the use of arbitrary screening devices (e.g., only white, working age males were considered "credit worthy" by some U.S. banks during certain times in the 1950s and 1960s when, at the going interest rate, the supply of loanable funds fell short of demand). Similarly the scarce goods can be allocated by favoritism or by corruption (i.e., special payments by the buyers to the sellers). When surpluses develop with fixed prices, goods can be allowed to pile up on inventory shelves while production remains at the same level; or they can be allocated by corruption (e.g., special discounts to favorites), and so forth.

Of course, *formal* rationing devices can also be used as allocating devices. These include not only the sumptuary laws discussed above, but also three important methods of distributing goods in situations of scarcity which have been adopted by many wartime (and some peacetime) authorities.[9]

(i) Point Rationing. Under the first method, a "point value" is placed on every rationed good. Each person with such points must pay not only the monetary price, but also the point value of the product. Sometimes commercial companies use this device to arouse interest in their products, distributing "green stamps" or "fast food coupons" and selling their products by requiring both points and money. Governments use this system in a more serious fashion by distributing points in specified amounts to each member of the population according to his or her membership in a specified group (e.g., over age 65, nursing mothers, or those working in heavy jobs in vital industries, etc.). A given point

[9]These various rationing systems are analyzed in much greater detail in Richard Gettell, "Rationing: A Pragmatic Problem for Economists," *American Economic Review,* 33, No. 1 (March 1943), pp. 260–71.

can be used for any of a number of products within the class of goods for which the points are valid. As relative scarcities change, either the point values or the monetary prices can be changed. During World War II in many countries such as the United States, clothing and certain other highly unstandarized commodities were rationed in this manner. In Eastern Europe today, those receiving foreign currency gifts from relatives abroad can spend such money only in special "foreign currency stores" where all sorts of scarce imported goods and, in some countries, scarce domestic goods can be purchased. In this case, foreign currency is a type of point ration coupon. If the product classes for which particular points can be used are defined broadly, few problems arise; if they are defined narrowly, certain consumers may end up with more points for goods in particular product class than they want and with a potential deficit in ration points for goods in another product class. A market for points between such product classes may or may not be allowed by the political authorities to develop.

(ii) Unit Rationing. Under the unit rationing method each consumer uses specified ration coupons to purchase only a given amount of *one* particular commodity (e.g., only for *X* kilos of sugar). As in point rationing all buyers pay not only the money price but a given number of ration coupons, which they receive according to their membership in particular groups. Again, when the supply of the scarce good changes, either the price of the good or the value of each coupon in terms of commodities can be changed so as to adapt supply to demand. Administration of such a program is more complicated than in the case of point rationing since separate stamps must be issued for separate commodities (although the task may be made more manageable by limiting the number of commodities covered by the rationing arrangement). A market between unit coupons for particular commodities may or may not be allowed to develop; in most cases, however, such trading is suppressed in the name of equity although analysis reveals this to be a very shaky argument.

(iii) Certificate or Administrative Rationing. In the case of certificate or administrative rationing each purchase must be approved by governmental authorities. During World War II in the United States a limited number of products were distributed in this way, including new automobiles, automobile tires, and new typewriters. Clearly such a rationing system is extremely costly to administer and is worthwhile to use only in situations where relatively costly products must be distributed. Given the rationale for such a rationing system, transfer of such certificates or goods purchased with the certificates is usually not permitted (although illegal "subletting" can occur in certain cases). Entry

into prestige universities is another situation where such certificate rationing is applied. It should be noted in passing that those administering such a certificate rationing system must have some method by which to arrive at their decisions and they may adopt criteria that resemble the other rationing systems. For instance, they may assign the good or service according to how long the person has been on the waiting list (a method used to allocate automobiles in Eastern Europe or subsidized apartments in certain cities all over the world). Or the administrators may assign points to various characteristics of the applicants and then allocate the goods according to the point totals (a method used to allocate admissions to elite U.S. universities or, in Switzerland, to give priority allocation of certain apartment spaces to those with particular health problems). Or they may allocate according to how much of the good or service the person has received in the past, trying to even the amount consumed by each person. Or they may allocate according to favoritism, arbitrary screening devices, and so forth.

Clearly most types of nonprice rationing do not permit either consumer *choice* or *sovereignty*. It should also be noticed that, contrary to the other cases where trade is structured to break the links between producers and consumers, nonprice allocation devices do not permit an easy calculation of the differences between the present production structure and that which would obtain under consumer sovereignty.

4. Consumption Institutions

Just as production decisions can be made in various types of units (in agriculture, these units can be family farms, collective farms such as Soviet *kolkhozi,* communes, or governmental ministries), so consumption decisions can be made by units other than individuals. The variety of these consumption units deserves brief attention.

Although in most modern economies the consumption decision unit is often the individual, in many cases the relevant decision-making unit is the family or some delegated member of the family. For instance, in the traditional early twentieth-century American or European household, the wife made most of the decisions about what foods were bought and consumed (usually trying, however, to take into account certain perferences expressed by other family members). In this situation an individual's choices of foods to eat were quite limited. With regard to food, the relevant consumption unit for many U.S. university students is the dormitory cafeteria where only a limited variety of food (allegedly poorly prepared) is served. For the institutionalized part of the population (those in prisons, hospitals, monasteries, or the armed services), the consumption unit is the relevant institution. In a number of nations, many people are living in cooperative groups (e.g., the kibbutzim in Israel, the Hutterites in America, the Society of Brothers in the United States and Europe) where the entire group is the most important consumption unit.

Less exotic examples occur in the consumption of *public goods* and certain other goods and services such as education where the relevant consumption unit in all modern nations most often is the local, state, or national government. In the discussion below, considerable attention is paid to the importance of such *public consumption.*

If the most important consumption unit is the family, the type of family often depends on the type of the economy. In gathering-hunting societies, the major consumption unit is quite often the elemental family (husband, wife, and children). In primitive agricultural societies, on the other hand, several generations can live together in an extended family so that the consumption unit is very much larger.[10]

In certain ways the consumption unit represents a conscious political choice and can be changed. As noted below, the most important change in the economic systems of the economically developed nations of the world since 1950 has been the dramatic rise in the share of consumption that is financed by taxes and decided upon by the government. The political choice of the consumption unit is not, however, without limits. For instance, in China during the Great Leap Forward, communes were introduced on a large scale in 1958. Not only was the work of all individuals directed by the commune (so that the commune also represented a change in the production unit) but food was served in large dining halls, clothes were doled out by commune officials, and both individual and family decision making about consumption was suppressed. Although communes lasted for some years, this radical change in the consumption unit was abandoned after some spectacular failures. This does not mean, of course, that less radical changes in the consumption unit could not occur or that such communes might not evolve more slowly in the future.

In analyzing consumption and consumption units, it is often useful to distinguish proximate and ultimate consumption. When analyzing consumption on the level of the family, we assume a given income and procede to examine how that income is spent and who are the ultimate enjoyers of the goods and services obtained. When analyzing consumption from a broader perspective, we know that various institutions such as government, philanthropies, churches, and insurance companies redistribute income and thus influence the consumption pattern. However, it is often extremely difficult to determine the distributional im-

---

[10]Empirical evidence on the relation of type of economy and family system is presented in Frederic L. Pryor, *The Origins of the Economy: A Comparative Study of Distribution in Primitive and Peasant Economies* (New York: Academic Press, 1977), chap. 1.

pact of such programs and institutions. For example, we can analyze the amount of education that is financed by private individuals and by redistributive agencies (e.g., the government) and then try to measure the relative importance of the consumption institution by the share of the service that it finances. However, this is looking only at immediate relationships; the real impact of the higher-level consumption unit (i.e., redistributive agency) can be measured only by determining what the total consumption of the given good or service would have been if that redistributive agency had not entered the picture (e.g., in the case where the government taxes people in order to obtain the funds to redistribute). Unfortunately, it is very difficult to make such analyses; we must have information about the elasticity of substitution between private and public expenditures, for which little data are available. This means that the following quantitative analysis of major changes in the consumption unit such as the increasing role of public consumption expenditures is incomplete and must be interpreted cautiously.

C. Some Evidence about Trade in Different Economic Systems

Certain hypotheses about the origins and development of trade institutions are discussed in Chapter 6. This analysis focuses on two propositions about the impact of trade institutions on the economic behavior of different countries in East and West. One of these propositions deals with domestic trade; the other, with foreign trade.

1. Domestic Trade

In the socialist, centrally administered economies of Eastern Europe, retail trade is carried out somewhat differently than in the capitalist, market economies of the OECD nations. For our purposes, several particular differences deserve notice.[11]

    a. In most Eastern European nations the lines of communication between consumers and producers are much less direct than in the capitalist, market economies. The production of a considerable share of consumer goods is planned by local or central governmental authorities; and information concerning surpluses and shortages of particular goods appears either to be less available or else to be less taken into account by those engaged in setting production goals.

---

[11]This discussion is drawn from the sources cited in the suggested readings for this chapter.

b. In most of these nations retail trade is characterized by relatively unchanging differential turnover taxes,[12] while in OECD nations retail trade is heavily taxed but the taxes are relatively uniform so that price ratios reflect more closely the marginal rates of transformation.

c. In most Eastern European nations, a considerable share of the retail prices are set by central authorities and are infrequently changed. In the capitalist, market economies, the prices are set by the sellers and are more responsive to changes in consumer demands. In some Western countries, the prices of particular goods are also much less uniform than in the East.[13]

d. In many Eastern European countries nonprice rationing devices play a more important role in the distribution of scarce goods and services. Such devices include local shortages (either deliberate or inadvertent), waiting-line procedures, distribution by favoritism, and so forth.

The system in many of the centrally administered nations of relatively unchanging prices and of extensive use of nonprice rationing devices means that their retail trade systems are not characterized by a high degree of consumer choice (since prices do not clear local markets). Without *consumer choice,* there cannot be *consumer sovereignty.* However, we should not fall into the logical trap of assuming that their pattern of production reflects less adequately the state of consumer demand than do production patterns in the market economies. The inexhaustible number of anecdotes about difficulties in finding what one wants to buy in Eastern Europe can spring solely from their incredibly inefficient retail systems (in contrast to China, where the retail system is allegedly much better); the proper goods can be available, but not at the right time or place.

One obvious inference to be drawn about the lack of a well-functioning consumer market is that shopping should be much more time

[12]Rates of turnover taxes have, unfortunately, received little empirical study. This generalization is drawn from the experience of the Soviet Union. Data for 1935 are presented in Franklyn D. Holzman, *Soviet Taxation* (Cambridge, Mass.: Harvard University Press, 1962), p. 149; data for the mid-1960s can be found in Daniel Gallik et al., *The Soviet Financial System: Structure, Operation, and Statistics,* U.S. Bureau of Census, International Population Statistics Report, Series P-90, No. 23 (Washington, D.C.: GPO, 1967), chap. 6.

[13]A fascinating paper by E. Scott Maynes et al., "Informationally Imperfect Markets: Implications for Consumers," presented at the convention of the American Economic Association, December 28, 1982, gives comparisons of the prices of a large number of consumer goods at different stores in the same U.S. cities. Such prices differ often by 100 percent for exactly the same goods; such price variation is not, to my knowledge, found in Eastern Europe (except, perhaps, in some free markets for agricultural goods).

TABLE 7–2
Shopping Times and Related Variables in the Mid-1960s

Country	Marketed Goods per Capita	Retail and Whole-Sale Personnel per 1,000 Population	Average Shopping and Marketing Time per Day (minutes)
Socialist, centrally administered economies			
Bulgaria	$212	18.1	29.24
Czechoslovakia	373	24.5	37.06
East Germany	460	37.5	33.82
Hungary	301	24.3	27.82
Poland	211	20.4	41.96
Soviet Union	341	19.7	40.76
Unweighted average		24.1	35.11
Yugoslavia			
Slovenia	298	{ 12.4	29.84
Serbia	150		40.16
Capitalist, market economies			
Belgium	$515	53.0	26.22
France	540	47.0	29.18
United States	802	71.1	27.90
West Germany	628	55.3	32.23
Unweighted average		56.6	28.88

Source: The data come from Frederic L. Pryor, "Some Costs and Benefits of Markets: An Empirical Study," *Quarterly Journal of Economics,* 91, No. 1 (February 1977), pp. 81–102.

consuming in East than in the West. Comparable information on shopping time is available from a multinational time budget study conducted under the auspices of UNESCO. Some relevant data are presented in Table 7–2.

At first glance our suspicions about shopping times appears verified, for the average daily shopping time in the East is roughly 25 percent higher than in the West. Since shopping is, in part, directly related to the amount of shopping that must be done and since the Western nations in the sample have a higher volume of marketed goods per capita, the higher shopping time in the East is even more notable. However, this is not quite the end of the story.

Shopping time depends, in part, on the number of available trade personnel to serve customers. The middle column of Table 7–2 shows that the retail and wholesale personnel per 1,000 population is considerably lower in the East than in the West. Regression experiments using a 21-nation sample reveal, indeed, that the centrally administered economies have only 53 percent as many retail personnel and 55 percent as many retail and wholesale personnel per capita as the market economies, holding income per capita constant.[14] There are also fewer retail stores per 1,000 population in Eastern Europe (a reflection of planners' preferences for larger outlets).

It is necessary to factor into the statistical analysis the relative number of trade personnel. Given the small size of the sample and a problem of multicolinearity (this is explained on Appendix A) between the explanatory variables, such a task must be carried out in a rather indirect fashion and the final results must be considered highly tentative.

The statistical calculations using as explanatory variables the marketed goods per capita, the trade personnel per 1,000 population, and the economic system reveal that the first two variables explain almost all of the difference in shopping time between the two groups of nations and that the systems variable per se explains very little.

Such an empirical result is quite disturbing in light of the theory that nonfunctioning consumer markets in centrally administered economies bring about more shopping time. However, before the theoretical evidence is discarded, several warning shots must be fired with regard to these empirical estimates. *First,* it is likely that in Western Europe, much more time is spent in shopping for pleasure than in Eastern Europe, so the shopping time data for the West are inflated. *Second,* the existence of shortages (especially for luxuries or for goods with many substitutes) can actually reduce shopping time if the shortages are known, since people won't even spend time looking. For instance, for many years in Prague people did not shop for potatoes except on Saturday since this was the only day this food was available. *Third,* the smaller range of quality variations among products in Eastern Europe reduces shopping time; that is, it is not necessary to look at many different types of television sets before making a decision (or investigating the price of a given set at many different stores). *Fourth,* other causal variables that possibly influence the results (e.g., the share of self-service stores, the number of retail outlets, etc.) are not included in the regression. *Finally,* the sample is very small to allow firm conclusions. Given these caveats, we cannot be completely sure that the systems variable makes no difference in shopping time, except insofar as the relative number of trade personnel is smaller; nevertheless, the results are worth pondering.

One last interesting experiment can be performed on these data to answer the following question: Do the centrally administered economies increase total hours of work at the expense of leisure by reducing the

---

[14]The regressions underlying this result, as well as the remainder of the discussion in this subsection, are drawn from Frederic L. Pryor, "Some Costs and Benefits of Markets: An Empirical Study," *Quarterly Journal of Economics,* 91, No. 1 (February 1977), pp. 81–102. The comparison of hours spent shopping to work hours saved by having fewer retail personnel are quite rough because of difficulties in handling part-time personnel.

number of trade personnel and requiring people to spend more time shopping? If one compares the total number of work hours saved in the socialist, centrally administered economies by having fewer trade personnel to the total number of additional hours that the citizens of these nations spend shopping (of course, holding the per capita GDP constant), one arrives at the startling conclusion that the two amounts of time are about the same. Or, to put the matter in somewhat different terms, the total work hours of trade personnel and hours spent shopping appear to be roughly the same in all economies with the same volume of marketed goods per capita, regardless of economic system.

2. Foreign Trade

The foreign trade systems of the centrally administered economies of Eastern Europe are also quite different from those in Western Europe. The following important differences can be observed:[15]

a.   In the East foreign trade is centrally planned using the system of material balances, while in the West the volume and composition of foreign trade is left primarily to market forces.

b.   Because of problems of currency convertibility, planners in the East often try to obtain bilateral balancing of exports and imports with individual nations.[16] In the West only overall balancing of exports and imports is usually of interest to policy makers.

c.   In the East for many years foreign trade was channeled through a small number of foreign trade enterprises that acted as a barrier in trade transactions between their country and the rest of the world. It was difficult for Western exporters to contact the buying companies directly; and it was difficult for Western importers to negotiate directly with the producing companies. Although this situation is slowly changing, the number of companies directly engaged in foreign trade is very much less in the East than in the West.

For these and other reasons, it is often argued that the centrally planned nations have a lower volume of foreign trade than market economies, other factors remaining constant.[17] Studies of the volume of

[15]These generalizations are drawn from the sources cited in the suggested readings to this chapter.

[16]The motives for such bilateral balancing are quite clear. However, there is some dispute about the degree to which such bilateral balancing is actually achieved, which appears relatively close to that of many Western nations.

[17]This argument is developed in considerable detail by Edward Hewett, "Foreign Trade Outcomes in Eastern and Western Economies," in Paul Marer and John Michael Montias, eds., *East European Integration and East-West Trade* (Bloomington: Indiana University Press, 1980), pp. 41–69.

foreign trade in East and West in the 1950s and early 1960s also verified this proposition. Some relevant data on this matter for 1970 are
presented in Table 7–3. In studying these data, two problems must be
borne in mind. First, the dollar value of trade for the Eastern European
nations is overstated by very roughly 10 percent.[18] Second, trade in both
parts of Europe has increased considerably more rapidly since 1970 than
GDP growth. Because these later years very much reflect the impact of
the series of oil price increases after 1973, it is believed that comparing
trade in 1970 permits us to isolate more carefully the impact of the
systems variable alone (at least until the various nations have adjusted
to the impact of the oil price shocks).

Since it is generally considered that foreign trade is relatively
more important in nations with higher level of economic development
and is relatively less important in nations with large domestic markets
(represented in terms of the population), any analysis of trade GDP
ratios in nations with different economic systems must include these
variables. From the data of Table 7–3 the following regression equation
can be calculated:

$$T/Y = 44.6^* + .136 \; Y/C - 3.91^* \; LPOP - 3.11 \; S \qquad \begin{array}{cc} R^2 & n \\ .5391 & 28 \end{array}$$
$$ (9.3) \quad (.069) \qquad (0.94) \qquad (2.89)$$

where

T/Y = ratio of trade to GDP in 1970 (both calculated in dollars)
Y/C = per capita GDP in a common currency in 1970
$LPOP$ = logarithm of the population
S = economic system (0 = market; 1 = centrally administered)
R^2 = coefficient of determination
n = sample size (Yugoslavia is omitted)
( ) = standard errors
* = statistical significance at the .95 degree of confidence

As theoretical evidence might suggest, the trade-GDP ratio is
directly proportional to the income per capita and is inversely proportional to the size of the domestic market (as measured by the population). Although the ratio of foreign trade to GDP is lower in the socialist,
centrally administered economies of Eastern Europe than in the capitalist, market economies of Western Europe, the calculated coefficient for
the systems variable is not statistically significant. However, as noted

[18]The problem of trade valuation, albeit without an exact estimate, is discussed by
Paul Marer, *Soviet and East European Foreign Trade, 1946–1969* (Bloomington: Indiana
University Press, 1972), app. C. The 10 percent datum cited in the text represents a very
rough estimate.

TABLE 7-3
The Relative Importance of Foreign Trade in East and West in 1970

Country	Relative Per Capita GDP in 1970	Population in 1970 (thousands)	Ratio of Trade to GDP in 1970
Socialist, centrally administered economies			
Bulgaria	37.3	8,980	12.6%
Czechoslovakia	62.0	14,339	8.8
East Germany	63.9	17,058	9.0
Hungary	42.7	10,338	11.4
Poland	35.4	32.473	6.5
Romania	31.2	20,244	6.3
Soviet Union	46.9	242,768	4.1
Unweighted average			8.4%
Yugoslavia	25.8	20,371	5.0%
Capitalist, market economies			
Australia	69.6	12,666	10.8%
Austria	63.1	7,447	14.2
Belgium	72.0	9,638	33.4
Canada	81.9	21,406	17.6
Denmark	83.3	4,929	19.7
Finland	63.1	4,606	17.8
France	73.2	50,670	10.4
West Germany	78.2	60,700	14.1
Greece	38.7	8,793	8.0
Ireland	40.5	2,954	22.8
Italy	49.2	53,565	11.2
Japan	59.2	103,430	6.5
Netherlands	68.7	13,032	29.4
New Zealand	64.6	2,820	14.2
Norway	68.4	3,877	24.2
Portugal	27.1	8,628	11.3
Spain	48.9	33,779	4.5
Sweden	86.6	8,043	20.7
Switzerland	72.4	6,627	26.8
United Kingdom	63.5	55,480	12.2
United States	100.0	204,879	4.2
Unweighted average			15.9%

Note: "Trade" is the arithmetic average of exports (f.o.b.) and imports (c.i.f.), both denominated in dollars. As noted in the text, trade for Eastern Europe is overstated. The GDP used in this ratio is calculated as the product of population, relative GDP per capita in dollars, and GDP in market prices for the United States in 1970. These ratios are quite different from similar calculations made in national currencies.

Sources: The sources of the GDP and population data are cited in Appendix D. The trade data come from UNESCO, *Handbook of International Trade and Development Statistics 1979* (New York: 1980).

above, the dollar value of trade in Eastern Europe is overstated. Correction of this factor and recalculation of the regression would probably confirm the proposition that foreign trade is relatively lower in the centrally planned economies.

A number of other propositions have been advanced linking the economic system to the composition and direction of foreign trade.[19] Although these matters cannot be discussed here, the discussion above should give some indication of one important issue in this debate.

D. Some Evidence on Consumption in Different Economic Systems

The brief description in the previous section of the retail systems in East and West suggests that we can find considerable differences in the patterns of consumption and consumption prices in the two sets of nations. Although one study outlined below does provide some empirical evidence on such questions, currently available data do not permit a very exact assessment of the situation. Given the available data, however, we can study a number of interesting developmental propositions about the causal forces underlying the origin of public consumption institutions and change of patterns of public consumption. Impact propositions about the differential effects of public and private consumption prove much more difficult to analyze from an empirical perspective because of data problems.

1. Aspects of Private Consumption in East and West

Before turning to public consumption, it is useful to pause briefly to examine private consumption in nations with different economic systems. However, comparing private consumption requires quite detailed data for a number of nations and, unfortunately, only one such study focusing on countries in both East and West appears to have been carried out in recent years.[20] It deals with the pattern of consumption in 30 capitalist, market economies plus four socialist nations in Eastern Europe: Hungary, Yugoslavia, Poland, and Romania. The first two nations have introduced certain market elements into their economies; the latter two have much more important elements of central administration.

[19]Several interesting empirical studies along these lines are Hewett, "Foreign Trade Outcomes"; and Peter Murrell, "An Evaluation of the Success of the Hungarian Economic Reform: An Analysis Using International Trade Data," *Journal of Comparative Economics,* 5, No. 4 (December 1981), pp. 352–67.

[20]Frederic L. Pryor, "A Quantitative Study of the Structure and Behavior of Consumption and Prices in Different Economic Systems," in Armin Bohnet, ed., *Preise in Sozialismus am Beispiel Ungarns* (forthcoming, 1984).

Holding price and income constant and examining 103 categories of goods and services for the year 1975, few important differences are found in the pattern of consumption in the market and centrally administered economies. Several reasons can be given to explain such a surprising result. *First,* so much variation in consumption occurs between different capitalist nations at the same level of development that the particular uniqueness of the socialist nations can not be isolated unless more causal variables could be held constant. *Second,* it is possible that if Bulgaria, Czechoslovakia, East Germany, and the Soviet Union were included, greater differences between the market and centrally administered nations could be isolated. *Third,* differences between the two sets of nations might also be noticeable only if the data could be disaggregated to a greater degree.

The same study also yields another surprising result; namely, in 1975, the structure of consumer prices was not greatly different between the 30 market economies and most of the socialist nations (Romania is an exception). Again, variations in prices between the capitalist nations are extremely great and this might mask differences between the two sets of nations.

Since the data on private consumption are limited, it seems more fruitful to turn to differences in public consumption in East and West.

2. Goods and Services That Are Publicly Financed

The preceding discussion in this chapter about market breakdowns suggests several important considerations to take into account in order to predict whether the good or service is publicly financed. We would certainly expect that public goods would be publicly financed, that production of goods with consumption externalities would be either publicly financed or subsidized, and that certain goods and services where risk considerations are important (e.g., health insurance) might also be financed through the fiscal system. However, upon reflection it becomes rapidly apparent that such public goods and services constitute only a small part of expenditures of the public sector in all nations. Further, it is very difficult to determine in a quantitative fashion the relative importance of consumption externalities in many cases or the degree to which risk skimming might become sufficiently important to warrant financing through the public sector. Consequently this line of approach does not seem very promising for empirical research, even though the theoretical implications are important.

Although a number of other hypotheses have been proposed to explain why certain goods and services are financed publicly, few have been statistically tested because the requisite data are difficult to obtain. The most recent large-scale empirical examination of this problem appears to be a detailed analysis of some 500 services financed by different towns and cities in the U.S. state of Minnesota.[21] In this study few of the investigated services manifest consumption externalities or public good features. The best predictor of whether or not a service is financed by a governmental unit is the size of the population served by that unit; that is, the larger the population, the more services are publicly financed. Although the authors of this study offer no satisfactory explanation of the underlying mechanisms, several factors can be conjectured. For instance, the larger the population served by the local government, the more heterogenous the population is likely to be; this in turn may increase the demand for the number of special services financed by the government. Further, the larger the population, the greater the possible economies of scale for the production of certain services, and therefore the greater the number of governmentally financed services.

In general, current knowledge of the causal forces underlying the specific goods and services produced and/or financed by the government is quite inadequate. Until much more detailed empirical investigations can be carried out, we must rest content with untested conjectures.

3. Determinants of the Volume of Public Expenditures

The most important systematic change in the capitalist, market economies in the last quarter century has been the increase in public expenditures. For instance, the average ratio of public expenditures (current, capital, and transfers) to the GNP in the OECD nations has risen from 28.5 percent in 1955–57 to 34.5 percent in 1967–69 to 41.4 percent in 1975–76.[22] Leading this increase has been the rise in "welfare state expenditures," that is, expenditures for education, health, and social welfare (which include income maintenance and old age pensions).

Comparable data on public consumption expenditures (i.e., current expenditures and transfers) are available for a group of countries in East and West for seven key areas. These expenditures as a percentage of gross production in factor costs are presented in Table 7–4. For the capitalist, market economies, the data reflect the dramatic upward trend just mentioned. It is noteworthy that in Eastern Europe, the share of total public expenditures in the GNP went in the opposite direction until 1970, at which time it began to follow trends in the West and rose. The relative importance of welfare state expenditures in these socialist, centrally administered economies appears to have risen, but much more slowly than in the West.

---

[21]Henry J. Schmandt and G. Ross Stevens, "Measuring Municipal Output," *National Tax Journal*, 12, No. 4 (1960), pp. 369–75.

[22]OECD, *Public Expenditure Trends* (Paris: 1978).

TABLE 7–4
Public Consumption Expenditures in East and West, 1956–76

	Percent of Gross Domestic Production							
	Adjusted Budget Expenditures				Welfare State Expenditures			
Nation[a]	1956	1962	1970	1976	1956	1962	1970	1976
Socialist, centrally administered economies								
East Germany	33%	30%	32%	36%	19%	20%	20%	22%
Czechoslovakia	31	27	26	33	20	18	19	24
Soviet Union	30	30	27	28	14	14	14	16
Hungary	23	19	18	28	11	12	11	20
Bulgaria	28	21	20	25	14	12	14	17
Poland	21	20	23	21	12	12	15	14
Romania	20	18	17	13	10	12	12	9
Unweighted average	28%	24%	23%	26%	14%	14%	15%	17%
Yugoslavia	27%	28%	28%	30%	13%	16%	18%	19%
Capitalist, market economies								
United States	20%	23%	26%	27%	8%	11%	14%	19%
West Germany	25	29	28	38	18	19	20	29
Austria	25	28	31	35	21	23	26	30
Italy	24	25	28	33	15	17	21	16
Ireland	21	18	24	34	16	14	18	26
Greece	17	18	24	24	8	10	14	13
Unweighted average	22%	24%	27%	32%	14%	16%	19%	22%

Note: Adjusted budget expenditures include current expenditures for administration, external security (defense and diplomacy), internal security (police and justice) research and development, education, health and welfare. The last three types of expenditures are aggregated as "welfare state expenditures." Expenditures for the first three types of expenditures represent rough estimates. None of the expenditure data include private expenditures for the same purposes. For the market economies, the data are calculated as a percentage of GDP in factor cost prices; for the centrally administered economies, GNP in factor cost prices.

[a]Nations are arranged roughly according to descending order of level of per capita GDP.

Sources: The data come from Frederic L. Pryor, Public Expenditures in Communist and Capitalist Nations (London: Allen and Unwin, 1968); and "Public Expenditure Trends in East and West," in Gustav Ranis et al., eds, Comparative Development Perspectives (Boulder Colo.: Westview Press, 1984), pp. 362–89.

These trends have attracted considerable attention and a number of hypotheses have been offered to explain the increasing relative importance of public expenditures. The most important causal factors that have been offered can be classified according to whether they focus on the demand or the supply side.[23]

[23]A much more complete list of causal factors can be found in the sources listed for Table 7–4. The empirical investigations on the data from East and West that are referred to in the following paragraphs also come from the same sources.

a. Important Demand Factors

(i) Economic System. On the basis of their ideology it might be argued that socialist nations would have a relatively higher level of public consumption expenditures. On the basis of the aggregative data in Tables 7–4 this proposition receives no empirical support.

(ii) Level of Development. The most famous early theorist on determinants of public expenditures is Adolph Wagner, who formulated a long-run "law" that the share of such expenditures rises with an increasing level of economic development.[24] In order to justify this proposition on theoretical grounds, Wagner divided public expenditures into two categories: (1) expenditures for internal and external security, and (2) expenditures on culture and welfare (which include education, health, culture, social welfare, public transportation, communication, and banking expenditures). For security expenditures he foresaw increases due to the shifts from offensive to standing defensive armies and, with regard to police expenditures, to the growing social frictions induced by increasing urbanization. For culture and welfare expenditures he essentially argued that such expenditures have an income elasticity of demand that is greater than unity and, further, that the public sector would increasingly encroach upon the private sector.

Although time series data for Western nations show a rising ratio of public expenditures to GNP as per capita income increases, the cross-section data presented in Table 7–4 offer no support for any relationship between per capita income and the relative importance of public consumption expenditures. However, as noted below, for certain individual public expenditures defined by function, such a relationship can be found.

b. Important Supply Factors

(i) Relative Productivity Effects. Because productivity in the provision of services is generally considered to rise more slowly than in the production of goods, and because wages in most governmental sectors keep pace with wages in the rest of the economy, the relative costs of a given volume of governmental services will rise. For making international comparisons, the data on wages in the governmental sector are not sufficiently detailed to allow us to take this factor into account. However, since wages in general are higher in nations with higher per capita GDPs, we would expect the share of the governmental sector to be higher in the nations with higher levels of development, other things being equal.

---

[24]Wagner's style is so murky that it is difficult to determine exactly what he means by his "law." An excellent summary of his ideas is Herbert Timm, "Das Gesetz der wachsenden Staatsuasgaben," *Finanzarchiv*, N.F., Band 21 (September 1961), pp. 201–47.

(ii) The "Displacement Effect." In a well-known book Alan Peacock and Jack Wiseman propose that the pattern of government expenditures over time reveals a ratchet effect that is related to the difficulty of raising tax rates except in periods of national emergency.[25] If tax rates are raised during the emergency, they can generally be maintained at this higher level after the emergency recedes, thus permitting the government to increase its expenditures. With the data in Table 7-4 this proposition can not be tested. However, a number of economists have used time series data to make the proper tests; in general, such evidence provides little support for the propositions.

(iii) Bureaucracy Effects. It is often argued that administrators of government bureaus are interested in increasing their personal power by attempting to persuade the legislature to increase the budget of the bureau. Although such an approach appears unpromising in explaining differences in public expenditures on an aggregative level, for particular expenditures it has some interesting implications that are briefly explored below.

(iv) A Voting Mechanism Approach. Recently Sam Peltzman has proposed an elegant mechanism to explain the growth of government expenditures. In essence, he argues that politicans in order to maximize their votes propose programs to tax a minority in order to subsidize a majority; and from such an approach he derives propositions such as the greater the income differences between the minority rich and the majority poor, the higher public expenditures and taxes will be.[26] Unfortunately, this type of approach does not apply to the one-party states found in Eastern Europe. It also does not appear to explain well the data for Western nations in the sample. For instance, welfare state expenditures are much higher in West Germany than in the United States, where the distribution of income is more unequal.

The conclusions from this brief survey can be easily summarized: It is difficult to find any convincing explanations of the determinants of aggregative public expenditures. On the other hand, much more success is obtained if we examine individual types of public expenditures, for example, by separating health, education, and welfare expenditures. Some data of this nature are presented in Table 7-5.

Education expenditures seem to be a function of per capita income. It is interesting to note that income elasticities appear much greater if

---

[25]Alan T. Peacock and Jack Wiseman, *The Growth of Public Expenditures in the United Kingdom* (Princeton, N.J.: Princeton University Press, 1961).

[26]Sam Peltzman, "The Growth of Government," *The Journal of Law and Economics,* 23, No. 2 (October 1980), pp. 204–89. The income distribution data refered to later in the paragraph come from Malcolm Sawyer, "Income Distribution in OECD Countries," *OECD Economic Outlook: Occasional Studies* (Paris: 1976).

TABLE 7–5
Education, Health, and Welfare Data in East and West, 1956 and 1976

Nation	Education 1956	Education 1976	Health 1956	Health 1976	Welfare 1956	Welfare 1976	Population 65 and over as Percent of Population from 15 through 64 — 1956	1976
Socialist, centrally administered economies								
East Germany	3.8%	4.9%	4.4%	5.1%	10.7%	11.7%	19.7%	26.0%
Czechoslovakia	3.8	3.9	4.2	3.8	11.9	16.3	12.7	18.8
Soviet Union	4.4	3.7	3.0	2.6	6.4	9.3	8.9	12.4
Hungary	2.7	3.4	2.6	5.3	5.6	11.6	12.7	19.3
Bulgaria	5.1	3.9	3.4	3.1	5.5	10.3	10.9	16.2
Poland	2.6	3.2	2.6	3.3	6.5	7.1	8.7	14.7
Romania	3.4	2.5	2.7	1.9	3.8	5.0	9.6	15.1
Unweighted average	3.7%	3.6%	3.3%	3.6%	7.2%	10.1%		
Yugoslavia	2.1%	4.8%	3.2%	4.5%	7.5%	10.0%	9.6%	13.3%
Capitalist, market economies								
United States	2.4%	5.0%	0.9%	2.9%	4.8%	11.3%	14.5%	16.4%
West Germany	2.2	3.8	2.6	5.1	13.1	20.6	14.8	22.9
Austria	2.5	4.6	2.8	4.6	15.5	21.1	17.1	24.4
Italy	2.7	5.0	3.0	6.1	9.8	14.8	13.2	17.6
Ireland	2.6	5.8	3.8	7.4	10.0	13.3	18.3	18.8
Greece	1.3	2.0	1.0	1.4	5.3	9.3	11.5	19.5
Unweighted average	2.3%	4.4%	2.4%	4.6%	9.8%	15.1%		

Note: As in Table 7–4, the data exclude privately financed expenditures for these purposes.

Sources: The expenditure data come from the sources cited in Table 7–4. The population data come from United Nations, *Demographic Yearbook* (New York: various issues); and OECD, *Labour Force Statistics* (Paris: various issues). For several of the centrally administered economies, the population data refer to 1975 instead of 1976; the data for the Soviet Union had, in part, to be estimated.

time series, rather than cross-section data, are used (at least in the West). This might be attributed to the fact that all nations face roughly the same technology at a given point in time; therefore, the educational demands to master such technology are roughly the same for all nations; over time, however, the level of technology rises and the educational demands rise accordingly.

For welfare expenditures an interesting bureaucratic phenomenon can be isolated. The longer the social security system has been in operation, the longer such a system has had to expand its operations to cover a larger share of the population and to give them greater monetary coverage. Combining this with the systems variable, we can calculate the following regressions:

$$1956: W/Y = 1.04 - \underset{(0.150)}{0.274} S + \underset{(0.0053)}{0.0209^*} YRS \quad \begin{matrix} R^2 & n \\ .5172 & 14 \end{matrix}$$

$$1976: W/Y = 1.93 - \underset{(0.166)}{0.364^*} S + \underset{(0.0058)}{0.0127^*} YRS \quad .4582 \quad 14$$

where

W/Y = ratio of welfare expenditures to gross production

S = economic system: 0 = market economy (including Yugoslavia); 1 = centrally administered economy

YRS = number of years separating the founding of the social insurance system and 1970

R^2 = coefficient of determination

n = size of sample

( ) = standard errors

* = statistical significance at the .05 level

Such results appear very interesting. It is noteworthy that economic system is negatively related to the welfare expenditures variable and, in 1976, to a significant extent. This means that state welfare expenditures as a share of GDP are lower in the socialist, centrally administered economies than in the capitalist, market economies. The bureaucratic variable performs as expected. An alternative explanation of differences in welfare expenditures is that such expenditures are greatly influenced by the relative number of pensioners in the system. Using the demographic variable presented in Table 7–5 and a systems variable, similar regressions can be run. For both years the calculated coefficient of the demographic variable is also statistically significant but the degree of explanatory power is much lower. In short, these results suggest that a supply variable (the length of time of operation of the social insurance system) seems to explain welfare expenditures better than an obvious demand variable (the relative important of the aged population); however, the sample is too small to allow an absolutely firm conclusion to be drawn. For health expenditures similar regressions can be calculated and the length of time of the operation of the social insurance system also appears to play an important role.

If the length of time of the operation of the social insurance variable is so important, we are quite justified in asking why the social insurance systems in various nations were established at different points in time. If we compare 25 leading nations in 1914, of which roughly half had social insurance systems, we find little relationship between the level of per capita income and the existence of such a

TABLE 7–6
Total Current Public and Private Welfare and Pension Expenditures
in the United States, 1957–58

	Percent of Factor Price GNP	Percent of Total Welfare and Pension Expenditures
Public funds		
Social insurance	3.56%	44%
Other	2.17	26
Private funds		
Philanthropy	0.24	3
Insurance and enterprise payments for short term losses	0.48	6
Insurance and enterprise payments for pensions	1.68	21
Total	8.14%	100%

Source: The data come from Frederic L. Pryor, *Public Expenditures in Communist and Capitalist Nations* (London: Allen and Unwin, 1968), p. 142.

system. However, it can be argued that such social insurance systems were strongly favored by workers and we can use as a measure of the degree of political mobilization of workers the percentage of the labor force enrolled in labor unions. In such an exercise, as discussed in Chapter 1, we find a highly significant and positive relationship between this kind of political mobilization and the existence of social insurance institutions.[27]

A number of other propositions about the determinants of other public expenditures have been proposed and tested on samples of nations in East and West. Still other propositions have been tested on an international sample and have focused on the degree to which governmental expenditures are carried out on the national or local governmental levels, that is, propositions that focus on the size of the consumption unit from a different perspective. The brief discussion above should, however, give a taste of this interesting literature.

Before turning to impact propositions, several additional features of these data must be noted. The data refer only to governmentally financed expenditures. However, in certain Western nations such as the United States, many such "public" expenditures are financed from other sources (including insurance companies, which act to "socialize" risk). An example of welfare expenditures in the United States is provided in Table 7–6. In the West, furthermore, private individuals make considerable expenditures for health and education; if we wish to consider

[27]This exercise is carried out in Frederic L. Pryor, *Public Expenditures in Communist and Capitalist Nations,* (London: Allen and Unwin, 1968), pp. 473–75.

total expenditures for such purposes, we must add these to the public expenditures. Finally, the composition of some of these expenditures is quite different in the two sets of nations. For instance, although the share of welfare expenditures directed to the elderly is about the same in both sets of nations, a much larger share of welfare expenditures appears to be directed to working age adults in the market economies and to children and youth in the centrally administered economies. The welfare expenditures to those of working age provide income support for unemployment and other vagaries of market economies.

4. Impacts of Public Expenditures

Two major impacts of public expenditures can be investigated. First, the source of financing of a good or service might affect the distribution of its consumption. Second, the source of financing of the good or service might affect the efficiency of production.

Some types of expenditures of consumption units broader than the family are specifically designed to equalize the distribution of income or consumption. Although the greatest share of such expenditures are made by governments, other organizations such as churches, philanthropic agencies, and insurance companies also participate (as shown in Table 7–6), and the total impact of public expenditures must take these into account as well.

Some dramatic examples of the impact of such redistributive expenditures can be seen in the field of health. For instance, infant mortality in the United Kingdom was considerably higher than in the United States from the 1920s through 1947. However, in 1948 when "socialized medicine" was introduced in the United Kingdom, the infant mortality rate dropped below that of the United States and has remained below ever since. Part of this drop was due to the fact that poorer families were receiving adequate prenatal and maternal care for the first time in their lives. Part may have also been due to the conscious geographical redistribution of medical services that accompanied the introduction of the national health service.[28]

Unfortunately, it is usually quite difficult to examine empirically and on an international basis other propositions about the impact of

[28]Of course, the public financing of health care does not necessary mean that health care distribution is geographically more evenly spread. For instance, the variation by region of the ratio of physicians to population is twice as great in the Soviet Union as in the United States (ibid., p. 161). It should also be noted that public financing per se may not lower infant mortality if other causal factors are in operation. For instance, in recent years the infant mortality in the Soviet Union has reached levels twice as high as in the West, a phenomenon that has been blamed partly on the medical care system and partly on the high rate of alcoholism among pregnant women and nursing mothers in that country.

consumption institutions, especially with regard to the efficiency of production. This is not only because few testable propositions exist but also because the requisite data are very difficult to obtain. Almost all of the studies along these lines deal with the impact of different methods of institutionalizing consumption in a single economy (e.g., the consumption of garbage collection services discussed in Chapter 1).

E. A Brief Summary

Although consumer sovereignty is often considered to be an important performance criterion for evaluating economic systems, some important objections to such a goal can be raised. However, this does not necessarily mean that guiding an economy by "planners' preferences" would be any better. The problem is confounded even further when it is realized that perfect consumer sovereignty may not be achievable in any economic system. Market breakdowns and risk problems can prevent a decentralized market economy from reaching this goal, while high information costs and lack of adequate mechanisms to reveal consumer preferences in nonprice distribution systems may also prevent a totally centralized economy from achieving it.

Trade institutions mediate between producers and consumers and can impede communication between these groups in a variety of ways. Rationing institutions, either formal or informal, are among the ways in which a wedge can be driven between consumers and producers. Data presented above show how the domestic trade institutions in Eastern Europe lead to more time spent in shopping by consumers; however, most if not all of this difference appears to be attributable to a policy decision in Eastern Europe to limit the number of wholesale and retail personnel, rather than to the institutions *per se.* Foreign trade is also institutionalized in a quite different fashion in the two economic systems. As a result, the volume of trade appears to be (although we can't be certain) lower in socialist, centralized economies than in capitalist, market economies of a similar size and level of economic development.

Consumption institutions can also vary considerably, especially as to the level at which consumption decisions are made. The single most important systemic change in the West in the last 25 years is the dramatic rise in the share of consumption decisions that are made at the governmental level. It is shown that relative public expenditures for education, health, and welfare in the market economies are equal to or greater than those in centrally administered economies. Certain supply and demand factors can be demonstrated to play important causal roles determining the relative level of such expenditures across systems.

SUGGESTED READINGS

A. Theoretical Approaches to Consumption

1. George H. Hildebrand, "Consumer Sovereignty in Modern Times," *American Economic Review*, 41, No. 2 (May 1951), pp. 19–33, outlines the major issues. However, the consumer sovereignity debate rages afresh in new garbs about every decade. In the *American Economic Review*, 52, No.2 (May 1962), pp. 262–90, there is an exchange of views between Tibor Skitovsky, Abram Bergson, and Jerome Rothenberg; in the *American Economic Review*, 62, No. 2 (May 1972), pp. 258–79, there is a debate between Abba Lerner and Herbert Gintis that introduces a quasi-Marxist perspective. Joan Robinson, "Consumer Sovereignty in a Planned Economy," in Alec Nove and D. M. Nuti, eds., *Socialist Economics* (Baltimore: Penguin Books, 1972), pp. 263–75, provides a somewhat different viewpoint on the problem.

2. John Kenneth Galbraith, *The New Industrial State* (Boston: Houghton Mifflin, 1967), chaps. 18–19, presents in condensed form the thesis originally made in his *The Affluent Society* (Boston: Houghton Mifflin, 1958) that consumer tastes are strongly manipulated by an industrial technostructure (i.e., managers) that is trying to even out production over time and raise profits. A summary of the theoretical criticism of these ideas is presented by Myron Sharpe, *John Kenneth Galbraith and the Lower Economics*, 2nd ed. (White Plains, N.Y.: IASP, 1974). An empirical test of Galbraith's ideas is carried out by Harold Demsetz, "Discussion," *American Economic Review*, 50 (May 1970), pp. 481–85; "Where Is the New Industrial State?" *Economic Inquiry*, 12, No. 1 (March 1974), pp. 1–2; and "Advertising in the Affluent Society," in Yale Brozen, ed., *Advertising and Society* (New York: New York University Press, 1974), pp. 67–78. See also W. S. Comanor and T. A. Wilson, *Advertising and Market Power* (Cambridge, Mass.: Harvard University Press, 1974).

3. The role of public goods in a theory of consumer sovereignty adds a complication. Richard Musgrave, *Fiscal Systems* (New Haven, Conn.: Yale University Press, 1969), chap. 1, outlines how it can be included. A neat diagrammatic analysis is presented by Paul Samuelson, "Diagrammatic Exposition of a Theory of Public Expenditures," *Review of Economics and Statistics*, 37 (November 1955), pp. 350–56.

B. Rationing Problems

1. Richard Gettell, "Rationing: A Pragmatic Problem for Economists," *American Economic Review*, 33 (March 1943), pp. 260–71, analyzes the various types of formal rationing devices.

2. During and after World War II a number of interesting essays on rationing problems appeared in economic journals all over the world. For the experience in the United States, J. A. Maxwell and M. N. Balcom, "Gasoline Rationing in the United States," *Quarterly Journal of Economics*, 60 (August 1946), pp. 561–87; and Vol. 61 (November 1946), pp. 125–55, provide an extremely interesting case study. For an overview of policy problems, see John Kenneth Galbraith, "The Strategy of Direct Controls in Economic Mobilization," *Review of Economics and Statistics*, 22 No. 1 (February 1951), pp. 12–17.

C. Consumption and Domestic Trade in Eastern Europe

1. Alec Nove, *The Soviet Economic System* (London: Allen and Unwin, 1977), chap. 10, pp. 149–72. This survey (which includes foreign trade) is for orientation purposes.

2. Marshall I. Goldman, *Soviet Marketing: Distribution in a Controlled Economy* (Glencoe, Ill.: Free Press, 1963), especially chaps. 2, 3, 7, and 8. There are a number of other monographs on the retail sector in Eastern Europe: Al Dimaio, *Soviet Urban Housing* (New York: Praeger, n.d.); Philip Hanson, *The Consumer in the Soviet Economy* (London: Macmillan, 1968); Philip Hanson, *Advertising in Socialism* (New York: IASP, 1974); NATO, *Economic Aspects of Life in the USSR* (Brussels: 1975); and V.I. Raitsin, *Planning the Standard of Living According to Consumption Norms* (White Plains, N.Y.: IASP, 1969).

3. A number of articles focus on particular aspects of the retail sector and consumption in Eastern Europe. Among the most useful are Imogene Edwards, "Automotive Trends in the USSR," and Gertrude E. Schroeder, "Consumption in the USSR: A Survey," in Morris Bornstein and Daniel Fusfeld, eds., *The Soviet Economy* (Homewood, Ill.: Richard D. Irwin, 1974), pp. 269–327; Marshall Goldman, "The Reluctant Consumer and Economic Fluctuations in the Soviet Union," *Journal of Political Economy,* 73, No. 4 (August 1965), pp. 366–88; Henry Morton, "Who Gets What, When, and How? Housing in the Soviet Union," *Soviet Studies,* 23 (April 1980), pp. 235–60; Dennis O'Hearn, "The Consumer Second Economy: Size and Effects," *Soviet Studies,* 23 (April 1980), pp. 218–34; Frederic L. Pryor, "Some Costs of Markets: An Empirical Study," *Quarterly Journal of Economics,* 91 (February 1977), pp. 81–102; Roger Skurski, "The Buyers' Market and Soviet Consumer Goods Distribution," *Slavic Review,* 31 (December 1972), pp. 817–30; Philip Weitzman, "Soviet Long-Term Consumption Planning," *Soviet Studies,* 24 (July 1974), pp. 305–22; or J.H. Walters, "Retailing in Poland," and M. Skobe, "Marketing and Advertising in Yugoslavia," in Montrose S. Sommers and Jerome B. Kernan, eds., *Comparative Marketing Systems* (New York: Appleton Century Crofts, 1968), pp. 289–307.

D. Public Consumption in East and West

1. Frederic L. Pryor, *Public Expenditures in Communist and Capitalist Nations* (Homewood, Ill.: Richard D. Irwin, 1968).

2. Frederic L. Pryor, "Interpretation of Public Expenditure Trends in East and West," in Gustav Ranis, ed., *Comparative Development Perspectives* (Boulder, Colo.: Westview Press, 1984), pp. 362–89.

E. Foreign Trade in Eastern Europe

1. A useful overview is Franklyn Holzman, "Foreign Trade Behavior of Centrally Planned Economies," in Morris Borstein, ed., *Comparative Economic Systems: Models and Cases,* 4th ed. (Homewood, Ill.: Richard D. Irwin, 1979), pp. 279–315, and readings, pp. 261–79.

2. A number of monographs and collections of articles on Eastern European trade have appeared. The most useful include Sander Ausch, *Theory and Practice of CMEA Cooperation* (Budapest: Akademiai Kiado, 1972); Alan Brown and Egon Neuberger, eds., *International Trade and Central Planning* (Berkeley: University of California Press, 1968); Jozef M. Brabant, *East European Cooperation: The Role of Money and Finance* (New York: Praeger, 1977); Franklyn Holzman, *Foreign Trade under Central Planning* (Cambridge, Mass.: Harvard University Press, 1974); Paul Marer and John Michael Montias, *East European Integration and East-West Trade* (Bloomington: Indiana University Press, 1980); Frederic L. Pryor, *The Communist Foreign Trade System* (Cambridge, Mass.: MIT Press, 1963); Peter Wiles, *Communist International Economics* (Oxford:

Blackwell, 1968); and Adam Zwass, *Monetary Cooperation between East and West* (White Plains, N.Y.: IASP, 1975)

    3. A useful survey on changes in the foreign trade systems is Alan Brown and Paul Marer, "Foreign Trade in the East European Reforms," in Morris Bornstein, ed., *Plan and Market* (New Haven, Conn.: Yale University Press, 1973), pp. 153–207.

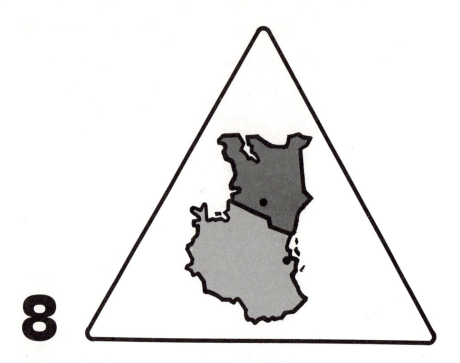

8

FACTOR ALLOCATION AND THE DISTRIBUTION OF INCOME

A. Introduction

Every economic system must allocate the factors of production in some manner. Although in some economies such allocation occurs primarily through a market, many other methods exist as well. For instance, labor can be allocated by coercion as in a slavery system or, for that matter, as in large organization where such commands are voluntarily accepted; land can be allocated by various types of inheritance mechanisms, by mechanisms associated with membership in restricted groups (e.g., the nobility in medieval Europe), or by various types of coercive measures (e.g., occupation and seizure); and capital can be allocated by a considerable variety of governmental administrative measures. Section B of this chapter deals briefly with certain types of factor allocation mechanisms and some major causal forces underlying their origins.

In addition, every economic system must distribute the resulting production in some manner. Income is an enforced claim—or property right—over some part of that production. The mechanisms by which such income is obtained depend in good part on the manner by which the factor is allocated. Of all property rights, income has generated the most interest and, for this reason, statistics on income are readily available. Therefore, this special aspect of property rights receives considerable attention in this chapter before more general issues of property rights are confronted in the next chapter.

Currently there are two types of theories about the distribution of income in systems where factors are allocated through markets. These deal respectively with the relative shares of different types of income (labor income, rents, profits, and interest income) and with the size distribution of income. Certain key institutional and policy aspects of both types of theories are reviewed.

B. Developmental Theories about Methods for Allocating Factors of Production

1. Labor

Every known human society features some type of division of labor. In many highly primitive economies, the most important division of labor is by sex, marital status, and age; thus the family and marriage systems serve as very important allocators of different types of labor.[1] Even though most members of a given sex perform the same type of work, this does not necessarily imply that all producers work only for and by themselves. Labor exchanges are a common feature of many tribal and peasant societies and occur either to obtain the help of others for tasks that one person cannot carry out alone or else to provide for sociability. These exchanges can be either informal (where two individuals exchange labor) or formal (where groups of individuals work first for one person, then for another in a predetermined order).

If occupations differ within the society, various institutions exist to allocate labor. Such allocation can rest on obvious coercion: The slave-

---

[1]The discussion about allocation of factors of production in primitive societies in this section draws heavily on Frederic L. Pryor, *The Origins of the Economy: A Comparative Study of Distribution in Primitive and Peasant Economies* (New York: Academic Press, 1977). The various theories and empirical results that are briefly mentioned receive much greater attention in this source.

holder uses force to direct his slave toward a task; the serfholder prevents his work force from taking up other occupations. The element of coercion can also be more masked: Guild systems operate to prevent the free entry into specific occupations; caste systems greatly limit the choice of occupations for any given individual; and, in the Soviet Union until the 1960s, workers on the collective farms (*kolkhozi*) could not leave the farm without permission from the farm leaders (since workers did not have the necessary internal passport required for travel). A still different method of allocating labor occurs in organizations where individuals are assigned particular jobs; the element of coercion is more difficult to define since the individual always has the option to resign from the organization (although, in some cases, such as the army, this option can only be exercised at discrete time intervals) or to bargain for some other job. Finally, of course, labor can be allocated through a market, a method that occurs not only in the capitalist, market economies of the West but also, as discussed briefly below, in all centrally administered, socialist economies of Eastern Europe with the possible exception of Albania.[2]

Up to now there are few rigorous theories about the origins of labor exchanges. The known facts of can be quickly summarized: Such exchanges more often occur in societies with very low levels of economic development, with relatively important lineage structures, and in agricultural economies (in contrast to herding, fishing, or hunting and gathering economies). Although theories can be formulated to "explain" these three relationships, in actuality social scientists are far from an understanding of the crucial causal elements.

For the origins of slavery, on the other hand, there are a plethora of theories. Many such theories stress that slavery is a stage experienced by almost all societies at a particular level of economic development, but is relatively infrequent at lower or higher levels of development. The *lower limit* occurs because the level of economic development must be sufficiently high for the slaves to produce a significant surplus that more than covers the cost of feeding and guarding them. From this approach, it would be clear that it is less expensive to procure adult slaves from other societies than to raise them from childhood in one's own society; and, thus, slave procurement from the outside occurs at lower levels of economic development than the raising of one's own slaves. (Contrary to most common propositions about slavery, this one

---

[2]A number of readings on labor markets in the centrally planned, socialist economies in Eastern Europe are presented in the suggested readings. It must be noted, however, that labor turnover between enterprises in most socialist nations appears quite low. Often the crucial labor market decisions on the part of the individual are the level of education that is chosen or that can be obtained, and the first job. In China, for instance, most individuals remain with a particular "unit" all of their working lives so that no real labor market appears to exist.

receives considerable empirical support). The *upper limit* occurs because at sufficiently high levels of economic development, a social "surplus" can be procured in ways other than forced labor. For instance, some have argued that after the population density increases and unclaimed land is no longer available (land is no longer *open*), a "surplus" can be more easily obtained by renting land out and collecting a rent.

The benefit/cost approach implicit in this stage-theory model has been extended in other directions. Some have stressed that slavery is most likely to occur where it is relatively inexpensive to prevent slaves from escaping (because the society is sedentary, or because the slave's homeland is far away, or because the slaves are a different race than their masters and can be easily identified). Still others have argued that slaves (or serfs) are most likely to be found in societies where sufficient empty land is available so that coercion must be used by landowners to retain a labor force.

The empirical evidence for most theories of the origins of slavery is quite weak. While it is true that slavery is generally not found in highly primitive societies, slavery is also not found in certain societies at all levels of economic development. Any "stage theory" of slavery thus specifies necessary, but not sufficient conditions, for the existence of this type of labor allocation. In agricultural societies, one empirical comparison of 36 societies reveals little relationship between slavery and either the level of development or the existence of *open* agricultural land.

In empirical investigations of the origins of slavery, two factors do provide some explanation for the occurrence of slavery. The *first* is a variable reflecting the degree of political centralization within the society; obviously coercive methods are difficult to maintain by individual slave owners alone and the aid of a centralized polity provides slaveholders useful assistance. The *second* is a variable reflecting the authoritarian nature of the family structure (especially concerning the power of men over women). According to this argument, where authoritarian relationships exist in one sphere of activity (the family), they are more easily introduced in other spheres (the economy). Such an approach also provides insight into the reasons why, in a number of societies, male slaves are forced to wear the clothes of women. However, this approach also raises the difficult question of why authoritarian relations arise at all in the family, which allegedly is a more "basic" institution than slavery.

Several important determinants of the existence of labor markets for unskilled workers are discussed in Chapter 6. In brief, there appears to be a positive correlation between the level of economic development and the occurrence of labor markets. Moreover, such markets are also more likely to be found in particular types of economies such as herding societies. The occurrence of labor markets in herding societies where the worker is paid in kind (often, in kine) refutes the assertions of many economists that a functioning market for goods is a necessary prerequisite for a labor market.

2. Land

In tribal societies, especially those where most food is obtained through hunting and gathering, personal property rights in a particular piece of land do not exist; rather, a certain territory is controlled by a particular group and an individual obtains the use of the land by virture of membership in this group. Such an arrangement occurs also in many peasant societies where the relevant group is usually political or familial. It is interesting to note that today in most centrally administered, socialist economies, a similar method of land allocation exists. That is, the use of agricultral land is obtained either by virtue of membership in the collective farm or by signing an employment contract to join a state farm. However, one major difference is that in many of these socialist nations, the government has the power to change the form of the group (e.g., to change a collective farm into a state farm), while in the peasant or tribal societies the particular groups are (or were) relatively autonomous and stable.

Attached to a piece of land are many property rights, such as the right to use the land, the right to decide what is planted on the land, the right to obtain a rent or tax if others use it, and so forth. These various rights can be transferred in quite different ways. In some societies, the right of use is inherited; in other societies, the children of present users are either allocated unused land or land that others have abandoned either voluntarily or through death. Unfortunately, few studies have attempted to sort out the factors influencing the type of processes by which the use of land is obtained through different kinds of group membership.

As noted in Chapter 6, land markets—either in the form of the renting of land or the buying and selling of land—emerge at relatively high levels of economic development. In that discussion both theoretical and empirical evidence is presented to show that such land markets are correlated not only with the level of economic development, but also with the form of marriage structure.

3. Capital

Capital allocation in this discussion refers only to the assignment of capital equipment (buildings, equipment and tools, and inventories) or the borrowing and lending of investable funds for obtaining capital equipment. In most tribal and peasant societies, capital equipment is produced either by the users themselves or by specialists (e.g., canoe builders) who are contracted and who receive payment (e.g., in food). Political allocation of capital equipment rarely occurs in these economies, except in the case of large-scale irrigation or temple-building projects which are usually constructed by coerced labor (slaves or members of the society coerced into such work for brief intervals). The latter type of capital creation is usually associated only with societies with relatively high levels of economic development and strong governments. Nonmarket "social allocations" of capital, such as mechanisms to transfer capital equipment or funds from one kin group to another outside a market, do not appear important in most primitive societies.

As noted in Chapter 6, the occurrence of capital markets (the borrowing and lending of investable funds of some interest rate) in primitive societies is associated with two factors: the level of economic development and the presence of capital-intensive means of production. In the proper environment, capital markets in primitive societies can become highly sophisticated; witness the early capital markets in Mesopotamia in the third millennium B.C.[3]

The growing role of capital markets in the allocation of capital is not, however, a one-way process. As argued in Chapter 3, capital markets have begun to decline in relative importance as an allocator of capital in market economies as nominally capitalist governments participate to an increased degree in the allocation of investable funds. Of course, in the centrally administered, socialist economies, governmental decisions concerning the creation and use of capital is the key allocative device for this factor of production.

C. Labor Markets and Labor Incentives

For production to take place, it is not enough just to get people to the various workplaces; measures must also be taken to get them to work with a certain degree of intensity. Both of these problems receive attention below.

1. Labor Markets

The capitalist, market economies rely primarily on the labor market to mobilize a labor force to carry out various jobs. This market is highly imperfect, due to high costs of information, the special activities of labor unions, and the many varied features by which labor-management rela-

---

[3]The discussion on these matters by Sidney Homer, *A History of Interest Rates,* 2nd ed. (New Brunswick, N.J.: Rutgers University Press, 1977), chaps. 1–2 is quite relevant and interesting.

tions are structured in the different nations. In some countries wages are determined primarily at the enterprise level; in other countries, at the industry level; and in still other countries, broad wage agreements between the employer organizations and the unions are hammered out at the national level. In some capitalist nations, the relative degree of unionization is low; in others it is high, but many different unions operate within a given enterprise or plant; and in still other countries, it is high and, for the most part, only one or two unions are represented at any single plant.

With certain exceptions, unemployment was low (less than a few percent of the labor force) in most economically developed capitalist, market economies from 1950 to the mid-1970s. However, in the late 1970s and early 1980s, unemployment rose in most of these nations to over 8 percent of the economically active. However, most of these countries maintained broad systems of unemployment compensation to support unemployed workers.

In most socialist, centrally administered economies of Eastern Europe, labor has been allocated through a type of centralized market in which the workers are free to work where they can find employment; however, wage guidelines are determined by the central government and enterprises are considerably restricted in the wages that they can offer. Previous chapters have contained brief discussions of certain features of this market. In particular, although statistics are not available, it appears that unemployment has remained low in most countries during the entire post–World War II period, even during the difficult times in the late 1970s and early 1980s when their economic growth declined sharply.

Although labor unions exist in these socialist nations, they do not participate in the setting of wages and, in most countries, have acted as little more than an arm of the government in helping to mediate disputes between workers and managers. In Poland in the late 1970s and early 1980s, disaffection with these official unions gave rise to Solidarity, a trade union independent of the government and which the overwhelming majority of Polish workers joined. In 1982, however, Solidarity was banned by the military government as inimical to the interests of the workers' state!

Yugoslavia, a socialist nation with strong market elements in its economy, also has an active labor market. The structuring of the labor market is complex in this nation because both labor unions and worker councils (discussed in the next chapter) are present. Wages are determined at the enterprise level. Over the entire decade of the 1970s, unemployment was high, averaging about 10 percent of the economically active.[4]

[4]International Labour Office, *Yearbook of Labour Statistics 1981* (Geneva: 1981), p. 326.

If labor is allocated primarily through some type of market, we can derive a number of propositions and can make empirical investigations to see if they are validated. One obvious implication of a market mechanism is that in the long run, for instance, more skilled labor must generally receive more remuneration than less skilled labor; otherwise, shortages for skilled labor would arise. Similarly, other compensating differentials (e.g., more pay for unpleasant work) can be derived on the same grounds. Although making these rather weak tests of a market mechanism raises problems when wages in particular industries or occupations are differentially influenced by union activities, these propositions appear to receive empirical support from the data in both capitalist and socialist nations of Europe.[5]

A stronger test of the operation of a labor market occurs with regard to interindustry wage differentials. Although many Eastern European economists claim that the wage structure in their economies are manipulated to accord with plan goals and specified priority sectors, a comparison of relative wage levels in comparable industries appears quite similar in nations from both East and West. This comparison has been carried out by ranking average wages in each sector for each country and then averaging these rank orders across nations with the same economic system. Such an exercise yields two important results: *First,* such rankings for each nation having a particular economic system are quite similar (as measured by the "coefficient of concordance," a statistic explained in Appendix A). *Second,* these average rankings are quite similar between systems, as shown by the data in Table 8–1. More specifically, correlating the rank orders for the two economic systems yields a Kendall rank order correlation coefficient of .67, which is statistically significant at the .05 level. The average skill levels required in each industry, the unpleasantness of the work, and other such factors undoubtedly underlie these striking similarities between and among the nations with different economic systems. Other types of comparisons of wage rates can also be made to show the similarity of operations of the labor markets in the two systems.

2. Labor Incentives

Although getting labor into particular industries is one part of the problem, another part is inducing the labor to work hard. Here we run into some difficult theoretical and empirical questions that, unfortunately, have received relatively little empirical attention. It is useful to attack

[5]A very interesting microeconomic study of such problems is M. Gardner Clark, "Comparative Wage Structure in the Steel Industry of the Soviet Union and Western Countries," *Proceedings of the Industrial Relations Research Association,* 13 (December 1960), pp. 266–88.

TABLE 8–1
Ranking of Average Wages and Salaries of Workers and Employees in East and West

ISIC No.	Industry	Average Rank Order (from Highest Average Earnings to Lowest) West, 1963	East, 1963–66
32	Petroleum and coal products	1	3
34	Primary metals	2	2
31	Chemicals	3	7
38	Transport equipment	4	4
36	Machinery except electrical, transport	5	5
10–9	Mining	6	1
28	Printing	7	15
27	Paper products	8	12
37	Electrical machinery	9	6
30	Rubber products	10	8
21	Beverages	11	16.5
35	Metal products	12	10
33	Stone, glass, clay products	13	9
39	Miscellaneous industries	14	11
22	Tobacco	15	18
20	Food processing	16	16.5
26	Furniture	17	14
25	Lumber products except furniture	18	13
29	Leather products	19	19
23	Textiles	20	20
24	Clothing	21	21
	Number of countries in sample	19	6
	Coefficient of concordance (both statistically significant at .05 level).	.59	.80

Note: The "West" includes 19 capitalist, market economies in Western Europe and North America; the East includes 6 centrally administered, socialist economies in Eastern Europe. ISIC stands for International Standard Industrial Classification.

Source: The data come from Frederic L. Pryor, *Property and Industrial Organization in Communist and Capitalist Nations* (Bloomington: Indiana University Press, 1973), p. 78.

the subject by focusing on several common distinctions between different types of incentives.

a. Positive and Negative Incentives

Positive incentives represent the "carrot." They include all sorts of monetary and nonmonetary rewards for good performance, such as individual and group bonuses, awards and honors, and so forth. Although comparable data on most types of positive incentives are not available,

Table 8–2
Bonus Systems for Production Workers in Different Nations

	All Production Workers	Payment Exclusively by the Time Worked	Group Bonuses	Personal Bonuses Excluding Piecework	Exclusively Piecework	Mixed Group and Personal Bonuses
				Payment Tied in Some Manner to Production		
Western European Nations						
Belgium	100%	79.3%	11.4%	7.0%	2.2%	1.4%
France	100	63.9	18.3	14.0	0.8	2.9
West Germany	100	59.6	13.8	11.4	8.9	6.2
Italy	100	61.9	15.8	8.3	1.0	13.0
Luxembourg	100	62.3	30.0	4.5	1.4	1.8
Netherlands	100	73.3	12.2	11.9	1.2	1.4
United States	100	75.5	8.2	8.5	2.2	5.5
Soviet Union	100	11.8	42.1	←	46.1	→

Note: The data for the three groups of nations are not completely comparable; nevertheless for rough comparisons between nations, they are adequate.

Sources: The Western European data come from Elisabeth Vlassenko, "La structure des salaires dans l'industrie et les services en 1978," *Les collections de l'INSEE*, Séries M, No. 90–91 (March 1981). The Soviet data are contained in the article by Marie Lavigne, "La prime socialiste," in her edited book *Travail et monnaie en système socialiste* (Paris: Economica, 1981), pp. 93–109. The data for the United States are drawn from a survey privately conducted by the author. Further details of this survey are contained in Frederic L. Pryor, "Incentives in Manufacturing—The Carrot and the Stick," *Monthly Labor Review*, July 1984.

we can make rough comparisons among nations from the data in Table 8–2 on percentage of production workers who receive monetary bonuses for good performance. It is noteworthy that roughly 90 percent of production workers in the Soviet Union receive such incentives, in contrast to roughly 30 percent in the Common Market nations of Western Europe and about 25 percent in the United States. Scattered data from Poland suggest that about 90 percent of their workers also receive such bonuses.

Negative incentives represent the "stick." They include firing workers for poor performance, subjecting them to public criticism, increasing the number of foremen and supervisors to crack down on shirking, and other types of punishments. Negative incentives (often called sanctions) usually accompany direct orders to perform some task. Comparable data on such negative incentives appear impossible to find. However, scattered evidence suggests that in most Eastern and Western European nations the rate of firing workers for poor job performance is very low (less than 1 or 2 percent), in contrast to the United States where about 5 percent of industrial workers lose their jobs each year for this reason.

b. Competitive and Cooperative Incentives

Competitive incentives encourage more effort by focusing on differential performance. A typical type of competitive incentive pits one person or one group against another person or group, the winner receiving either monetary or nonmonetary rewards. Cooperative incentives, on the other hand, encourage more effort by increasing individual participation in, and identification with, work groups.[6] An example of a cooperative incentive is the "quality circle" found in Japanese factories, where workers participate in meetings set up by the firm to discuss their work and make suggestions for improvements. Comparable data on the use on such incentives are not available.

c. Material versus Moral Incentives

While material and moral incentives are often discussed in the literature, these terms seem to vary greatly in meaning. The most common usages found are discussed below.

(i) Monetary versus Nonmonetary Incentives. The most extreme monetary incentive is, of course, piecework, where the worker is paid exclusively on what he or she produces (in contrast, a time rate gives no incentive to the worker to work hard at all). However, less drastic types of monetary incentive schemes are also in common use, such as combinations of time rates and piecework or bonuses for exceeding certain production norms (or fines for falling short of such norms). Monetary bonuses can also be based on other aspects of production, for example, bonuses (or fines) based on punctuality, cutting costs, saving materials, or simply subjective appraisals of "good work." It should be noted that monetary bonuses can be given not only for individual work but also for group work. The above remarks about the data from Table 8–2 suggest that such monetary incentives are used more heavily in the socialist, centrally administered economies than the capitalist, market economies. Nonmonetary incentives include pats on the back (or criticism) by supervisors, awards such as the "Hero of Work" awards found in many Eastern European nations, public commendation (or criticism), stories in the newspaper about particular workers, and so forth. It is noteworthy that many types of incentive schemes are difficult to classify as monetary or nonmonetary such as nonmonetary rewards that have monetary value (e.g., priority places in vacation homes or extra rations).

---

[6]A useful collection of empirical studies on the impact of such types of *participatory* incentives is Arnold S. Tannenbaum, *Control in Organizations* (New York: McGraw-Hill, 1968).

(ii) Individual versus Group Incentives. Bonuses (or fines) given to particular individuals for particular work have already been discussed. Group bonuses (or fines) can be given on the basis of a variety of indicators of group efforts such as total production or sales, total profits (various profit-sharing devices), savings in material costs, and so forth. Allegedly the group incentives foster a sense of participation and are supposed to lead to peer pressure for greater performance, although this common supposition has relatively little empirical support. From the data in Table 8–2 we can see that the mix between personal and group bonuses varies greatly between nations with the same economic system. Further, although a higher percentage of Soviet workers receive group bonuses, the ratio of group to individual bonuses is higher in some of the Western European nations.

(iii) Market versus Nonmarket Incentive Systems. Market incentives include all manipulations of prices, wages, rents, and interest rates. Nonmarket incentives include exhortations, manipulation of tastes and values through use of the mass media, peer pressure (either informal or formal, as in the case of group criticism sessions), devices to increase the identification of workers with their enterprise (e.g., various types of human relations devices), direct orders combined with various sanctions, and so forth. Although comparable data are not available, it should be clear that moral incentives in this sense are not restricted to any particular type of economic system, but rather can be found in all. It must be added, however, that certain types of nonmarket systems of labor allocation appear to be peculiar to the agricultural sector of socialist, centrally administered nations. These include: official policies making it difficult to leave the agricultural sector (e.g., China during most of the period following socialization of agriculture or the Soviet Union until the 1970s); mobilizing urban workers for particular agricultural tasks (such as the 1970 sugar campaign in Cuba to harvest 10 million tons); and instituting a generalized system of short-run "brigades" of clerical workers, students, and so forth, for work in areas experiencing agricultural labor shortages.

(iv) Sloth versus High Effort. Moral incentives can also be defined in terms of results; that is, moral incentives are those that induce all to give their utmost. This approach, which is often used in ideological discussions, leaves open the question of determining whether workers are giving their utmost; it does not, therefore, seem very useful unless the degree of "utmost effort" can be quantified.

Given this diversity of meanings, it should be clear that generalizations about differences between economic systems with regard to moral and material incentives should be made carefully. A further problem arises because of variations in incentive systems over time. In several socialist countries in particular periods, dramatic but only temporary steps were taken to move toward an extensive nationwide system of moral incentives; for instance, wage differentials were considerably reduced and much greater emphasis was placed on various types of nonmarket incentives. Examples of such interludes include China during the Great Leap Forward in 1958 or the Cultural Revolution in the mid-1960s; and Cuba in the mid and late 1960s, when certain parts of the labor force were drafted into quasi-military work groups.

This brief review suggests that variation in the use of different types of incentive schemes to increase the intensity of work varies considerably among nations with the same economic system. The only firm generalization we can make is that to increase work efforts of blue-collar workers, positive monetary incentives appear to be used in the centrally administered, socialist economies more than in the capitalist, market economies and, in addition, these socialist nations appear to rely somewhat more on nonmarket incentives as well.

Of course, the use of various types of incentives (positive or negative, competitive or cooperative, material or moral) does not at all imply that such incentives are effective. For instance, the bluntness of certain types of moral incentives means they are not be suited for many purposes. Certainly "jawboning" by political leaders has not often proved useful in inducing harder work or, in the market economies, more spending or lower prices. Further, although moral incentives can possibly increase work effort, the direction in which such effort is occurring is often difficult to control. Thus increased effort in one sector can interfere with supply and demand relations in other sectors of the economy (a situation occurring in Cuba during the campaign for 10 million tons of harvested sugar). Finally, for any type of bonus to be effective, it must be carefully structured. In the economic literature of Eastern Europe one finds considerable complaint that the incentives are not effective because workers consider the bonuses as part of their base salary and that the indicators on which such bonuses are based do not encourage the proper type of work.

It is unfortunate that our evidence on the effectiveness of particular types of incentives is anecdotal. Until the subject is studied more systematically, however, we must content ourselves with such scattered data.

d. Managerial Incentives

Motivating managers to work hard and in the proper manner also deserves consideration, for the problems are qualitatively similar but quantitatively different from those just discussed. One important part of the problem concerns the way in which managerial behavior is monitored and this involves the proper choice of indicators on which the incentive is based. For instance, should positive, monetary incentives for managers be based on gross production, or sales, or profits, or savings in costs of the enterprise? If the price system does not reflect the forces of supply and demand, bonuses based on cost savings or profits might not produce results beneficial for the rest of the economy. Thus, many socialist, centrally administered economies have relied on rather crude output measures as the indicator for setting bonuses. A vast number of articles and books (some are noted in the suggested readings at the end of the chapter) provide examples to show that basing bonuses on tons produced means that the managers produce very heavy products, that basing bonuses on a grass output index means managers may produce goods that are hard to sell, and so forth.

Another important part of the incentive problem for managers is selecting the proper bonus formula, a matter discussed in the management literature in both East and West. Using output Y as our bonus indicator, the most simple compensation (C) formula has a fixed portion (S for salary) and a variable part (based on some fraction q of Y):

$$C = S + q\,Y.$$

Some authors have suggested that a simple bonus based on the differences between actual (Y) and planned production (Y_p) is more effective, but it can be easily shown that this is the same as a simple output bonus

$$C = S + q\,(Y - Y_p) = [S - qY_p] + q\,Y,$$

since the part of the formula in the brackets is fixed and the second part is variable upon output.

In order to obtain advance information on what will be produced, some Eastern European nations (as well as capitalist firms) have experimented with counterplan bonuses, in which one part of the bonus is based on the difference between planned production and the counterplan (Y_c, which is the amount of production that is promised by the manager after he has received the plan), while another part of the bonus is based on the difference between actual production and the counterplan. However, by examining the formula and rearranging the terms, we see that this simple type of approach makes little sense:

$$C = S + q(Y_c - Y_p) + r\,(Y - Y_c) = [S - qY_p] + rY + (q - r)\,Y_c.$$

The part in the brackets of the rearranged formula is fixed, the second part depends on output, and the third part depends on the counterplan. If $q > r$, the managers will select the largest believable counterplan, even though they have no intention of producing that amount. If $q < r$, they will select the lowest believable counterplan, even though they have no intention of producing that amount.

One way of escaping such problems is to make the bonus system asymmetric, that is, varying the bonus coefficient according to output. For instance, compensation for a normed output bonus would look like this:

$$C = S + r(Y - Y_p) \quad \text{if } Y \geq Y_p \quad r \neq s$$
$$C = S + s(Y - Y_p) \quad \text{if } Y < Y_p.$$

An asymmetric counterplan bonus system now becomes interesting. The formulae are now

$$C = S + q(Y_c - Y_p) + r(Y - Y_c) = [S - qY_p] + rY + (q - r)Y_c \quad \text{if } Y \geq Y_c$$
$$C = S + q(Y_c - Y_p) \neq s(Y - Y_c) = [S - qY_p] + sY + (q - s)Y_c \quad \text{if } Y < Y_c$$
$$0 < r < q < s.$$

The part in brackets of the rearranged formula is fixed: the second part depends on output, and the third part depends on the counterplan. It can be easily shown that such bonus formulae lead to relatively accurate counterplans, at least if there is no uncertainty in the system. Suppose, for instance, that managers assess their production capabilities and the risks associated with various levels of production and, as a result, they wish to produce Y for the period, no matter what plan they receive. What counterplan should they send up? If they are thinking about sending up a counterplan that is less than Y (i.e., $Y > Y_c$), the bonus formula would induce them to select the largest counterplan possible, or $Y_c = Y$. If they are thinking of producing less than the counterplan (i.e., $Y < Y_c$), the formula would induce them to select the lowest counterplan possible, or $Y_c = Y$. Thus in either case managers find it worthwhile to select the counterplan that represents their desired production Y. Therefore, the counterplan provides some very useful information for the planner about the managers' real intentions.

The problem is, however, more complicated for two reasons. First, managers do not know exactly how much they will be able to produce and thus will alter their behavior for making both production decisions and counterplans.[7] Second, this kind of approach neglects the strategic behavior in which managers engage to make their lives easier. For instance, they constantly fight for a lower plan. Further, they make sure not to exceed the plan by very much, for if they have a very large overfulfillment of the plan, in the next period the plan handed down from the center will be set very much higher (the ratchet effect). A

---

[7]Some of the major studies covering these problems are presented in the suggested readings at the end of the chapter.

rather intricate game occurs between managers and their superiors which is not captured in this static type of analysis.

These issues are only part of a larger discussion in the theoretical literature about the structuring of incentives of subordinates so as to reduce their subversion of the planning process and to achieve consistency with the goals of the superiors (the principal-agent problem). Many of the results obtained depend quite critically on the assumptions made about the environment and the constraints of the environment in which the process occurs and are, therefore, difficult to summarize. Nevertheless, some of the important issues involved should be clear from this brief exposition.

D. The Distribution of Income

1. Shares of Factor Incomes

Factor income shares refer to the relative importance of income accruing to the owners of labor, land, and capital in the total national income. In economies with factor mobility, active factor markets, and a price for each factor, it is not difficult to determine the respective shares of income from labor and property. However, in societies lacking such markets (e.g., in peasant societies with no market for land), such a statistical task is often very much more difficult.

As noted above, in the centrally administered, socialist economies the markets for land and capital are relatively inconsequential. Personal income stems from four primary sources: (1) official wages and salaries or income from agricultural cooperatives, (2) the monetary value of various perquisites, (3) income from the "second economy" (the "underground economy") and various illegal activities, and (4) the monetary value of home-produced goods and services. Therefore, it should come as no surprise that property income (which accounts for roughly one-fifth to one-third of national income in most capitalist, market economies) is very low in the centrally administered, socialist economies and is probably declining even more from decade to decade.

Turning to the capitalist, market economies, there are a number of propositions about the behavior of factor income shares that deserve brief review.

a. Marginal Productivity Theory

The marginal productivity theory of factor payment, which has supported mainstream economics in the West since the writings of Ricardo, really makes no prediction about the behavior of factor shares.

This is because the share of labor or property income depends upon the elasticity of output with regard to particular factor inputs (i.e., upon the form of the aggregate production function), which is an empirical rather than a theoretical matter.[8]

b. Marxist Theory

A vulgar interpretation of Marx suggests that the share of property incomes rises and the share of labor income falls over the course of capitalist development. This is because wages are tending toward the subsistence level while labor productivity increases, so that the number of hours that the worker works to produce his own subsistence decreases in relation to his total working day. Such an interpretation is misleading because Marx specifically noted that the subsistence income is a social, not a physiological, concept. If the subsistence income rises at the same rate as productivity, then the share of labor income remains constant. Attempts to verify empirically this interpretation are not successful because the labor share of income appears to have increased over the long term, at least for the nations shown in Table 8–3. In the post–World War II era, this trend also appears evident among the OECD nations as a whole.[9]

c. Neo-Marxist Theory

A neo-Marxist approach emphasizes that the relative importance of the labor income share depends upon the relative strength of labor and capital in the class struggle. It is, of course, difficult to find indicators of relative strength of these two groups that are independent of the income indicators. If you hypothesize that the working class is relatively weaker during periods of recession when unemployment is high, then you could argue that the labor share in the national income should be lower during these difficult periods. However, exactly the reverse appears to be the case since aggregate profits are considerably more sensitive to business conditions than aggregate wages. Another type of indicator of the strength of the working class relates to union activity; however, there does not appear to be a significant relationship between the presence of unions and the relative importance of labor income.[10]

---

[8]Assume a homogeneous production function: $Q = f(L,K)$, where labor (L) is paid its marginal productivity and capital (K) receives the remainder. The elasticity of output with regard to labor is $e = [\delta Q/\delta L]\ (L/Q)$. The income share of $L = [L(\delta Q/\delta L)]/Q = e$.

[9]Data on this matter are presented in Frederic L. Pryor, *Property and Industrial Organization in Communist and Capitalist Nations* (Bloomington: Indiana University Press, 1973), p. 72.

[10]Albert Rees, *The Economics of Trade Unions* (Chicago: University of Chicago Press, 1962).

TABLE 8–3
Shares of Property Income (%P) in the National Income

United States		United Kingdom		France		Germany	
Period	%P	Period	%P	Period	%P	Period	%P
1900–09	30.6%	1900–09	40.6%			1900–09	28.3%
1905–14	30.7	1905–14	42.3	1913	34.0%	1905–13	29.1
1910–19	31.9						
1915–24	29.8						
1920–29	28.4	1920–29	30.8	1920–29	30.7		
1925–34	26.8	1925–34	29.9	1929–38	29.4	1925–34	6.8
1930–39	23.4	1930–39	28.9			1929–38	28.4
1934–43	24.2	1935–44	27.6				
1939–48	24.3	1940–49	22.8				
1944–53	23.8						
1949–57	23.8	1949–54	20.5	1952–56	20.6	1950–59	26.5

Note: Property and labor income are defined before taxes. Altough great pains were taken so that the data for a given nation are comparable for the entire time period, the data are not completely comparable between nations.

Source: The data are from Frederic L. Pryor, *Property and Industrial Organization in Communist and Capitalist Nations* (Bloomington: Indiana University Press, 1973), p. 70.

d. Kalecki's Approach

Michael Kalecki has suggested that the labor share should be smaller in those economies with a greater degree of monopoly. Attempts to test this notion using data on average industrial concentration ratios have not provided any empirical support.[11]

Although other theories have been proposed, their empirical support is as weak as for the theories reviewed above. At the present time we really have no convincing explanation of the changing shares of labor and capital income in the capitalist, market economies. Unfortunately, this means we are left from his brief discussion with only the banal proposition that the share of the property income is lower in economies in which there is very little private property.

2. The Size Distribution of Income

In this discussion attention is focused on the empirical determination of the size distribution of income. Since such data are not available for most societies in the past or for primitive economies, only current capitalist and socialist nations can serve as examples.

---

[11]See Pryor, *Property and Industrial Organization,* app. A–6.

a. Measuring the Inequality of Income

In the current economic literature we find a large number of different measures of inequality of the size distribution of income. Some of these are measures of central tendency that are part of the statistical lore of all social scientists such as measures of standard deviation, variance, or log variance (the variance of the logarithm of income).[12] Others are descriptive statistics that are used more for convenience than for theoretical purity, such as quartile ratios (the ratio of income of a unit in the 75th percentile to the 25th percentile), decile ratios (the ratio of income of a unit in the 90th percentile to the 10th percentile), and the gini coefficient (which is explained in Figure 8–1). Still other measures of inequality rest on assumptions about the share of the individual utilities of income at different income levels or about particular characteristics of the social utility function. It could be argued that none of these measures of inequality is very useful, and that what we really need is a measure of the share of the population whose income is below some minimum standard; unfortunately, comparable data on this are not available.

A nightmare of conceptual problems arises in the specification of the inequality for empirical comparisions. What is the income unit to be chosen? For the most part, family units are chosen; however, this does not take into account the number of people in the family. What type of income should be included? For the most part, only legal monetary income is included; however, this does not take into account the large share of nonmonetary income that is received in certain households or the influence of taxes and government transfers in kind or illegal income. Using different definitions of the income unit and the type of income, one study shows a spread of gini coefficients from .30 to .48 for the same sample of families in the United States during the late 1950s.[13] For instance, the inequality of income is higher among adult units (i.e., individual adults) than among family units; income is also more unequal in comparisons where income is defined strictly as money income, rather than money income plus home production plus nonmonetary transfers less federal income taxes; further, income is more unequal in comparisons between families as a unit than when the number of children in each family is taken into account (by calculating for each family the income per "adult equivalents" with the children given fractional values of the adults). The time period in which income is measured provides another difficulty: One study shows that the gini coefficient of

---

[12]The variance is explained in footnote 15. The log variance is often used because the logarithm of the curve empirically describing the relationship between individual incomes and the number of people with such an income approximates the normal distribution.

[13]These experiments are made by James N. Morgan et al., *Income and Welfare in the United States* (New York: McGraw-Hill, 1962), chap. 20.

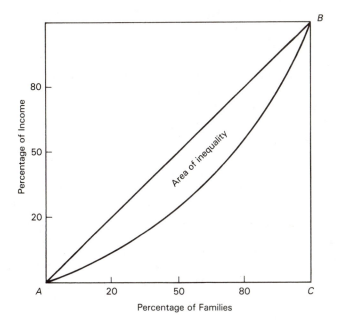

FIGURE 8–1
Calculation of the Gini Coefficient

   If we line up all income units from poorest to richest and plot their cumulated income as a percentage of total income, the result is called a Lorenz curve.
   If income of all income units is equal, the Lorenz curve is the straight 45° line *AB;* that is, the poorest 20 percent receive 20 percent of all income; the poorest 50 percent, 50 percent; and so forth. However, the Lorenz curve lies below this line of perfect equality because the poorest 20 percent receive less than 20 percent of all income, and so on.
   The difference between the line *AB* and the Lorenz curve is called the area of inequality. The ratio of the area of inequality to the triangle *ABC* is the gini coefficient. If the gini coefficient is equal to zero, there is complete equality of income; if it is equal to one, then all income units have an income of zero except the one unit that receives all income.

inequality for lifetime income is roughly one half the value of this coefficient when income for a single year is examined.[14]

b. Major Causal Factors Underlying the Inequality of Income

Let us define total individual income (Y) as the sum of labor income (W) and property income (P) and consider the standard formula of the variance of a sum:[15]

[14]Robert Summers, *An Econometric Investigation of the Size Distribution of Lifetime Average Annual Income,* Technical Report No. 31, Department of Economics, Stanford University (Stanford, Calif.: 1956).

[15]The variance of a distribution is a measure of dispersion around the mean. More

$$\text{var } Y = \text{var } W + \text{var } P + 2r(W,P) \, [(\text{var } W)(\text{var } P)]^{1/2},$$

where r (W,P) is the correlation coefficient between the two types of income. This tells us that income inequality (measured in terms of the variance) is a function of the inequality of labor income, the inequality of property income, and the correlation between these two types of income. We can also, if we wish, investigate the variance of labor or property income in terms of the inequality of the distribution of the factors, the inequality of the factor returns (i.e., wages or profit rates), and the correlation between the distribution of the factor ownership and its return.

A great many propositions have been offered to explain the inequalities of labor income. Some of these propositions relate this inequality to the inequalities of labor characteristics, such as the distribution of talents or of education and training. Others focus upon features of the economy; for example, smaller inequalities of labor incomes are associated with higher levels of economic development and with smaller sizes of the national labor markets. Still others focus on the impact of particular institutions; for example, the behavior of labor unions leads to greater equality of labor incomes within the unionized sphere and greater inequalities of labor incomes between union and nonunion workers.

Table 8–4 presents some roughly comparable data on the distribution of legal monetary labor incomes for a group of countries in East and West. The incomes in different percentiles of the wage distribution are calculated as a percentage of the median income. For each column, regression equations are then calculated relating that percentage of median income to the per capita GNP calculated in a common currency, the size of the national labor markets, and the economic system.[16] From these regressions, further calculations are made (presented at the bottom of the table) of standardized values for both groups of nations.

From these calculations two important conclusions can be drawn: (1) Legal monetary labor incomes are more equally distributed in the socialist than the capitalist nations, and (2) labor income inequalities

---

exactly, it is the average of the squared distance of all points to the mean. If a simple average of the differences of a group of points with their mean is calculated, the result is zero since positive and negative differences cancel each other out. The average of the squared differences signifies that all distances from the mean are defined as some positive amount or zero.

[16]The size of the labor market influences the size distribution of income in the following way: If a nation is sufficiently large that it has, in effect, several separate labor markets (say, one in the northern part of the nation and another in the southern part), and if the average wage in these different markets is different, the overall size distribution of income will be more unequal than if the labor markets have the same average wage (i.e., than if there is only one integrated labor market for the nation as a whole).

TABLE 8–4
The Size Distribution of Legal Wages and Salaries in East and West Around 1960

| Country[a] | Year | Wages and Salaries as a Percent of Median Wages and Salaries | | | |
		95th Percentile	90th Percentile	25th Percentile	15th Percentile
Socialist					
Czechoslovakia	1964	165%	145%	85%	79%
East Germany	1959	180	151	86	77
Hungary	1964	180	155	83	74
Soviet Union	1959	245	195	69	61
Poland	1960	200	170	76	64
Bulgaria	1962	172	150	86	79
Yugoslavia	1963	200	166	80	71
Capitalist					
United States	1959	206%	167%	75%	60%
New Zealand	1960/1	178	150	83	67
Australia	1959/60	185	157	84	66
Sweden	1959	200	165	78	62
Canada	1960/1	205	166	79	59
Belgium	1964	206	164	84	76
France	1963	282	205	73	60
United Kingdom	1960/1	200	162	80	71
West Germany	1957	205	165	77	55
Denmark	1956	200	160	82	65
Austria	1959/60	210	170	80	70
Finland	1960	250	200	73	56
Japan	1955	270	211	64	50
Spain	1964	220	180	75	62
Standardized for income and population					
($1000 GNP per capita, 40,000,000 population)					
Socialist Nations		202	169	77	69
Capitalist Nations		238	189	71	58
($2000 GNP per capita, 40,000,000 population)					
Socialist Nations		184	155	82	73
Capitalist Nations		216	173	76	61

[a]The nations are arranged in descending order of per capita GNP.

Source: The data come from Frederic L. Pryor, *Property and Industrial Organization in Communist and Capitalist Nations* (Bloomington: Indiana University Press, 1973), pp. 83–84.

are inversely related to the level of per capita GNP. The regressions underlying these standardized calculations also reveal an expected inverse relationship between the size of the national labor market and the degree of inequality of labor incomes.

The causal factors underlying the differences between economic systems are difficult to isolate. One common explanation revolves around differences in the distribution of skills in the two economic systems. However, given the relatively similar share of public education expenditures in the GNP of countries in both East and West that is shown in Table 7–5, differences in the inequalities of education and training do not seem to be the important causal factor. Three more likely explanations can be offered. *First,* the socialist, centrally administered economies have a greater standardization of wage scales. *Second,* they have taken deliberate steps to reduce the gap between wages and salaries of blue- and white-collar workers. *Third,* the data understate the degree of labor income inequality in the socialist nations because of the exclusion of nonmonetary income, a matter to which we return shortly.

With regard to the variance of property income, a major factor is the distribution of property ownership. Again, a number of theories to explain these inequalities, especially in capitalist market economies, have been proposed.

Some of these theories focus on the relationship between income and factors influencing savings.[17] For instance, if higher-income groups obtain greater earnings from their wealth than lower-income wealth holders, than wealth (and savings) are likely to be more unequally distributed. Further, the ratio of the amount of wealth passed on to heirs to lifetime income is also important: if this ratio is roughly constant among income groups, wealth is more equally distributed than if this ratio is higher for the rich.

Certain institutional features of the economy relating to the inheritance system also have important influences on the distribution of wealth. For instance, the degree to which wealth can be transferred at death intact to heirs (i.e., without being diminished by taxes) appears positively related to the inequality of wealth. Further, the distribution of a parent's wealth by primogeniture (where most goes to one heir) makes for greater inequality than equal division of the property to all heirs. Unfortunately, there is little empirical evidence with which to test these or other propositions about the distribution of property income.

With regard to the relationship between labor and property income in market economies, few theories or facts are readily available with which to investigate such matters. Basically, the problem is whether or not the rich are idle or working. It appears that in the United States and certain other market economies, there is a strong positive correlation between labor and property incomes, while in certain economies in

[17]Empirical and theoretical evidence for this point is presented in James E. Meade, *Efficiency, Equality, and the Ownership of Property* (London: Allen and Unwin, 1964). A simulation of some of the other propositions presented in this paragraph can be found in Pryor, *Property and Industrial Organization,* chap. 4.

the past there was an inverse correlation. For instance, it is reported that in nineteenth-century China, many people receiving land ownership with rentals large enough for subsistence immediately stopped working and tried to live as gentry.

If we put these various sources of income equality together, several propositions emerge. First, it appears that legal, monetary income is more equally distributed in the centrally administered, socialist economies than in the capitalist, market economies. Part of this is due to the fact that property incomes are not important in the socialist nations and the inequality of substantial property income is a source of overall income inequality. In the United States, for instance, one study shows that the gini coefficient of income inequality is .38 for all income, but declines to .35 when just labor income is considered. A more important part of the differences in inequality of legal income in the two economic systems is due to the fact that legal labor income is more equally distributed in the socialist, centrally administered economies, as shown in Table 8–3. This can also be seen in the gini coefficients. The gini coefficient of labor incomes in the United States is noted above; in Eastern Europe this coefficient is about .30 (a figure which is also roughly equal to the gini coefficient of *all* legal incomes of the urban population in the Soviet Union[18]).

Second, income inequality appears inversely related to the level of economic development, at least in capitalist, market economies. Although time series comparisons of the distribution of income are extremely difficult to make, the current available empirical evidence appears to support this proposition.[19] For the United States, for instance, Kuznets argues that the share of income accounted for by the top 1 or 5 percent of the population has decreased considerably between 1913 and 1948; and according to governmental calculations covering all income groups, the income shares of the poorest 20 and 40 percent of the population has increased between 1929 and 1970 while the share of the richest 20 percent declined during the same period. For Western European nations, scattered data for various nations appear to show similar trends. Certain cross-section evidence between states in the United States also appears to show an inverse relationship between income inequalities and the level of economic development, even when the

[18]Gini coefficients for the Soviet Union have been estimated by Gur Ofer in a forthcoming paper.

[19]The statements in this paragraph are based on data found in U.S. Bureau of the Census, *Historical Statistics of the United States: Colonial Times to 1970* (Washington, D.C.: GPO, 1975), pp. 301–2; Simon Kuznets, "Quantitative Aspects of the Economic Growth of Nations, VIII: Distribution of Income by Size," *Economic Development and Cultural Change*, 9, No. 1 (January 1963), Part 2, pp. 1–79; and David I. Verway, "A Ranking of States by Inequality using Census and Tax Data," *The Review of Economics and Statistics*, 48, No. 4 (August 1966), pp. 312–22.

rural-urban distribution and the racial mix are held constant. Such cross-section relationships do not, however, appear to hold true between countries. Although the meaning of these various time series and cross-section relationships is not entirely clear, such data suggest that the Marxist proposition about the development of capitalism being accompanied by an increasing inequality of income is not supported by the available evidence.

Third, certain governmental policies also appear to influence the distribution of income. These include, of course, redistributive programs of taxing high-income units and transfering such income to low-income units through various types of social welfare programs. However, there is also indication that many types of governmental programs increase income inequality. For instance, South African apartheid regulations forbidding black workers from being hired for certain skilled jobs mean that black workers are crowded into a narrow range of unskilled and low-paying jobs while white workers have a possible choice of a variety of higher-paying jobs. It seems highly likely that a lifting of such regulations would result in greater similarity of incomes between the two groups. Certain economists have also argued that import substitution development strategies have led to the creation of artificial domestic monopolies (whose gains are shared by the owners and the workers fortunate enough to have employment in these industries) and that the income distribution would be more equal if freer trade were permitted. Scattered empirical evidence on these matters appears to support this contention.

Finally, it should be noted that certain institutions such as labor unions may also influence the distribution of income. Since reasons are offered above to suggest that union activity acts in one manner to increase income inequality and in another manner to decrease income equality, resolution of this confusion awaits empirical research. A greater role of various types of monetary incentives to encourage hard work might also increase income inequality, but these matters have not received much empirical investigation.

Unfortunately, the various propositions and empirical comparisons are not the end of the story for they focus attention primarily on monetary income. The data do not include the value of income in kind (such as job prequisites) which, for such socialist nations as the Soviet Union, appear to be an extremely important source of income.[20] Nor do the data include illegal incomes which also appear appreciable in a number of socialist nations.

Given the number of popular stories about such dubious matters in

[20]Certain evidence on this matter for the Soviet Union is found in: Michael Voslensky, *La nomenklatura: Les privilégiés en U.R.S.S.* (Paris: Belfond,1980); and Konstantin Simis, *USSR: The Corrupt Society* (New York: Simon & Schuster, 1982).

centrally administered economies (or, for that matter, the humorous Soviet curse, "May you live within your income!"), it seems useful to ponder the implication of two of Katsenelinboigen's four laws of nonofficial income in centrally administered economies.[21] (i) The higher the position a person occupies in the social and political hierarchy, the higher the ratio of payments in kind and perquisites to the official monetary income; (ii) further, the higher the position in the hierarchy, the greater the percentage of bribes in total income. Although job perquisites occur in market economies as well, they are much less necessary because the scarcity of particular goods and services is less acute and many such privileges (e.g., to shop in a store that stocks fresh fruits at all times or to buy imported goods) have no value. Bribery, of course, also occurs in market economies but since products are usually distributed through a market, such bribes are not necessary to obtain scarce goods and, instead, they usually occur in transactions with the government where nonmarket allocative methods are used.

To gain some perspective on these ideas, C. Morrison has performed an extremely interesting and useful statistical experiment.[22] Starting with official data on the distribution of family income for a group of socialist and capitalist nations, he has subtracted income tax paid and has added cash transfers and an estimate of home-produced goods to arrive at an estimate of net family income. Then he has made two additional adjustments: The first is a rough adjustment to take into account the fact that higher-income families are generally larger (many low-income "families" consist of just one person); this adjustment is made on the basis of scattered data on average family size at different income levels in different nations. The second is a rough adjustment to take into account that legal monetary income in socialist nations represents an increasingly smaller share of total income as income rises; this is made by assuming that such nonmonetary or illegal income represents 50 percent of official monetary income of the top 10 percent of the income receivers.

Given these adjustments, the total income distributions of the various socialist, centrally administered economies look very similar to those in the capttalist nations. The gini coefficients are in the same range as those in the market economies and the major difference seem to be that the relative incomes of low-income households (deciles 1 to 4) are higher in the Eastern European nations. Of course, this is a rather uncontrolled

[21]Aron Katsenelinboigen, "Corruption in the USSR: Some Methodological Notes," *Papers of the 1982 International Conference on Corruption,* forthcoming. Katsenelinboigen's "laws" are actually conjectures based on personal observations of the Soviet Union. Although they have not been verified in a formal sense, they seem quite reasonable.

[22]C. Morrison, "Income Distribution in Eastern European Countries and the West," *Journal of Comparative Economics,* 8, No. 2 (June 1984).

experiment (e.g., the relative levels of development are not held constant) and is based on an assumption that cannot be empirically verified. However, it suggests that in general, income inequalities are not greatly different in the two economic systems when all sources of income are taken into account, even though the income extremes are greater in the capitalist, market economies. Until more data are available and more research has been carried out, this controversial and tentative proposition represents the best guess that we have on these matters.

Since the income distribution data for Eastern Europe are so scattered, it is difficult to generalize about changes over time. Another of Katsenelinboigen's laws is that the less tyrannical and authoritarian the leadership in a centrally administered economy, the more it uses corruption of lower-level employees as a method of increasing the power of the people on top. This suggests that increasing income inequality would accompany any political liberalization in these countries. Unfortunately, only anecdotal evidence is available to support this proposition.

3. The Impact of an Unequal Income Distribution

Most of the discussion above has focused on development propositions, that is, the factors underlying unequal income distributions. It would be useful to discuss the impact of an equal income distribution on the rest of the economy, particularly on the other performance indicators.

In the economic literature one finds occasional studies of this questions. For instance, Richard Easterlin has brought together public opinion data showing that the degree of self-declared "happiness" is not related to the average level of economic development of a nation.[23] Indeed, the average degree of happiness appears roughly similar across nations and, furthermore, has remained roughly constant over time. Of importance to us, he shows that such self-declared "happiness" is not related to one's income in some absolute sense, but rather to one's relative position in the income distribution.

There are, however, many other questions that can be asked about the impact of income inequality. For instance, to what degree is an unequal income distribution correlated with economic growth? Some economists have argued that greater inequality of income leads to more saving and investment and, hence, to faster growth. Others have claimed that greater income inequality leads to less growth because more senseless conspicuous consumption occurs, the average level of health is lower because the poorest part of the population is much sicker, and so forth. The issue has not yet been resolved.

[23]Richard Easterlin, "Does Economic Growth Improve the Human Lot?" in Paul David et al., eds., *Nations and Households in Economic Growth* (New York: Academic Press, 1974), pp. 89–120.

To what degree is an unequal income distribution correlated with static efficiency? A number of development economists have argued that if the wage structure is distorted so that urban workers receive much higher incomes than those in the rural area, producers adopt technologies that are inappropriate to the factor proportions in that economy. As a result, large cities are flooded with people from the countryside who remain unemployed for long periods and live in slums at the edge of the city while searching for the high-wage jobs.

Other important questions can be raised, for example, about the impact of income inequality on various types of economic stability. For none of these issues are definitive answers available; they number among the many fascinating problems in comparative economics awaiting serious empirical research.

E. A Brief Summary

Over time, a variety of arrangements for the allocation of factors of production have been used. A critical aspect of these arrangements is the method by which claims on production (or income from production) resulting from the use of these factors are distributed.

The allocation of labor in the socialist, centrally administered economies through a market mechanism bears many similarities with the labor market in the West. There are two major differences: (1) Labor unions in the socialist nations do not play a role in wage setting and are, for the most part, instruments of government rather than independent agencies; and (2) unemployment of labor is lower in the socialist, centrally administered economies.

In both economic systems, proper incentives to encourage intense and productive work by labor raise many difficulties. Although economically developed nations in both systems appear to rely primarily on material incentives, the socialist, centrally administered economies appear to place much greater emphasis on positive incentives such as wage and salary bonuses. There are, however, a number of dilemmas in structuring such bonuses so as to encourage the proper activities.

The two economic systems differ considerably in certain factors influencing the size distribution of income. On the one hand, as a consequence of differences in the ownership of the means of production, property incomes are an important share of national income in the capitalist nations and a very small share of national income in the socialist, centrally administered nations of Eastern Europe. Although the relative importance of property income appears to be declining in the capitalist economies, such income still plays an important role in the size distribution of income. On the other hand, as a consequence of localized scarcity of goods and services in the socialist, centrally administered economies, nonmonetary income appears to play a more important role in their size distribution of income than in the West. It appears that the gini coefficients of income inequality are roughly similar in the two systems, even though income extremes appear greater in the market economies. However, this evaluation is quite tentative because of the difficulties in making proper comparisons.

SUGGESTED READINGS

A. The Emergence of Factor Markets

1. Frederic L. Pryor, *The Origins of the Economy* (New York: Academic Press, 1977), chap. 5, pp. 103–48.

2. Two studies that present some interesting historical materials on the origins of factor markets are Karl Polanyi, *The Great Transformation* (Boston: Beacon Press, 1957), chap. 6, pp. 68–76 and 163–66; and E. H. Phelps Brown, *The Economics of Labor* (New Haven, Conn.: Yale University Press, 1961), chap. 2.

B. The Market for Labor in the Soviet Union

1. Alec Nove, *The Soviet Economic System* (London: Allen and Unwin, 1978), chap. 8.

2. Emily Clark Brown, *Soviet Trade Unions and Labor Relations* (Cambridge, Mass.: Harvard University Press, 1966), especially chaps. 2–3, pp. 11–71. See also her essay "Continuity and Change in the Soviet Labor Market," in Morris Bornstein and Daniel Fusfeld, eds., *The Soviet Economy,* 4th ed. (Homewood, Ill.: Richard D. Irwin, 1974), pp. 168–96.

3. The problem of unemployment in centrally administered economies is discussed in Morris Bornstein, "Unemployment in Capitalist Regulated Market Economies and in Socialist Centrally Planned Economies," in his *Comparative Economic Systems: Models and Cases,* 4th ed. (Homewood, Ill.: Richard D. Irwin, 1979), pp. 412–21. On the same topic but somewhat outdated are A. Oxenfeldt and E. Van Den Haag, "Unemployment in Planned and Capitalist Economies," *Quarterly Journal of Economics,* 68 (February 1954), pp. 43–60; the flurry of arguments about this article in *Quarterly Journal of Economics* 69 (August 1955), pp. 452–64; George Feiwel, "Causes and Consequences of Disguised Industrial Unemployment in a Socialist Economy," *Soviet Studies,* 26, No. 3 (July 1974), pp. 344–62; and Peter Wiles, "A Note on Soviet Unemployment in U.S. Definitions," *Soviet Studies,* 23, No. 2 (April 1972), pp. 619–28.

4. Other aspects of the Soviet labor market are discussed in various articles in Arkadius Kahan and Blair Ruble, eds., *Industrial Labor in the USSR* (New York: Pergamon Press, 1979). For special aspects, see S. Swianieweicz, *Forced Labor and Economic Development* (London: Oxford University Press 1965); Arvid Brodersen, *The Soviet Worker* (New York: Random House, 1966); Mary McAuley, *Labor Disputes in Soviet Russia, 1957–65* (Oxford: Clarendon Press, 1969); and Wolfgang Teckenberg, "Labor Turnover and Job Satisfaction: Indicators of Industrial Conflict in the USSR," *Soviet Studies,* 30, No. 2 (April 1978), pp. 193–212.

5. The subject of the role of women in the Soviet economy is analyzed by Norton Dodge, *Women in the Soviet Economy* (Baltimore: Johns Hopkins, 1966); Gail Lepidus, *Women in the USSR* (Berkeley: University of California Press, 1978); John P. Morony, "Do Women Earn Less under Capitalism," in his *Income Inequality* (Lexington, Mass.: Heath, 1978), pp. 43–65; and Alastair McAuley, *Women's Work and Wages in the Soviet Union* (London: Allen and Unwin, 1981).

C. Labor Market Institutions and Problems in Market Economies

1. Peter Wiles, *Economic Institutions Compared* (New York: John Wiley, 1977), chap. 7, pp. 161–79. This survey of different types of unions in a variety of nations is very useful. For a fascinating comparison of the United Kingdom and Japan, see Ronald Dore, *British Factory, Japanese Factory* (Berkeley: University of California Press, 1973). Other studies of the Japanese system are Robert E. Cole, "Industrial Relations in Japan," in Morris Bornstein, ed., *Comparative Economic Systems: Models and Cases,* 3rd ed. (Homewood, Ill.: Richard D. Irwin, 1974), pp. 93–116; and Arthur Whitehill and Shin-ichi Takezawa, *The Other Worker* (Honolulu: East-West Center Press, 1968).

2. A. Rees, "Union Influence on Relative Earnings," chap. 4 in his *The Economics of Trade Unions* (Chicago: University of Chicago Press, 1968), pp. 69–99.

3. E.H. Phelps Brown, "The Fixing of Rates of Pay: Collective Bargaining and Public Regulation," in his *Economics of Labor,* pp. 157–206.

4. John T. Dunlop, "The Task of Contemporary Wage Theory," in George Taylor and Frank Pierson, eds., *New Concepts in Wage Determination* (New York: McGraw-Hill, 1957), pp. 127–38. This essay presents some interesting empirical evidence for a theory of wages not based on considerations of marginal productivity.

5. It might be noted that despite the many studies of unemployment in the West, the measurement of unemployment raises problems that are seldom recognized. These problems are discussed by Julius Shiskin, *Monthly Labor Review,* February 1976; and Julius Shiskin and R. L. Stein, *Monthly Labor Review,* August 1975. Unemployment statistics in various capitalist economies are compared by J. Moy and C. Sorentino, *Monthly Labor Review,* April 1977.

D. Wages and the Distribution of Income

1. Frederic L. Pryor, "Property and Labor Income: Some Empirical Reflections," in his *Property and Industrial Organization in Communist and Capitalist Nations* (Bloomington: Indiana University Press, 1973),pp. 67–90.

2. M. Gardner Clark, "Comparative Wage Structure in the Steel Industry of the Soviet Union and Western Countries," *Proceedings of the Industrial Relations Research Association,* 13 (December 1960), pp. 266–88. This is a fascinating comparison of wage structures on a micro level. A broader view of the Soviet wage structure is provided by Leonard Joel Kirsch, *Soviet Wages* (Cambridge, Mass.: MIT Press, 1972), pp. 1–42. Four specialized studies of interest are Janet Chapman, "Soviet Wages under Socialism," in Alan Abouchar, ed., *The Socialist Price Mechanism* (Durham: Duke University Press, 1977), pp. 246–82; Karl Eugen Waediken, "Income Distribution in Soviet Agriculture," *Soviet Studies,* 27, No. 1 (January 1975), pp. 3–27; Harold Wachtel, *Workers' Management and Workers' Wages in Yugoslavia* (Ithaca, N.Y.: Cornell University Press, 1973), chaps. 5–8; and Jan Adam, "Systems of Wage Regulation in

the Soviet Bloc," *Soviet Studies,* 28, No. 1 (January 1976), pp. 91–110. The last selection compares all of Eastern European wage control systems after the economic reforms. Some interesting general issues are raised by Alberto Chilian, "Income Distribution under Soviet Type Socialism: An Interpretive Framework," *Journal of Comparative Economics,* 4, No. 1 (March 1980), pp. 1–19; and by some essays in Zvi Griliches, ed., *Income Distribution and Economic Inequality* (New York: John Wiley, 1978).

3. Irving B. Kravis, "Relative Income Shares in Fact and Theory," *American Economic Review,* 49, No. 5 (December 1959), pp. 917–49. This is a more detailed treatment of a critical issue in distribution theory.

E. Worker Incentives

1. Frederic L. Pryor, "Incentives in Manufacturing—The Carrot and the Stick," *Monthly Labor Review,* July 1984.

2. P. Wiles, *Economic Institutions Compared,* chap. 2, pp. 15–32, surveys a wide variety of incentive systems.

3. Several reviews of incentive systems in Cuba and China, where considerable experimentation has taken place, are Robert M. Bernardo, *The Theory of Moral Incentives in Cuba* (University, ALA: University of Alabama Press, 1971), chap. 3, pp. 48–79; and Carl Riskin, "Workers' Incentives in Chinese Industry," in U.S. Congress, Joint Economic Committee, *China: A Reassessment of the Economy* (Washington, D.C.: GPO, 1975), pp. 1199–225. A more theoretical piece by the same author is his "Maoism and Motivation," *Bulletin of Concerned Asian Scholars,* June 1973, pp. 10–24. See also Charles Hoffmann, *The Chiness Worker* (Albany: SUNY Press, 1975).

4. The technical literature on incentive systems is interesting but difficult since a certain amount of mathematical sophistication is required. Most of the important problems concerning consistent incentives are reviewed in the various articles contained in a special issue of *Journal of Comparative Economics,* 3, No. 3 (September 1979). See also Theodore Groves, "On Theories of Incentive Compatable Choice with Compensation," in Werner Hildebrand, ed., *Advances in Economic Theory* (Cambridge: Cambridge University Press, 1982), pp. 1–31; and Jean-Jacques Laffont and Eric Mascher, "The Theory of Incentives: An Overview," pp. 31–94 in the same volume. A number of problems concerning incentives in situations of uncertainty are discussed by Michael Keren, "On the Tautness of Plans," *The Review of Economic Studies,* 39, (October 1972), pp. 469–86; and "The Incentive Effects of Plan Targets and Priorities in a Disaggregated Model," *Journal of Comparative Economics,* 3, No. 1 (March 1979), pp. 1–26.

F. Some Broader Issues

1. Frederic L. Pryor, "Two Notes on the Distribution of Property Holding," in *Property and Industrial Organization,* chap. 4, pp. 90–132. This covers the role of inheritance and mate selection on the distribution of income.

2. Mervyn Matthews, "Top Incomes in the USSR: Toward a Definition of the Soviet Elite," in NATO, *Economic Aspects of Life in the USSR* (Brussels: 1975), pp. 131–58; Alec Nove, "Is there a Ruling Class in the USSR?" *Soviet Studies,* 27, No. 3 (October 1975), pp. 615–38; Michael Voslensky, *La nomenklatura: Les privilégiés en U.R.S.S.* (Paris: Belfond, 1980); Konstantin Simis, *USSR: The Corrupt Society* (New York: Simon & Schuster, 1982).

3. The relationship of income inequalities and social stratification in socialist societies are treated in a number of monographs including David Lane, *The End of Inequality?* (Baltimore: Penguin, 1971); Frank Parkin, *Class Inequality and Political Order* (New York: Holt, Rinehart & Winston, 1971); Zev Katz, *Patterns of Social Mobility in the USSR* (Cambridge: MIT Press, 1973); Mervyn Matthews, *Class and Society in Soviet Russia* (New York: Walker, 1972); Murray Yanowitch, *Social and Economic Inequality in the Soviet Union* (White Plains, N.Y.: M. E. Sharpe, 1977). In addition to these, there are a number of studies of social stratification and inequality in Eastern Europe.

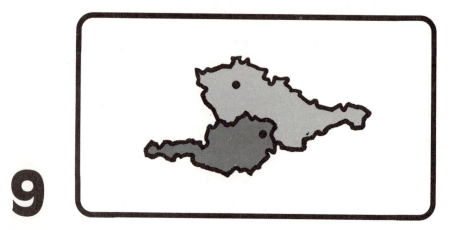

9

SOME ECONOMICS OF PROPERTY RELATIONS

A. Introduction

In the last six chapters we have focused primarily on performance indicators for the economy as a whole. Such an approach permits separation of systemic factors from policy influences on economic outcomes. However, this orientation means that we must often neglect a number of important microeconomic questions of comparative economics concerning particular institutions, epecially those dealing with property relations.

In countries with the same economic system certain economic institutions exhibit vast differences in their property right configurations; this raises a number of interesting economic issues. Further, the intimate connection between property rights and economic power permits certain political considerations to be discussed in a systematic fashion.

The analysis of the economics of property in this chapter has three purposes: (1) to give a more complete view of economic systems by dealing with both developmental and impact propositions of property relations; (2) to show how the analytic framework of this guidebook is related to a considerable literature on "the property rights approach," which is an important new development in economics; and (3) to grapple with a set of issues playing a central role in traditional Marxist analysis.

The next section deals with the definition of two key concepts: *property* and *centralization.* The following two sections survey a number of developmental and impact propositions about property. Although few are discussed in great detail, the outlines of this vast literature should become clearer to those who wish to explore particular aspects.

B. Key Concepts

1. Property

Property is a bundle of rights or set of relations between people with regard to some good, service, or "thing"; such rights must have economic value and must be enforced in some societally recognized manner.[1]

This is a broad definition that focuses on real (rather than moral) rights and that emphasizes the choices open to individuals and the direct constraints limiting their actions. Thus the definition concerns those rights on which actual behavior is based. Since economics deals with the implications of individuals maximizing their perceived self-interests with a constrained set of choices, the appropriateness of this definition to economic analysis should be quite apparent. Such a concept has also been given alternative labels such as *economic power, decision making,* and *control.* Several aspects of this definition deserve brief attention.

The *bundle* can consist of one or more rights; and the composition of the bundle can be quite different from one economic system to another. An illustration of this can be seen in Table 9-1, where the levels of decision-making rights in coal mining are specified for two countries calling themselves "socialist."

The *rights or set of relations* have several important implications. *First,* person A's rights over, or claim to, some good, service, or "thing" (hereafter C) implies an important relationship with some other person B. More specifically, it means that B has some duty or that B is sub-

---

[1]The various definitions outlined in this section are discussed in much greater detail in Frederic L. Pryor, *Property and Industrial Organization in Communist and Capitalist Nations* (Bloomington: Indiana University Press, 1973), chaps. 1 and 8, and app. A–1.

TABLE 9–1
Formal Decision-Making Powers in Government-Owned Coal Mining Enterprises in Two Socialist Nations in the Middle 1960s

Decision	Soviet Union			Yugoslavia		
	H	M	W	H	M	W
Production						
1. Overall volume of production	H					W
2. Assortment of coal produced	H				M	
3. Noncoal goods produced	H					W
4. Total labor to be used	H	M			M	W
5. Types of labor to be employed		M			M	
6. Labor productivity norms	H				M	
7. Major raw materials to be used	H				M	
8. Production techniques	H	M			M	W
9. Important buyers of products	H	M			M	
10. Important suppliers of raw materials	H	M			M	
Financial						
1. Goals for total profit or loss	H					W
2. Goals for total wage bill	H				M	W
3. Wage rate	H			H	M	W
4. Goals for total costs of materials	H			H	M	
5. Goals for overall costs	H					W
6. Major investments	H					W
7. Investment finance sources	H			H	M	
8. Prices	H			H	M	W
9. Working capital	H					W
10. Type of accounting system	H			H		
Organizational						
1. Most important organizational changes	H	M			M	W
2. Management techniques		M			M	
3. Selection of key personnel	H	M			M	
4. Methods of labor relations	H			H	M	W
5. Types of bonuses	H	M		H	M	W

Note: H = higher authority; M = enterprise manager and his subordinates; and W = councils of workers' representatives or unions. The higher authorities include state planning organs, ministries, trusts and other intermediate authorities, and city and regional economic organs. This table includes only the most important decisions; no matter how centralized a production hierarchy may be, the enterprise managers are permitted to make certain decisions. It should also be stressed that this table covers only the formal decision-making powers; the actual exercise of particular powers may be quite different.

Source: The data come from Frederic L. Pryor, *Property and Industrial Organization in Communist and Capitalist Nations* (Bloomington: Indiana University Press, 1973), p. 25.

jected to A's claims with regard to C. *Second,* these rights, claims, or competencies of A over C are enforceable. Unless some mechanism of enforceability is present, property rights in the sense of this definition do not exist. *Third,* such rights, claims, or competencies can arise in a variety of ways including purchase, membership in a particular group, occupation of some position or office, and so forth. *Fourth,* this definition of property focuses on the relations between people, rather than between people and particular goods, services, or things per se.

Economic value is used in its broadest meaning. On the production side such value includes opportunity costs; on the consumption side it includes welfare arising from consumption. Although an obvious indicator of value is the price at which something can be sold in the marketplace, many goods, services, or things cannot be sold but nevertheless permit an economic value to be imputed. For other reasons, the market price may not reflect the true value.

One particularly important subset of property rights is the right to use a particular good, service, or thing to obtain income, other than by means of labor. Such income rights are designated hereafter as *ownership.* The income derived from the holding of these rights can be obtained by particular types of levies (e.g., rents, lease payments, taxes, etc.),[2] or by using the good, service, or thing to produce something sold on the market for profit. Such a definition of ownership is somewhat different from the legal definition (which focuses on the holding of a legal instrument containing provisions enforceable by the courts) because many types of income rights rest on more informal mechanisms. For instance, the government of the Soviet Union holds formal title to all agricultural land within its boundaries, while in some other Eastern European nations, many of the formal land ownership titles are held by cooperatives. However, agricultural institutions, policies, and income distribution mechanisms in agriculture during the 1970s were very similar in most of these nations; clearly the formal legal definitions of ownership made little difference in behavior.

Another particularly important subset of property rights includes simply the rights to use (and to dispose of) goods, services, or things with regard to production or exchange; these are designated as *control rights* (which others have called *decision-making* or *custodial rights*). Such control rights may arise either as a result of ownership; or they may be delegated to the holder by others; or they may adhere to an office that the holder occupies. Control rights can be exercised in several different ways as giving orders, manipulating incentives, or affecting the way in which decisions are made by others. Thus managers of enterprises possess control rights in that they can effectively direct the actions of others, exercising by virtue of their offices various powers with

---

[2]From such an approach it can be argued that governments have ownership rights in "private" corporations since they have a claim on net income. However, such an argument neglects the incidence of such taxes. Although there is considerable dispute about the incidence of profits taxes, it appears that a very large share of such taxes are passed on to the consumers or the workers, so that after–tax corporate profits are not greatly affected in the long run by these taxes.

which they can secure conformity to their desires. Such managers may possess these control rights independently of whether they have any personal ownership in the enterprise.

For certain purposes in studying property rights it is also useful to distinguish the ways in which they are acquired (e.g., through exchange or purchase, or through assignment in some manner such as by virtue of membership in a group); the manner in which such property rights are held (e.g., in an absolute fashion so that they cannot be taken back, or in a conditional fashion so that they can be withdrawn under certain conditions); and the ways in which such rights are disposed (e.g., whether they are alienable to anyone or inalienable so that the next holder of these rights is specified beforehand, independently of the desires of the present holder). The traditional *absolute property rights* in capitalism are acquired in exchange, held in an absolute fashion, and are alienable. Much different are *stewardship rights,* which are obtained by assignment, exercised in a conditional fashion, and are inalienable (e.g., the nonowner manager of an enterprise). Still different are *corporate rights* (e.g., rights exercised by the management board of a cooperative), which are obtained by assignment, exercised in an absolute fashion, and are inalienable.

For derivation of interesting development or impact propositions, many different ways of classifying property rights can also be specified. However, this brief discussion should give some flavor of the possibilities.

2. Centralization and Other Configurational Elements

So far, individual property rights have been the focus of attention; however, property rights do not exist in a vacuum, but rather in some configuration or structure. This means that we must consider the relationship between different property rights bundles if we wish to understand the functioning of the system. In another context, this means that lines of communications between property right holders and also various types of incentives offered by one property right holder to another (this is a particular type of communication) are very important in the functioning of the system as whole. Certain aspects of this theme are discussed in Chapter 8.

Within organizations several different types of configurational arrangements can be specified. For instance, in the centrally administered economies (or, for that matter, in very large multiplant corporations in the West), there is considerable debate about the relative advantages of organizing production along product lines (e.g., so that all plants producing automobiles are under the direction of a single manager), or on a regional basis (so that all plants in a particular region are under the direction of a single manager), or on a functional basis (where specific subunits of all plants such as accounting departments, sales units, and purchasing departments are under a single manager).

A still different type of configurational problem withinin an organization concerns the levels of the administrative pyramid and the span of control exercised at each level. Thus the hierarchy can be tall and narrow, with people at each level controlling relatively few subunits; or short and broad, with people at each level controlling many subunits. In a tall-narrow pyramid, lines of communication between the top and bottom are very long, but control exercised at each level can be thorough. In a low-broad pyramid, communication lines between the top and bottom are short, but control exercised over subunits is much weaker because the superiors can focus less of their time on each subunt.

Other types of problems about the configuration of property rights are more tied to the economic system. For instance, in capitalist nations there is considerable debate about whether the boards of directors of large enterprises should be forced by law to have representatives of labor unions and consumers as voting members. Or in Eastern Europe. for instance, there is considerable disagreement about the configuration of property rights in agriculture, particularly the optimal mix of cooperative (*kolkhoz*), state (*sovkhoz*), and private farms.

One configurational element of systems of property rights receiving considerable attention in both East and West is the degree of centralization. Unfortunately, *centralization* is one of those vague terms which, like *socialism*, has many different and conflicting meanings. In order to know what is being discussed in the various propositions about centralization, it seems useful to sort out some of the most important ways in which this ambiguous term has been used by various analysts.

a. Processes of Interaction

Some of these definitions of centralization focus directly on the degree to which effective control of an organization is exercised by those at the top.

i. One special definition concerns the degree of detail by which commands and instructions are issued by higher to lower decision-making bodies. The less detailed the commands, the greater the discretion that can be exercised by a lower unit and, hence, the greater the decentralization.

ii. A second special definition focuses on the relative degree of vertical versus horizontal interaction of members of an organization. Vertical interactions denote dealings between subordinates and superiors within an organizational hierarchy; horizontal interactions denote dealings between members who have no formal power relationship vis-à-vis each other and who deal with each other from positions of relative equality. A preponderance of horizontal interactions denotes decentralization.

iii. A third special definition focuses on the organizational level where responsibility for decisions is placed, or where initiative taken, or where control is exercised (of course, these may not be the same). In a decentralized organization members at all levels of the hierarchy share in the exercise of responsibility, control and initiative.

b. Participation in Decision Making

Another set of definitions of centralization focuses on whether or not people at particular levels are permitted to participate in the process by which decisions are made.

i. One special definition focuses on the degree to which jobs are routinized, that is, where activity is structured and competencies are delineated so that the person doing the job has little choice as what task should be performed or how they should be done. A decentralized structure features a preponderance of nonroutinized jobs.

ii. A second definition focuses on participation or influence of members of an organization in the decision making concerning important organization policies. This is similar to the previous definition in that it concerns the degree to which individuals can affect the control that is exercised over them; however, it covers broader issues. Decentralization is manifested by a high degree of participation by members at all levels of the hierarchy. In the discussion below, this definition is called *hierarchical centralization.*

iii. A third special definition is quantitative and focuses on the number of property rights that are exercised by the system as a whole. This approach suggests that the property rights exercised within an organization are not equal to the theoretical number which could be exercised. Greater or more intense participation of members of an organization results in more potential property rights being used (or a decrease in the decisions that are "made" by not being taken). The set of property rights can expand by increasing the effective use of the physical resources, or by increasing the use of psychic resources (e.g., by increasing motivation to participate and by strengthening feelings of participation). Such greater participation reflects a greater decentralization.

c. Structural Variables

A final set of definitions directs attention to some formal structural elements and several quite different approaches are taken.

i. One special definition focuses on the degree to which the operations of a system or an organization are carried out primarily in one place or are dispersed over an entire geographical area. Such dispersion represents geographical decentralization.

ii. A second special definition directs attention on the degree of vertical mobility of people or organizational units within the system. A high degree of vertical mobility means that positions with many property rights are held by many people or subunits over time; this represents a decentralization.

iii. A third special definition considers the degree to which functional specialization occurs, that is, whether the exercising of a particular function is placed in one person or department or is spread around. Thus the personnel function is decentralized when each department or division handles these matters for itself.

iv. A final special definition focuses on the degree to which a system features large organization units that control many resources, or the degree to which an organization features large subunits. This contrasts to a system or organization where property rights are exercised by a large number of small organizations or subunits.

Marching through ten definitions is a tedious exercise, but it leads to several useful morals: Any developmental proposition focusing on the causal forces underlying centralization or on the impact of centralization upon the rest of the economy deserves careful scrutiny as to what phenomena are being discussed. Further, any description of the "economic reform" of a particular nation that mentions centralization deserves careful scrutiny to see which definition is being employed.

C. Developmental Propositions about Property Rights

A vast number of propositions about the origins and causal forces influencing the development of property rights have been proposed. By judiciously sampling among these, perspective can be gained on this discussion.

1. Differences in the Degree of Public Ownership

Perhaps the single best-known proposition in comparative economics is the Marxist notion that capitalist systems will eventually become socialist, that is, that the private ownership of the means of production will be replaced by public ownership. Marx based this proposition on several dysfunctional elements which he saw in the operation of capitalist market economies and, to give a flavor of his argument, it is useful to list some of the most important of them: a polarization of society in capitalists and proletariat (i.e., those with and those without ownership of the means of production); an increasing "centralization" of the ownership of the means of production into ever fewer hands; a falling labor income share in the national income with a concomitant widening of income differential between the workers and the owners of capital; a falling rate of profit; an increasingly severe business cycle and a secular increase in the rate of unemployment; and an increasing awareness on the part of the workers of differences between the current operation of the economic system and its potential if it were organized in a different fashion. Since many of these dysfunctional elements are discussed empiricaly in previous chapters or in the remainder of this chapter, it is not necessary to discuss their truth at this point.

Given these allegedly malign features of developed capitalist economies, Marx, Engels, and many of their followers foresaw the change from private to public ownership occurring rather suddenly as the achievement of a revolution of the proletariat:

> The monopoly of capital becomes a fetter upon the mode of production, which has sprung up and flourished along with, and under it. Centralization of the means of production and socialization of labor at last reach a point where they became incompatable with their capitalist integument. This integument is burst asunder. The knell of private property sounds. The expropriators are expropriated.[3]

Joseph Schumpeter and his followers foresee the change from private to public ownership as a much more gradual process.[4] They trace the cause of such slow socialization of the means of production to a gradual weakening of the ideological defense of private ownership as the entrepreneurial function of enterprises becomes increasingly bureaucratized. That is, as long as single entrepreneurs risk their own fortunes to develop new products, processes, and methods of marketing, capitalism can be easily justified on an ideological basis. However, as this entrepreneurial function is taken over by the enterprise bureaucracy and financed by borrowing or by internally generated funds, as enterprises become increasingly administered by hired managers who are not large stockholders in their companies, and as the communications media of the nation become increasingly dominated by people who are not large property owners, the ideological defenses of the capitalist system become weaker.

[3]Karl Marx, "Historical Tendency of Capitalist Accumulation," *Capital,* vol. I, chap. 32.

[4]Joseph Schumpeter, *Capitalism, Socialism, and Democracy* (New York; Harper and Bros., 1950).

Since data on public ownership over time are scattered, it is difficult to gain perspective on current trends throughout the capitalist world to test these ideas.[5] However, the main lines appear clear: After the wave of nationalization following World War II, the relative share of public ownership has remained relatively steady. In some Western nations such as Austria or the United Kingdom, it has declined slightly; in other Western countries such as United States, this share has slightly increased, irrespective of the political party in power. In France, the relative importance of public ownership remained roughly constant until the wave of nationalizations following the Socialist Party victory in the elections of 1981; given the enormous losses that the newly nationalized firms sustained thereafter, the future of this recent nationalization remains in doubt.

If we look at changes in public ownership in capitalist nations over a longer time period, the scenario of changes from private to public ownership appears quite different from the script written by Marx, Engels, or Schumpeter. In Italy, much nationalization occurred during the Great Depression of the 1930s in an attempt of the Mussolini government to preserve employment by preventing private firms from going bankrupt. In France, much nationalization occurred in the immediate postwar years in the takeover of enterprises owned by French collaborators with the Nazis; another burst of nationalization occurred in the early 1980's with the election of a socialist government. In Austria, nationalization was forced upon the nation by the Soviet Union, which occupied part of Austria until the middle 1950s. In the United Kingdom the relative degree of nationalization seems to depend upon the political party in power: the Conservatives have denationalized certain industries (e.g., steel) that were previously nationalized by the Labour Party. In the United States the relative increase in public ownership appears to have occurred either as the result of expansion of existing nationalized enterprises or as an attempt to preserve certain financially weak industries that are deemed vital (e.g., the railroads) from bankruptcy. Governmental purchase of such ailing enterprises is sometimes called *lemon socialism.*

One rather interesting recent change in ownership has been noted by Peter Drucker,[6] who presents data for the United States showing that an increasing share of ownership of the means of production is held

---

[5]The data presented in this section are drawn from Pryor, *Property and Industrial Organization*, chaps. 5–6.

[6]Peter F. Drucker, *The Unseen Revolution: How Pension Plan Socialism Came to America* (New York: Harper & Row, 1976). An interesting book by Jeremy Rifkin and Randy Barber, *The North Will Rise Again: Pension Politics and Power in the 1980's* (Boston: Beacon Press, 1978), documents how labor unions have been unable to use their pension plan funds to influence managerial decisions on the geographical location of new plants and outlines a strategy for how this might be changed.

by pension funds. Since these pension funds are, in turn, owned by the workers, he designates this phenomenon *pension plan socialism*. Unfortunately, charting this trend for countries other than the United States is difficult because data on a comparable basis are not readily available. It should be noted, however, that Drucker's notion is a variant of the traditional finance-capital argument, that is, that over time financial intermediaries hold an increasingly larger share of national wealth. This latter hypothesis has attracted considerable attention but up to now its empirical support has not been very impressive for most capitalist nations.[7]

Before leaving the topic of public ownership, however, it is useful to consider briefly a related question: Why are some sectors and branches of the economy more characterized by public ownership than others?[8] On this topic a number of hypotheses have been offered: (1) A standard conjecture is that greater public ownership should occur in sectors featuring important economies of scale. If the minimum efficient scale of production in a particular industry is such that an enterprise of this size exercises considerable market power (i.e., monopoly power), then this industry is a target for nationalization, especially since large enterprise size is often associated with illegitimate political power. (2) A second argument is that nationalization is more likely when an industry has important positive or negative externalities. (3) Another hypothesis is that nationalization is more likely to occur in industries that are major suppliers to the government (e.g., munitions or aircraft producers). (4) Still others have posited greater nationalization in industries where "unearned income" is important, for example, where rents are high or where the degree of industrial concentration is great. (5) A final group has argued that greater nationalization occurs where the industry controls a "commanding height" of the economy, that is, where an important element of national sovereignty is involved (e.g., the postal service) or where one industry serves as a major supplier to many other industries. (6) Of course, skeptics might argue that none such factors are important and that the degree of nationalization in any sector or branch is relatively random, depending in each instance on quite specific and different political and economic factors.

The data in Table 9–2 for nationalization in major economic sectors of a number of nations show very similar patterns of relative na-

---

[7]The literature on finance capital stems from a seminal study by Rudolf Hilferding, *Das Finanzkapital* (Frankfurt: Europaeische Verlagsanstalt, 1968 [orig. publ. 1910]). The most extensive empirical test of these ideas is a comparative study by Raymond W. Goldsmith, *Financial Structure and Development* New Haven, Conn.: Yale University Press, 1969).

[8]This discussion is a considerable condensation of the analysis presented in Pryor, *Property and Industrial Organization,* chap. 2.

TABLE 9–2
Nationalization Ratios for Major Economic Sectors

Economic Sector	West Germany 1950	Japan 1960	Switzerland 1960	United States 1960	France 1954	Sweden 1960	Israel 1959	United Kingdom 1962	Yugoslavia 1953[a]	Austria 1966[b]	Finland 1965[c]	Bulgaria 1956	Poland 1960	Soviet Union 1959	East Germany 1964
Total	9%	10%	11%	15%	17%	20%	24%	25%	30%	31%	34%	37%	48%	59%	71%
Total excluding agriculture, forestry, fishing	12	14	12	16	22	22	28	26	75	33	36	92	84	96	80
Utilities[d] (electricity, gas water, sanitation)	43	20	60	28	83	71	100	} 70	100	100	53	100	100	100	100
Transportation and communication	74	42	63	18	69	53	32		100	78	59	100	96	100	96
Services (public administration, defense, professions, other)	33	40	31	46	41	56	61	87	86	59	77	97	90	98	84
Construction	0	14	6	12	1	12	6	8	100	4	31	96	90	100	67
Manufacturing and mining	1	0	1	1	8	4	2	9	72	25	14	85	83	93	84
Commerce and finance	0	0	2	1	5	5	1	2[e]	79	18	3	96	53	92	55
Agriculture, forestry, fishing	2	1	3	1	1[e]	5	1	2	3	6	17	6	8	14	17

Note: The "nationalization ratio" is the ratio of the economically active population in publicly owned enterprises and units to the total economically active population in the corresponding branch or sector.

[a] Enterprises owned by Workers' Councils are considered as government ownership because profit distribution was still quite limited in 1953.

[b] Ratios are calculated from GNP data rather than from labor-force data.

[c] Ratios are calculated from aggregate wage data rather than from labor-force data.

[d] For Bulgaria, East Germany, Poland, the Soviet Union and Yugoslavia, only electricity production is included and the other utilities are included in the services or in manufacturing.

[e] Estimated by the author.

Source: Adapted from Frederic L. Pryor, Property and Industrial Organization in Communist and Capitalist Nations (Bloomington: Indiana University Press, 1973), pp. 46–47.

tionalization (i.e., ranking of nationalization ratios of each sector). The coefficient of concordance (which measures the extent to which the rank orderings of sectors by relative nationalization are similar in the various countries in the sample) is statistically significant; this means that the skeptic's hypothesis is refuted. Unfortunately, we do not have enough sectors to test easily any of the other hypotheses listed above.

The data in Table 9–3 for nationalization in major branches of manufacturing and mining also show a very strong pattern and the coefficient of concordance of relative nationalization is statistically significant. Furthermore, it is possible to operationalize some of the hypotheses offered above and to test them with these data. The results are rather disappointing in that several hypotheses seem to work: the natural monopoly argument (where natural monopoly is measured by the average size of enterprise in each branch), the unearned income hypotheses (where the weighted four-digit concentration ratios of the branch represent such unearned income), and the commanding heights argument (as measured by the volume of branch sales to other branches) all appear to explain the data. The reason for this is, of course, that the indicators used to measure these three phenomena are highly correlated with each other; that is, the various characteristics of "heavy industry" are interrelated.

2. Theories about the Structuring of Property Rights

Social scientists have offered a considerable number of developmental theories about the structuring of property rights. However, it is difficult to gain an overview of these theories: Many of them deal with very different and unrelated aspects of reality. Further, relatively few have received serious empirical examination and, therefore, it is difficult to sort out those which are useful so as to link them to a more general theoretical framework. In addition, most of the propositions focus on the changes of property rights in capitalist, market economies so that little comparative perspective between changes in different economic systems can be gained. Therefore, in this section only a sampling of some of the most interesting developmental propositions can be presented; they await synthesis into a broader framework.

a. Centralization and Concentration of Capital

Of crucial importance to the Marxist theory are propositions that productive units (establishments and enterprises) are becoming increasingly larger and, further, that a given number (e.g., the top 100) of the largest enterprises are controlling an increasingly larger share of production and assets in the manufacturing sector. In Marxist terminology, there is an increasing "centralization" and "concentration" of capital; in non-Marxist terminology, the average size of productive units and the *agglomeration ratio* are increasing. Certain Marxists (and others) also argue that the degree of monopolization (i.e., *industrial concentration*) is increasing in capitalist nations.

Underlying these propositions is an assumption that modern industry is characterized by considerable economies of scale. Thus an enterprise larger than others in its industry has lower average costs and, in the long run, will be able to drive the others out of business, other things remaining the same.

Is the average size of productive establishments and enterprises in manufacturing really rising? The empirical evidence is not completely clear, primarily because of problems in measuring and defining the average size of manufacturing establishment or enterprise. For instance, in the United States in 1963, 68 percent of all manufacturing establishments had less than 20 worker and employees. If these minifactories are included in our calculation of average establishment size, the average number of workers and employees in all industrial establishments was 53; if they are excluded, the average establishment size was 152. To complicate comparisons over time, the number of such minifactories has varied considerably from year to year. In order to sidestep such problems, it seems useful to define some type of cutoff limit on factory size to avoid undue influence on the "average" by such plants. Once such a limit is selected, then the proposition that the average sizes of industrial establishment and enterprise is increasing over time appears validated, although this increase over the last half century has been relatively slow.[9]

Trends in the agglomeration ratio in individual capitalist, market economies appear mixed. In the United States, the top 100 manufacturing enterprises controlled about 40 percent of manufacturing assets from 1900 to 1950. Between 1950 and 1980, this ratio rose to roughly 45 percent (having reached a high of about 49 percent in the early 1970s). Data for shorter time periods for Western European nations show increases in some countries and decreases in others, although it is probable that in the last decade and a half, the trend has deliberately fostered industrial mergers. Since multinational enterprises appear to be growing faster than strictly domestic enterprises, the agglomeration ratio for the worldwide capitalist system is probably increasing. Ideological interpretation of the increasing agglomeration ratio raises problems because in many cases these large "capitalist" multinationals are state owned (e.g., Renault).

[9]Data on the sizes of industrial enterprises and establishments are presented in ibid., chaps. 5–6. The data on agglomeration ratios and agglomeration ratios presented below also come from the same source, chap. 6.

TABLE 9–3
Nationalization Ratios for Major Branches of Mining and Manufacturing

Branch	ISIC No.	Japan 1960	Greece 1963	Switzerland 1960	United States 1960	West Germany 1950	Norway 1964	France 1954[a]	Israel 1965[b]	Finland 1963[c]	Poland 1960[a]	East Germany 1964[a]	Hungary 1966	Bulgaria 1956
Total		0%	0%	1%	1%	1%	6%	9%	9%	13%	79%	83%	84%	85%
Highest-range nationalization ratios														
Mining and quarrying	10–19	0	3	2	0	12	23	64*	24	59	100	100	100	100
Transport equipment	38	0	1	2*	6	3	15	17	25	34	95	99	97	93*
Middle-range nationalization ratios														
Petroleum and coal products	32	0	1	0	0	0	18	64*	0	65	100	100	100	100
Primary metals	34	0	0	0	0	2	26	0	0	22	100	100	99	100
Chemicals	31	0	0	1	1	0	0	8	29	29	88	93	91*	96†
Printing and publishing	28	2	3	0	1	0	1	6	8	3	75	74	99	94
Machinery except electrical, transport	36	0	0	2*	0	1	0	7	11	19	96	82	92	93*
Tobacco products	22	100	1	0	0	0	0	99	5*	0	62*	96	98†	96‡
Stone, glass, clay products	33	0	0	0	0	1	2	0	10	1	87	91	97	96
Electrical machinery	37	0	0	2*	0	0	2	0	8	5	93	86	96	93*

Lowest-range nationalization ratios

Sector													
Beverages	21	0	0	0	0	8	0	18	5*	62*	91	98†	96‡
Metal products except machinery	35	0	0	5	0	14	0	7	3	61	95	75	58
Food processing	20	0	0	1	0	3	0	0	5*	62*	53	98†	96‡
Paper and pulp products	27	0	0	0	0	1	0	24	0	74	84	89	100
Textiles	23	0	0	0	0	1	0	0	5	94	86	98	92
Lumber products except furniture	25	0	0	0	0	3	0	11	2**	66†	58*	64‡‡	100
Rubber products	30	0	0	0	0	0	0	0	0	89	98	91*	96†
Miscellaneous	39	0	0	1	0	0	0	4	4	27	84	42	94
Clothing and footwear	24	0	0	2	0	1	0	1	6	39	70	50	38
Furniture	26	0	0	0	0	0	0	4	2**	66†	58*	64‡‡	62
Leather products except footwear	29	0	0	0	0	0	0	1	1	48	42	61	53

Note: The "nationalization ratio" is defined in the first note to Table 9–2 and in the text. When the nationalization ratio is followed by some typographic sign such as an asterisk or a dagger, the original sources supplied nationalization data for several branches combined. The combined nationalization ratio is used for the estimate for each sector; and the sectors which were combined are indicated by the same typographic sign.

[a]Mining and manufacturing are defined slightly differently than in Table 9–2.

[b]These data are for a different year than the previous table and the sector is defined somewhat differently.

[c]Ratios are calculated on labor force rather than aggregate wage data, as in Table 9-2.

Source: Adapted from Frederic L. Pryor, *Property and Industrial Organization in Communist and Capitalist Nations* (Bloomington: Indiana University Press, 1973), pp. 48–49.

Data on the degree of monopolization are more scattered; however, it appears that changes in industrial concentration in a very limited sense of the term are not very spectacular. A convenient measure of such concentration is the four-firm, four-digit concentration ratio, that is, the share of shipments accounted for by the top four firms in an industry defined on a four-digit level in the national industrial classification. For the United States, for instance, industrial concentration has remained about constant for over half a century. Unfortunately, such long time series are not available for most Western European nations although in some countries there may be a slow upward trend in industrial concentration. However, it should be noted that these concentration ratios are generally calculated without taking into consideration world trade. Given the dramatic increase in world trade, especially in the decade of the 1970s, market competition has increased, even though the concentration ratios (in a narrow meaning) have remained the same. For instance, although the three largest automobile manufacturers in the United States control almost all of domestic production, the increasing sales of foreign automobiles provide an important new competitive element so that the alleged ill-effects of nominally high industrial concentration are substantially modified. Thus the capitalist world appears to have increasing agglomeration accompanied by an effectively decreasing industrial concentration.

A more general approach along the same lines as the above propositions concerns the increasing "organization" of capitalist, market economies. Among these, the most coherent and stimulating propositions have been argued recently by Mancur Olson.[10] He focuses his attention on "private interest groups" of all sorts which organize themselves as "distributive coalitions" to exclude competition in some particular line of endeavor in order to raise their incomes (e.g., unions, professional associations, cartels, lobbies, farm organizations, "guilds," etc.). In pursuing these private ends, economic growth, efficiency, and flexibility for the economy as a whole are lowered. He further argues that stable societies with unchanged geographic boundaries and with domestic peace tend to accumulate more such distributive coalitions over time. Although the evidence he brings forth to bear directly on these propositions is primarily theoretical, he derives a number of interesting conclusions which he uses to gain insight into a number of economic megaphenomena such as the differential growth of nations, stagflation and recession, as well as a number of social phenomena.

Testing such a theory in a rigorous fashion raises a number of problems. It is difficult to measure these distributive coalitions directly

---

[10]Mancur Olson, *The Rise and Decline of Nations: Economic Growth, Stagflation, and Social Rigidities* (New Haven, Conn.: Yale Univeristy Press, 1982).

since many organizations wishing to act as distributive coalitions do not manage to fulfill their aims. Thus one often needs highly detailed information to decide what such an organization has actually managed to do and whether or not the economy is being reorganized. On a macro scale, however, testing is much easier. Olson uses the theory to explain that World War II, which destroyed the organizational infrastructure of redistributional coalitions in certain nations such as Germany, Japan, and France, led to much faster economic growth in the succeeding decades in these nations than in countries such as the United Kingdom or the United States where such groups continued their operations undisturbed for many decades. Econometric evidence to support in a broad fashion in this relationship between distributional coalitions, World War II, and subsequent differential growth patterns is quite mixed.[11]

b.   Separation of Ownership and Control

An important change in the configuration of property rights in capitalist nations over the last century has been a separation of *ownership rights* from *control rights* over the same set of goods, services, and things. On both theoretical and empirical grounds a wide variety of social scientists such as Karl Marx, Alfred Marshall, Thorstein Veblen, V.I. Lenin, John Maynard Keynes, Adolf Berle, Gardiner C. Means, James Burnam, Joseph Schumpeter, Ralf Dahrendorf, John Kenneth Galbraith, and Daniel Bell have argued in favor of this proposition.[12] Most importantly, as industrial enterprises become larger, it becomes increasingly difficult for one person or group to control a large share of the voting stock. Further, as the level of technology rises, industrial management becomes increasingly more complex and requires specialized training and knowledge. Moreover, as stock markets become more developed, it becomes increasingly easier for individual investors to spread their risks by investing in a portfolio of firms, rather than a single enterprise. Finally, the rise of financial intermediaries controlling large blocks of stock directly or as trustees dilutes participation of owners in enterprise management.

These forces shift effective control over industrial enterprises from the stockholders to the top managers. Such managers participate on the board of directors and dominate the selection of directors, who are supposed to watch over the activities of the managers. Associated with this

[11]This evidence is presented in Dennis C. Mueller, *The Political Economy of Growth* (New Haven, Conn.: Yale University Press, 1982), especially in the esasays by Kwang Choi, Frederic L. Pryor, and Peter Murrell.

[12]A history of doctrine is presented by Daniel Bell, *The Coming of Post-Industrial Society* (New York: Basic Books, 1973). A poignant example of the way in which labor unions are unable to use their pension funds to achieve certain goals because of the role of financial intermediaries is provided by Rifkin and Barber, *The North Will Rise.*

separation of ownership and control is the rise of a "new class" whose power lies not in their personal wealth but in their position within production organizations, that is, the property rights (control rights) they control by virtue of their job position.[13]

Without a great deal of detailed information, it is difficult to determine who dominates in a board of directors. The various empirical studies of the separation of ownership and control must rely on imperfect proxy measures and, for this reason, leave something to be desired. For what the data are worth, they suggest that roughly 70 to 80 percent of the largest enterprises in the United States, the United Kingdom, and Australia can be considered manager dominated; this figure appears lower in certain other capitalist, market economies.[14] Since these imperfect measures of the separation of ownership and control appear to be increasing over time, the proposition seems validated.

Is it possible to speak of a separation of ownership and control in the centrally administered, socialist economies? Since all power exercised in these economies is by virtue of position rather than ownership, ownership and control appear totally separated in a formal sense. However, if the government (which owns the means of production) is defined as the set of most powerful politicians, then we can discuss the separation of ownership and control in socialist, centrally administered economies.

Following this approach, several methods of analyzing empirically the separation of ownership and control in centrally administered economies can be specified. *First,* such separation can be said to increase when the enterprise managers have greater decision-making autonomy and superior organs interfere less into key production decisions, a phenomenon reflecting an increased decentralization in several meanings of this word. *Second,* such separation can also be said to occur when enterprise managers are able to increase their autonomy from the political sphere overseeing their actions or to increase their political power at the expense of other power groups, phenomena that are sometimes labeled *managerialism.*

Generalizing about trends in the separation of ownership and control in Eastern Europe raises a difficulty in that changes in the configuration of property rights have been quite different in the various Eastern European nations. In Hungary, for instance, decentralization in the sense of fewer commands from the center has occurred since 1969; however, the degree to which managerialism has increased is open to some

---

[13]A review of relevant literature and an analysis of its weak points is provided by Frederic L. Pryor, "The 'New Class': The Concept, the Hypothesis, and the Idea as a Research Tool," *The American Journal of Economics and Sociology,* 40 (October 1981), pp. 367–81.

[14]These and other data are presented by Pryor, *Property and Industrial Organization,* chap. 6.

doubt. Yugoslavia has tried to avoid the separation of ownership and control by placing both control rights and ownership rights into the hands of a workers' council, which directs the enterprise and distributes a share of the profits to the workers; however, this nation cannot be considered a centrally administered economy. In other countries such as the Soviet Union, very few types of decentralization or, for that matter, managerialism appear to have occurred in the period between 1950 and 1980. If a separation of ownership and control does occur more extensively in the 1980s in these socialist, centrally administered nations, it seems likely to occur more with regard to various types of decentralization than to managerialism since there is now little evidence to suggest that the various Communist parties would voluntarily relinquish their power to the managers.

c. The Rise of the "New Property" and the "Rent-Seeking Economy"

The propositions covered in this brief subsection have a number of common elements with those of the previous two subsections. However, the starting point and the focus are quite different. For the most part they concern only capitalist economies, although in some cases they can be extended to socialist, centrally administered economies.

One key idea underlying the "new property" is that in order to win elections in democratic societies, politicians often make a number of promises of assistance to special groups with particular influence on the election. Such assistance comes in the form of tax breaks, special governmental financial assistance, measures raising prices, and so forth, all measures which lower slightly the real income of the general population. Since the benefits fall to a well-organized minority and the imperceptible burdens are borne by an unorganized majority, the benefit cost ratio of votes gained to votes lost is positive.[15] Although such an approach runs into certain difficulties in explaining expenditures because taxes and public expenditures are quite visible, it may be more applicable to explain the growth of government regulations, franchises, tax rebates, and similar measures where static efficiency losses occur which have no visible indicator. If a special-interest group succeeds in obtaining a tariff against foreign imports, the domestic price of the product usually rises; but many voters know nothing of the tariff and, as a result, do not link their own legislative representative to the price rise. Thus the politician gains the votes of the organized minority that is helped and does not lose votes from the unorganized majority that is harmed.

According to the next step in the argument, over the years such a

[15]This idea and a very elegant variant are analyzed by Sam Peltzman, "The Growth of Government," *Journal of Law and Economics*, 23, No. 2 (October 1980), pp. 204–89.

series of special-interest legislation tends to accumulate and, as a result, the nature of property is changed. Private property rights are no longer absolute and unbounded, but rather are constrained by a variety of different types of government regulation that become increasingly complex. Equally important, such government actions provide a rich source of income and the economic system moves from a profit-seeking society to rent-seeking society,[16] that is, a society where differences in income are due to the ability to obtain special governmental concessions. Ownership of wealth in physical property becomes less important; ownership or control of wealth in terms of special governmental beneficence becomes more important.

Another aspect of this change in property rights is manifested by governmental restrictions on managerial rights with regard to the work environment (e.g., health regulations and standards for worker safety), to the physical environment (e.g., antipollution laws), and to the product that is produced (e.g., consumer product safety regulations). These have an impact on manufacturers as a group, not just specific enterprises.

It is unfortunate that most analyses of the nature of the "new property" simply document what has happened, rather than attempt to examine empirically the causal roots of the phenomenon. Further, most studies of the "rent-seeking society" focus upon the impact of such actions on the economy. In short, in most of the analysis of the new property or rent seeking, the causal forces underlying the changes in property relations are unexamined. Nevertheless, the congruence of this approach with the previously discussed approach by Mancur Olson should be readily apparent. A major task of those following this approach is to specify and test propositions dealing with different changes occurring in particular sectors of the economy.

d. Control over the Work Environment

A major change in property rights occurring in a number of Western European capitalist, market economies in the period following World War II concerns the relative property rights of workers and employers with regard to specific jobs. As noted briefly in Chapter 8, in most of these nations it has become extremely difficult to fire a worker for poor performance (in contrast to the United States, where about 5 percent of the manufacturing work force is fired each year for this reason).[17] Although such language is imprecise, it is often said that the workers now "own their jobs."

[16]Many examples are provided in various essays in James M. Buchanan, et al., eds., *Toward a Theory of the Rent-Seeking Society* (College Station: Texas A&M University Press, 1980).

[17]See Frederic L. Pryor, "Incentives in Manufacturing—The Carrot and the Stick," *Monthly Labor Review,* July 1984.

In addition, in some market economies worker councils have been established which are composed of representatives of labor, management, and the owners, and which set policy on certain aspects of enterprise life. In other countries the representatives of workers participate on enterprise boards of directors.[18] A well-known example of this movement is the West German system of *codetermination,* which has been increasing in size and scope since the late 1940s.

Workers in some countries now participate in decision making on particular problems at lower levels of the enterprise hierarchy. Sometimes such participation takes the form of *quality circles,* which are set up by management to encourage workers to make and implement suggestions for improvements; in other cases, such committees are more independent of management.

This greater participation in managerial decisions represents an important change in the configuration of control rights (in one sense, a decentralization). In certain instances, these various forms of worker participation have also been accompanied by profit-sharing schemes that represent a major change in ownership rights as well.

Despite the importance of this change in property rights, we have no credible theory of why it is occurring, or why such changes have occurred in some countries and not in others. As in the case of the "new property" and the "rent-seeking society," the focus of economic analysis has been on the impact of the changes, rather than on the causal forces underlying the changes.

e. Property Right Configurations in Agriculture

The agricultural sector features a wide variety of institutions for accomplishing the same tasks. It is useful to consider some of the major propositions, not only for their own sake but also to gain perspective on other facets of problems revolving around the configuration of property rights.

One interesting type of analysis concerns the centralization of property rights in the entire agricultural sector, primarily in preindustrial agricultural societies of the past. Such a question served as the first important problem to be analyzed by comparative economist since it began to be studied in the fifth century B.C. One of the earliest participants in the discussion was Herodotus, who documented the fact that in the West (i.e., Europe), property rights were more absolute, while in the East (Asia) property rights were more dependent upon the will of the ruler. He also speculated upon the underlying causes and, since his time, a vast literature on the subject has arisen. Marxist analysts desig-

---

[18]A useful summary of these trends is contained in G. David Garson, ed., *Worker Self Management in Industry: The West European Experience* (New York: Praeger, 1977).

nate such centralized agricultural the "Asian mode of production" and non-Marxists use such labels as "Oriental depotism," although in both cases a general economic system is examined which is not confined to Asia or the Orient.[19]

The most elaborate theory about the origins of this centralization has been advanced by Karl Wittfogel.[20] In a fascinating study he argues that the major causal force is insufficient rainfall and the necessity to develop large-scale irrigation systems. Since such systems, according to the theory, require central direction, the control of such a system also imparts political power as well.

The thrust of empirical analysis of this theory has been the examination of selected centralized and decentralized agricultural societies in order to specify the conditions underlying the presence of irrigation agriculture and the linkages between the control of such irrigation systems and the rest of the society and economy. Since a number of highly centralized precapitalist economies did not have irrigation systems, a series of other causal factors have been elaborated. In addition, the relatively simple notion of centralization that Wittfogel used in his analysis has been broadened to include other forms of centralization as well.

The net result of these efforts to explain centralization of property rights in precapitalist economies has been to produce a literature that is theoretically shapeless. The definitions of centralization used in this discussion need to be clearly distinguished; the hypotheses need to be specified in a manner that they are testable; and the empirical analysis needs to be carried out on a group of societies chosen randomly, rather than selected case studies chosen to prove the point of the author.

Other problems concerning the configuration of property rights in agriculture have received considerable recent attention. Some of the propositions deal with microeconomic problems. For instance, why do we find a great deal of scattering of plots under the control of a single farming unit in some societies and relatively consolidated plots in other societies?[21] A number of proposals have been advanced; for example, the scattering is found in societies with highly varying microclimates and represents a form of risk diversification; or the scattering is found in

[19]A history of doctrine for the last 1,000 years on this question is presented by Lawrence Krader, *The Asiatic Mode of Production: Sources, Development, and Critique in the Writings of Karl Marx* (Assen, Netherlands: Van Gorcum, 1975). For a review of recent ideas on the topic, see Frederic L. Pryor, "The Asian Mode of Production as an Economic System," *Journal of Comparative Economics*, 4, No. 4 (December 1980), pp. 420–42.

[20]Karl A. Wittfogel, *Oriental Despotism: A Comparative Study of Total Power* (New Haven, Conn.: Yale University Press, 1957). See also Theodore E. Downing and McGuire Gibson, eds., *Irrigation's Impact on Society* (Tucson: University of Arizona Press, 1974).

[21]A review of this literature is contained in Frederic L. Pryor, "An International Perspective on Land Scattering," *Explorations in Economic History*, 19, No. 3 (1982), pp. 216–30.

societies with relatively short growing seasons and, by taking advantage of the different harvesting and planting periods in different locations, reduces the necessity to hire outside labor for peak periods that would occur if plots were consolidated and harvesting to be done at a single time.

Some of the propositions deal with property relations as reflected in contractual arrangements.[22] For instance, in rental contracts, why do we find sharecropping in one area and fixed rents in another? It can be demonstrated mathematically that if both the price of agricultural goods and the quantity of agricultural production are fluctuating, sharecropping contracts provide less combined risk to landlords and tenants than fixed-rent contracts. Therefore, one would expect to find more sharecropping in riskier agricultural situations. Others have argued that sharecropping is more likely in situations where the crop features relatively fixed proportions of production inputs in contrast to situations where these matters are uncertain and individual choices as to inputs makes a considerable difference. Other types of microeconomic propositions deal with such problems as why in nonslave economies one generally finds cotton produced by small holders (either landowners or renters) while sugar is produced in plantations.[23]

Still other propositions deal with property relations on a macro scale. For instance, under what conditions are *feudal* property relations introduced or do such property relations disintegrate. For this matter, one finds a plethora of hypotheses in the historical literature; unfortunately, most of the evidence seems to be based on case studies of Western European nations, rather than a comparative analysis of many countries.[24]

3. General Theories of the Dynamics of Property Right Changes

One of the important reasons for the comparative study of economic systems is to gain perspective on large-scale institutional changes. Unfortunately, no completely satisfactory general theory of the dynamics of property right configurations has yet been advanced.

---

[22]The literature on these topics is reviewed in Frederic L. Pryor, "An Analysis of Risk Arising from Different Tenancy Contracts" (forthcoming); and Frederic L. Pryor, "The Choice of the Sharecropping Contract" (forthcoming).

[23]This problem is brilliantly analyzed by Ralph Schlomowitz, "Plantations and Smallholdings: Comparative Perspectives from the World Cotton and Sugar Cane Economies, 1865–1939," *Agricultural History*, 58, No. 1 (January 1984), pp. 1–17.

[24]These propositions are summarized in Frederic L. Pryor, "Feudalism as an Economic System: A Review Article," *Journal of Comparative Economics*, 4, No. 1 (March 1980), pp. 56–77.

As noted above, the Marxist theory of property right changes is based on dysfunctional elements ("contradictions") in the economy arising from misalignment of the level of economic development ("the forces of production") and the forms of property ownership ("the relations of production"). Marx and Engels did not seriously apply such an approach to precapitalist societies (indeed their attempts to do so raises some enormous theoretical problems[25]), but they used this general approach primarily to explain property changes in capitalism (many of the propositions are discussed in previous chapters of this guidebook). This approach is seldom used by Marxists to examine socialist economies because, according to classical Marxist doctrines, communist economies feature no such dysfunctional elements (which are unresolvable) and problems of socialist economies reflect merely transitional difficulties. In brief, although some Marxists claim generality for their approach, its application has been primarily limited to one economic system.

The neoclassical theory of property right changes stresses the notion that property rights and institutions are constantly in adjustment to achieve greater production efficiency, given the level of technology.[26] This happens because the profit motive induces entrepreneurs to make such changes. When defining efficiency, neoclassical theorists lay great stress on taking into account the costs of information, of negotiation, and of enforcing contracts; they also focus attention on the riskiness of situations and on the methods by which such risk can be spread. It is difficult to test this theory on a macroeconomic level, for it lends itself primarily to very specific situations; thus it lacks the grand sweep of the Marxist property theory. Indeed, its applicability to the systemic level is open to doubt. For instance, it appears to contradict the notions previously discussed that we are moving away from well-functioning markets toward a rent-seeking society and an economy where market action is increasingly hindered by the operation of distributional coalitions. Although the previously discussed explanations of these phenomena leave much to be desired, such rent-seeking notions appear to capture on a descriptive level an important reality in the economic life of capitalist, market economies that is denied by the neoclassical approach.

What alternatives are available to those who reject both the Marxist and the neoclassical theories as too simplistic? Since a large share of the specific theories on causal elements underlying the creation or the development of particular property rights remain untested, the "sieve of reality" cannot be employed to reduce the volume. This means that

---

[25]These are analyzed in detail by Frederic L. Pryor, "The Classification and Analysis of Precapitalist Economic Systems by Marx and Engels," *History of Political Economy*, 10, No. 4 (1982), pp. 521–42.

[26]This approach and its shortcomings are analyzed lucidly by Douglass C. North, *Structure and Change in Economic History* (New York: W. W. Norton, 1981).

before any theory claiming generality can be accepted, social scientists must begin to test empirically the most important propositions. The armchair theorizing about large-scale changes in property rights configurations has led to an intellectual chaos that does not seem curable by additional armchair theorizing which would raise the volume but not the quality of the argument. However, by trying emprically to isolate common causal elements in different property right changes, a more solid base is provided for the creation of more adequate general theories about large-scale changes in property rights in different economic systems. Currently, however, such a theory does not appear on the horizon.

D. Impact Theories of Property Right Configurations

How does the configuration of property rights affect economic performance? Many previous chapters have dealt with this question on a systematic level; however, such questions can be asked of particular institutions as well. By reviewing a series of different types of studies, it is possible to gain an appreciation of the contours of this approach. Since the various studies surveyed below fall much more into the traditions of mainstream economics, this review of impact propositions can be carried out much more quickly than the developmental propositions.

1. The Economics of Producer Cooperatives

Although a vast number of theoretical studies have been made to examine the behavior of producer cooperatives,[27] almost none of the hundreds of contradictory propositions proposed have been examined empirically. Without wading through these studies, some appreciation of the theoretical approach can be gained by examining a very simple and early model proposed by Benjamin Ward. He considers the behavior of a producer cooperative in the short run with the following properties: The manager of the cooperative is trying to maximize net income (income after expenses) per worker; the cooperative can painlessly take on new members or fire old members; the only variable input is labor; each person works a specified numer of hours so that the labor input is reflected by a change in the number of workers; there is no uncertainty; there is only one product; there are no production quotas; the only role of the government is to charge the cooperative a rental charge on the

[27]This extensive literature is summarized by Frederic L. Pryor, "The Economics of Production Cooperatives: A Reader's Guide," *The Annals of Public and Cooperative Economy*, 54, No. 2 (April 1983), pp. 133–73. The model discussed in the text is by Benjamin Ward, "The Firm in Illyria: Market Syndicalism," *American Economic Review*, 48 (1958), pp. 566–89.

equipment; and the price of the product is constant unless otherwise specified.

Income maximization consists of setting production at a level such that marginal costs per worker (MC/L) are equal to marginal revenue per worker (MR/L). (Marginal costs and revenues are divided by the number of workers because maximizing net income *per worker* requires attention to the changes in costs and revenue per worker when another worker is added to the labor force.) This maximization process is shown in Figure 9–1, where cost and revenue functions are presented. To simplify, assume that the cooperative produces the good out of air so that there are no raw material costs. This means that the only cost is the rent (R) and therefore that the total cost per worker (X) can be represented by a rectangular hyperbola ($X = TC/L = R/L$). The marginal cost per worker is the derivative of this function; that is, $dX/dL = -R/L^2$. In Figure 9-1 curve X represents the original total cost/worker function and curve X' represents the same curve after the rent has been increased. The marginal cost per worker is represented by the slope of the tangent to this total cost curve; at any given L^* the tangent to X' is steeper than the tangent of X (β is smaller than α).

Total revenue per worker (Y) is equal to price (P) times quantity sold (Q) divided by the labor supply; and the quantity, in turn, is a function only of the labor input. Since the price is constant, the Y curve has the same shape as the curve for average labor productivity (Q/L), i.e., it has an outwardly bowed shape. The marginal revenue per worker is the derivative of this function and can be easily determined as: $dY/dL = \frac{P}{L} [dQ/dL - (Q/L)]$. If the price increases, curve Y shifts upward to Y'. The marginal revenue per worker is represented in the figure by the slope of the tangent to the Y curve; at any given L^* the tangent to Y' is steeper than the tangent to Y (γ is smaller than α).

To maximize income per worker, we must pick that place on the diagram where the difference between total revenue per worker and total cost per worker is greatest. This is also the point where the tangents of curves X and Y are equal. This is drawn in the diagram as the perpendicular at L^*.

If the fixed costs (i.e., the rent) increase, the average cost curve (the X curve) shifts upward. Examining the diagram to find the L at which the tangents of the X' and the Y curve are equal, you will see that it lies to the right of L^*. That is, the new income-maximizing point is such that production increases. This is in contrast to the behavior of a profit-maximizing capitalist firm where an increase in fixed costs does not bring about any change in the short run, except if such a change is sufficiently great that the variable costs are not covered (in which case, production would cease). If the wage outside the cooperative rises, no

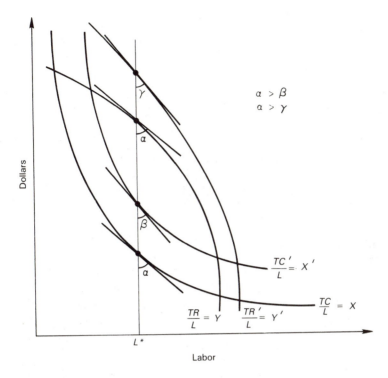

FIGURE 9–1
Graphical Representation of the Ward Model

change in production occurs (this assumes that revenue per capita in the cooperative is still higher than the wage) since neither curve changes. In other words, since labor payments are a residual, wages are not a cost; this is in contrast to the behavior of a profit-maximizing, capitalist firm where wages are a cost that would reduce production. If the price of the good increases, the marginal revenue curve shifts upwards and, to maximize net income per worker, production should be reduced; this is in contrast to a profit-maximizing, capitalist firm whose production would increase.

Because the short-run backward-bending supply curve of the producer cooperative has the potential to introduce considerable market instabilities, great theoretical attention has been paid to this problem. If there is perfect competition between production cooperatives, new cooperatives will enter the market and the price will fall so that the long-run equilibrium is the same as for the profit-maximizing, capitalist firm. If more than one variable factor is employed, or more than one product is produced, the supply curve is, in most cases, no longer backward-bending.

A vast proliferation of different models with different assumptions has been proposed that permit decision making in the cooperative on a decentralized basis so that work-leisure tradeoffs can be made, that introduce risk,[28] that change the maximand, that change the nature of the market structure, and so forth.

This type of analysis has been carried out not only on pure producer cooperatives, but on other types of organizations such as Soviet collective farms (where production quotas set by the government are important) groups where the income is divided according to the number of people independently of the work performed, hospitals, and government bureaucracies.[29] It is regrettable that most of these studies are strictly theoretical and that little attempt has been made to subject the various hypotheses to empirical test.

2. The Impact of Public Ownership and Government Regulation

There is a growing empirical literature on the effects of government ownership. In most cases the theoretical structure is rather simple: A number of general factors influencing behavior in particular environments are specified (e.g., size of enterprise, distance from transportation facilities, climate, or average wage in the relevant area); performance indicators are defined (e.g., profits, total factor productivity, or prices); data on public and private enterprises are collected; and some type of regression analysis is carried out in which a dummy variable indicating the type of ownership is included. The garbage collection example discussed in Chapter 1 could serve as a typical example of these studies; a number of others have, however, been made for a variety of enterprises in quite different sectors of the economy.[30] Such studies seem to have

[28]A considerable number of such propositions are summarized by John P. Bonin, "On the Theory of the Competitive Labor-Managed Firm under Price Uncertainty: A Correction," *Journal of Comparative Economics,* 4, No. 3 (September 1980), pp. 331–37.

[29]Many of these studies are summarized in Pryor, "Economics of Production Cooperatives." For an empirical study of groups dividing income equally, see L. Dwight Israelsen, "An Economic Analysis of the United Order," *Brigham Young University Studies,* 18, No. 4 (Summer 1978), pp. 536–61. For an empirical study of hospitals, see Martin S. Feldstein, *Economic Analysis for Health Service Efficiency* (Chicago: Markham, 1968). For impact propositions of government bureaucracies, see William Niskanen, *Bureaucracy and Representative Government* (Chicago: Aldine Press, 1971); or William Orzechowski, "Economic Models of Bureaucracy: Survey, Extensions, and Evidence," in Thomas E. Borcherding, ed., *Budgets and Bureaucrats: The Sources of Government Growth* (Durham, N.C.: Duke University Press, 1977), pp. 229–60. A number of other studies of this genre are collected by Eirik G. Furubotn and Svetozar Pejovich, eds., *The Economics of Property Rights* (Cambridge, Mass.: Ballinger, 1974).

[30]The empirical evidence is summarized by Robert M. Spann, "Public versus Private Provision of Governmental Services" in Borcherding, ed., *Budgets and Bureaucrats,* pp. 71–89.

been carried out for primarily capitalist, market economies; in general they indicate lower performance on the part of publicly owned enterprises than privately owned enterprises. Such results do not lend themselves to easy interpretation, for in many cases it appears that the publicly owned enterprises are mandated to have a different objective function than a private firm. For instance, the post office in most countries is forced to serve all individuals at the same price, regardless of the cost (rural delivery is much more expensive than urban delivery); a private enterprise mail carrier can focus only on the most profitable routes, leaving the high-cost routes to public enterprises. Or public water suppliers provide higher service levels than private water suppliers.[31]

It should be added that studies in this genre are not confined to just differential behavior of public versus private enterprises.[32] Empirical research has, for instance, been carried out in differential behavior of stock banks versus mutual savings banks, farm renters versus farm owners, enterprises characterized by owner control versus manager control, and so forth.

The studies concerning the impact of government regulation have been theoretically more sophisticated since it is necessary to specify the nature of the intervention as well as the differential impact that it might have.[33] Some of these studies show that government regulation has little influence at all on enterprise behavior; most others indicate that such regulations act to raise costs and prices. Again, some problems arise as to the interpretation of such results. For instance, environmental protection regulations are bound to raise costs; however, it is felt

[31]Susan Feigenbaum and Ronald Teeples, "Private versus Public Water Delivery," *Review of Economics and Statistics,* 65, No. 4 (November 1983), pp. 672–8.

[32]Examples of studies mentioned in the text include Alfred Nicols, "Stock versus Mutual Savings and Loan Associations: Some Evidence of Differences in Behavior," *American Economic Review,* 57 (May 1967), pp. 337–46; Virgil L. Hurlburt, *Use of Farm Resources as Conditioned by Tenure Arrangements,* Research Bulletin 215 (University of Nebraska College of Agriculture and Home Economics, April 1964); and Walter G. Miller, "Comparative Efficiency of Farm Tenure Classes in the Combination of Resources," *Agricultural Economic Research,* 11, No. 1 (January 1959), pp. 6–16. The results of various studies on the impact of the separation of ownership and control are quite contradictory; many such studies are summarized in Pryor, *Property and Industrial Organization,* chap. 6.

[33]The literature on these matters is vast, of which a good example is the pioneering work of H. Averch and L. Johnson, "The Firm under Regulatory Constraint," *American Economic Review,* 70, No. 5 (December 1962), pp. 1052–69. Some representative empirical studies of the impact of regulation are George J. Stigler and Claire Friedland, "What Can Regulators Regulate? The Case of Electricity," *The Journal of Law and Economics,* 5 (October 1962), pp. 1–16; and Sam Peltzman, *Regulation of Automobile Safety* (Washington, D.C.: American Enterprise Institute for Public Policy Research, 1975). The literature on the impact of government ownership is also vast; an example of the sophisticated studies that are being carried out is Louis D. Alessi, "An Economic Analysis of Government Ownership and Regulation: Theory and the Evidence from the Electric Power Industry," *Public Choice,* 19, No. 1 (Fall 1974), pp. 1–43.

that the gains to the environment outweigh the higher costs to the consumers of the product.

3. Other Types of Studies

Most of the other studies tracing the impact of various configurations of property rights focus on relatively microeconomic problems. It is worthwhile to consider several examples.

Some of these studies deal with incentive problems and with questions such as, What are the differential effects of share cropping versus fixed rent contracts? Or what are the differential effects of piece-rate versus time-rate contracts? In both cases, most work has focused up to now on the theoretical aspects so that testable propositions can be derived. Economists are beginning to carry out interesting empirical comparisons in this area which tie in closely with work carried out in other disciplines, especially psychology, about the impact of particular incentive arrangements.

Other studies deal with the impact of particular institutions on the distribution of income and wealth. For instance, how do inheritance and marriage patterns influence these distributions? Given the complexity of modeling these arrangements, simulation techniques are often employed to explore such questions and they show, for instance, that equal division of property among heirs has a dramatic influence on the distribution of income (as does the pattern of lifetime savings); but that the marriage institutions have little impact on the final equilibrium.[34] Empirical work has begun to investigate the actual institutions and patterns of the particular economic systems.

A third example of such impact studies can be drawn from a much different area, namely, organization theory and the relationship between particular success indicators and the configuration of property rights, particularly "centralization." For instance, Table 9–4 contains a series of commonly held propositions about differential behavior of "centralized" and "decentralized" organizations. Unfortunately, the definitions of these crucial terms are not very clear; and the models by which they are derived appear more intuitive than rigorous. Nevertheless, this summation of the conventional wisdom about the impact of these configurations of property rights does suggest some interesting propositions that can be empirically tested; indeed, some organizational theorists have begun to carry out some interesting empirical work.

A final example of studies of the impact of institutions lies in the area of macroeconomics. In Chapter 8 brief mention was made of the research on the impact of labor unions on the wage structure. In a quite

---

[34]See Pryor, *Property and Industrial Organization*, chap. 4.

TABLE 9–4
Alleged Advantages and Disadvantages of Centralization and Decentralization

Centralized Organization	
Advantages	*Disadvantages*
1. Uniformity of standards and activities among organizational units.	1. Stretching communication lines to the breaking point.
2. Utilizing the talents of outstanding executives by the entire organization.	2. Excessive demands on executives' time.
3. Uniformity of decisions.	3. Undesirably "personalizing" management policy by concentrating authority in a few hands.
4. Consistency of operating.	
5. Cost savings due to elimination of overlapping or duplicated activities.	4. Forcing top executives to develop a breadth of interest that is beyond their capacity.

Decentralized Organization	
Advantages	*Disadvantages*
1. More manageable scope of operations.	1. Lack of uniformity in policy and procedures.
2. Development of more executives capable of decisive action in setting and administering policy.	2. Difficulty in finding executives able and willing to assume primary responsibility.
3. Shortening lines of authority and communication, thus increasing efficiency.	3. Acceptance of second rate executives in top jobs, simply because they are available and in line.
4. Vesting decision-making responsibility in the individuals closest to situations.	4. Poor coordination between decentralized units.
5. Creation of more chains of promotions.	5. Interunit rivalry interfering with operations.

Source: This list was drawn up by the Research Institute of America and presented in an analysis by Aaren Uris, "Centralization versus Decentralization," in Franklin G. Moore, ed., *A Management Sourcebook* (New York: Harper & Row, 1964), pp. 261–67.

different area, development and agricultural economists are studying the impact of land reforms to determine how such dramatic changes in ownership and control influence production, productivity, growth, and other indicators.[35] Considerable empirical and theoretical work has also been carried out to determine the impact of the plantation form of agriculture, not only upon economic variables but also upon political variables such as the potential for revolution.[36]

[35]Good examples of this literature are William R. Cline, *Economic Consequences of a Land Reform in Brazil* (Amsterdam: North Holland, 1970); and Steven N. S. Cheung, *The Theory of Share Tenancy* (Chicago: University of Chicago Press, 1969).

[36]Examples of this genre are Bruce Russett, "Inequality and Instability: The Relations of Land Tenure to Politics," *World Politics,* 16 (April 1964), pp. 442–55; Jeffrey Paige, *Agrarian Revolution: Social Movements and Export Agriculture in the Underdeveloped World* (New York: Free Press, 1975). Other such studies are summarized in Frederic L. Pryor, "The Plantation Economy as an Economic System: A Review Article," *Journal of Comparative Economics,* 6, No. 3 (September 1982), pp. 288–317.

4. A Note

This brief discussion should give some indication of the type of work that is being carried out. Again, it should be emphasized that there is no uniform analytical framework nor, it should be added, statistical methodology that is followed. The intellectual purposes underlying such work also differ considerably, ranging from quite policy-oriented studies to highly theoretical work. Unfortunately no propositions have emerged that can be employed usefully to generalize about a wide range of impact phenomena, either on a theoretical and empirical level; however, work in this area is still in its infancy.

E. Some Reflections

Starting with a broad definition of property rights, this chapter touches on a considerable number of propositions concerning the causal forces underlying the emergence, distribution, pattern, and development of property rights, as well as a number of propositions concerning the impact of particular configurations of property rights on the rest of the economy and society. Throughout the discussion emphasis is placed on the comparative evidence from which some notion of the validity of the proposition can be gained. This is not, however, the only way of examining property rights.

The mainstream literature on property rights that has been published since the mid 1960s has provided some useful insights. With regard to impact propositions, this neoclassical approach has given rise to a number of sophisticated empirical studies of considerable value. With regard to development propositions, however, the results have been less promising. It is unfortunate that the overwhelming bulk of the neoclassical property rights literature is primarily theoretical with casual examples offered to demonstrate "empirical relevance." Although the "new property rights" literature has a rigorous theoretical foundation, many of the underlying assumptions have not been carefully tested; further, its relevance to the serious problems with which we have been dealing has yet to be empirically demonstrated.

The Marxist literature on property rights has dealt with broader questions than have the neoclassical studies. Nevertheless, many important Marxist propositions have received little empirical support. Others have not been subjected to serious empirical analysis and, therefore, we must be very cautious in considering them.

Without an overriding theoretical framework with which to approach the subject, the literature on property rights reviewed in this chapter has a somewhat formless quality. To a considerable extent, this is due to the very different types of models or theoretical considerations from which the propositions have been derived. However, the fact that many have been subjected to empirical test and have been found promising gives them a certain degree of credibility. In short, the various property rights theories discussed in this chapter must be taken as "work in progress" toward a more general theory of property.

SELECTED READINGS

A. Definitions and Approaches

1. Frederic L. Pryor, *Property and Industrialization in Communist and Capitalist Nations* (Bloomington: Indiana University Press, 1973).

2. Eirik Furubotn and Svetozar Pejovich, "Property Rights and Economic Theory: A Survey of Recent Literature," *Journal of Economic Literature,* 10, No. 5 (December 1972), pp. 1137–68. This is an extensive survey of the emerging economic theory of property rights. A number of articles illustrating this approach are reprinted in Furubotn and Pejovich, eds. *The Economics of Property Rights* (Cambridge, Mass.: Ballinger, 1974). The "new property rights approach" is subjected to some interesting criticism by Douglass North, *Structure and Change in Economic History* (New York: W. W. Norton, 1981).

3. The Marxist approach toward property (primarily developmental propositions) is embodied in Marx's broader theory of economic development. A recent book by G. A. Cohen, *Karl Marx's Theory of History* (Princeton, N.J.: Princeton University Press, 1978), lucidly outlines this general approach. Paul Sweezy, *The Theory of Capitalist Development* (New York: Monthly Review Press, 1956), presents a useful summary of Marx's special theory of capitalism. For a critique of Marx's general theory of property rights see Frederic L. Pryor, "The Classification and Analysis of Precapitalist Economic System by Marx and Engels," *History of Political Economy,* 10, No. 4 (1982).

B. Trends in Propery Rights in the West

1. Charles A. Reich, "The New Property," *The Public Interest,* Number 3 (Spring 1966), pp. 57–90. A more extended discussion can be found in his article with the same title in *Yale Law Journal,* 73 (April 1964), pp. 733–87. This is a study of particular property relations that are becoming increasingly more important.

2. Robert J. Larner, *Management Control and the Large Corporation* (Cambridge, Mass.: Dunellen, 1970), chaps. 1–2, pp. 1–24. Among other things Larner provides a succinct statement of the Berle-Means approach, which can be read in greater detail in Adolf A. Berle, *Power without Property* (New York: Harcourt Brace, 1959), esp. pp. 27–76. Larner's results in testing implications of the Berle-Means approach run exactly counter to the results of R. Joseph Monsen, John S. Chiu, and David E. Cooley, "The Effect of Separation of Ownership and Control on the Performance of the Large Firm," *Quarterly Journal of Economics,* 72 (August 1968), pp. 435–51.

3. Considerable materials exist on the nature and behavior of public enterprise, not only in socialist nations but also in capitalist, market economies. Case study materials for a number of nations can be found in William G. Shep-

herd, ed., *Public Enterprise* (Lexington, Mass.: D. C. Heath, 1976); Stuart Holland, ed., *The State as Entrepreneur* (White Plains, N.Y.: IASP, 1973); and Raymond Vernon, ed., *Big Business and the State* (Cambridge, Mass.: Harvard University Press, 1974). Detailed discussions of the British experience can be found in Richard Pryke, *Public Enterprise in Practice: The British Experience of Nationalization over Two Decades* (London: MacGibbon and Key, 1971); and William G. Shepherd, *Economic Performance under Public Ownership* (New Haven, Conn.: Yale University Press, 1965).

C. Models and Statistical Analysis

The references in footnotes 29 through 36 provide materials for the considerable number of different propositons that are discussed.

D. Worker Ownership and Control

1. The theoretical literature on worker-managed enterprises is vast; a summary and a bibliography of over 120 items is presented in Frederic L. Pryor, "Producer Cooperatives: A Reader's Gude," *The Annals of Public and Co-operative Economy*, 54, No. 2 (April 1983), pp. 133–73. The most elaborate theoretical analysis of the behavior of worker-managed enterprises is Jaroslav Vanek, *The General Theory of Labor-Managed Market Economies* (Ithaca, N.Y.: Cornell University Press, 1970). More humanistic analyses of the behavior and necessity of worker councils are found in Branko Horvat et al., *Self-Governing Socialism: A Reader* (White Plains, N.Y.: IASP, 1975).

2. The empirical material on production cooperatives and worker-managed enterprises in capitalist nations is scanty. Several useful collections of case studies are Darek C. Jones and Jan Svejnar, eds., *Participatory and Self-Managed Firms* (Lexington, Mass.: D. C. Heath, 1982); G. David Garson, ed., *Workers' Self-Mangement in Industry: The West European Experience* (New York: Praeger, 1977); and Adolf Sturmthal, *Workers' Councils* (Cambridge, Mass.: Harvard University Press, 1964). An interesting case study is Juan G. Espinosa and Andrew S. Zimbalist, *Economic Democracy: Workers Participation in Chilean Industry, 1970–73* (New York: Academic Press, 1978).

3. Some useful studies of the operation of the Yugoslav system of worker management are David Granick, *Enterprise Guidance in Eastern Europe* (Princeton, N.J.: Princeton University Press, 1975), chaps. 11–12, pp. 323–94; Ichak Adizes, *Industrial Democracy: Yugoslav Style* (New York: Free Press, 1971); Ichak Adizes and Elisabeth Mann Borges, eds., *Self Management: New Dimensions to Democracy* (Santa Barbara, Calif.: ABC-Clio, 1975); Jiri Kolaja, *Workers' Councils: The Yugoslav Experience* (New York: Praeger, 1965); International Labour Office, *Workers' Management in Yugoslavia* (Geneva: 1962); Josep Obrodovich and William N. Dunn, eds., *Workers' Self-Management and Organizational Power in Yugoslavia* (Pittsburgh: University of Pittsburgh, 1978); and Howard Wachtel, *Workers' Management and Workers' Wages in Yugoslavia* (Ithaca, N.Y.: Cornell University Press, 1973).

10

OTHER DIRECTIONS

The first nine chapters of this guidebook have led you through a number of topics, particularly concerning the economic performance of capitalist, market economies and of socialist, centrally administered economies at relatively high levels of economic development. Although a certain amount of pure theory was presented along the way so that the empirical materials could be correctly interpreted, primary attention was given to the derivation of testable developmental and impact propositions and the ways in which the available data can be used to put such theories to a serious empirical test. A considerable amount of the discussion was organized around a number of impact propositions that focus on the relationship between the economic system and particular performance indicators such as economic growth, dynamic efficiency, economic stability, static efficiency, consumer sovereignty, and the distribution of income. In Chapter 9 a number of propositions related to the development of economic institutions also received attention.

A major purpose behind this discussion is to show you how systemic comparisons of institutions and economic systems can be made so you can learn more about the actual functioning of the economy. Although many questions that are raised cannot be answered, you should be able to see what kind of information is needed to answer them and how such data can be employed to obtain answers. The list of suggested readings at the end of each chapter should also help you in finding materials that will enable you to explore by yourself many of the unanswered questions as well as materials relating particular theoretical issues to the organization or performance of different economies, particularly the Soviet Union.

No guidebook can be complete without unduly expanding its size and cost. Nevertheless, it is worthwhile to consider briefly the kinds of issues that either do not receive due attention in this study or are inadequately treated because of the unsatisfactory state of our knowledge.

A. Theory

One important direction of investigation is the development of more adequate models with which to describe the behavior of different economic systems. At the present time the theoretical models developed for description of capitalist, market economies are becoming increasingly more refined; however, the theoretical models developed for description of centrally administered, socialist economies are still in their infancy; and there are almost no theoretical models at all for the description of precapitalist economies. Although a great deal of theorizing about noncapitalist economies is rigorous and interesting,[1] most such studies deal with a narrow range of problems and, it should be added, focus primarily on impact propositions.

One cause of the problems in analyzing noncapitalist economies that allocate resources with institutions other than the market can be traced to the lack of an adequate general theory of institutions with regard to their development or to their impact. Another cause lies in the difficulties of developing models of these other economic systems that can actually be empirically tested with the available data. In many cases, such data are not available and we are left swimming in a sea of contradictory theories and propositions.

[1]Two excellent examples are John Michael Montias, *The Structure of Economic Systems* (New Haven, Conn.: Yale University Press, 1976); and the essays in Judith Thornton, *Economic Analysis of the Soviet-Type System* (Cambridge: Cambridge University Press, 1976).

Still another aspect of this lack of a adequate theory of economic systems can be seen by considering a question raised in Chapter 1: What is an economic system? The general answer suggested in that chapter is that an economic system is any entity defined in any manner that has analytical relevance or convenience. For the rest of this guidebook, a major share of the discussion focuses on propositions relating to economic systems defined according to one set of major characteristics (i.e., capitalist, market versus socialist, centrally administered).

It is, of course, quite easy to define economic systems in terms of certain *combinations* of particular features or traits. For instance, we can focus attention on criteria such as the degree to which the property structure has a relatively high or low degree of "centralization" and the degree to which material or moral incentives are stressed, and construct two-by-two typologies into which we can place various actual economies (e.g., the United States has low "centralization" and high stress on material incentives; Cuba during the mid-1960s had high "centralization" and high stress on moral incentives, etc.). However, it should be noted that there are very few propositions or models that take into account the *interaction* of two or more systemic elements. This problem is even more acute when we consider interrelations between three important systemic elements: the property structure, the information structure, and the incentive structure. Although this apparently useful threefold distinction of systemic elements has been made for some years, very few interesting or worthwhile hypotheses have been generated from such a scheme. In sum, theories about the interactions of systemic elements are lacking and, therefore, most attention is paid to theories that have a unidimensional definition of economic system.

The need for more adequate theorizing must be accompanied by the empirical testing of such theories. The latter task is necessary not only "to keep the theorists honest," but also to prevent the development of a vast literature that deals either with issues that can never be tested or with issues so trivial that they shouldn't be tested. An example of such a development occurs in the study of labor-managed firms and, in many respects, much of the so-called "theoretical" literature is little more than an exercise in applied mathematics deserving to be pruned from the journals designed for those who are interested in real economic problems.

The lack of adequate theory is a problem not only for economic theorists, but for anyone who is called upon to make judgments about various aspects of different economic systems. For instance, what should be the proper mix of market and plan elements in our own economic system? In many instances, such judgments are made on ideological grounds which, in turn, implies some type of theory about the functioning of the economy. Unfortunately, a great deal of ideological theorizing is based neither on any facts nor on any serious or realistic appraisal of the situation.

The factual materials and the results of the statistical analysis presented in the previous chapters can aid us in making certain types of judgments in a more serious fashion. However, such results cover only a limited range of phenomena and there are many gaps in our knowledge. To utilize such empirical analyses to the fullest extent, they must be placed in some type of theoretical framework, for often isolated facts prove more disorienting than helpful.

B. Extensions of the Approach

1. Other Nations

An embarrassing aspect of the lack of adequate models or systems labels becomes quite apparent when we consider the economies of the world and try to make some meaningful classification of these 215 entities into different economic systems. One useful place to start is to consider those nations that are "socialist."

Although a number of economic definitions of *socialism* are presented in Chapter 1, let us abandon these for a short while and employ a more political definition using three criteria: (a) nations with "centralized" power structures (operationally, nations with a single political party), (b) nations whose governments (and single party) have a socialist ideology borrowing heavily from orthodox Marxism-Leninism, and (c) governments whose actual policies have been influenced by their ideology.[2] It is, of course, often difficult to distinguish a statist from a socialist ideology or to determine exactly what governments are doing, in contrast to what they are saying. In order to show which are the most ambiguous cases, it is also useful to divide socialist countries into "core countries" where the single party and socialist ideology seem strongly entrenched and "penumbra countries" where the political system seems less stable. Such an exercise is carried out in Table 10–1, where 38 "socialist" nations in the world in 1980 are listed (in 1983 Grenada would be dropped from the list of penumbra countries). The importance of these nations in the world economy can be judged from the summary data presented in Table 10–2.

[2]This type of hurried approach hides many serious problems, which are discussed with considerable insight by Stephen White, "What Is a Communist System," *Studies in Comparative Communism,* 16, No. 4 (Winter 1983), pp. 247–65; and by Peter Wiles and Alan Smith, "The General View, Especially from Moscow," in Peter Wiles, ed., *The New Communist Third World* (New York: St. Martin's Press, 1982), pp. 13–53. See also the discussion by various authors in Charles K. Wilber and Kenneth P. Jameson, eds., *Socialist Models of Development* (Oxford: Pergamon Press, 1981).

Several important aspect of the results should be readily apparent: Many of the nations appearing to be "socialist" according to the political criteria discussed above are not "socialist" according to the economic criteria discussed in Chapter 1 such as the degree of public ownership, the relative importance of public expenditures, or the relative importance of central economic administration or planning. In terms of economic policy, such as greater attention to education or health, there appears to be little difference between these nations and comparable

TABLE 10–1
Scoreboard of "Socialism" for 1980

Country	Land Area 1975 (1,000 sq. km.)	Population 1975 (1,000's)	Index, Per Capita GDP, 1970 (U.S.A. = 100)
Core Countries			
Afghanistan, Democratic Republic	648	16,665	4.9
Albania, Socialist People's Republic	29	2,424	18
Bulgaria, People's Republic	111	8,721	37
China, People's Republic	9,562	879,217	10
Cuba, Republic	115	9,332	21
Czechoslovak Socialist Republic	128	14,802	62
German Democractic Republic	108	16,850	64
Hungarian People's Republic	93	10,541	43
Kampuchea, People's Republic	181	8,110	7.3
Korea, Democratic People's Republic	121	15,852	11
Lao People's Democratic Republic	237	3,303	4.2
Mongolian People's Republic	1,565	1,444	8
Polish People's Republic	313	34,022	35
Romania, Socialist Republic	238	21,245	31
Soviet Union	22,402	254,393	47
Vietnam, Socialist Republic	330	46,546	13
Yugoslavia, Socialist Federal Republic	256	21,352	26
Subtotal	36,437	1,364,819	20
Penumbra Countries			
Algeria, Democratic and Popular Republic	2,382	16,776	15
Angola, People's Republic	1,247	6,260	15
Benin, People's Republic	113	3,112	4.4
Burma, Socialist Republic	677	30,170	4.4
Congo, People's Republic	342	1,352	11
Ethiopia	1,222	27,465	4.0
Guinea, People's Revolutionary Republic	246	4,416	4.3
Guinea-Bissau, Republic	36	525	14
Guyana, Cooperative Republic	215	781	17
Grenada, State	0.3	105	17
Iraq, Republic	435	11,124	17
Libya, Socialist People's Arab Jamahiriya	1,760	2,430	53
Madagascar, Democratic Republic	587	7,675	7.0

TABLE 10–1 (continued)

Country	Land Area 1975 (1,000 sq. km.)	Population 1975 (1,000's)	Index, Per Capita GDP, 1970 (U.S.A. = 100)
Penumbra Countries (continued)			
Mali	1,204	5,807	2.9
Mozambique, People's Republic	802	9,203	12
Nicaragua, Republic	30	2,155	20
Seychelles, Republic	0.2	58	7.0
Somali Democratic Republic	72	3,045	4.6
Syrian Arab Republic	185	7,355	13
Tanzania, United Republic	945	15,312	5.3
Yemen, People's Democratic Republic	333	1,690	6.0
Subtotal	12,869.5	156,816	8.9
Total	49,306.5	1,521,635	19

Note: The criteria for inclusion in this table are (a) single-party system, (b) socialist ideology, borrowing heavily from orthodox Marxism-Leninism, and (c) actual governmental policies influenced by ideology. This Marxist-Leninist element is particularly strong in all of the core countries and such penumbra countries as Angola, Benin, Congo, Ethiopia, Guyana, Grenada (up to 1983), Madagascar, Mozambique, and Yemen; in the other countries this socialist ideology draws from several sources. It is difficult, however, to classify many nations and some may prefer to remove certain countries in the list or to include other nations such as Zambia or Zimbabwe. Certain nations such as Ghana once had a strong Marxist-Leninist ideological orientation but have changed over the years and are not included in the above list. Several small island nations (e.g., Cape Verde, São Tomé) are also omitted from this table.

The GDP data come from Irving Kravis et al., "Real GDP per Capita for More Than One Hundred Countries," *The Economic Journal,* 88, No. 2 (June 1978), pp. 215–42, and other sources cited in Appendix D. Given the nature of the estimating procedures, especially for the nations with low per capita incomes, index data should be interpreted as indicating only broad orders of magnitudes. For countries not covered in the sources cited, estimates were made so that the world sample includes 215 nations. For many countries, however, these estimates are little better than guesses; the per capita GDP estimates for Albania, China, Cuba, Mongolia, Seychelles, and Vietnam fall into this category.

Sources: Information about the political nature of the countries in the world comes from Arthur S. Banks and William Overstreet, *Political Handbook of the World: 1981* (New York: McGraw-Hill, 1981); and Richard F. Starr, ed., *Yearbook of International Communist Affairs* (Stanford, Calif.: Hoover Institution Press, 1978). Land area and population data come from United Nations, *1979 Demographic Yearbook* (New York: 1980).

"capitalist" nations.[3] Indeed, it is quite difficult to discover any way in which many of them are "socialist," except nominally.

Although many of these 38 nations may not be "socialist" in any significant fashion, what are their economic systems? Why and how did these systems evolve in the manner that they have developed? Into how many groups must these 38 nations be divided in order to distinguish their economic performance?

[3]The differences in health and educational standards in the nations mentioned in Table 10-1 and a comparison group of nations is carried out by Frederic L. Pryor, "Review of Socialist Models of Development," *Journal of Comparative Economics,* 7, No. 2 (June 1983), pp. 201–7.

TABLE 10–2
Summary of the Scoreboard for 1980

Country Group	Percentage of World		
	Land Area	*Population*	*GDP*
Core countries	27%	34%	27%
Penumbra countries	9	4	1
Both core and penumbra countries	36	38	28

Source: The data come from Table 10–1.

From this perspective, it also makes little sense to lump the 177 remaining nations into one basket entitled "capitalist, market economies." Not only do these economies feature varying mixtures of capitalist and socialist elements but in many qualitative respects they are quite different. For instance, a number of political scientists have begun to examine various aspects of corporatism, which appears to be an important feature in certain Western European economies.[4] At present, unfortunately, the degree to which the "classical" functioning of the market has been modified by corporatistic elements is quite unclear.

This problem of classification can be viewed profitably from a different angle. One surprising result of the empirical analysis of this guidebook is the similarity in performance between nations in the two sets of economic systems into which the economically developed nations are divided. Economic growth, dynamic efficiency, stability of production, consumption expenditures (both public and private), and the distribution of income appear quite similar. Although inflation is less in the socialist, centrally administered economies and although static efficiency appears greater in the capitalist, market economies, the similarities between the systems appear more striking than the differences.

These empirical results could arise for several reasons. The empirical analysis might have been too crude to isolate the crucial differences. But these similarities might also be due to the fact that the division of economic systems into two groups is insufficient. In short, there is no very satisfactory way of distinguishing the economic systems of the various nations in the world in a manner that is helpful for analyzing their differential performance on major performance indicators or determining how their institutions developed in the manner in which they evolved. Nor is there any satisfactory way of predicting in a systematic fashion how they will develop in the future and whether they may actually become socialist in a meaningful economic definition of the term or whether the trend will turn toward a purer form of capitalism.

[4]These problems are explored by various authors in Suzanne D. Berger, *Organizing Interests in Western Europe: Pluralism, Corporatism, and the Transformation of Politics* (Cambridge: Cambridge University Press, 1981).

2. Other Sectors

For the most part this guidebook has adopted a macroeconomic viewpoint. However, in many cases it is also useful to make microeconomic comparison of different economies, for example, on the basis of a single sector or economic function. For instance, although factories in many countries appear to resemble each other,[5] agricultural systems may differ greatly. Comparative analysis of the origins or impact of their land tenure systems, or farm size, or governmental methods for encouraging technological progress on the farms, or mechanisms for transferring rural workers to urban areas would provide considerable insight into the operation of different economic systems, not to mention aid to policy makers. Other comparative analyses in the fields of banking, or transportation, or provision of services, or industrial policy that are not covered in this guidebook might also be worthwhile and interesting.

3. Other Times

Comparative analyses of the type discussed in this guidebook are not, of course, bound by time. In the field of economic development, considerable insight has been gained by examining the development process in the past of "successful" and "nonsuccessful" industrializers and, undoubtedly, much more can be learned from such exercises.

C. The Borderline with Other Disciplines

In this guidebook relatively little attention has been focused on the reciprocal influences between the economy and either the polity or the society. Although some of the discussion of public expenditures or of various developmental propositions touched on these issues, they are not systematically attacked. Of course, these problems are very difficult to handle in a rigorous fashion, particularly because analysis in the fields of comparative politics or comparative sociology are not often based on formal terms of models from which testable hypotheses can be derived. Thus the chasm between economics and these other disciplines becomes difficult to bridge.

This problem can also be viewed from a different perspective. Although certain Marxist scholars see a direct causal relation between the economy and both the polity and the society (the first being the "base"

---

[5]Appearances are very deceiving, however. For two interesting comparisons that reveal some fundamental differences, see Ronald P. Dore, *British Factory, Japanese Factory: The Origins of National Diversity in Industrial Relations* (Berkeley: University of California Press, 1973); or David Granick, *Managerial Comparisons of Four Developed Countries* (Cambridge, Mass.: MIT Press, 1972).

and the latter two being part of the "superstructure"), both Marx and Engels had more sophisticated views and saw reciprocal influences.[6] The degree of reciprocity, however, is a deep problem for which we still have relatively little systematic evidence. Given the multitude of theories that allow almost any speculative opinion, it is certainly high time to approach the problem more empirically.

The roles of ideology and the reciprocal influences of the ways in which people perceive the economy and the actual structure and operation of the economy are also not discussed in this guidebook except in passing. However, the subject is important and also worthy of attention. It is also a problem lying on the fascinating borderline between economics and other social sciences which has received little systematic empirical research in the entire economic literature.

D. An Overview

Throughout this guidebook a series of propositions about the comparative behavior of nations with different economic systems are discussed; many are also tested empirically. Several broader issues require brief discussion, for they incorporate the three morals of this book.

1. The Bases for Our Judgments

Despite the ideological conviction with which most people judge differences in the economic performance between economic systems, most of these judgments appear ill founded in reality. These impact questions form a major focus of this analysis and, as noted above, the similarities appear more important than the differences. However, current knowledge about many aspects of economic performance is still limited. Sometimes the basic facts are lacking, data regarding the actual economic efficiency of the two systems or the distribution of real income (including nonmonetary income). Sometimes the underlying causes are unclear, for example, why growth rates or degrees of fluctuation of production are similar in the two major systems.

2. The Extent of Our Knowledge

Knowledge about the origins of particular institutions and the reasons why certain nations have ended up with particular institutions or economic systems is also limited. These developmental questions formed

---

[6]On this problem the discussion of G. A. Cohen, *Karl Marx's Theory of History: A Defense* (Princeton University Press, 1978), is particularly illuminating.

another major focus of this study. Why, for instance, do certain nations have sharecropping systems in agriculture while others have fixed rent systems and still others have very little land rental? Why have some nations chosen particular growth strategies and not others? A thousand other "why" questions could be added.

3. The Use of Comparative Analyses

The comparative method as used in this book provides some extremely useful information to help you to answer the impact and developmental questions outlined above. An important problem in comparative analysis is to include as many of the major causal factors as possible so that, in examining the impact of one such factor, all others can be held constant. Although there are a number of books and articles giving advice on how to carry out such analyses, many offer counsels of perfection that are impossible to achieve. For anything to be accomplished, some critical tradeoffs need to be made; and the real problem is usually to draw conclusions from admittedly imperfect comparisons that do not do violence to the data at hand.

In short, this guidebook has presented a set of questions and a method by which to answer some of them. It has placed great emphasis on the testing of propositions drawn from theory or ideology, on trying to determine the reality of our presuppositions by confronting them with the best available data.

If you are dissatisfied with the results or if you wish to investigate other questions with the same methods, then your course of action is clear. Put down this guidebook and explore the territory by yourself. Now is the time to begin.

A

NOTES ON THE STATISTICAL ANALYSES

Regression analysis is an attempt to fit an equation to a set of data so as to show the relationship between two or more variables. An example is shown by a linear equataion of the following form:

$$Y = a + b_1X_1 + b_2X_2 \ldots,$$

where Y is the variable to be explained (the *dependent variable*), the X's are the explanatory variables (the *independent variables*), and the lowercase letters represent the coefficients that are calculated.

To obtain the data set for the regression analysis, a sample is drawn (in this guidebook, the sample is drawn from the set of developed capitalist and socialist nations on the planet). For each observation (in this case, each country), the values for the X and Y variables are used.

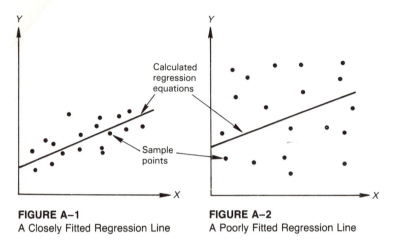

FIGURE A–1
A Closely Fitted Regression Line

FIGURE A–2
A Poorly Fitted Regression Line

A. Simple Regression Analysis

The most simple linear equation has but one independent variable and is represented in Figures A–1 and A–2. The actual calculation of the regression requires use of a mathematical technique to select the set of coefficients that permits the "best fitting" curves to be established. The criteria for "best fitting" are tricky and are discussed in statistics texts.

In Figure A–1 you see a situation where X and Y appear strongly related. A statistic to show how much is "explained" (in the sense that if you are given X, how well can you predict Y) is the *coefficient of determination* (R^2), which runs from 1.00 (a perfect fit) to .00 (the points are randomly distributed and the calculated curve is useless for prediction). The numerical value of R^2 represents the ratio of the variation of Y (more exactly, the variance of Y) which is "explained" by X. In Figure A–2, the R^2 is much lower. The R^2 can be low either because your sample is not very representative or because you have not specified the relationship in the correct manner (see below) or because the relationship between the variables is weak.

The coefficients a and b are calculated from the regression analysis. If $X = 0$, then $Y = a$. For every unit that X changes, Y changes by b.

If the R^2 is low, then the hypothesized relationship and the calculated coefficients may be incorrect. If you have specified the statistical relationship properly, then you can gain some idea of the degree of confidence to be placed in the calculated coefficients examining the *standard errors* that are placed in parentheses below the coefficients. If the calculated coefficient is very small in relation to the standard error, then it is common to *reject* any causal relation between the two variables. In actuality, this low ratio indicates either that the "actual value" of the coefficient is very much different from the calculated value (because the sample selected is not very representative of the wider universe from which it has been drawn) or that the causal relation has been misspecified (see below). If, on the other hand, the ratio of the calculated coefficient to the standard error is quite high, then you can have some confidence that the calculated coefficient is relatively accurate and that the hypothesized relationship is correct. More precisely, if you have specified the relationship correctly and if the ratio of the calculated regression coefficient to this standard error is greater than about 2.1, then you have a certainty that 19 times out of 20 the relationship portrayed by the coefficient is not caused by chance but rather represents a "real" relationship. (In the text, an asterisk is placed above those calculated coefficients that meet this test.) In Figure A–2, it is highly unlikely that the b coefficient would meet this test.

The *standard error of estimate (SEE)* is a statistic that directly tells you how well you can predict Y, given X. The larger the *SEE*, the less certain your prediction will be.

A simple regression does not need to be linear. You can, for instance, calculate a regression of the following form: logarithm $Y = a + b X^2$. In this case, the logarithm of Y is treated in the same manner as Y is handled in the linear regressions; similarly, X^2 is treated in the same manner as X in the linear regressions.

B. Specification and Interpretation Errors

Although you may be correct in believing that Y is related to X, you may be incorrect in specifying the form of the relation. In Figure A–3, for instance, the regression is calculated in a linear form; however,

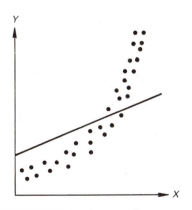

FIGURE A–3
An Incorrectly Specified Regression Line

graphing the sample points reveals that the relationship is curvilinear and you would have obtained a better fit (and better predictions) if you had calculated a relationship such as logarithm $Y = a + b X$. This is one type of *specification error*.

You may, however, be incorrect in believing that Y is related to X; rather, Y may be related to Z instead. In many such cases calculating a regression $Y = a + b X$ results in a very low R^2 and a very low ratio of calculated coefficient to standard error, and you reject the result because the criterion specified above is not met. However, sometimes your regression may look quite promising, which represents a case of spurious correlation. In this case Z is related not only to Y but to X, so that there is a meaningless correlation between X and Y. For example, one ingenious statistician showed that there is a direct relation between the birth rate in Sweden and the number of storks. This came about because the number of storks is inversely related to urbanization and urbanization is inversely related to the birth rate and *not* because the fewer number of storks brought fewer babies to Swedish couples. This is a second type of misspecification error.

Although the regression may show a strong relationship between two variables, Y and X, it does not indicate the direction of causality. That is, X may cause Y, Y may cause X, or there may be a mutual causation. It is only from theoretical reasoning that the direction of causality is determined. If you have misspecified the regression so as to include variables that mutually cause one another or where the direction of causality goes from the variable that has been designated as the dependent variable to the independent variable, the regression results can be easily misinterpreted. In interpreting all regressions, it is important to investigate this third type of specification error by asking yourself if the causation runs from the "independent" to the "dependent" variables or vice versa.

One last problem of interpretation concerns the "rejection" of certain results because the test revolving around the ratio of the calculated coefficient to the standard error is not met. Although the 19 out of 20 probability standard that is used throughout this gudebook permits you in most cases to avoid accepting spurious correlations, it can also result in your rejecting certain hypothesized causal relationships that actually occur but that do not pass the test because not all causal variables underlying a particular situation are specified.

C. Multiple Regression Analysis

The above discussion is conducted in terms of two variables. However, the same statistical techniques can be employed if there are two or more independent (causal) variables. However, in this case, a number of coefficients and their *standard errors* are calculated (there is still only one *standard error of estimate* and one *coefficient of determination*).

The interpretation of a multiple regression is slightly more complicated. Given a regression $Y = a + bX + cZ$, the calculated coefficient b represents the impact of X on Y when Z is held constant; similarly c represents the impact of Z on Y when X is held constant.

Usual regression techniques require that the independent variables X and Z be independent of each other. If they are related, you have *multicollinearity,* and the usual mathematical techniques of calculating the various statistics yield standard errors that are too large and, in some cases, coefficients that are biased.

In the multiple regressions presented in the text, *dummy variables* are sometimes used. A dummy variable is a variable like any other but has only two values, for example, 0 when the nation has a capitalist, market economy and 1 when the nation has a socialist, centrally administered economy. (Since Yugoslavia does not fall in either category, it is omitted from such regressions). The calculated coefficient of the dummy variable should be interpreted in the same manner as any other calculated coefficient. In the case of the regressions presented in the text, it shows the impact of the economic system on the dependent variable. Further, when the ratio of the calculated coefficient to the standard error is less than 2.1, the hypothesized causal relationship is *rejected.*

One manner of portraying the action of a dummy variable on a two-dimensional diagram is to consider it to be a *shift variable,* that is, a variable that shifts the value of the dependent variable upward or downward an amount specified by the value of the calculated regression coefficient for the dummy variable. This is shown in Figure A–4, where the predicted value of Y is on the upper or lower line, depending on whether the dummy variable has a value of 1 or 0.

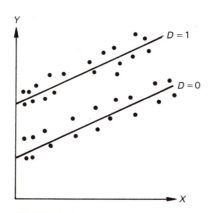

FIGURE A–4
An Example of a Shift Variable

Figure A–4 also reveals one danger in using dummy variables in the analysis of the impact of economic systems, namely, the hidden assumption that the two economic systems act in the same manner except for the shift. However, it is quite possible that the slope of the relationship between the other causal variables and the dependent variable will be different as well. For each of the regressions reported in this guidebook, statistical tests were made to see if this occurred. In no case did this seem to happen and, therefore, little attention is paid to the problem which, in other circumstances, can be quite serious.

D. Rank Order Correlations

The use of dummy variable is one example of how noncontinuous variables can be handled in the same manner as continuous variables. Another example, which is used in several chapters of this guidebook, occurs with the use of rank order correlations.

Suppose that you take 20 manufacturing sectors in a given nation and rank them according to several characteristics such as average level of wages and capital intensity. You can then determine the degree to which the two rank orderings are related to each other by calculating a rank order correlation coeficient whose square, like the coefficient of determination, ranges from .00 (the two rank orderings are totally unrelated to each other) to 1.00 (the two rank orderings are exactly the same). Similarly, such a coefficient can be calculated for the rank orderings of a particular characteristic for the same set of 20 industries for two different countries.

A *coefficient of concordance* is a generalized rank order coefficient; that is, it shows the degree to which the rank orderings for many different countries or many different characteristics are related to each other (i.e., to some sort of "average rank ordering" for the entire sample). The concordance coefficient ranges from .00 (a totally random pattern) to 1.00 (all rank orderings are the same).

B

GLOSSARY

Agglomeration ratio The share of assets or sales in an economic sector or industry accounted for by the largest of a specified number of enterprises (e.g., by the largest 100 enterprises).

Capital Buildings, machines, tools, and inventories that contribute to production.

Capitalism An *economic system* where the means of production (capital) are predominantly owned by individuals, rather than by the government. Other criteria such as the allocation of resources through a market are also often used (see Chapter 1, Section C–3). *Regulated capitalism* is a capitalist economic system in which certain decisions by producers are limited by laws and governmental decrees.

Centralization Ten definitions are presented in Chapter 9, Section B–2.

Communism An *economic system* characterized by all people receiving goods and services according to their needs and participating in producting according to their abilities. Only the model of this economic system has been described; it has not been realized.

Competitive model A theoretical description of an ecnomic system where all goods and services are allocated through a market and where no producer or consumer has an appreciable influence on the price. The ownership of the means of production in such a model is not an essential element.

Concentration ratio A measure of the degree of monopoly that is usually calculated by determining the ratio of the value of sales of the four largest producers to total sales of that product or industry.

Concordance coefficient See Appendix A, Section D.

Consumer sovereignty or **consumer efficiency** A pattern of production of consumer goods that is determined by the aggregation of consumer wants. More technically, no change can be made in the production pattern or in the goods and services consumed by any given person so as to raise the utility of one person without reducing the utility of another person.

Codetermination A system of governance of enterprises found in the Federal Republic of Germany (West Germany), where representatives of the workers in the enterprise participate on the board of directors and can vote on policy issues.

Coefficient of determination See Appendix A, Section A.

Corporatism An economic system where production of particular industries or industrial sectors in controlled by a single large organization so that there is no competition within that industry or sector.

Developmental proposition A proposition concerning the origins of some institution or concerning the forces influencing its development or magnitude.

Diminishing returns A circumstance in which production increases in ever smaller amounts as an additional amount of one type of factor of production (e.g., labor) is added to the production process while the other factors of production are held constant.

Dynamic efficiency: A term with a number of meanings. In this guidebook it is defined in terms of total factor productivity, that is, the change in output occurring with a specified change in factor inputs.

Echo cycle A business cycle that recurs with an ever diminishing impact.

Economic system In Chapter 1, Section C–2, this is defined as those parts of political, social, and ecnomic institutions, organizations, laws, rules, and beliefs that interact in a manner directly or indirectly to affect production, consumption, distribution, or exchange. An *ideal* economic system is a theoretical model of such a system.

Economies of scale Economies that occur when the percentage increase in production is higher than the percentage increase in the *factors of production*, when these factors are maintained in a given production.

Edgeworth box diagram A diagram (beloved of teachers of economic theory) by which properties of static efficiency can be easily demonstrated in a rigorous fashion.

Enterprise A business organization consisting of one or more *establishments* under common ownership and control.

Establishment A business or industrial unit at a single physical location that produces goods or services. It can consist of several "plants" or "factories," as long as they are located together and under a single mangagement.

Externalities Costs or benefits that accrue to a producer or a consumer that are not contracted or paid for (e.g., costs caused by pollution by others) and that are not transmitted through the market.

Factors of production Generally defined as land, labor, and *capital*.

GDP Gross domestic product, which is the money value of the total production of goods and services of a nation. This can be valued in terms of prices on the market (market price GDP) or in terms of wages, rents, and profits which the factors of production receive (factor price GDP). The market and factor price GDPs differ primarily by indirect taxes and subsidies. If depreciation is removed from GDP, the net domestic product (NDP) is obtained.

GNP The money value of total consumption, investment, government expenditures on goods and services, and net exports (exports minus imports). It differs in value from the GDP by the amount of income obtained from or paid to foreigners, an aggregate that is generally small in relation to total GNP.

Impact proposition A proposition about the economic effect of a particular institution, policy, or variable.

Index number problem A problem arising when aggregating a set of outputs or inputs. A key difficulty is the property choice of weights since different weights can give quite different indicators of aggregate behavior.

Institution Defined in Chapter 1, Section C–1, as a pattern of recurrent and regularized relations between two or more people who are carrying out some economic function (production, distribution or exchange, consumption). Such relations are shaped by the values of the particpants, norms regularizing the interaction, sanctions and rewards, and the specific motives of the individuals involved.

Kolkhoz A cooperative farm in the Soviet Union. All net income (income after paying for expenses) is divided among the members.

Macroeconomics The study of the determination of economic aggregates such as total output, the price level, or total employment.

Market breakdown Circumstances where the allocation of resources in a market system does not meet the standards of static efficiency or of consumer sovereignty.

Marginal rate of substitution of two factors The least number of units of one factor that can replace a unit of another factor in the production process such that the volume of production remains constant.

Microeconomics The study of the allocation of resources and distribution of income.

Mixed economic system A vague term, generally considered to be an economic system where elements of capitalism and socialism are combined in some unspecified fashion.

Opportunity cost The cost of using resources for a certain purpose, measured by the benefits or revenues foregone by not using them in their best alternative use.

Participation ratio The ratio of people of a particular age and sex who are in the labor force or looking for such work to the total number of people of that age and sex.

Performance criteria or indicators Particular indicators selected by the analyst to evaluate the performance of an economy. In this guidebook six performance indicators (discussed in Chapter 2, Section C) are chosen.

Policy cycle   Systematic variations in the economic policies of a government; for example, just before an election, public expenditures are increased.

Production possibilities curve   A curve describing the maximum amount of a set of goods or services when a given technology and amount of factors of production are assumed. The production possibilities curve defines the locus of production where static efficiency is achieved.

Property   Defined in Chapter 9, Section B–1, as a bundle of rights or set of relations between people with regard to some good, service, or "thing"; such rights must have economic value and must be enforced in some societally recognized manner.

Public good   Defined in Chapter 7, Section B–2 as goods and services characterized by nonjoint (or nonrival) consumption and the inability of the producer to exclude from the enjoyment of benefits those who have not paid for them.

Quality circle   A technique used in factors in Japan and other nations to increase productivity where the workers participate in discussions designed to elicit suggestions and behavior for improving the quantity and quality of production.

Rank order correlation coefficient   See Appendix A, Section D.

Shadow prices   A set of prices that are derived from the solution of a linear programming problem and that indicate the relative scarcities of the factors, goods, or services under examination.

Socialism   An *economic system* where the means of production are predominantly owned by the government, rather than by individuals. Other criteria such as the use of nonprice methods to allocate resources are also often used (see Chapter 1, Section C–3).

Sovkhoz   A farm in the Soviet Union that is run like a factory and where the farmers receive a wage.

Standard deviation   The square root of the *variance*.

Standard error   See Appendix A.

Static efficiency   An arrangement of *factors of production* and of the production pattern such that no rearrangement of factors or production tasks can bring about an increase in the production of one good without decreasing the production of another good. In short, the *production possibility curve* has been reached.

Strategic behavior   Economic behavior that does not follow market or administrative signals but is designed to mislead others so that profits can be gained from behavior influenced in this manner.

Transfer prices   Fictitious prices used for accounting purposes to price of goods and services passed from one division of an organization to another.

Underemployment   A situation where labor in an enterprise is not used to its fullest capacity.

Variance   A measurement of dispersion of a set of points around their mean value. More specifically, it is the sum of squares of the distances of the various points from the mean, divided by the number of points.

C

CARRYING OUT COMPARATIVE RESEARCH: SOME BIBLIOGRAPHIC AIDS

A. Introduction

Surveys of general sources used in economic research can be found in Ralph L. Andreano et al., *The Student Economist's Handbook: A Guide to Sources* (Cambridge, Mass: Schenkman Publ., 1967); or Charles Helppie et al., *Research Guide in Economics* (Morristown, N.J.: General Learning Press, 1974).

B. Articles

Articles in the field of comparative economics are listed in the standard bibliographical sources: the PAIS (Public Affairs Information Service) index, the *Social Science Citation Index*, the *Index of Economic Articles* (published by the American Economic Association), and the *Journal of Economic Literature,* which appears four times a year.

For empirical analyses of the current state of individual socialist economies, an excellent place to start are the yearly compendia of articles published by Joint Economic Committee of the U.S. Congress. These are generally published annually and, from 1976 through 1982, consisted of *Soviet Economy in the 1980's: Problems and Prospects* (1982); *East European Economic Assessment* (1981); *Soviet Economy in a Time of Change* (1979); *Chinese Economy Post-Mao* (1978); *East European Economies Post-Helsinki* (1977); and *Soviet Economy in a New Perspective* (1976).

C. Statistics

A difficult task in testing any proposition is finding comparable statistics; and the problem is complicated when nations are being compared. Although the national statistical yearbooks and the specialized statistical publications of the nations of the world contain a great deal of data, comparability is limited. A number of international and other agencies have attempted to make comparable certain types of statistics. Although often quite useful, these sources must be used cautiously and attention must be paid to the definitions employed by various nations.

Several major bibliographic aids can be used for locating international statistics:

SISCIS, *Subject Index to Sources of Comparative International Statistics* (Beckenham, Kent: CBP, 1978).

Index to International Statistics (Washington, D.C.: Congressional Information Service.) Unfortunately, this excellent index starts only in 1983.

United Nations, Statistical Office. *Directory of International Statistics* (New York: 1975).

Paul Wasserman and Jacqueline O'Brien, *Statistical Sources,* 7th ed. (Detroit: Gale Research Co., 1982).

For worldwide statistics, the United Nations and its member agencies publish data. These data vary in comparability, depending on the agency and the type of statistics. For instance, data from the FAO appear carelessly compiled, while those of the World Bank are carefully done. Similarly, aggregate national accounts data are not comparable between socialist and capitalist nations, while demographic statistics are, for the most part, comparable. The major compilations, usually issued on an annual basis, are the following:

Food and Agricultural Organization, *Production Yearbook.*
Food and Agricultural Organization, *Trade Yearbook.*
International Labour Organization, *Yearbook of Labour Statistics.*
International Monetary Fund, *Balance of Payments Yearbook.*
International Monetary Fund, *Government Finance Statistics Yearbook.*
International Monetary Fund, *International Financial Statistics.*
UNCTAD, *Handbook of International Trade and Development Statistics.*
UNESCO, *Statistical Yearbook.*
United Nations, *Demographic Statistics.*
United Nations, *Statistical Yearbook.*
United Nations, *Yearbook of Industrial Statistics.*
United Nations, *Yearbook of International Trade Statistics.*
United Nations, *Yearbook of National Account Statistics.*
World Bank, *World Tables.*
World Health Organization, *World Health Statistics.*

Member organizations of the United Nations also publish special statistical yearbooks for Latin America and also Asia and the Pacific nations, as well as special collections of statistics on energy production and usage, trade in engineering products, construction, transport statistics, and so forth.

Among the intergovernmental agencies, the OECD (Organization for Economic Cooperation and Development) and the EEC (European Economic Community) generally publish the most comparable and reliable statistical compilations, but these focus primarily on the nations belonging to these organizations. The Council for Mutual Economic Assistance publishes statistics for its member nations (mostly in Eastern Europe) but comparability problems arise. Although this yearbook appears in Russian, English translations are available.

Several compendia have been produced by governments or individuals that contain more or less comparable statistics including two by B. R. Mitchell: *European Historical Statistics* (New York: Columbia University Press, 1975); and *International Historical Statistics: Africa and Asia* (New York: New York University Press, 1982).

D

NOTES ON THE DATA SOURCES OF THE TABLES

A. GDP in Comparable Prices

These data come from Irving B. Kravis, Alan Heston, and Robert Summers, "Real GDP *Per Capita* for More than One Hundred Countries," *Economic Journal*, 88, No. 2 (June 1978), pp. 215–42.; Irving B. Kravis, Alan Heston, and Robert Summers, *World Product and Income* (Baltimore: Johns Hopkins University Press, 1982), p. 10; and Frederic L. Pryor, "Comparable G.N.P.'s per Capita: An Addendum," *Economic Journal*, 89, No. 3 (September 1979), pp. 666–69.

B. National Account, Price, and Production Data

Data for the OECD nations come from OECD, *National Accounts in O.E.C.D. Countries* (Paris: 1970); and OECD, *National Accounts*, Vols. 1 and 2 (Paris: 1982). These are supplemented by several other OEDC publications as well as different national sources for certain countries.

Data for Yugoslavia come not only from the above-cited OECD sources, but also from Vinod Dubey, ed., *Yugoslavia: Development with Decentralization,* World Bank Country Economic Report (Baltimore: Johns Hopkins University Press, 1975); United Nations, *Yearbook of National Accounts Statistics* (New York: annual); and several other sources.

For the socialist, centrally planned economies, data come primarily from the the U.S. Joint Economic Committee volumes cited in Appendix C, Section B. These are supplemented by United Nations, *Yearbook of National Account Statistics* (New York: annual); a series of publications by Thad P. Alton and his associates at the Research Project on National Income in East Central Europe; and Wolfgang F. Stolper and Karl Roskamp, *The Structure of the East German Economy* (Cambridge, Mass.: Harvard University Press, 1960. Price data are derived from data presented in Thad P. Alton et al., *Official and Alternative Consumer Price Indices in Eastern Europe, Selected Years, 1960–1981,* O.P. 73, (New York: 1982); and U.S. Congress, *USSR: Measures of Economic Growth and Development, 1950–80* (Washington, D.C.: GPO, 1982).

The most aggregative production data for Eastern Europe are GNPs; for the OECD nations, GDPs. This should make almost no difference in the results covering a 30-year period.

All growth rates of production are calculated by fitting exponential curves to the various series. The annual increases in prices are calculated from the end points the series.

C. Population and Labor Force

The population data come either from United Nations, *Demographic Yearbook* (New York: annual) or from OECD, *Labour Force Statistics* (Paris: annual).

Labour Force Statistics is also the main source for the labor force statistics of the OECD nations. In passing, it should be noted that the OECD data are somewhat different for certain countries than that found in International Labour Office, *1950–2000 Labour Force: Estimates and Projections* (Geneva: 1977); the source of the discrepancies could not be determined.

For Eastern Europe, the labor force data come from various U.S. Congress Joint Economic Committee sources cited in Appendix C, the ILO source cited in the previous paragraph, and from various country studies of the U.S. Department of Commerce.

D. Trade Data

These data come from UNESCO, *Handbook of International Trade and Development Statistics 1979* (New York: 1980).

E

FURTHER DISCUSSION
OF THE USES OF LINEAR
PROGRAMMING

Chapter 5 sketches the use of linear programming for solving the "transportation problem." In this appendix several other simple theoretical examples are presented in a geometrical form, combined with a brief analysis of how such a problem could be solved in a real-life situation. Several actual applications of linear programming to the real world are also very briefly discussed. More extended nontechnical descriptions of the use of linear programming can be found in the suggested readings at the end of Chapter 5.

A. The Choice of Technique in a One-Factor Economy

For simplicity let us suppose that an economy consists of only two sectors (producing commodities S and F) and one factor of production, labor, which is available in a prespecified amount. Further, let us assume that there are several ways to produce each commodity, but that each method requires not only labor but also a certain amount of the other product as an input (e.g., it takes electricity to produce steel and steel to produce electricity) in some fixed proportion. Your problem is to select the methods of production such that the two goods are produced in a specified fixed proportion and that net production of each (i.e., the amount of the commodity left over for consumption after some of it has been used up in the production of the other commodity) is maximized.

This is illustrated in Figure E–1, where the various production possibilities are shown in solid lines. More specifically, points $A_1 \ldots A_7$ show the amounts of production (a positive value) occurring and the amount of inputs of the other product used (a negative value) if all labor is placed in that sector. For instance, if all labor is placed in industry F and if production method A_1 is selected, then 225 F's are produced and, in the process, 40 S's are used up. Similarly, if all labor resources are placed in industry S and if the production method is A_4, 125 S's are produced, but 25 F's are used up.

Labor does not need to be placed exclusively in the production of one product. If it is divided between production methods A_1 and A_4, then production lies somewhere on the locus of points connecting the end points of the two vectors. Further, since it is desirable to produce a positive net amount of each product, labor should be distributed so that the point of this locus lies in the upper right-hand quadrant where both S and F are positive.

All of these production vectors for a given product are linear and require labor and the input of the other product in fixed proportions. In order to maximize their combined production, the particular methods for producing them should be selected such that no change of technique for producing one of them will permit more of one product to be made without a reduction of the production of the other good. In geometric terms, we connect the end points of the various production vectors and select the line lying farthest to the right. In the diagram three combinations of different techniques to produce F and S are displayed. It is apparent that the combination of production methods A_2 and A_5 is clearly superior to the other combinations of techniques. It is noteworthy that the "best" solution line is never crossed by any other solution line at any point.

If the state planning commission has information about all of the different production methods, then it can select the best combination in this manner: If few products and techniques are involved, graphical methods can be used; if a larger number of products and techniques are involved, then mathematical techniques must be employed. In cases where a great many products and techniques must be taken into account, the problem would be very difficult to solve, even with the largest computer. However, certain iterative techniques that structure a "dialogue" between the state planning commission and the enterprises are

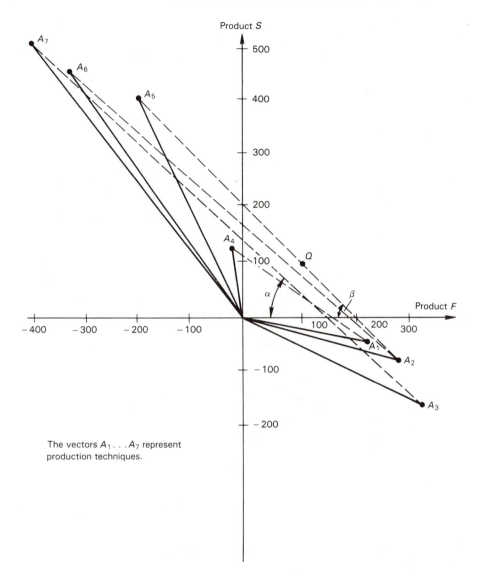

FIGURE E–1
Choice of Production Techniques Using One Factor of Production

available such that the correct solution is obtained. For the particular problem at hand, one such dialogue has been proposed by E. Malinvaud. To give a concrete example of what might be involved, Malinvaud's technique is briefly examined.[1]

The planning commission starts with a feasible plan (i.e., one that

[1]The exposition of Malinvaud's solution follows the analysis of Benjamin N. Ward, *The Socialist Economy: A Study of Organizational Alternatives* (New York: Random House, 1967), chap. 3.

incorporates its knowledge of one production technique in every industry and that does not demand more than the labor available); for purposes of illustration, let us assume that these techniques are A_3 and A_7.
Using these technologies the planners then find a set of prices that
reflect the rate at which production of F and S can be substituted; this is
the slope of the line connecting the two production vectors and is designated in Figure E–1 as α.

The planning commission then announces these prices to each sector and asks them to choose the method of production to maximize the
value added per unit of labor at the assigned prices. Both the S and the
F industries then examine the various technologies available to them
and select the one that permits the farthest outward parallel shift of the
price (i.e., the line with the slope of α that is the farthest to the right
when it is extended in the northeast quadrant. In the case of industry S,
this is production method A_5; in the case of industry F, this is production
A_2. These industries then announce these production methods to the
planning commission, which then calculates a new set of prices based on
the rates of substitution of S and F using these techniques; in the diagram this is the β of the line connecting these two vectors. The process
is repeated until there is no change in the technologies chosen between
the last two iterations; in the example at hand, this occurs after the first
iteration. It can be demonstrated mathematically that such an iterative
method will converge toward the final solution and, moreover, each
tentative solution is better than the last.

This iteration scheme has several useful features. First the planning commission requires very little information—just one technology
per sector; and the problem it must solve—calculation of relative
prices—is relatively simple. Second, the process can be stopped short of
full optimality with the assurance that the stopping point represents an
improvement over the plans generated by previous iterations. Further,
the solution can be reached in a finite number of steps. Finally, the
introduction of prices gives the system flexibility and allows the search
toward optimality to be decentralized. The final prices that emerge are
those that induce the enterprises in each industry to select the proper
technique. In the solution of linear programming problems, such prices
emerge as part of the solution to the physical allocation problem. They
are called *shadow prices* and, if used, can lead to an optimal solution of
the choice of production without any direct commands by the central
planning bureau about the choice of technology being issued.

It should be noted that such an iterative procedure to derive
shadow prices and an optimal allocation of resources assumes that enterprises answer the questions posed to them in an honest fashion. However, an enterprise director might engage in *strategic behavior* in order
to hide production reserves so that he or she will not need to work very

hard in the future. In this case, the optimality properties of the dialogue break down. This problem of strategic behavior is not just a theoretical possibility, as noted in Chapter 5 in the example of the Czechoslovak price reform in the mid-1960s.

Once the optimal combination of production method is selected (using either linear programming techniques or this iteration method), the planning commission then chooses the exact production mix it wishes of the two commodities. If, for example, it wishes to produce the commodities at a ratio of one to one, then the final net output plan is set at Q.

B. The Introduction of Many Factors of Production

The nature of the problem can be changed by introducing many factors of production. For simplicity, let us continue to assume only two products F and S and that they are not needed to produce each other. Let us further assume that there are five factors of production (capital, unskilled labor, and three kinds of skilled labor) and that there is only one method for producing each good, which requires fixed proportions of particular factors of production. Finally, only specified amounts of each factor are available.

The problem is to produce the goods in a prespecified fixed proportion and maximize production of each, given the various constraints imposed by different amounts of the many factors of production. In this example, problems arise because there may not be the proper mix of factors of production to employ them all and to make as many of one good as desired. Such a situation is shown in Figure E–2.

If unskilled labor is the only constraint to production and we have all the skilled labor and capital that we want, then the economy could either produce 140 units of F or 110 units of S, or any combination of F and S along line 1. If, on the other hand, capital is the only constraint on production and if we have all the skilled and unskilled labor that we want, the economy could produce either 100 units of F or 150 units of S, or any combination of F and S along line 2. If to produce S we require a particular type of labor skill C for which only a limited amount exists so that a maximum of 80 units can be produced, then line 3 represents this constraint (since this skill is not used at all in producing commodity F). Further assume that to produce F, we need labor skills A and B (not used in producing S) and that these are limited so that production of F is constrained according to line 4 by skilled labor A and according to line 5 by skilled labor B.

It should be clear that production is feasible only within the different constraints; this maximum production taking all constraints into

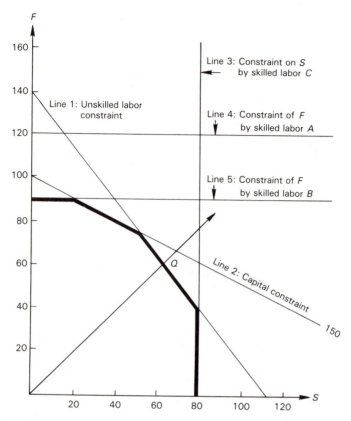

FIGURE E–2
Determination of Output with Many Different Input Constraints

account is indicated by the heavy black line. It should also be clear that the curve bounding this feasible set is none other than the concave production possibility curve. If the planners wish to produce the two goods in a proportion of one to one, then the maximum that they can produce is designated by point Q. Here, the ultimate constraining input is unskilled labor.

If the planning commission possesses data about all of the various constraints for all of the various products in the economy, it can determine the maximum production of a set of goods in a particular proportion by mathematical techniques. With a large number of products and constraints, this can become very difficult to solve, even with a large computer. However, it is also possible to solve the problem through a dialogue between the planning commission and the enterprises of the type discussed above.

C. Many Factors of Production, Many Techniques

The two examples above are rather simple. As we approach the real world, the linear programming problem becomes progressively more complicated; and this, in turn, means either that the planners must process increasing amounts of information for processing in increasingly more powerful computers or else that we must design increasingly sophisticated dialogues between the center and the periphery in order to solve the problem in an iterative fashion. A number of methods of conducting such a nationwide dialogue have been analyzed in the literature and it is useful to give an example.

One method has been proposed by the Soviet economist L.V. Kantorovich.[2] He asssumes that the planning commission has data about all scarce resources plus information on one technology for the production of each good; and he posits the goal of the commission to be the maximization of the volume of output as measured in a bundle of goods in a fixed proporition. The commission solves a linear programming problem that maximizes the volume of output (goods in a fixed proportion), from which it derives shadow prices representing the scarcity of the resources and which it announces to the enterprises. The enterprises use linear programming techniques to select a technology that, given the prices announced by the center, allows them to maximizes their profits. After these technologies are transmitted to the planning commission, the central authorities then resolve the linear programming problem to maximize production using this new technology set, deriving a new set of shadow prices of resources which are announced to the enterprises. The process is continued until the enterprises no longer choose different technologies, a situation reached when their profits using the announced prices are zero.

One major difficulty to this solution is that the problem to be solved by the planning commission can rapidly become too large to handle. Other types of dialogues have been proposed that reformulate the types of problems solved by the planning commission and the enterprises[3] or where the planning commission assigns quantities to the enterprises and receives cost data in return.[4] Another problem arises when enterprises engage in strategic behavior in order to influence the final shadow prices that are announced.

When several layers of government are involved, an interesting

[2]Leonid Kantorovitch, *The Best Use of Economic Resources* (Oxford: Pergamon Press, 1965).

[3]George B. Dantzig, *Linear Programming and Extensions* (Princeton, N.J.: Princeton University Press, 1963), chap. 23.

[4]János Kornai and Tamás Lipták, "Two Level Planning," *Econometrica*, 23 (January 1965) pp. 141–69.

question is raised as to the best way to partition the economy to conduct the planning exercise in the optimal fashion. For instance, should the planning commission send its instructions to production ministries that break down the plan and send them to the enterprises? Or should the planning commission send its instructions to territorial governmental units, who then break down the plan and send them to the enterprises? The type of dialogue conducted influences the optimal arrangement.[5]

D. Some Evaluations

Looking at linear programming problems in an abstract manner, everything looks rather simple. In all cases the problem to be solved is framed in terms of maximizing or minimizing some linear "objective function" (e.g., an index with fixed weights) where the various technologies to produce a given product are defined in a linear fashion (each technology features fixed proportions) and where the economy faces linear constraints (e.g., absolute limits of labor, capital, and land).

The various proposed procedures for solving such problems—either directly or iteratively in terms of a dialogue between the center and the enterprises—differ greatly according to the information required at each level, the type and quantity of information exchanged between level, the size of the problem to be solved by each units, and the speed at which such a process converges.

We cannot evaluate the net benefits of employing linear programming techniques until we can determine the cost of information and information processing, as well as the importance of arriving at a rapid solution. Two factors should, however, be emphasized: *First,* Many economic processes involve nonlinearities, so that the use of linear approximations may not allow us obtain complete efficiency. However, although we have no assurance that the marginal conditions discussed above will be completely met (especially if the iterative process is cut off before completion), we do know that in all normal cases, the final solution will be more efficient than that achieved with input-output methods.

Second, solving a linear programming problem becomes very, very difficult if many products, technologies, and factors of production are involved; therefore, the use of such techniques is confined to fairly small-scale problems. The discussions about use of such techniques for the economy as a whole, with dialogues between the center and the enterprises, helps us to understand the theoretical potentialities of the method if information and computational costs are very low. Such na-

---

[5]These problems are discussed by Michael Keren, "Industrial versus Regional Partitioning of Soviet Planning Organization: A Comparison," *Economics of Planning,* 4, No. 3 (1964), pp. 143–60.

tionwide systems have not been implemented because these two crucial assumptions are not met.

E. A Few "Real-World" Applications

Linear programming techniques have been applied to solve actual problems for allocating resources in the most efficient way in a variety of situations. The classical linear programming problem discussed in Chapter 5 about the minimization of transportation costs between many different warehouses and retail outlets has been solved in many different contexts. Another well-known linear programming problem concerns the minimization of the cost of food. It employs information about the calories and the various vitamins and minerals in each food and requires that minimum nutritional standards be met for each type of vitamin and mineral. Many hospitals have used such an approach to reduce food costs. Another linear programming problem that has been often solved in different contexts requires us to maxmize production of a bundle of goods requiring the use of various machines, where a given machine may be used in the manufacture of part of several products and where the capacity of each machine is known.

In the last decade linear programming has become part of the tool kit of operations research specialists who are working on problems of production.[6] In addition, certain linear programming techniques have been used in the setting out of development plans for developing nations.[7] Further, such techniques have been used quite successfully for aiding in the planning of particular segments within larger plans, especially for foreign trade in Hungary and Poland.[8] As computing costs become increasingly lower, the costs of information may prove the most important constraint on large-scale usage of such techniques.

[6]Examples for many different problems are given by Dantzig, *Linear Programming.*

[7]Some examples are described by Hollis B. Chenery and Paul G. Clark, *Interindustry Economics* (New York: John Wiley, 1959), chap. 11.

[8]Examples are provided by Janos Kornai, *Mathematical Planning of Structural Decisions* (Amsterdam: North Holland, 1967); and Economic Commission of Europe, *Economic Planning in Europe* (Geneva: 1965). For the Soviet Union a number of interesting examples in different sectors are discussed by Michael Ellman, *Planning Problems in the USSR* (Cambridge: Cambridge University Press, 1973).

INDEX